Holt MUSIC

TEACHER'S EDITION Grade 4

Eunice Boardman Meske
Professor of Music and Education
University of Wisconsin—Madison
Madison, Wisconsin

Barbara Andress
Professor of Music Education
Arizona State University
Tempe, Arizona

Mary P. Pautz
Assistant Professor of Music
  Education
University of Wisconsin—Milwaukee
Milwaukee, Wisconsin

Fred Willman
Professor of Music and Education
University of Missouri—St. Louis
St. Louis, Missouri

TEXAS EDUCATION AGENCY
Textbook Division

Readability Level Designation
State Textbook Adoption of <u>November 1988</u>
(To be filed in the Textbook Division no later than
5:00 p.m. on April 11, 1988)

Name of Publishing Company ___HOLT, RINEHART AND WINSTON, INC.___

Signed _Larry Hoss_   SOUTHWEST REGIONAL MANAGER
                (Name and Title of Company Official)

Name of Texas Depository ___SOUTHWEST SCHOOL BOOK DEPOSITORY___

Multiple List (Enter title & author)	Edition & Copyright	Name of Formula	Readability Level
HOLT MUSIC, Grade 4 Boardman and Andress	1988	Harris-Jacobson	3.6

Holt, Rinehart and Winston, Publishers
New York, Toronto, Mexico City, London, Sydney, Tokyo

Acknowledgments for previously copyrighted material
and credits for photographs and art begin on page 380.
ISBN 0-03-005294-7
7890 032 98765432

HOLT MUSIC

It's the leader of the band!

CONSIDER THE ADVANTAGES . . .

☐ *Dozens of the world's finest songs in each level—the songs your students want to sing!*

☐ *Exciting activities that enable students to interact with the music and acquire musical knowledge.*

☐ *Exceptionally motivating listening lessons that really get students involved in learning.*

☐ *Flexibly organized Teacher's Editions, rich with background information and no-nonsense teaching strategies.*

☐ *A wealth of supplementary materials that enhance, extend, and enrich.*

Music That Motivates

Every song in HOLT MUSIC builds on the natural enthusiasm students have for singing, dancing—expressing themselves in creative ways! You'll find hundreds and hundreds of authentic songs that students really *want* to sing—songs with built-in appeal.

Choose from a rich variety of songs: contemporary, traditional, American and European folk, classical, holiday music, and more.

Just look at some of these favorites:

Weave Me the Sunshine
Peace Like a River
School Days
Pop! Goes the Weasel
Sleigh Bells
The Happy Wanderer
My Name Is Yon Yonson
So Long, Farewell
The Unicorn
We're Off to See the Wizard

Lively, colorful photographs and illustrations provide the perfect visual accompaniment.

Music to Learn From

Songs throughout HOLT MUSIC develop note-reading skills and apply them as a basis for instrumental accompaniment and vocal exploration.

Each song provides a point of departure for creative involvement in learning.

Unique graphic devices that look like the music sounds introduce basic note-reading skills and reinforce concepts of melody and rhythm.

Illustrations ease the transition to standard notation.

Music to Interact With

Engaging activities help students understand, relate to, and interact with music right from the start. These activities are more than entertaining—they're truly *instructive,* designed to strengthen and enhance musical understanding.

"Measure a Rhythm

What do these things measure?

Here is a rhythm ruler.
What do you think it will measure?

One of These Does Not Belong

Listen to the music.
- You will hear four pieces of music in each set.
- Three of the pieces are the same kind of music.
- One is different!
- Can you pick the one that does not belong?

A

Peach Tree, Peonies and Cranes, Shen Ch'üan (1682-1758), The Metropolitan Museum of Art.

The Unsweet Suite

Create a **movement** for this suite.
Choose a title.
Make your music suggest the idea of the title.

201

Words and Music

Here are some words made into a poem.
Add rhythm and harmony to make a song.

How I Get Cool
by Richard J. Smith

What a hot and muggy day.
I think I'm going to roast.
What a drippy, sweaty day.
I feel like buttered toast.

These concrete steps are sizzly-hot.
They're cooking my backside.
The heat is coming through my soles.
My toes are almost fried.

On days like this, scorchy days,
Here's how I get cool.
I eat three cherry popsicles
And swim in City Pool.

My Puppy
by Richard J. Smith

My puppy can be my very best friend.
He'll lick me and play games for hours on end.
Sometimes he'll kiss me right on the nose,
And try to snuggle under my clothes.

Sometimes I like my puppy a lot.
Sometimes I do and sometimes not.
I guess with my puppy it's good and it's bad.
He makes me happy, and he makes me mad.

Add rhythm and melody to make a song.

193

Irresistible activities inspire singing, clapping, making up melodies and rhymes, and more—the true exhilaration of musical expression. Many activities involve poetry or related arts.

Short instrumental experiences begin at Kindergarten, employing readily available instruments.

Music Worth Listening To

Many activities call upon students to move to rhythms and melodic patterns or to listen critically and make judgments about mood, instrumentation, melody, and form.

Listening lessons in HOLT MUSIC keep students tuned in with appealing graphics, follow-along activities, and professional performances. Recordings use a wide variety of vocal and instrumental sounds to heighten awareness of form, mood, melody, and musical styles.

The focus is on active participation to make music exciting, involving, and fun!

The listening selections include a wide variety of musical styles and eras.

Thinking About Music

Both activities and listening lessons supply ample opportunities to develop and reinforce thinking skills. Exercises are designed to improve students' ability to think, through analysis and evaluation, comparison and contrast, choosing alternatives, and more.

Music That's Realistic to Teach!

Whatever your musical background, you'll find all the backup help you need in HOLT MUSIC Teacher's Editions: concrete information, strategies you can rely on, and solid, flexible lesson plans with many optional suggestions. Every page is designed to bring musical understanding and appreciation within reach of all your students.

Each lesson begins with a clear objective and a complete list of program materials, including a detailed summary of recordings and the voices and instruments used.

A special logo signals when activity sheets are available for the lesson.

Each of the extension lessons in Unit 2 is cross-referenced to a core lesson.

"Introducing the Lesson" includes a simple-to-perform motivator that leads naturally into the lesson content.

"Developing the Lesson" gives step-by-step teaching suggestions to ensure that the lesson objective is met. Commentary and questions to the student are highlighted in boldface type.

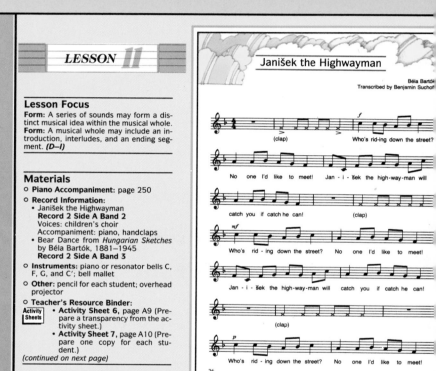

LESSON 11

Lesson Focus
Form: A series of sounds may form a distinct musical idea within the musical whole.
Form: A musical whole may include an introduction, interludes, and an ending segment. **(D–I)**

Materials
○ **Piano Accompaniment:** page 250
○ **Record Information:**
  • Janišek the Highwayman
    Record 2 Side A Band 2
    Voices: children's choir
    Accompaniment: piano, handclaps
  • Bear Dance from *Hungarian Sketches* by Béla Bartók, 1881–1945
    Record 2 Side A Band 3
○ **Instruments:** piano or resonator bells C, F, G, and C'; bell mallet
○ **Other:** pencil for each student; overhead projector
○ **Teacher's Resource Binder:**
  Activity Sheets • **Activity Sheet 6,** page A9 (Prepare a transparency from the activity sheet.)
  • **Activity Sheet 7,** page A10 (Prepare one copy for each student.)
(continued on next page)

Introducing the Lesson

Clap the following pattern and ask the class to echo you several times until they can perform it easily.

Play the recording of "Janišek the Highwayman" through the first musical statement of the song as students follow it in their books on page 26. **Did you hear the pattern we clapped earlier?** (Yes, it was also clapped on the recording.) **What other instrument played this rhythmic pattern?** (piano)

Developing the Lesson

1. Display the transparency of Activity Sheet 6 (*Janišek the Highwayman*). Play the complete recording of "Janišek the Highwayman."

Help the class discover that the piece consists of one main melody (**A**) repeated several times. Variety is provided by the introduction interludes, and the coda.

2. Practice the patterns shown on page 27 "Play" the C–G pattern by patting both hands on the left knee and the F–C pattern by patting both hands on the right knee. (Patting the patterns will help prepare the class to play them on the resonator bells or on the piano Choose one or two students to perform the patterns on the bells or the piano while you sing the song. The others may continue to "play" the patterns on their knees.

3. Invite the class to sing the song as new player add the piano/bell part.

4. Explain that Bartók often composed short pieces based on a single melody. **How did h**

Freedom of choice is truly yours—lesson plans are designed for maximum flexibility. Each level is divided into two units. Unit 1, the core, contains 60 lessons for a minimum program. Unit 2 contains four chapters for reinforcement, enrichment, and special performances.

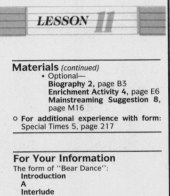

Materials *(continued)*
• Optional—
   Biography 2, page B3
   Enrichment Activity 4, page E6
   Mainstreaming Suggestion 8, page M16
○ **For additional experience with form:**
   Special Times 5, page 217

For Your Information
The form of "Bear Dance":
   Introduction
   A
   Interlude
   A
   Interlude
   A
   Interlude
   A
   Interlude
   A

vary the melody in "Janišek the Highwayman" to make his music more interesting? (The melody gets softer each time it is heard.)

OPTIONAL

Closing the Lesson
Distribute a copy of Activity Sheet 7 *(Bear Dance)* and a pencil to each student. **Listen to another piece by Bartók. As each new number is called, listen for the instruments shown in each numbered box.**

Play the recording of "Bear Dance." Explain that this piece has only one main melody, as does "Janišek the Highwayman." **This time Bartók changed the melody by using different instruments.** Ask the class to listen again and decide which section is the main melody (the A section), the introduction, interlude, and the coda. They should write the correct label in each box as they

listen again. **You may not need to use all the labels.** Play the recording as many times as necessary to complete the call chart and verify student responses. (See **For Your Information** for correct answers.)

When a score is given in graphic notation in the pupil book, the music notation appears on the teacher's page.

"For Your Information" provides a quick, convenient reference for background information about lesson contents.

A colored band designates the core pages. Optional steps are labeled with a logo.

"Closing the Lesson" offers activities to apply what has been learned.

Special logos indicate when performance cassettes and rehearsal cassettes are available.

Music That's Manageable

The **Teacher's Resource Binder** makes classroom management uncommonly convenient. Blackline masters help teachers structure the course to match individual preferences.

Teachers who use the **Kodaly** approach will find creative teaching ideas and fun-filled student charts— all correlated to HOLT MUSIC.

The **Orff** activities will delight your class with chants, games, and lively instrumental arrangements.

The **Biography** series brings music personalities to life.

A complete set of **Evaluations** provides a comprehensive testing program for HOLT MUSIC.

Students who are especially interested in music or who are academically gifted will find plenty of challenges in the **Enrichment** ideas.

Students will love working with the call charts, games, puzzles, costume patterns, and other idea-packed **Activity Sheets**. These blackline masters are designed to supplement, extend, and enrich the basic lesson plans.

Mainstreaming activities ensure that involvement in music learning is an important part of every child's day.

Relating music to other areas of learning becomes a snap with **Curriculum Correlation** teaching suggestions and charts.

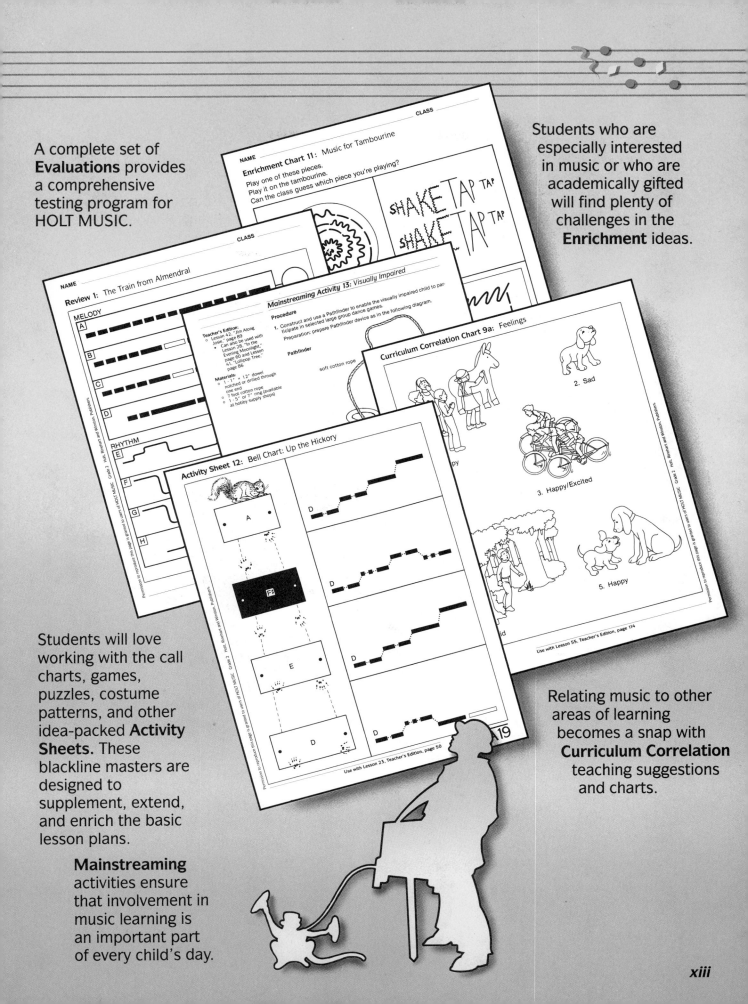

NAME _____   CLASS _____

Enrichment Chart 11: Music for Tambourine

Play one of these pieces.
Play it on the tambourine.
Can the class guess which piece you're playing?

SHAKE TAP TAP
SHAKE TAP TAP

NAME _____   CLASS _____

Review 1: The Train from Almendral

MELODY

RHYTHM

Mainstreaming Activity 13: Visually Impaired

Procedure

1. Construct and use a Pathfinder to enable the visually impaired child to participate in selected large group dance games.
   Preparation: prepare Pathfinder device as in the following diagram.

Pathfinder

soft cotton rope

Teacher's Edition:
○ Lesson 42, "Jim Along Josie," page 89
   • Can also be used with Lesson 28, "In the Evening Moonlight," page 60 and Lesson 41, "Lollipop Tree," page 86

Materials:
○ 1 · 1" · 12" dowel notched or drilled through one end
○ 7 foot cotton rope
○ 1 · 5" or 7" ring (available at hobby supply shops)

Curriculum Correlation Chart 9a: Feelings

2. Sad

3. Happy/Excited

5. Happy

Use with Lesson 55, Teacher's Edition, page 114

Activity Sheet 12: Bell Chart: Up the Hickory

A

F♯

E

D

D

D

D

D

Use with Lesson 23, Teacher's Edition, page 50

A19

Recordings

A set of first-quality recordings serves a dual purpose: to give students a model for performance and to provide a valuable instrumental and vocal resource. Dual-track stereo allows separation of recorded voice and accompaniment. Recordings are digitally mastered.

A sturdy carrying case includes an index cross-referenced to lessons in the Teacher's Edition.

Song and listening selections appear in lesson order.

Extra Features!

Performance cassettes contain instrumental tracks specially edited for optimum sound in public performance.

Rehearsal cassettes for Grades 4-8 help students learn part songs by hearing each vocal part alone.

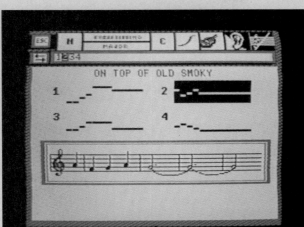

Wait Until You Hear This! music software uses songs from HOLT MUSIC to encourage active experimentation with musical elements. Students can rearrange phrases, alter rhythms, tempo, and timbre, and change key or mode to create new musical works. Three separate programs are available: Grades K-2, 3-5, and 6-8.

The *Holiday Song Book* includes lyrics and piano accompaniments for an additional 50 songs celebrating a year's worth of holidays — Mother's Day, Columbus Day, the Fourth of July, and more.

COMPONENTS CHART

	K	1	2	3	4	5	6	7	8
Pupil Book		✓	✓	✓	✓	✓	✓	✓	✓
Jumbo Book	✓	✓							
Teacher's Edition	✓	✓	✓	✓	✓	✓	✓	✓	✓
Recordings	✓	✓	✓	✓	✓	✓	✓	✓	✓
Teacher's Resource Binder	✓	✓	✓	✓	✓	✓	✓	✓	✓
Holiday Song Book	✓	✓	✓	✓	✓	✓	✓	✓	✓
Computer Software	✓	✓	✓	✓	✓	✓	✓	✓	✓
Performance Cassettes	✓	✓	✓	✓	✓	✓	✓	✓	✓
Rehearsal Cassettes				✓	✓	✓	✓	✓	✓

HOLT MUSIC offers you a total package for your classroom needs. A list of components is given in the chart at the left.

TABLE OF CONTENTS

CORE UNIT 1 — Music to Explore.....4

UNIT 2 More Music to Explore.....134

Special Times 210

Meet the Authors

Eunice Boardman Meske is Director of the School of Music and Professor of Music and Education at the University of Wisconsin, Madison. She works with university students in a "lab school" where she and her students teach grades K-8. Meske holds a Ph.D. from the University of Illinois.

EUNICE BOARDMAN MESKE

BARBARA ANDRESS

Barbara Andress is Professor in the School of Music at Arizona State University, Tempe. She received a B.A. and M.A. in education from Arizona State University. Andress has taught general music and instrumental music and for over twenty years was a district music supervisor.

Mary Pautz is Assistant Professor of Music Education at the University of Wisconsin, Milwaukee. In addition to teaching music education methods, she also teaches elementary music classes as part of a practicum for music majors. Pautz is a doctoral candidate at the University of Wisconsin, Madison.

MARY PAUTZ

FRED WILLMAN

Fred Willman is Professor of Music Education at the University of Missouri, St. Louis. William holds a Ph.D. from the University of North Dakota, Grand Forks. He has worked extensively in the development of computer software for use in music education.

Consultants

Nancy Archer
Forest Park Elementary School
Fort Wayne, Indiana

Joan Z. Fyfe
Jericho Public Schools
Jericho, New York

Jeanne Hook
Albuquerque Public Schools
Albuquerque, New Mexico

Danette Littleton
University of Tennessee at Chattanooga
Chattanooga, Tennessee

Barbara Reeder Lundquist
University of Washington
Seattle, Washington

Ollie McFarland
Detroit Public Schools
Detroit, Michigan

Faith Norwood
Harnett County School District
North Carolina

Linda K. Price
Richardson Independent School District
Richardson, Texas

Buryl Red
Composer and Arranger
New York, New York

Dawn L. Reynolds
District of Columbia Public Schools
Washington, D.C.

Morris Stevens
A.N. McCallum High School
Austin, Texas

Jack Noble White
Texas Boys Choir
Fort Worth, Texas

Contributing Writers

Hilary Apfelstadt
University of North Carolina
at Greensboro
Greensboro, North Carolina

Pat and Tom Cuthbertson
Professional Writers
Santa Cruz, California

Louise Huberty
(*Special Kodaly Consultant*)
Milwaukee Public Schools
Milwaukee, Wisconsin

Susan Kenney
Brigham Young University
Salt Lake City, Utah

Diane Persellin
Trinity University
San Antonio, Texas

Janet Montgomery
Ithaca College
Ithaca, New York

Richard O'Hearn
Western Michigan University
Kalamazoo, Michigan

Arvida Steen
(*Special Orff Consultant*)
The Blake School
Minneapolis, Minnesota

Field Test Sites

While HOLT MUSIC was being developed, parts of the program were field tested by 25 teachers in 18 states. These teachers played a crucial role in the program's development. Their comments, suggestions, and classroom experiences helped HOLT MUSIC become the workable, exciting program it is. Our grateful appreciation goes to the following teachers who used our materials in their classrooms.

ARKANSAS
Judy Harkrader
Vilonia Elementary School
Vilonia

COLORADO
Nancylee Summerville
Hutchinson Elementary School
Lakewood

Robert Horsky
Goldrick Elementary School
Denver

Joan Tally
Eiber Elementary School
Lakewood

Germaine Johnson
University of Northern Colorado
  Laboratory School
Greeley

GEORGIA
Angela Tonsmeire
Cartersville Elementary School
Cartersville

Nancy Clayton
Norman Park Elementary School
Norman Park

INDIANA
Nancy Archer
Forest Park Elementary School
Fort Wayne

Elizabeth Staples
School #92
Indianapolis

Pat Gillooly
School #90
Indianapolis

KANSAS
Shelli Kadel
El Paso Elementary School
Derby

KENTUCKY
Patricia Weihe
Wright Elementary School
Shelbyville

MASSACHUSETTS
Marya Rusinak
Kennedy School
Brockton

MISSISSIPPI
Dottie Dudley
Crestwood Elementary School
Meridian

Mira Frances Hays
Forest Seperate School District
Forest

MISSOURI
Elizabeth Hutcherson
Parker Road Elementary School
Florissant

NEW JERSEY
Lorna Milbauer
North Cliff School
Englewood Cliffs

NEW YORK
Ruthetta S. Smikle
Hillary Park Academy
Buffalo

NORTH CAROLINA
Julie Young
Burgaw Elementary School
Burgaw

OKLAHOMA
Cindy Newell
Washington Irving Elementary School
Durant

OREGON
Larry Verdoorn
Hall Elementary School
Gresham

PENNSYLVANIA
Marianne Zimmerman
Steele School
Harrisburg

TENNESSEE
Sarah Davis
Powell Elementary School
Powell

WEST VIRGINIA
Eva Ledbetter
Cross Lanes Elementary School
Cross Lanes

WISCONSIN
Jill Kuespert Anderson
Lannon Elementary School
Lannon

A Guide To Holt Music

The HOLT MUSIC program can help you provide rich and enjoyable experiences for all of your students. The information given below will help you get acquainted with the Pupil Book, the Teacher's Edition, the Teacher's Resource Binder, and the Recordings.

Organization Of The Program

Each level of HOLT MUSIC is divided into two units. Unit 1, "Music to Explore," is the "core" unit. The core lessons are divided into four quarters, or chapters, of fifteen lessons each. Each quarter ends with an evaluation. If time for music class is limited, we suggest that you concentrate on the core, which provides a comprehensive program in itself.

Unit 2, "More Music to Explore," contains an additional four chapters for review, reinforcement, extension of core concepts, and seasonal music. Lessons in Unit 2 are cross-referenced in the Teacher's Edition to lessons in Unit 1. However, these cross-references are only suggestions; you will also be guided by the interests of your students and available class time.

Types Of Lessons In The Book

☐ **Song lessons**—Most lessons in the program are song-based lessons. Song lessons are identified by a gray band above and below the title. Usually both the music and the words are in the Pupil Book. However, in certain lessons only the words appear in the Pupil Book, and it is expected that students will learn the song by listening. Students are not expected to be able to read all of the musical notations that appear in their books. The lesson sequence is designed so that they will gradually acquire the skill to do so as they progress through the grades. For this reason it is strongly recommended that the core unit be followed in page order.

☐ **Listening lessons**—These lessons are built around a recording of a classical, folk, or contemporary work. Listening lessons featured in the Pupil Book are identified by a logo. Complete titles, composers, and performer credits are listed in the "Materials" section of the Teacher's Edition.

Many of the listening lessons have a chart or an illustration designed to help guide the children through the listening experience. In some lessons the recording includes "call numbers"—spoken numbers recorded over the music. The call numbers correspond to the numbers on the chart and help to focus attention on important features as the music continues.

☐ **Activities**—Many activity-based lessons are included in HOLT MUSIC. The type of activity in the Pupil Book is identified by a special logo: a quill pen and an ink bottle for creative activities, a

French horn for performance activities, and a human figure for activities involving movement.

The activity is always structured in some way; for example, a poem, a story, or a picture in the Pupil Book might serve as a focal point for creative exploration, or the students could be invited to explore certain sounds on instruments.

Using The Recordings

The recordings are essential teaching aids for HOLT MUSIC. The song recordings may be used in various ways: to help students learn words and melody if songs are beyond their current reading level; and to provide examples of appropriate tempo, diction, expression, and vocal tone quality. For teaching flexibility, song recordings have voices on one channel and instruments on the other. By turning the balance control completely to the right, you will hear instruments only. The grooves between all selections are locked.

Special Helps For The Teacher

☐ The **Scope and Sequence Chart,** page xxviii–3, summarizes concepts, terms, and skills covered in each grade level.

☐ The teacher's **Glossary,** page 378, gives definitions of musical terms used in the text.

☐ Complete **Classified and Alphabetical Indexes,** starting on page 383, provide a convenient way to locate songs, poems, listening lessons, and particular skills and concepts.

☐ Step-by-step **lesson plans** are provided for each page of the Pupil Book. The **Lesson Focus** indicates the concept to be studied and gives, in abbreviated form, an indication of the primary behavior and mode stressed. **P–I,** for example, means "perform" in the "ikonic mode." (See "The Generative Approach to Music Learning," page xxvi.)

☐ The **Teacher's Resource Binder** includes Activity Sheets, Biographies, Evaluations, and suggestions for Curriculum Correlation, Enrichment, Kodaly, Mainstreaming, and Orff. All binder materials are cross-referenced to lessons in the Teacher's Edition. This enables you to adapt or expand individual lessons to fit your special needs.

☐ **Instrumental accompaniments**—Most songs contain chord names for autoharp or guitar accompaniment, and many lesson plans include accompaniments for students to perform on classroom instruments. Piano accompaniments, provided in the back of the Teacher's Edition, are cross-referenced to each lesson plan. The piano score includes markers showing where a new line begins in the Pupil Book. The symbol $\overset{2}{\mathbf{v}}$ above the score, for example, indicates that the second line of music in the Pupil Book begins at this point.

To the Classroom Teacher

The classroom teacher's role in music education varies from school to school. Whatever the situation in your district, the classroom teacher is vital to the success of the total music program.

Many teachers approach music with mixed feelings: enthusiasm, apprehension, curiosity, or insecurity. These attitudes are influenced by the musical knowledge the teacher possesses, the memory of music in his or her own school experience, and by heavy demands on the teacher's time.

HOLT MUSIC welcomes the classroom teacher's participation. The suggestions that follow are provided with the hope that they will alleviate fears and encourage the teacher to enjoy and learn music with the students.

1 "I Don't Know How To Teach Music!"

Every classroom teacher can teach music with HOLT MUSIC—if he or she is willing to learn with the students and read through the lessons in the Teacher's Edition. The "generative" approach used in HOLT MUSIC can help the teacher learn along with the students.

Music presents a special challenge because of the need to occasionally demonstrate by singing, moving, or playing. HOLT MUSIC helps the teacher as much as possible with

- comprehensive, easily understood lesson plans
- quality demonstration recordings
- a teaching sequence that works
- appealing songs, listening lessons, and poetry
- activities that are fun for students to do

2 "There Isn't Time To Teach Music!"

The pressure for students to achieve in all curricular areas is intense. However, music can be interspersed throughout the school day. Sing a song to begin or end the day; create an instrumental accompaniment to enrich a story; share the music from the culture being highlighted in social studies.

The Curriculum Correlation section in the Teacher's Resource Binder provides many suggestions for integrating music into your day. To expand class time for music, set up music centers where small groups may work on their own.

However, a scheduled time devoted to music is just as important as time scheduled for other subjects. Just as reading throughout the day does not take the place of reading class, neither should the use of music throughout the day be considered sufficient. To achieve an understanding of music there must be a sequential course of study.

3 "I Don't Have Time To Hunt For Materials!"

The authors of HOLT MUSIC have gathered and organized all materials for you. You will find

- Complete lesson plans that include a lesson focus, an introduction, a development and a conclusion. Usually a lesson can be completed in 20 to 30 minutes.
- Integration of all types of activities—listening lessons, dances, creative experiences, and songs—within a lesson.
- Boldfaced dialogue in the lesson plans that may help you in presenting the lesson, especially if you are not familiar with musical concepts and terms.

4 "The Kids Will Laugh If I Sing!"

Students may need encouragement at first. However, young people will eventually sing if a positive atmosphere is created. Common teaching errors that hinder singing include

- expecting students to sing before they are ready (A new song must be heard several times before the students sing it.)
- expecting students to sing too loud

The students may laugh the first time they hear you sing. You are not alone: They are even more likely to laugh at a music specialist who has a trained voice! If you can laugh with the class and proceed with the song, the laughter is soon forgotten and the music enjoyed. Or if you prefer, you can rely on the recordings. By adjusting the balance on the stereo, the voice only may be heard; this is especially helpful in teaching a new song.

5 "What Will I Do With the Boys?"

There is nothing inherent in the genes of boys that causes them to have an aversion to music! Often they will be the most enthusiastic supporters. Expect all students to enjoy music; expect everyone to learn. You will find that an activity-based, hands-on experience in music will spark enthusiasm in both boys and girls. They will never tire of opportunities to play bells and autoharps, to use props such as streamers, wands, and balloons, or to work with the activity sheets provided in the Teacher's Resource Binder.

6 "I Can't Play the Piano!"

While playing the piano is helpful, it is not essential for teaching music. Instead, you can play the recordings or use autoharp accompaniments.

7 "I Remember How I Hated Music When I Was In School!"

Teachers who have had pleasant experiences with music are likely to approach music teaching with enthusiasm. Others, unfortunately, may have less pleasant memories. What was it in the experience that caused the bad feelings? You can prevent another generation from having unpleasant experiences by avoiding those stressful practices you recall.

The Generative Approach To Music Learning

HOLT MUSIC's generative approach is based on the recognition that

Learning begins with a "need to know." Real learning occurs only to the extent that the student willingly makes a commitment to the act of learning. Learning based on intrinsic "need to know" goals, which the learner personally identifies, is more permanent than learning based on extrinsic goals such as rewards or adult approval.

Learning leads to more learning. Once the student is personally committed to learning, each achievement is "generative"; it provides the foundation and the impetus for further learning.

Learning is future-oriented. The student who becomes enthralled with the learning process continues to seek opportunities to learn as long as each experience leads toward personal independence and self-actualization. Music learning thus approached allows the learner to become

☐ more deeply involved in the aesthetic experience

☐ aware of music as an avenue of one's own personal expression

☐ musically independent

The Generative Instructional Theory

The Generative Instructional Theory recognizes that music learning, whether formal or informal, involves four components. These components include

1. The musical concept to be learned. Musical understanding emerges gradually as the learner develops musical concepts, that is, principles or ways of categorizing musical sounds.

Concepts stressed in the generative approach include

☐ those related to musical elements
  ■ pitch (melody and harmony)
  ■ duration (rhythm and tempo) ■ dynamics
  ■ articulation ■ timbre (qualities of sound)
☐ those that reflect the way musical elements are organized into a complete musical statement that has ■ form ■ texture ■ an expressive nature ■ a cultural context (time and place)

The Scope and Sequence chart beginning on page xxviii gives the concepts covered in HOLT MUSIC.

2. A musical example that embodies the concept to be learned. Examples are selected for their musical value reflecting

  ■ diverse musical heritages
  ■ diverse times and places
  ■ many forms of human emotion
  ■ many different combinations of voices and instruments

3. A musical behavior through which the learner interacts with music, gradually developing essential musical concepts by
  ■ performing music through singing and playing

  ■ describing music through moving, visualizing, and verbalizing
  ■ creating music through improvisation or composition

4. A conceptual mode that enables the learner to communicate understanding and move through three stages of conceptualization:

☐ **The enactive mode:** The learner begins to associate concept with example through observation, manipulation, and experimentation. Understanding is "acted-out" as the student interacts directly and nonverbally with the musical sound.

☐ **The ikonic mode:** The learner internalizes musical sound images that can be recalled even when the musical sound is absent. The learner demonstrates understanding through pictorial representations that "look like" the music sounds or with simple verbal imagery such as up-down, longer-shorter, or smooth-jerky.

☐ **The symbolic mode:** The learner builds on previous enactive and ikonic experiences until verbal and musical symbols gradually become associated with the sound.

The Lesson Focus

Lesson plans in HOLT MUSIC are built on the recognition that these four components must be present in order for learning to take place. The **Lesson Focus** for each plan identifies the concept, the behavior, and the conceptual mode. An example follows.

Lesson Focus
Melody: A series of pitches may move up, down, or remain the same. *(P–I)*

■ The **behavior** is identified at the end of the concept statement by the first letter.
  P Perform (singing/playing)
  D Describe (move/verbalize/visualize)
  C Create (improvise/compose)
■ The **conceptual mode** at which it is expected that most students will be functioning in this lesson is identified by the second capital letter.
  E Enactive *I* Ikonic *S* Symbolic

Thus in the example given above, the designation *(P–I)* at the end of the concept statement indicates that the behavior stressed in the lesson is **Perform** and that the students will be primarily using the **Ikonic** mode in that lesson.

The Generative Approach To Music Reading

Lessons that help develop music-reading skills are an integral part of any learning sequence that leads toward musical independence. The generative approach to music reading used in HOLT MUSIC

☐ is based on a cyclic process that takes the learner through three stages corresponding to the three modes of conceptualization (See chart.)

☐ provides a lesson sequence that recognizes that a learner may be functioning at different stages of the cycle simultaneously—for example, a student might be reading simple rhythms from notation (symbolic stage) while associating melodies with ikons (ikonic stage) and learning harmonies aurally (enactive stage).

☐ presents each new skill in relation to the musical whole, rather than through pattern drill alone.

☐ distinguishes between sight-reading (playing an instrument from notation) and sight-singing.

Reading Rhythm

The generative approach to reading rhythm

☐ recognizes that reading of rhythm depends on the perception of durational relationships
☐ is based on a two-dimensional approach
 ■ sensing durations within the melodic rhythm in relation to the underlying beat, and
 ■ sensing durations in the melodic rhythm in relation to the shortest sound within that rhythm

The **additive approach** described above is used because

☐ it is the rhythmic relationship to which the young person seems to respond most readily
☐ it allows the student to solve rhythmic problems by using addition rather than division
☐ it is the basis for rhythmic organization used in the music of many non-Western cultures, as well as in much of the popular music of today.

Reading Melody

The generative approach to reading melody

☐ begins with melodies based on major or minor modes because these are most familiar to the contemporary American child
☐ uses the body scale (see below) to help the beginning student internalize pitch relationships
☐ stresses the hearing and performing of melodies in relation to the underlying harmony
☐ makes use of scale numbers to describe tonal relationships because numbers

 ■ provide the learner with a way of internalizing and recalling melodic pitches in relation to a tonal center
 ■ build on a numerical concept that most children have when this stage is introduced
 ■ allow for meaningful transfer to the reading of staff notation
 ■ are commonly used to describe chord structure, thus helping the student to understand the relation of melody to harmony

---

Lessons that develop reading skills take the student through the three conceptual modes.

ENACTIVE MODE The student performs the rhythm of a melody and metric grouping by imitating what is heard.

IKONIC MODE The student associates rhythms with ikons that represent duration in relation to

 ■ the shortest sound ■ the beat and accent

As the student associates these ikons with sound patterns, vocabulary is introduced to describe

 ■ sounds that make up the melodic rhythm (short, long, lo-ong)

short short long short short long lo–ong

 ■ sounds in relation to the beat (shorter than, longer than)

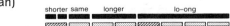

shorter same longer lo–ong

 ■ the accent (moves in twos, moves in threes)

moves in twos moves in threes

SYMBOLIC MODE The process is completed as the child transfers the ability to read ikons to reading traditional music notation.

ENACTIVE MODE The student performs in response to melodies heard. During this stage the body scale is introduced, providing the child with another means of sensing and responding to pitch relationships.

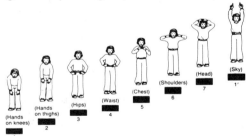

IKONIC MODE The child first associates melodies with ikons that represent the up-down, step-skip relationship of pitches. Later, pitches are labeled with scale numbers to show their relationship to the tonal center.

SYMBOLIC MODE The student transfers the ability to read a new melody from scale numbers to staff notation.

Scope and Sequence

As students grow in their understanding of musical concepts, they acquire skills for manipulating their own musical environments. Page numbers following each concept statement guide the teacher to lessons in HOLT MUSIC, Level 4, that focus on that concept. Boldfaced numbers represent lessons where that concept is dealt with as a primary focus of the lesson. Other numbers indicate

Concepts	Ikon	Musical Symbol
RHYTHM		
■ Music may be comparatively fast or slow, depending on the speed of the underlying pulse. *Pages:* 48–49, **88–89**, 161–162, **172–173**		
■ Music may become faster or slower by changing the speed of the underlying pulse. *Pages:* 6–7, 92–93, 124–125, **172–173**		
■ Music may move in relation to the underlying steady beat or shortest pulse. *Pages:* 50–51, 54–55, 86–87, 128–129, 142–143, 153, 164–165, 184		
■ A series of beats may be organized into regular or irregular groupings by stressing certain beats. *Pages:* **54–55, 72–73, 74–75, 76–77,** 196–197, 198–199, 200		
■ Individual sounds and silences within a rhythmic line may be longer than, shorter than, or the same as other sounds within the line. *Pages:* 147, **194**		
■ Individual sounds and silences within a rhythmic line may be longer than, shorter than, or the same as the underlying steady beat or shortest pulse. *Pages:* **14–15, 16–17,** 28–29, 38–39, **78–79, 80–81,** 154–155, **175, 176, 177,** 196–197, 200, 212–213, 216, 219, 222, **229,** 232–233		
■ Accented sounds within a rhythmic line may sound with, before, or after the accented underlying beat. *Pages:* 44–45, 50–51, 114–115, 170–171, 178–179, 224–225		
MELODY		
■ A series of pitches may move up, down, or remain the same. *Pages:* 14–15, 40–41, 74–75, 90–91, 106–107, 124–125, 145, 150–151, 154–155, 164–165, 166–167, 196–197, 200 **224**		
■ A series of pitches may move up or down by steps or skips. *Pages:* 6–7, 14–15, **18–19,** 20–21, 26–27, **32–33,** 110–111, 120–121, 140, 141, 161–162, 170–171, **175, 176,** 203, 210–211, 216, 217		
■ Each pitch within a melody moves in relation to a home tone. *Pages:* **24–25, 44–45, 70–71, 82–83, 84–85,** 108–109, 218		
■ A series of pitches bounded by the octave "belong together," forming a tonal set. *Pages:* **20–21, 22–23, 24–25, 82–83, 84–85, 108–109, 110–111, 112–113, 114–115,** 185, **186,** 219, 223		
■ A melody may be relatively high or low. *Pages:* 70–71, **137, 138,** 161		
■ Individual pitches, when compared to each other, may be higher, lower, or the same. *Pages:* 86–87		
TIMBRE		
■ The quality of a sound is determined by the sound source. *Pages:* 38–39, **58–59,** 76–77, 124–125, **190–191,** 196–197, 201, 230		
■ The quality of a sound is affected by the material, shape, and size of the source. *Pages:* 36–37, **60–65, 66–67,** 195		
■ The quality of a sound is affected by the way the sound is produced. *Pages:* **60–65, 66–67,** 158–159, **195,** 198–199		
■ The total sound is affected by the number and qualities of sounds occurring at the same time. *Pages:* 38–39, **56–57,** 96–97, 116–117, 218		

lessons where the concept is dealt with, but not as the primary focus.

The skills list gives a sampling of representative behaviors for Level 4. Page numbers listed give only one example of a lesson where that skill is developed. For a comprehensive listing of skills, refer to the Classified Index of Activities and Skills, page 385.

Terms for Grade 4	Skills/Behaviors for Grade 4	
beat tempo melodic rhythm shortest sound meter Adagio—Allegro—Andante—Largo syncopation pulse rest meter signature	**Perform**	Sing, chant, and move with emphasis on accurate rhythm. *Throughout* Chant or sing rhythms of songs at varying tempos. *6–7* Sing or play repeated phrases on classroom instruments. *54–55* Clap the melodic rhythm against the shortest sound. *175* Maintain a steady beat with body movements when singing. *177*
	Describe	Use movement to demonstrate knowledge of up-and-down skips. *14–15* Verbally compare music that moves in threes and fours. *54–55* Use conducting patterns to show beat groupings. *72–73* Add short sounds together to show the length of sounds. *80–81*
	Create	Improvise melodies using appropriate rhythm to reflect verbal images. *94–95* Create a variety of rhythm patterns for performance on percussion instruments. *194*
echo pitch range melodic contour tonal center scale skip—step	**Perform**	Sing and play melodies by ear or by reading scale numbers. *Throughout* Perform two-part songs, demonstrating accurate pitch and familiarity with scale skips. *32–33* Play melodies on resonator bells by reading notation. *84–85*
	Describe	Recognize pitches occurring on the tonal center. *24–25* Use knowledge of scale numbers and letter names to identify major scales and tonal centers used in songs. *108–109* Verbally compare major and minor scales. *114–115* Show the contour of a melody through movement. *175* Improvise melodies vocally. *147*
	Create	Improvise accompaniments on classroom instruments, using the pitches of a pentatonic scale. *186* Create an introduction, interlude, or coda to a song. *224–225*
autoharp, guitar, trumpet, violin, harmonica, organ, gamelan, voice percussion (pitched and nonpitched) such as drums, timpani, cymbals, metallophones, piano woodwinds such as bassoon, clarinet, oboe, flute strings such as violin, viola, cello, bass brass such as trombone, tuba, trumpet, French horn	**Perform**	Perform melodies to suggest sounds of orchestral instruments. *64–65* Play the autoharp using appropriate tone quality. *142–143*
	Describe	Categorize instruments by orchestral family. *60–61* Identify instruments heard within an orchestral piece. *190–191*
	Create	Improvise music on instruments of students' devising. *196–197*

	Concepts	Ikon	Musical Symbol
DYNAM-ICS	■ Music may be comparatively loud or soft. *Pages:* **12–13, 90–91,** 161–162, **187,** 196–197, 200 ■ Music may become louder or softer. *Pages:* 6–7, 26–27, 92–93, 142–143, 166–167, **187,** 232–233		*f*　　*p*
ARTICU-LATION	■ A series of sounds may move from one to the next in either a smoothly connected or a detached manner. *Pages:* 10–11, **90–91,** 92–93, 161–162, 166–167, 212–213, 222 ■ The quality of a sound is affected by the way the sound begins, continues, and ends. *Pages:* 190–191		
HARMONY	■ Chords and melody may move simultaneously in relation to each other. *Pages:* 8–9, 32–33, 36–37, **40–41, 42–43,** 44–45, 56–57, **118–119, 120–121, 122–123,** 138, **139, 140, 141, 142–143, 144, 145, 146, 147, 148, 149,** 170–171, 184, 196–197, **203,** 219, 222 ■ Two or more pitches may be sounded simultaneously. *Pages:* 12–13, 40–41, 64–65, 66–67, 120–121, 137 ■ Two or more musical lines may occur simultaneously. *Pages:* 6–7, 46–47, 56–57, 106–107, 112–113, 116–117, **150–151, 152–153, 218, 220,** 221, 224–225, **226–228**		
TEX-TURE	■ Musical quality is affected by the distance between the musical lines. *Pages:* 38–39, 166–167 ■ Musical quality is affected by the number of or degree of contrast between musical lines occurring simultaneously. *Pages:* 60–61, 96–97, **166–167, 200,** 218		
FORM	■ A musical whole begins, continues, and ends. *Pages:* 96–97, 149, 161–162, 196–197, 200, 229, **230–231** ■ A musical whole is a combination of smaller segments. *Pages:* 8–9, 24–25, **36–37,** 54–55, 114–115, 164–165, 176–177 ■ A musical whole may be made up of same, varied, or contrasting segments. *Pages:* 6–7, 12–13, **18–19,** 22–23, **28–29, 31, 52–53, 92–93, 102–103, 104–105, 106–107, 116–117,** 122–123, 124–125, 147, 166–167, **178–179,** 188–189, **193,** 201, **202,** 212–213, **214–215, 217,** 221, 226–227, 234–235 ■ A series of sounds may form a distinct musical idea within the musical whole. *Pages:* **26–27,** 148, **190–191** ■ A musical whole may include an introduction, interludes, and an ending segment. *Pages:* **26–27,** 118–119, 142–143, 190–191, 200, **217**		
EXPRESSION	■ Musical elements are combined into a whole to express a musical or extramusical idea. *Pages:* **8–9, 10–11, 46–47, 48–49,** 56–57, **94–95, 96–97,** 114–115, **124–125,** 130–131, **136,** 139, 152–153, **154–155, 158–159,** 160, **161–163, 164–165, 168–169, 170–171,** 192, 193, 202, **204–205, 208–209, 210–211, 212–213, 216,** 219, **232–233, 234–235** ■ The expressiveness of music is affected by the way timbre, dynamics, articulation, rhythm, melody, harmony, form, tempo, and texture contribute to the musical whole. *Pages:* 6, 17, **38–39,** 54–55, **92–93, 196–197, 201**		
TIME & PLACE	■ The way musical elements are combined into a whole reflects the origin of the music. *Pages:* 50–51, 52–53, 166–167, **180–181, 182–183, 185,** 188–189, **198–199, 222,** 223, 229 ■ A particular use of timbre, dynamics, articulation, rhythm, melody, harmony, and form reflects the origin of the musical whole. *Pages:* 36–37, 46–47, 76–77, **184,** 219		

Terms for Grade 4	Skills/Behaviors for Grade 4	
very soft—medium loud—very loud pianissimo—mezzoforte—fortissimo	**Perform**	Sing and play songs, carefully observing dynamic markings. *90–91*
	Describe	Discuss variations in volume, using traditional musical terms. *187*
	Create	Improvise a melody and accompaniment for poetry, selecting appropriate dynamics to help express ideas. *12–13*
legato staccato marcato	**Perform**	Sing a song using appropriate articulations. *90–91*
	Describe	Devise visual representation to demonstrate the effect of articulation on the expression of a composition. *168*
	Create	Compose music and perform with appropriate articulation to express the ideas in a poem. *161–162*
chord chord symbols harmonic changes I–IV–V7 chords interval pentatonic unison accompaniment root major minor descant	**Perform**	Sing a three-part round, using a bell accompaniment. *40–41* Accompany a melody on the autoharp, using the I and V7 chords. *141* Maintain own part when singing a two-part song. *226–227*
	Describe	Identify places where chords must be changed when accompanying a melody (I, IV, V7). *44–45* Identify the chords required to accompany a song. *140*
	Create	Plan a coda for a song to be played by autoharp. *142–143* Compose harmony for an original melody. *193*
canon round	**Describe**	Identify varying musical textures heard in a composition. *166–167*
	Create	Improvise patterns on percussion instruments; combine them in different ways to create varying textures. *198–199*
suite march theme—variations phrase repeat *D.C. al Fine* first and second endings Introduction, Interlude, and Coda movement chorale refrain—verse trio section bridge	**Perform**	Use knowledge of same and different phrases to learn to sing or play a new song. *103*
	Describe	Use geometric shapes to show the order of phrases and whether they are the same, similar, or different. *28–29* Identify the main melodies and distinguish the introductions, interludes, and codas heard in instrument compositions. *217*
	Create	Compose original pieces by combining an extramusical form, such as poetry, with music. *193*
mood expressiveness	**Perform**	Sing and play songs expressively. *Throughout* Perform rhythm and melody in ways that express specific feelings and emotions. *8–9*
	Describe	Identify ways composers combine various elements to express musical ideas. *92–93* Discuss the effect of musical elements on mood. *164–165*
	Create	Improvise accompaniments to express ideas based on poetry, drama, and song. *94–95*
mariachi steel drum ensemble cowboy song waltz square dance	**Perform**	Sing, play, clap, and move to music and dances that reflect different ethnic traditions and historic periods. *50–51* Perform foreign-language songs with awareness of word meaning and correct pronunciation. *229*
	Describe	Discuss various aspects of music existing among other cultures and nations. *180–181*

3

Unit 1

Unit Overview

Unit I, Music to Explore, focuses on a variety of fundamental musical concepts. Students explore songs, recorded listening selections, dance, drama, and poetry in new and creative ways. The lessons progressively call upon the students to use the skills they have previously acquired.

In the First Quarter students become aware of the effect of self-expression on music. They discover ways that music can be varied, and they explore scale steps and tonal centers in songs. From a variety of musical styles, students learn how to find rhythm patterns in music.

In the Second Quarter, the students learn how rhythm and melody are interrelated. They explore music and dances of other cultures and begin to work with basic chord changes. The instruments of the orchestra are identified, and sounds are categorized by timbre.

Music To Explore

The Third Quarter further explores the role of rhythm in music. The students practice basic conducting patterns, and they learn to determine those notes that move with the beat. Students learn to internalize by *thinking* a pitch or melody and continue to expand their knowledge of musical concepts through the study of theme and variations

Form is introduced in the Fourth Quarter, and similarities and differences in phrases are noted. Students compose a canon, an introduction, an interlude, a coda, and an accompaniment to a song. They identify the themes from "Cattle" by Virgil Thomson. Various aspects of musical notation, including dotted quarter notes, are considered. Melodies and scales are transposed, major and minor scales are compared, and rhythm patterns are further explored.

Lesson Focus

Expression: The expressiveness of music is affected by the way timbre, dynamics, articulation, rhythm, melody, harmony, and form contribute to the musical whole. *(P–E)*

Materials

○ **No Piano Accompaniment**

○ **Record Information:**
  • Merry Are the Bells
  Record 1 Side A Band 1
  Voices: children's choir
  Accompaniment: glockenspiel, chimes, music box, carillon, gamelan, tuned Chinese gongs, English hand bells

○ **Instruments:** resonator bells and xylophones C, D, F♯, G, A, B, and D′; mallets

○ **Teacher's Resource Binder:**
  [Activity Sheets] • **Activity Sheet 1,** page A4 (Prepare several copies.)
  • Optional—
  Curriculum Correlation 1, page C2

(continued on next page)

The First Quarter

Introducing the Lesson

Clap a steady beat as you meet the students at the door. As they enter the room, ask them to softly clap your beat. As the students stand by their chairs, clap louder, softer, faster, and slower. Return to a moderate tempo and perform the chant "Along, Long, Long" for the class as they continue to softly clap the beat. (See **For Your Information.**)

Developing the Lesson

1. Teach the chant by asking the students to repeat it after you. When they know the chant, explore ways in which it can be varied musically. Discuss how each variation affects the chant.

   • Dynamics: Begin chanting softly, become gradually louder, then get softer again.

   • Tempo: Chant fast, then slow.
   • Melody: Call on several volunteers to improvise a melody on any two pitches for the final words. The class may echo the melody pattern.
   • Harmony: Divide the class into two groups. Ask the first group to repeatedly sing "So long" on E♭. The second group may then join in, singing the same phrase on G (a third higher). Both groups should continue to sing "So long" several times together, then gradually slow down to end the chant.
   • Form: Clap the rhythm of the first phrase. **How many times do you hear this pattern?** (once) **When do you hear contrasting patterns?** (next four phrases)

2. **Can you find the words on page 6 that describe some of the musical elements we've just used?** (tempo, melody, harmony, dynamics, rhythm, form)

Merry Are the Bells

English Round

Mer - ry are the bells and mer - ry would they ring;
Gai - ly o'er the house - tops, gai - ly through the streets

mer - ry is my - self and mer - ry would I sing.
sound the ring - ing bells as mer - ry friends do meet.

With a mer - ry ding, dong, hap - py, strong, and free and a

mer - ry, mer - ry sing song, hap - py let us be!

Materials *(continued)*

Kodaly Activity 9, page K13
**Mainstreaming Suggestions 1
and 2,** page M7
Orff Activity 1, page O2

○ **For additional experience with time
and place:** Describe 14, page 184

For Your Information

Chanting rhythm for "Along, Long, Long":

As I was go-ing a - long, long, long,

A - sing-ing a com - i - cal song, song, song,

The lane that I took was so long, long, long.

And so I went sing-ing a - long.

So long. So long. So

(Repeat and fade out)

---

3. Play the recording of "Merry Are the Bells." Ask the students to open their books to page 7 and to follow the melody as they listen. Invite them to sing the song.

4. Invite the class to move to the music. Students may sit on the floor in an open space. Identify each of five students as a leader of a chain dance. One at a time the leaders should weave in and out among the class, gently tapping a new seated student at the beginning of each phrase. When tapped, that student takes the hand of the last person in the chain. Each leader should acquire four new members for every repetition of the song. Repeat the song until the entire class has joined the chain. Encourage the students to try a variety of weaving and swooping movements as they sing and move.

OPTIONAL

Closing the Lesson

Set up resonator bells and xylophones C♯, D, F♯, G, A, B, and D'. Distribute a copy of Activity Sheet 1 *(Merry Are the Bells)* to each of the performers. They may add the instrumental parts while the rest of the class sings and dances to "Merry Are the Bells."

Lesson Focus

Expression: Musical elements are combined into a whole to express a musical or extramusical idea. *(D–E)*

Materials

○ **No Piano Accompaniment**

○ **Record Information:**
  • Merry Are the Bells
    (Record 1 Side 1 Band 1)
  • How Di Do
  Record 1 Side A Band 2
    Voices: man, children's choir
    Accompaniment: fiddle, 5-string banjo, guitar, double bass
  • Tennessee Wig Walk
    by Larry Coleman and Norman Gimbel
    Record 1 Side A Band 3
    Russ Morgan and His Orchestra

○ **Teacher's Resource Binder:**
  • Optional—
    Enrichment Activity 1, page E2
    Kodaly Activity 7, page K10
    Mainstreaming Suggestion 3, page M9

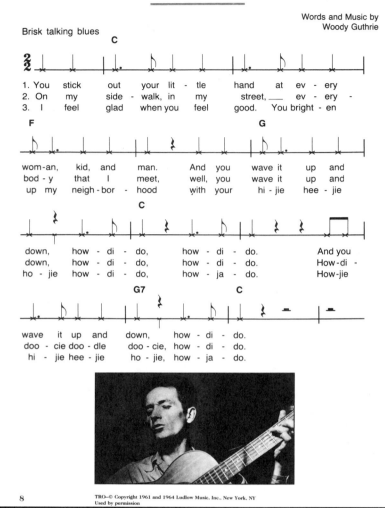

How Di Do

Words and Music by
Woody Guthrie

Brisk talking blues

1. You stick out your lit - tle hand at ev - ery
2. On my side - walk, in my street, __ ev - ery -
3. I feel glad when you feel good. You bright - en

wom-an, kid, and man. And you wave it up and
bod - y that I meet, well, you wave it up and
up my neigh - bor - hood with your hi - jie hee - jie

down, how - di - do, how - di - do. And you
down, how - di - do, how - di - do. How-di
ho - jie how - di - do, how - ja - do. How-jie

wave it up and down, how - di - do.
doo - cie doo - dle doo - cie, how - di - do.
hi - jie hee - jie ho - jie, how - ja - do.

8   TRO—© Copyright 1961 and 1964 Ludlow Music, Inc., New York, NY
Used by permission

Introducing the Lesson

Review the song, "Merry Are the Bells" (page 7). Teach the students a harmony part that may be sung with the melody.

Ding,   dong.   Ding,   dong,   ding.

Use this part to also create an introduction and a special ending.

Developing the Lesson

1. Discuss how music helps us enjoy our friends and how there are many ways we can "musically play together." Ask the students to open their books to pages 8–9 and to follow the words as they listen to the recording of "How Di Do." **What is different about this song?** (There is harmony but no melody; the performer just speaks the words.) **Could you tell by looking at the notes on the staff that there**

was to be no melody? (Yes, because there are x's instead of regular notes.) Explain that music written with x's shows speech instead of melody. Sometimes music for drummers is also written this way.

2. Ask the class to listen again, paying special attention to the rhythm. They may then perform the "talking blues" with the recording.

3. Continue musically playing together by introducing "Tennessee Wig Walk." Listen to the recording and help the class discover the order of the sections **(A A B A).**

4. Have the students form a double circle, with each set of partners facing one another. Perform the dance as follows:
Section A
  • Step right; close right; step right; close right. Clap on the last close. (Note: Partners will be moving away from each other.)

Refrain

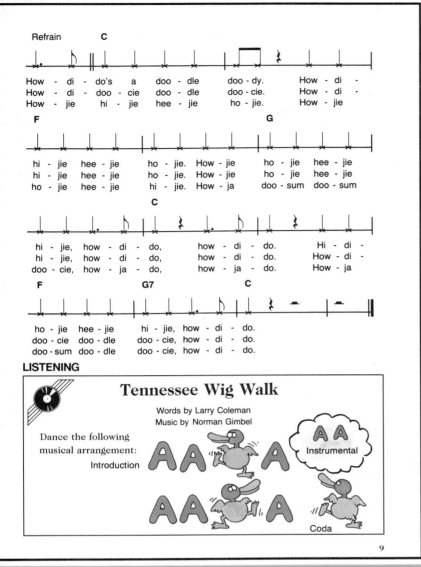

C

How - di - do's a doo - dle doo - dy. How - di -
How - di - doo - cie doo - dle doo - cie. How - di -
How - jie hi - jie hee - jie ho - jie. How - jie

F   G

hi - jie hee - jie ho - jie. How - jie ho - jie hee - jie
hi - jie hee - jie ho - jie. How - jie ho - jie hee - jie
ho - jie hee - jie hi - jie. How - ja doo - sum doo - sum

C

hi - jie, how - di - do, how - di - do. Hi - di -
hi - jie, how - di - do, how - di - do. How - di -
doo - cie, how - ja - do, how - ja - do. How - ja

F   G7   C

ho - jie hee - jie hi - jie, how - di - do.
doo - cie doo - dle doo - cie, how - di - do.
doo - sum doo - dle doo - cie, how - di - do.

LISTENING

Tennessee Wig Walk

Words by Larry Coleman
Music by Norman Gimbel

Dance the following
musical arrangement:

Introduction

Instrumental

Coda

9

For Your Information
Words for "Tennessee Wig Walk":
Section A, Verse 1
I'm a bowlegged chicken; I'm a
Knock-kneed hen.
Never been so happy since I
Don't know when. I
Walk with a wiggle and a
Giggle and a squawk,
Doing the Tennessee Wig Walk!
Section A, Verse 2
Hear a tune on a fiddle on a
Hardwood floor. Though I'm
Broke and weary and my
Back is sore, I
Walk with a wiggle and a
Giggle and a squawk,
Doing the Tennessee Wig Walk!
Section B
Put your toes together, your
Knees apart;
Bend your back, get
Ready, and start.
Flap your elbows
Just for luck; and then you
Wiggle and waddle like a baby duck.
Section A, Verse 3
Won't you dance with me honey, tap your
Toes and glide. And we'll
Always be together,
Side by side.
Walk with a wiggle and a
Giggle and a squawk,
Doing the Tennessee Wig Walk!

- Repeat, this time stepping to the left.
- "Suzy Q" (swivel on balls of feet) for eight beats. Move to the right to a new partner. Step with the right foot, swing the left foot, and spin around once.
- Clap thighs; clap hands; clap new partner's hands.

Section B
Take positions suggested by the words of the song. On the words "I walk with a wiggle," improvise a silly duck walk, moving to the right around the circle. Stop at the end of the verse and face a new partner.

Closing the Lesson OPTIONAL

As the students dance to the recording, they will soon learn the words. Encourage them to sing as they dance.

Lesson Focus

Expression: Musical elements are combined into a whole to express a musical or extramusical idea. *(C–I)*

Materials

○ **Piano Accompaniment:** page 238
○ **Record Information:**
  • Weave Me the Sunshine
    Record 1 Side A Band 4
    Voices: solo child, children's choir
    Accompaniment: oboe, guitar, electric piano, electric bass, percussion
○ **Teacher's Resource Binder:**
  • Optional—
    Orff Activity 2, page O2
○ **For additional experience with expression:** Describe 2, page 161

For Your Information

Wassily Kandinsky is primarily known as a painter. He also liked to express his feelings in words, creating wonderful poems that suggest images just as his paintings do.

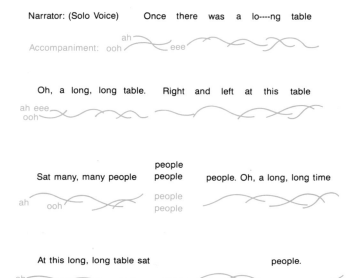

Table

by Wassily Kandinsky

Once there was a long table. Oh, a long,
long table. Right and left at this table
sat many, many, many
people.
people,
people,
people.
Oh, a long, long time at this
long, long table sat people.

10

Introducing the Lesson

Poetry expresses interesting ideas, just as music does. Read the poem, "Table." Explain that Kandinsky was also very concerned about creating a visual impact. **Can you discover the visual impact he was trying to create?** (The words of the poem make a picture of a table.)

Developing the Lesson

1. Perform this poem using musical sounds to help express the words and ideas in the poem. Follow the musical setting of the poem on the page. Select a narrator to expressively speak the words. The remaining students should form a vocal choir to help musically express important words such as "long" and "people." The choir sustains long-sounding dissonant pitches on the syllables "ooh," "ah," and "ee." Each member of the choir sustains the sound for one breath, then begins the next breath on another randomly selected pitch. The group begins to chatter "people," creating short, choppy sounds when indicated in the score. They then return to the long, sustained sounds to complete the performance.

2. Ask the class to look at the words for "Weave Me the Sunshine" (page 11). **What are the important words in this song?** (hope, new tomorrow, only you) **What do you think the words "weave me the sunshine out of the falling rain" mean?** (Make something good happen even if things look sad or bad.)

3. Play the record and ask the students to follow the music as they listen. Comment on the fact that this song is a little more difficult than

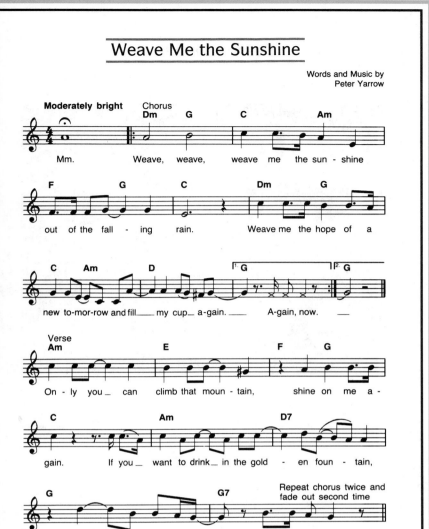

Weave Me the Sunshine

Words and Music by
Peter Yarrow

Moderately bright   Chorus

Mm. Weave, weave, weave me the sun - shine

out of the fall - ing rain. Weave me the hope of a

new to-mor-row and fill___ my cup_ a-gain.___ A-gain, now. ___

Verse

On - ly you_ can climb that moun - tain, shine on me a -

gain. If you_ want to drink_ in the gold - en foun - tain,

Repeat chorus twice and
fade out second time

shine ___ on me a-gain.___ Sing it with me.

11

many they have learned because there is little repetition. **How many times do you think you will need to listen to the song before you can sing it without help from the recording?** Allow the students to offer their ideas; play the recording as many times as they suggest. Then ask them to try singing the song without the record.

Closing the Lesson

Remind the students of the musical-elements discussion in Lesson 1 (page 6). Ask the class to suggest ways their performance of "Weave Me the Sunshine" might be changed to express different ideas. Experiment with different tempos, changes in dynamics, and different kinds of articulation—short (*staccato*) or sustained (*legato*)—for different sections of the song.

Lesson Focus

Dynamics: Music may be comparatively loud or soft. *(D—S)*

Materials

○ **Piano Accompaniment:** page 240

○ **Record Information:**
  • Peace Like a River

📼 **Record 1 Side A Band 5**
  Voices: children's choir
  Accompaniment: piano, electric organ, electric guitar, electric bass, percussion
  • *String Quartet in C Major* ("Emperor"), Second Movement
  by Franz Joseph Haydn (**hide**-n), 1732–1809
  Record 1 Side A Band 6
  The Budapest String Quartet

○ **Instruments:** autoharp or guitar

○ **Teacher's Resource Binder:**

| Activity Sheets | • **Activity Sheet 2**, page A5 |

  • Optional—
  Curriculum Correlation 2, page C2

○ **For additional experience with expression:** Perform 1–7, pages 136–143

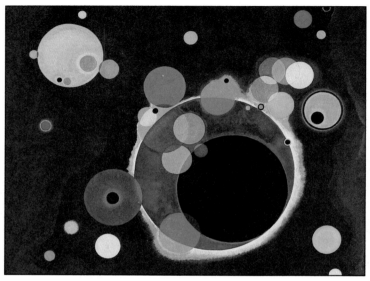

Peace Like a River

Old Southern Hymn

Several Circles by Kandinsky, Collection, Solomon R. Guggenheim Museum, New York.

```
         F              F7                    Bb           F
mp  1. I've got   peace like  a riv-er,   I've got   peace like  a riv-er,
f   2. I've got   joy like  a foun-tain,  I've got   joy like  a foun-tain,
mf  3. I've got   love like  the o-cean,  I've got   love like  the o-cean,

         C7        F          G7              C
    I've got   peace like  a riv-er  in  my   soul.
    I've got   joy like  a foun-tain  in  my   soul.
    I've got   love like  the o-cean  in  my   soul.
```

12

Introducing the Lesson

Ask the students to look at the Kandinsky painting on page 12 of their books. Inform them that the painting is the work of the artist whose poem they learned in the previous lesson.

Explain that color was of great interest to Kandinsky and that this interest is reflected in his poems as well as in his paintings. The following excerpts are examples of his poetry.

Blue, blue got up, got up and fell . . .(from "Seeing")

In the yellow sand walked a little, thin red man . . . (from "Water")

Within the bluish wavelet tosses, the torn and shredded scarlet cloth . . . (from "Hymn")

There are pale blue spots on the yellow glare. Only my eyes saw the pale blue spots . . . (from "Spring")

Ask the students to create sentences using "color words" to "paint" an idea.

Strum an Em or Dm chord on the autoharp (or guitar) as the students read their sentences aloud. After listening to each other's ideas, invite a few of the students to improvise a melody for their idea while you continue the one-chord accompaniment.

Developing the Lesson

1. Explain that poets often use similes to "paint" word pictures. (A simile is when one object or idea is likened to another, such as: "Like a branch on a tree, I keep reaching to be free. . . .") **Look at "Peace Like a River"on**

LISTENING

String Quartet in C Major, ("Emperor")

Second Movement

by Franz Joseph Haydn

Listen to the music. The **form** is **theme and variations**. The main idea, played by the violin, is followed by:

Variation I — violin duet
Variation II — cello plays the melody
Variation III — viola plays the melody
Variation IV — melody played an octave higher
         by 1st violin

Would the mood of this music be the same if it were played by a quartet of woodwind instruments?

13

page 12. Where are the similes in these lyrics? ("peace like a river," "joy like a fountain," "love like the ocean") The students will discover that the lyrics are almost entirely made up of similes.

2. **Is there such a thing as a "musical simile"?** Play the recording. Help the class to recognize that the melody and rhythm of each phrase are similar to the first phrase. Challenge the students to sing the song without the recording.

3. Focus attention on the dynamic markings as the recording is played again. Ask the children to decide the meaning of each marking by listening to the singers as they perform each verse. Decide that *mp* means medium soft; *f* means loud; and *mf* means medium loud. **Why do you think the markings were placed in this order?** (Perhaps the composer felt that soft

was most appropriate for "peace"; that joy "like a fountain" should swell up loudly; and that the feeling of love would also be intense but more personal and therefore only medium loud.) Ask the class to perform the song using these dynamics to help express the ideas of the lyrics.

Closing the Lesson

Instrumental music can also express ideas of quiet joy. Use Activity Sheet 2 *(Haydn String Quartet in C Major)* or the brief description on the pupil page. Play the recording of the "Emperor" quartet, guiding the students to follow the boxes on the activity sheet. After listening to the recording, ask the class to identify the way in which each variation was similar to yet different from the first statement of the theme. Discuss the question at the bottom of page 13.

"Measure" a Rhythm

What do these things measure?

Here is a rhythm ruler.
What do you think it will measure?

Can you measure the sounds in the rhythm pattern?

Can you measure the length of each note?

14

Lesson Focus

Rhythm: Individual sounds and silences within a rhythmic line may be longer than, shorter than, or the same as the underlying shortest pulse. *(D–I)*

Materials

○ **No Piano Accompaniment**

○ **Record Information:**
  • Sweetly Sings the Donkey
    Record 1 Side A Band 7
    Voices: children's choir
    Accompaniment: recorder, bassoon, harpsichord
  • Why Shouldn't My Goose?
    Record 1 Side A Band 8
    Voices: boy's choir
    Accompaniment: two crumhorns, viola da gamba, regal organ

○ **Other:** overhead projector; black overhead pen

○ **Teacher's Resource Binder:**
  Activity Sheets • **Activity Sheet 3,** page A6 (Prepare a transparency from the activity sheet.)

(continued on next page)

Introducing the Lesson

Ask the class to open their books and answer the question at the top of page 14. After they have identified each measuring instrument, ask them to look at the rhythm ruler. Conclude that it measures the length of sounds. The second rhythm ruler shows a rhythm pattern. **How will you know how long to make each sound?** ("Measure" it against the shortest sound units marked on the rhythm ruler.) Help the class describe the length of each sound in relation to the shortest sound.

Establish the shortest sound by tapping against your thigh. Ask the students to chant the pattern using the words "short" and "long."

Have the students look at the last rhythm ruler. Help them discover that it shows the same pattern they just performed, now shown with notes.

Developing the Lesson

1. **Look at the songs on page 15. Which pattern did you just perform?** (first part of "Why Shouldn't My Goose?") Display the transparency prepared from Activity Sheet 3 *(Rhythm Ruler)*. **Tell me how to fill in the rhythm ruler to show the length of each note for the rest of the song.** The ruler should look like this:

   Chant this rhythm pattern. Then return to "Why Shouldn't My Goose?" on page 15. Chant the rhythm with words.

2. Help the class learn the melody. Notice places where it stays the same, skips, or steps up or down. Establish tonality by singing 1–5, 3–1, 5–1'. Challenge the students to sing the mel-

Why Shouldn't My Goose?

Traditional Round

Why should-n't my goose grow as fat as thy goose,

When I paid for my goose twice as much as thine?

Sweetly Sings the Donkey

Old English Round

Sweet-ly sings the don - key at the break of day.

If you do not feed him, this is what he'll say:

"Hee - haw! Hee-haw! Hee - haw, hee-haw, hee-haw!"

15

Materials *(continued)*
• Optional—
Enrichment Activity 2, page E2
Kodaly Activities 2 and 12,
pages K2 and K19
**Mainstreaming Suggestions 4,
5**, pages M9, M11
Orff Activity 3, page O3

o **For additional experience with rhythm:**
Describe 9, page 176

ody independently. Listen to the recording and correct any mistakes.

3. Return to the transparency. **Can you perform the rhythm of this song? What does the ruler measure when the box is empty?** (a rest) Have the class chant the rhythm on "ch."

4. Draw attention to the notes and rests at the bottom of the transparency. Ask the students to tell you which note or rest to draw in each box to show with notes the rhythm they just performed. Compare their picture with the notes for the song "Why Shouldn't My Goose?" on page 15. **Were you right?**

Closing the Lesson

Help the students learn the melody of "Sweetly Sings the Donkey" by listening to the recording.

As I sing the song, stand when the melody makes a big skip up. (on "hee") Sit when the melody makes a big skip down. (on "haw") When the students can readily do this, ask them to sing the song while continuing to stand and sit on each "hee haw."

Return to both songs at a later time and help the students learn to sing them as rounds.

Lesson Focus

Rhythm: Individual sounds and silences within a rhythmic line may be longer than, shorter than, or the same as the underlying shortest pulse. *(D—I)*

Materials

o **No Piano Accompaniment**

o **Record Information:**
  - Sweetly Sings the Donkey **(Record 1 Side A Band 7)**
  - Kookaburra **Record 1 Side B Band 1** Voices: children's choir Accompaniment: string quartet

o **Instruments:** a variety of mallet instruments, as presented on pupil page

o **Other:** pencil; transparency prepared from Activity Sheet 3; overhead projector

o **Teacher's Resource Binder:**

  Activity Sheets
  - **Activity Sheet 4,** page A7 (Prepare a copy for each student.)
  - Optional—
    Curriculum Correlation 12, page C28
    Kodaly Activities 1 and 3, pages K2 and K5
    Mainstreaming Suggestion 5, page M11

o **For additional experience with rhythm:** Describe 8, page 175

Introducing the Lesson

Distribute a pencil and a copy of Activity Sheet 4 *(Measure a Rhythm)* to each student. Remind the class of the previously completed activity (page 14) in which they measured the length of sounds with the rhythm ruler. **Listen as I sing "Sweetly Sings the Donkey"** (page 15). **Draw lines to show the length of each sound. How long will you make the first sound?** (equal to one short sound)

Sing the song several times as the students draw vertical lines to show the length of each sound. When they have finished, display the transparency prepared from Activity Sheet 3 so the students can check their work.

Developing the Lesson

1. **That wasn't too hard because you knew the song. Can you draw the rhythm of a new song?** Tap the shortest sound and sing "Kookaburra." **What kind of a sound does the rhythm of the song begin with?** (with the shortest sound) Sing the song several times as the students draw the melodic rhythm.

2. When the students have finished drawing the rhythm, display the transparency prepared from Activity Sheet 3. Have them exchange patterns with their neighbors. Sing the song while they check their friends' patterns. **Did you find any problems?** (They may check against the transparency to correct any errors.)

3. Ask the class to turn to page 16 and sing the song as they follow the notation.

4. Challenge the students to become independent musicians by learning the instrumental parts on page 17. **How will the rhythm of the**

For Your Information
Rhythm rulers for "Kookaburra":

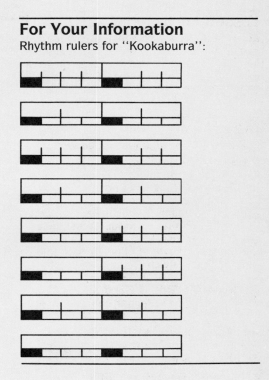

Alto Xylophone I part move? (Some notes will be twice as long as the shortest sound; others will be four times as long.) **How does the melody move?** (stays on the same pitch)

5. **Look at the Alto Xylophone II part. How is this pattern like the first alto xylophone part?** (same rhythm) **How is it different?** (uses two pitches)

6. Choose two students to practice the two patterns; then ask the class to sing Verse 1 as they play the accompaniment. Two other students may accompany Verse 2.

Closing the Lesson OPTIONAL

Learn as many patterns as possible, depending on the number of instruments available, the ability of the students, and the amount of time you have.

Lesson Focus

Form: A musical whole may be made up of same, varied, or contrasting segments.
Melody: A series of pitches may move up or down by steps or skips. *(D–I)*

Materials

○ **Piano Accompaniment:** page 244

○ **Record Information:**
  • The Silver Birch
    Record 1 Side B Band 2
    Voices: children's choir
    Accompaniment: balalaika, mandolin, guitar, cimbalom, double bass, accordion, percussion
  • *Symphony No. 4,* Fourth Movement, by Peter Ilyich Tchaikovsky (cheye-**koff**-skee), 1840–1893
    Record 1 Side B Band 3
    The New York Philharmonic
    Leonard Bernstein, conductor

○ **Instruments:** resonator bells E, F♯, G, A, and B; bell mallet; drum

○ **Other:** pencil

○ **Teacher's Resource Binder:**
  | Activity Sheets | • **Activity Sheet 5,** page A8 (Prepare one copy for each student.) |

  • Optional—
    Biography 1, page B1

(continued on next page)

LISTENING

Symphony No. 4
Fourth Movement
by Peter Ilyich Tchaikovsky

People plan trips.

Composers plan musical trips.

Can you map Tchaikovsky's musical trip?

18

Introducing the Lesson *OPTIONAL*

If you were going on a trip to a place that you'd never been to before, you would probably "map out" the trip. What decisions would you make? (Students may offer a variety of answers.) Composers often "map out" a new composition. They decide about the number of themes, their order, and whether they wish to repeat a theme. Composers must also decide whether to create new themes or borrow from melodies they know. Peter Tchaikovsky was a Russian composer who knew many folk songs. When he was mapping out his Fourth Symphony, he decided to use a folk song as one of his four themes.

Developing the Lesson

1. **Open your books to page 19. You will find a folk song Tchaikovsky knew.** Examine the melodic rhythm of "The Silver Birch." Review the relationship of each note to the eighth note as shown by the rhythm ruler at the top of the page. Ask the class to tap the shortest sound while a few students tap the melodic rhythm on the drums.

2. Examine the melody and guide the class to discover that Phrases 1 and 2 are the same, as are Phrases 3 and 4. Ask a student to play the first phrase on the resonator bells. (See **Materials.**) Then have the class sing the phrase with the words. Use the same procedure to learn the remaining phrases. Play the recording and correct any problems. Sing the complete song.

3. **Listen to Tchaikovsky's music. Does he use our song for Theme 1?** (no) Play the recording through the first theme. **Is it used in his second theme?** (yes) Play through Theme 2.

The Silver Birch

Words adapted by
Marcella Bannon

Russian Folk Tune

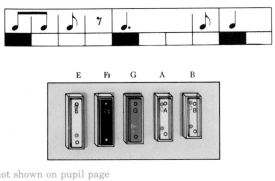

Chords not shown on pupil page

Em

Moderately

D   Em

Sil - ver birch a - lone in a mead - ow,

Em   D   Em

stand - ing all a - lone in a mead - ow.

Bm   D   Em

Soon a shep - herd boy comes stroll - ing.

Bm   D   Em

With his sheep and goats, he's stroll - ing.

19

From GROWING WITH MUSIC SERIES, Book 4, Wilson, et al (Englewood Cliffs, NJ: Prentice-Hall, Inc. © 1966)

Materials *(continued)*

Curriculum Correlation 12, page C26
Kodaly Activity 16, page K25
Orff Activity 10, page O17

○ **For additional experience with rhythm:**
Special Times 14, page 229

For Your Information

The four themes of Tchaikovsky's *Symphony No. 4 Fourth Movement:*

Theme 1

Theme 2

Theme 3

Theme 4

4. Can you make a "map" of this musical trip? Distribute Activity Sheet 5 *(Symphony No. 4)*. Each row of boxes on the map represents one of the four themes in the movement. **The composer moves from Theme 1 to Theme 2. What could Tchaikovsky have done next?** (gone to Theme 3, repeated Theme 2, returned to Theme 1) Tell the class to listen and then put an "X" in the box that shows the choice Tchaikovsky made. Play the recording through the third theme. **Where should you have put your "X"?** (third box in first row to show return of theme)

Closing the Lesson

Replay the recording as needed, guiding the students to complete their maps. Discuss their answers and put the correct answer, as shown on the diagram, on the chalkboard.

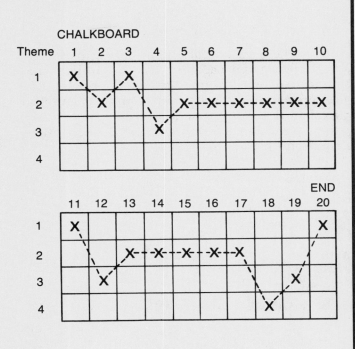

CHALKBOARD

Lesson Focus

Melody: A series of pitches, bounded by the octave, "belong together," forming a tonal set. *(P–S)*

Materials

- ○ **Piano Accompaniment:** page 246
- ○ **Record Information:**
  - • School Days
  - **Record 1 Side B Band 4**
    Voices: children's choir
    Accompaniment: piano, percussion
  - • Lullaby Round
    Record 1 Side B Band 5
    Voices: children's choir
    Accompaniment: harp, celesta
- ○ **Teacher's Resource Binder:**
  Evaluation • Optional—
    Checkpoint 1, page Ev2
    Kodaly Activities 3, 15,
    pages K5, K22
- ○ **For additional experience with melody:**
  Special Times 12, page 224

Singing Warm-Ups

Introducing the Lesson

Focus the students' attention on the picture at the top of pupil page 20. **Why do athletes and dancers exercise before starting their activities?** (to prevent injury and to warm up their muscles) Explain that musicians do exercises to warm up their fingers and their vocal chords. **Let's warm up. Echo me.** Perform the following patterns in the key of C while doing the body scale motions. (See page xxvii for the body scale.)

```
1 2 3 4 5 6 7 1'
1 3 5 3 1
1 2 3 4 5 3 1
5 4 3 2 1
```

Developing the Lesson

1. Have the class warm up their "music-reading muscles" by singing the patterns on page 20.

2. Ask the students to look at the songs on pages 20 and 21. **Which song includes these patterns?** ("Lullaby Round") **How do you know?** (It moves mostly by steps, like the warm-ups.) **How does the beginning of "School Days" move?** (mostly by skips) **Which song will be easier to sing with numbers?** ("Lullaby Round" will be, because it moves mostly by steps.)

3. Ask the class to demonstrate their ability to sing with scale numbers by singing "Lullaby Round." Establish the starting pitch on C and identify it as "1."

4. After the students have sung the song with numbers, ask them to do the body scale motions while they listen to the recording. **Where will you start?** (1—at the knees) Next, invite the class to sing "Lullaby Round" while doing the body scale.

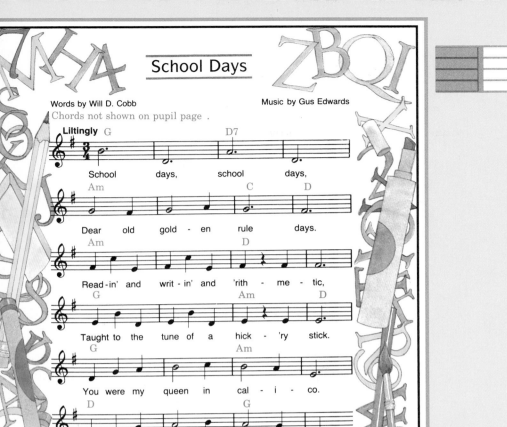

School Days

Words by Will D. Cobb

Music by Gus Edwards

Chords not shown on pupil page .

School days, school days,

Dear old gold - en rule days.

Read - in' and writ - in' and 'rith - me - tic,

Taught to the tune of a hick - 'ry stick.

You were my queen in cal - i - co.

I was your bash - ful, bare - foot beau,

And you wrote on my slate, "I love you, Joe,"

When we were a cou - ple of kids. _____

21

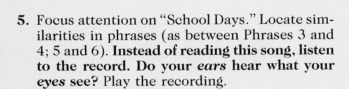

5. Focus attention on "School Days." Locate similarities in phrases (as between Phrases 3 and 4; 5 and 6). **Instead of reading this song, listen to the record. Do your *ears* hear what your *eyes* see?** Play the recording.

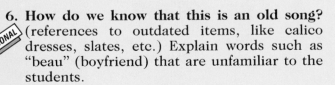

6. How do we know that this is an old song? (references to outdated items, like calico dresses, slates, etc.) Explain words such as "beau" (boyfriend) that are unfamiliar to the students.

Closing the Lesson

Encourage the students to listen to the recording of "School Days" as often as necessary to learn it well enough to sing at home. **Find out if your parents or your grandparents ever sang this song when they were in school.**

Lesson Focus

Melody: A series of pitches bounded by the octave ''belong together,'' forming a tonal set. *(P—I)*

Materials

○ **Piano Accompaniments:** pages 241 and 248

○ **Record Information:**
 • Peace Like a River
  (Record 1 Side A Band 5)
 • Why Shouldn't My Goose?
  (Record 1 Side A Band 8)
 • Lullaby Round
  (Record 1 Side B Band 5)
 • Pop goes the Weasel
  Record 1 Side B Band 6
  Voices: children's choir
  Accompaniment: synthesizer, percussion, sound effects
 • Three Jolly Fisherman
  Record 1 Side B Band 7
  Voices: children's choir
  Accompaniment: bass clarinet, trumpet, viola, electric harpsichord, percussion
 • *Variations on Pop Goes the Weasel* by Lucien Caillet (kie-**yay**), 1891 —
  Record 2 Side A Band 1
  Washington Symphony Orchestra
  Howard Mitchell, conductor

(continued on next page)

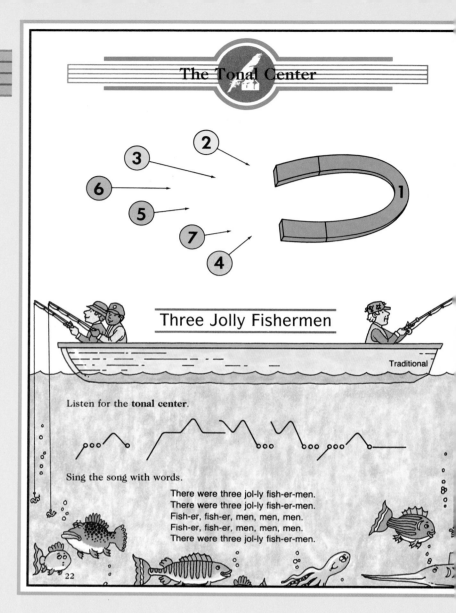

The Tonal Center

Three Jolly Fishermen

Traditional

Listen for the **tonal center**.

Sing the song with words.

There were three jol-ly fish-er-men.
There were three jol-ly fish-er-men.
Fish-er, fish-er, men, men, men.
Fish-er, fish-er, men, men, men.
There were three jol-ly fish-er-men.

22

Introducing the Lesson

I have some mystery melodies for you. I will sing the last part of a song you know, but I'll use numbers instead of words. Can you "name that tune"? Enjoy singing each song together after the class identifies it.

("Peace Like a River") 5 6 1 1 1 3 3 2 2 1

("Why Shouldn't My Goose?") 5 5 5 5 1'
5 4 3 2 1

("Lullaby Round") 4 4 3   6 6 5   4 4 3 3 2 2 1

Developing the Lesson

1. **Each song ended on the same step of the scale. What was it?** ("1") Sing the examples again for students who were not sure. **We call this pitch the tonal center.** Explain how most melodies have a tonal center that acts as a magnet. It seems to "pull" the melody to that pitch, especially at the end. **Here is the tonal center for a new song.** Play the F resonator bell. Ask the class to listen to the recording of "Three Jolly Fishermen." (See page 25 for complete song.) Play the F again. **Does that pitch pull the melody to end on it?** (yes)

2. Focus the students' attention on the "picture" of the melody of "Three Jolly Fishermen" on pupil page 22. Explain that each circle stands for the tonal center. Ask the students to follow the picture with their fingers. **Can you "stay with" the music?** Play the recording. Have the students identify the words that are sung on the tonal center. ("were three jol-" and "men") **Listen again before you answer.**

3. Give one student the F bell to play each time the tonal center occurs in the first verse. Choose other students for Verses 2 and 3.

OPTIONAL

Pop Goes the Weasel

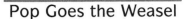

Traditional

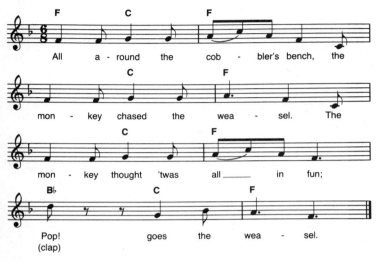

All a-round the cob-bler's bench, the
mon-key chased the wea-sel. The
mon-key thought 'twas all ____ in fun;
Pop! goes the wea-sel.
(clap)

LISTENING

"Variations on Pop Goes the Weasel"
by Lucien Caillet

23

Materials *(continued)*

○ **Instruments:** resonator bell F; bell mallet
○ **Teacher's Resource Binder:**
  • Optional—
  Curriculum Correlation 3, page C5
  Kodaly Activities 10, 11, and 12, pages K16, K19
○ **For additional experience with expression:** Create 1, page 192

For Your Information

Form for *Variations on Pop Goes the Weasel:*

Introduction—snatches of melody, full orchestra
Theme—"Pop Goes the Weasel," 6/8, orchestra
Variation 1—fugue, theme enters 5 times, variety of instruments
Variation 2—minuet, change of meter to 3/4, violins and brass
Variation 3—played in gypsy style, change to slower tempo, minor key
Variation 4—played in "music box" style, 3/4, violin, flute, piccolo, and glockenspiel
Variation 5—played in jazz style, 2/4, violins, trumpets, other brass
Coda

---

4. Ask the class to listen to another song. Play the recording of "Pop Goes the Weasel." **Be ready to sing the tonal center when the song ends.**

5. Tell the students to follow the music on page 23 as the recording is played again. Challenge them to sing only the tonal center aloud and to "think" all the other words. Repeat the activity, asking them to now sing all the other words and be silent on the tonal center!

Closing the Lesson

Tell the class that a composer decided to borrow "Pop Goes the Weasel" just as Tchaikovsky borrowed "The Silver Birch" (page 19). Have them listen again to the *Symphony No. 4* and recall the ways Tchaikovsky made the theme interesting by varying it. Play the recording of Caillet's *Variations on Pop Goes the Weasel.* **What does this composer do to help keep the theme interesting?** (varies the instruments, tempo, dynamics, melody, and rhythm) **Look at page 23 as you listen. Can you identify the picture that matches each variation?** (See **For Your Information**.) Focus the students' attention on the "Pop!" while listening to the composition one more time.

Lesson Focus

Melody: Each pitch within a melody moves in relation to a home tone.
Melody: A series of pitches bounded by the octave ''belong together,'' forming a tonal set. *(P–S)*

Materials

○ **Piano Accompaniment:** page 242
○ **Record Information:**
  • Three Jolly Fishermen
    (Record 1 Side B Band 7)
  • Pop Goes the Weasel
    (Record 1 Side B Band 6)
  • Bye Bye, Blackbird
    Record 2 Side A Band 2
    Voices: children's choir
    Accompaniment: trumpet, tenor saxophone, trombone, guitar, double bass, piano, percussion
○ **Instruments:** resonator bell F; bell mallet
○ **Teacher's Resource Binder:**
  • Optional—
    Curriculum Correlation 4, page C5
    Mainstreaming Suggestion 6, page M13
○ **For additional experience with expression:** Describe 6, page 170

Bye Bye, Blackbird

Words by Mort Dixon

Music by Ray Henderson

Chords not shown on pupil page

Pack up all my cares and woe, Here I go, sing-ing low.
Bye bye, black - bird.
Where some-bod - y waits for me, Sug-ar's sweet, so is she.
Bye bye, black - bird.

24

Introducing the Lesson

Review "Three Jolly Fishermen" and "Pop Goes the Weasel" (page 22). Perform each song in various ways: singing only the words that occur on the tonal center; singing all other words and remaining silent on the tonal center; allowing one student to play the appropriate bell each time the tonal center is heard.

Developing the Lesson

1. Ask the class to look at the song on pages 24–25 of their books. **There are no circles to show the tonal center. Can your ears tell you which pitch is the tonal center?** Ask the class to warm up by singing 1–3–5–1. **I'm going to sing the song. Be ready to sing the tonal center when I finish.** When you have finished singing the song and the students have sung the tonal center, ask them if the song ended on "1." (yes) **Is the note that represents the tonal center on a line or in a space?** (in a space—the first) Ask the students to listen again and raise their hands each time they see and hear the tonal center. **Will you raise your hand for the first note?** (No, because it starts on 3.)

2. Help the students sing the first section, using numbers as they follow the notation. (Each section is eight measures long.)

3. **Look at Section 2. What do you notice about it that will help you learn it?** (It has the same shape as Section 1 but starts higher, on 4 instead of 3.)

4. Examine Section 3. Call attention to the sharp (♯), which alters the last pitch in Measure 20 (on the word "me"). **This symbol tells us to alter the sound of that pitch by raising it**

No one here can love and un-der-stand me.

Oh, what hard-luck sto-ries they all hand me.

Make my bed and light the light. I'll ar-rive late to-night.

Black - bird, bye bye.

25

1. There were three jol-ly fish-er-men,—— There
2. The first one's name was A-bra-ham,—— The
3. The second one's name was I - saac,—— The
4. The third one's name was Ja - cob,—— The
5. They all sailed up to Jer-i-cho,—— They

were three jol-ly fish-er-men,
first one's name was A - bra - ham,
second one's name was I - saac,
third one's name was Ja - cob,
all sailed up to Jer-i-cho,

Fish - er, fish - er, men - men - men,
A - bra, A - bra, ham - ham - ham,
I, I, zak - zak - zak,
Jay, Jay, cub - cub - cub,
Jer - ry, Jer - ry, co - co - co,

Fish - er, fish - er, men - men - men, There
A - bra, A - bra, ham - ham - ham, The
I, I, zak - zak - zak, The
Jay, Jay, cub - cub - cub, The
Jer - ry, Jer - ry, co - co - co, They

were three jol-ly fish-er-men.
first one's name was A - bra - ham.
second one's name was I - saac.
third one's name was Ja - cob.
all sailed up to Jer-i-cho.

slightly. Explain that it will also be called "1" but to remember that it is a "raised 1."

5. Complete the song after discussing the similarity of the last section to Sections 1 and 2. Decide that the form of the song is **A A′ B A″**. (Each prime indicates a slightly different alteration of the original section.) When the students have studied and sung each section, ask them to perform the song with the recording. Adjust the balance on the recording so that only the instrumental accompaniment is heard.

Closing the Lesson *OPTIONAL*

This time, I'll sing the song. I will stop after each section. Your task is to sing the tonal center each time. Can you do it?

Lesson Focus

Form: A series of sounds may form a distinct musical idea within the musical whole.
Form: A musical whole may include an introduction, interludes, and an ending segment. *(D–I)*

Materials

○ **Piano Accompaniment:** page 250
○ **Record Information:**
  • Janišek the Highwayman
  Record 2 Side A Band 3
  Voices: children's choir
  Accompaniment: piano, handclaps
  • Bear Dance from *Hungarian Sketches*
  by Béla Bartók, 1881–1945
  Record 2 Side A Band 4
  Washington National Symphony
  Howard Mitchell, conductor
○ **Instruments:** piano or resonator bells C, F, G, and C′; bell mallet
○ **Other:** pencil for each student; overhead projector
○ **Teacher's Resource Binder:**

[Activity Sheets]
  • **Activity Sheet 6,** page A9 (Prepare a transparency from the activity sheet.)
  • **Activity Sheet 7,** page A10 (Prepare one copy for each student.)

(continued on next page)

Janišek the Highwayman

Béla Bartók
Transcribed by Benjamin Suchoff

(clap)   Who's rid-ing down the street?

No one I'd like to meet! Jan-i-šek the high-way-man will

catch you if catch he can!   (clap)

Who's rid-ing down the street? No one I'd like to meet!

Jan-i-šek the high-way-man will catch you if catch he can!

(clap)

Who's rid-ing down the street? No one I'd like to meet!

26

Introducing the Lesson

Clap the following pattern and ask the class to echo you several times until they can perform it easily.

Play the recording of "Janišek the Highwayman" through the first musical statement of the song as students follow it in their books on page 26. **Did you hear the pattern we clapped earlier?** (Yes, it was also clapped on the recording.) **What other instrument played this rhythmic pattern?** (piano)

Developing the Lesson

1. Display the transparency of Activity Sheet 6 (*Janišek the Highwayman*). Play the complete recording of "Janišek the Highwayman."

Help the class discover that the piece consists of one main melody (**A**) repeated several times. Variety is provided by the introduction, interludes, and the coda.

2. Practice the patterns shown on page 27. "Play" the **C–G** pattern by patting both hands on the left knee and the **F–C** pattern by patting both hands on the right knee. (Patting the patterns will help prepare the class to play them on the resonator bells or on the piano.) Choose one or two students to perform the patterns on the bells or the piano while you sing the song. The others may continue to "play" the patterns on their knees.

3. Invite the class to sing the song as new players add the piano/bell part.

4. Explain that Bartók often composed short pieces based on a single melody. **How did he**

OPTIONAL

Jan - i - šek the high-way-man will catch you if catch he can!

(clap)

Play these patterns on resonator bells or piano.

Introduction and First interlude

Second **interlude**

Coda

G
C

C
F

How did Bartók vary his single melody in "Janišek the Highwayman"?
How did he vary the single melody used in "Bear Dance"?

27

Materials *(continued)*
- Optional—
  Biography 2, page B3
  Enrichment Activity 4, page E6
  Kodaly Activity 12, page K19
  Mainstreaming Suggestions 5, 8, pages M11, M16

○ **For additional experience with form:** Special Times 5, page 217

For Your Information
The form of "Bear Dance":
  Introduction
  A
  Interlude
  A
  Interlude
  A
  Interlude
  A
  Interlude
  A

vary the melody in "Janišek the Highwayman" to make his music more interesting? (The melody gets softer each time it is heard.)

Closing the Lesson

Distribute a copy of Activity Sheet 7 *(Bear Dance)* and a pencil to each student. **Listen to another piece by Bartók. As each new number is called, listen for the instruments shown in each numbered box.**

Play the recording of "Bear Dance." Explain that this piece has only one main melody, as does "Janišek the Highwayman." **This time Bartók changed the melody by using different instruments.** Ask the class to listen again and decide which section is the main melody (the **A** section), the introduction, interlude, and the coda. They should write the correct label in each box as they

listen again. **You may not need to use all the labels. Play the recording as many times as necessary to complete the call chart and verify student responses.** (See **For Your Information** for correct answers.)

Lesson Focus

Form: A musical whole may be made up of same, varied, or contrasting segments. *(D–S)*

Materials

○ **Piano Accompaniment:** page 252
○ **Record Information:**
  • Wells Fargo Wagon
  📼 **Record 2 Side A Band 5**
    Voices: solo man, solo woman, solo child, children's choir
    Accompaniment: small show orchestra
○ **Instruments:** woodblock and mallet or whip (The whip is a hinged wooden instrument that simulates the sound of a whip being cracked.)
○ **Other:** coconut shells for as many students as possible; cutout, colored geometric shapes as described below (You may wish to prepare a large classroom set or one set for each student.)
  small circles: 3 red, 3 pink
  small squares: 2 dark and 2 light blue
  small triangles: 2 dark and 2 light green
  large rectangles: 1 white, 1 yellow, 1 orange

(continued on next page)

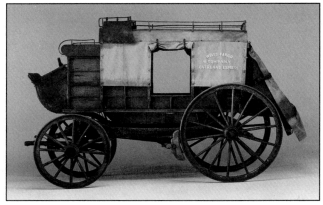

The Wells Fargo Wagon

From "The Music Man"
By Meredith Willson

Chords not shown on pupil page

1. O - ho the Wells Far - go Wag - on is a - com - in' down the street.
2. O - ho the Wells Far - go Wag - on is a - com - in' down the street.

Oh, please let it be for me._____
Oh, don't let him pass my door._____

O - ho the Wells Far - go Wag - on is a - com - in' down the street.
O - ho the Wells Far - go Wag - on is a - com - in' down the street.

© 1957, 1959. © Renewed 1985, 1987 FRANK MUSIC CORP.
and THE ESTATE OF MEREDITH WILLSON
International Copyright Secured All Rights Reserved

28

Introducing the Lesson

Ask the class to open their books to page 28 and follow the notation as they listen to the recording of "Wells Fargo Wagon."

Distribute coconut shells to as many students as possible. (See **Materials**.) As they listen again to the recording, have them use the pattern found at the end of the song (page 30) as an accompaniment.

Developing the Lesson

1. Help the class discover all the rests that occur on the first beat of a measure. As the class listens to the recording a third time, add the whip, woodblock, or a handclap during each of these rests. Then invite the class to sing the song independently.

2. Guide the students to describe the length of each 4-bar phrase by tracing a clockwise circle in the air, beginning at the bottom of the circle for each phrase. Have the students imitate you throughout the song. **Look at the music. How long was each phrase we traced in the air?** (4 measures) **Are there phrases that are exactly like or similar to Phrase 1?** (Every 4-bar phrase that begins with the pattern below and contains an eighth rest on the first beat of the second bar is similar but not exactly the same.) **How many phrases are not like the first one?** (two) **Are they the same or similar?** (similar) **How?** (The melody is seesaw-like.)

Materials (continued)
large rectangles with wavy edges: 1 white, 1 yellow, 1 orange
large rectangles with jagged edges: 1 white, 1 yellow, 1 orange

○ **Teacher's Resource Binder:**
  • Optional—
  Mainstreaming Suggestion 6, page M13

○ **For additional experience with form:** Describe 11, page 178

For Your Information
Form of "Wells Fargo Wagon":

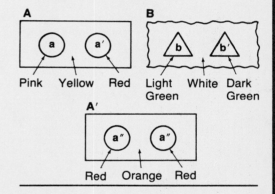

3. Display a complete set of geometric shapes. (See **Materials.**) Choose several students to arrange the smaller geometric shapes to show the sequence of the phrases. (Similar phrases should be shown by using the same shape, but a different shade of the color. Different phrases should be shown with different shapes. See **For Your Information** for a correct arrangement.)

4. Help the students determine the large form of "Wells Fargo Wagon" by looking at the small form. **Which groups of phrases are alike or similar?** (The first two phrases are similar to the last two phrases.) Choose a student to arrange large geometric shapes to show this form. Then place the smaller shapes on top of the appropriate larger shapes.

Closing the Lesson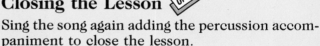

Sing the song again adding the percussion accompaniment to close the lesson.

It could be   cur - tains,   or dish - es, or a   dou - ble boil - er.
It could be   some-thin'   from some-one who is   no   re - la - tion.

Or it   could be ___ some-thin' spe-cial just for   me. _____
But it   could be ___ some-thin' spe-cial just for   me. _____

Add this pattern as an accompaniment. Use a woodblock or coconut shells:

(clip clop, clip clop, clip clop, clip clop)

Chords not shown on pupil page

Do Your Ears Hang Low?

Traditional

1. Do your ears hang low? Do they wob-ble to and fro?
2. Do your ears flip flop? Can you use them for a mop?

Can you tie them in a knot?— Can you tie them in a bow?
Are they string-y at the bot-tom? Are they cur-ly on the top?

Can you flip them o'er your shoul-der like a Con-ti-nen-tal sol-dier?
Can you use them for a swat-ter? Can you use them for a blot-ter?

Do your ears hang low?
Do your ears flip flop?

Add this rhythm pattern to the song.

LISTENING

Turkey in the Straw

Traditional
Listen to "Turkey in the Straw."
Compare it with the melody of
"Do Your Ears Hang Low?" What
do you notice?

31

Lesson Focus
Form: A musical whole may be made up of same, varied, or contrasting segments. *(D–I)*

Materials
○ **Piano Accompaniment:** page 245
○ **Record Information:**
  • Do Your Ears Hang Low?
    Record 2 Side A Band 6
    Voices: children's choir
    Accompaniment: French horn, trumpet, trombone, tuba, percussion
  • Turkey in the Straw
    Record 2 Side A Band 7
    Arranged by Buryl Red
○ **Teacher's Resource Binder:**
  • Optional—
    Mainstreaming Suggestion 3, page M9
○ **For additional experience with form and expression:** Create 2, page 193; Special Times 16, page 232

For Your Information
Form of "Do Your Ears Hang Low?":
Introduction, Verse 1, Verse 2, Coda
Form of "Turkey in the Straw":
Introduction, AB, AB, AB, Coda

Introducing the Lesson
Invite the students to tap the rhythm pattern shown in the pupil book by tapping two fingers in the palm of their other hand.

Play the recording of "Do Your Ears Hang Low?" and ask them to continue tapping the pattern throughout the song.

Developing the Lesson
1. Play the recording again using the same pattern. Clap during the introduction and return to tapping with two fingers for the remainder of the song.

2. Discuss the form heard on the recording: introduction, verse, verse, coda. Help the students realize that there are no contrasting melodies. Ask the class to perform the complete song without the recording, providing their own handclapping introduction.

3. Play the recording of "Turkey in the Straw." **What do you notice about the melody of this music?** (It is almost the same as "Do Your Ears Hang Low?" except that "Turkey in the Straw" contains an additional section—a refrain.)

Closing the Lesson

Discuss the fact that folk music is often changed or varied by different people for different uses. **What other folk songs do we know that have been used in varied ways?** Remind the class of "The Silver Birch," which was altered by Tchaikovsky (page 19) and "Pop Goes the Weasel," which was altered by Caillet (page 23).

31

Lesson Focus

Melody: A series of pitches may move up or down by steps or skips. *(D–E)*

Materials

○ **Piano Accompaniment:** page 256

○ **Record Information:**
- The Happy Wanderer
  Record 2 Side A Band 8
  Voices: children's choir
  Accompaniment: small show orchestra

○ **Instrument:** autoharp

○ **Teacher's Resource Binder:**
- Optional—
  Mainstreaming Suggestion 10, page M18

○ **For additional experience with melody:** Describe 8, page 175

The Happy Wanderer

Words By Antonia Ridge

Music by Friedrich W. Moller

In marching tempo

1. I love to go a - wan - der - ing
2. I love to wan - der by the stream

A - long the moun - tain track. _____
That danc - es in the sun. _____

And as I go, I love to sing,
So joy - ous - ly it calls to me,

My knap - sack on my back. _____
"Come! Join my hap - py song." _____

32

Introducing the Lesson

Ask the class to return to page 6 of their books. **Sometimes it's a good idea to stop and think about all the things that we have learned so far! If we've learned them well, we will be able to use that knowledge to learn even more.** Review the meaning of each word and ask the students to describe activities they have done that involved each musical element. **Look at the song on pages 32–33. Let's explore the music with our eyes and then with our ears. What can you tell about the song by looking at it?** List on the chalkboard possible suggestions that the class could make:

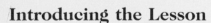

- the expressiveness (lighthearted, happy)
- the tempo (probably a quick, steady beat)
- the volume (robust, full)
- the melody (mostly steps except for "Valderi, Valdera")
- the form (two big parts: verse and refrain)

When the students have exhausted their suggestions, play the recording. After listening they may wish to add other elements to the list.

Developing the Lesson

1. **Look at the melody of the refrain. What happens each time the words "Valderi, Valdera" are sung?** (They always start on the same pitch but take a bigger skip each time.) **Echo me! Sing while showing the body scale.** (See **For Your Information.**) Have the class follow the notation and sing the refrain with numbers first, then with words.

5	5	7	(5	5	7)
5	5	1'	(5	5	1')
5	5	2'	(5	5	2')
5	5	3'	(5	5	3')

2. Next, study the verse. Examine the melody for each phrase: Phrase 1 moves mostly by steps;

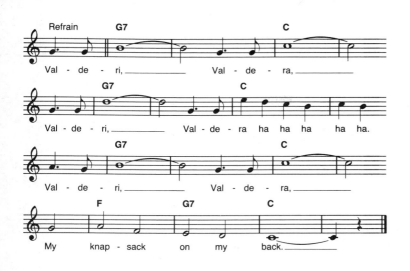

Refrain

G7   C

Val - de - ri, _____ Val - de - ra, _____

G7   C

Val - de - ri, _____ Val - de - ra ha ha ha ha ha.

G7   C

Val - de - ri, _____ Val - de - ra, _____

F   G7   C

My   knap - sack   on   my   back. _____

3. I wave my hat to all I meet
And they wave back to me.
And blackbirds call so loud and sweet
From every greenwood tree.
Refrain

4. High overhead, the skylark wing;
They never rest at home.
But just like me they love to sing,
As o'er the world we roam.
Refrain

For Your Information

The body scale for high 1–2–3:

1   2   3

Phrase 2 uses only 3 pitches; Phrase 3 moves by skips. Discover that the last phrase of the verse is the same as the last phrase of the refrain. Challenge the class to sing the verse with numbers, then with words.

3. Play the recording. Ask the students to evaluate their own performance. **Do you need to correct errors?** Play the recording again as needed.

Closing the Lesson

Call attention to the chord symbols. **Which chord letter represents the tonal center?** (C) **How do you know?** (C is the chord that is used most frequently. The song starts and ends with the C chord.) Choose a student to play an autoharp accompaniment. That student is to set the tempo and establish the feel for the home tone by playing an introduction. Strum once per measure: C C G7 G7 C C.

Invite four students to line up and play the autoharp — one student for each verse. When the students are sure of the melody, add a harmonizing part to the refrain by inserting an echo.

Val - de - ri, _____ Val - de -

(echo) Val - de - ri,

ra, _____ Val - de -

Val - de - ra,

ri, _____ Val - de -

Val - de - ri.

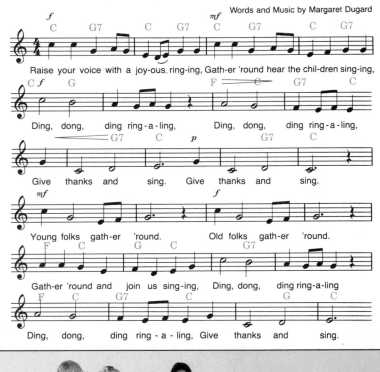

LESSON 15

Lesson Focus

Evaluation: Review and test concepts and skills studied in the First Quarter. *(D–S)*

Materials

○ **Piano Accompaniment:** page 268
○ **Record Information:**
  • Gather 'Round
    Record 2 Side A Band 9
    Voices: children's choir
    Accompaniment: harp, pipe organ, percussion
  • Waltz in D♭ Major ("Minute Waltz") by Frederic Chopin (**show**-pan), 1810–1849
    Record 2 Side A Band 10
    Alexander Brailowsky, pianist
○ **Instruments:** resonator bells C and C'; bell mallets
○ **Other:** a pencil for each student
○ **Teacher's Resource Binder:**

  Evaluation
  • **Review 1,** page Ev4 (Prepare one copy for each student.)
  • Musical Progress Report 1, page Ev5

Introducing the Lesson

Review "Peace Like a River" (page 12) and "Weave Me the Sunshine" (page 11). Discuss the expressiveness and the meaning of each of the songs. Direct the students' attention to "Gather 'Round" on page 34. Sing it or play the recording. **How is this song similar to the two songs we just reviewed?** (All the songs have expressive texts and melodies; all are songs of hope or thanksgiving.) **Can you think of other songs with similar texts?** (Answers will vary.)

Developing the Lesson

1. **How should we perform "Gather 'Round" to help express the feelings of its words?** Guide the students to conclude that they must make decisions about tempo and dynamics. Ask them to explain the dynamic markings on the song. (See **For Your Information.**)

2. Play the recording again as the students softly tap the shortest sound. **Do the words "Raise your voice" move with the shortest sound?** (no) **Listen again. How much longer is each word?** (twice as long) **Which words do move with the shortest sound?** ("with a," "-ous" of "joyous," "hear the," "ring-a," and "gather")

3. Ask the students to listen once more to the song and determine the word that has the longest sound (the last word, "sing"; it is eight times as long as the shortest sound). Enjoy singing the song. Explain that later on the class will add a harmony part.

4. Administer the evaluation for the First Quarter. Distribute a pencil and Review 1 (*Hurdle 1*). Explain that it is a good idea for everyone to stop periodically, and assess his or her musical progress. **It is like running a race and jumping one hurdle at a time.**

34

Give thanks ____ and sing.

Can you learn this part to sing with "Gather 'Round"? Sing it with numbers. The first pitch is "5."

Ding, dong, ding ring - a - ling, Ding, dong, ding ring - a - ling,

Give thanks and sing. Give thanks and sing.

LISTENING

Waltz in D♭ Major

Minute Waltz

by Frederic Chopin

Frederic Chopin wrote many waltzes for piano. They are named after their tonal centers. Some of the waltzes have nicknames. The *Waltz in D♭ Major* is also called the "Minute Waltz." Can you guess why?

35

For Your Information

Dynamic markings:

f	*(forte)*	=	loud
mf	*(mezzo forte)*	=	medium loud
<	*(crescendo)*	=	gradually louder
>	*(decrescendo)*	=	gradually softer
p	*(piano)*	=	soft

Answers to Review 1:
1. Check students' work.
2. Raise, your, Gath-er, Ding, thanks, thanks, sing, Young, Old, Ding, thanks, thanks
3a. 3; 3b. A B A; 3c. No

5. Read through the directions with the class. **Look at the song "Gather 'Round" on page 34. Use the rhythm ruler on your Review sheets to show the length of the notes for the first twelve measures of the song. The first two measures have been done for you.** Repeat the song as necessary, as the class completes their rhythm rulers.

6. **"Gather 'Round" has a tonal center that draws other pitches to it.** Remind the class of the discoveries they made when learning "Three Jolly Fishermen," "Pop Goes the Weasel," and "Bye Bye Blackbird." **This is low 1.** (Play the C bell.) **And this is high 1.** (Play C'.) Ask the students to listen to the song and write the words that use the low or high tonal center in the spaces on their activity sheets. Play the bells once more (C and C') and sing the song or play the recording so that the students may check their work.

7. **Composers make choices. One of those choices is to determine the form of a piece of music by deciding how many *sections* their piece will have. Another choice is to determine which sections will be the same and which will be different.** Play the recording of the "Minute Waltz," and ask the students to circle the correct answers on their Review sheets.

Closing the Lesson

When the students know the song well, challenge them to learn the harmony part on page 35. Add it to the last eight measures of the song.

Use the information gained from this lesson, as well as from observations made throughout the quarter, to complete a copy of Musical Progress Report 1 for each student. This may be used as a report to parents, as well as a permanent record for your files.

Lesson Focus

Form: A musical whole is a combination of smaller segments. *(D–I)*

Materials

○ **No Piano Accompaniment**

○ **Record Information:**
  • Meringue Boom
    Record 2 Side B Band 1
  • *Jesusita en Chihuahua*
    Record 2 Side B Band 2
    Voices: children's choir
    Accompaniment: two trumpets, violin, guitar, double bass, marimba

○ **For additional experience with time and place** Special Times 10 and 11, pages 222-223

The Second Quarter

LISTENING

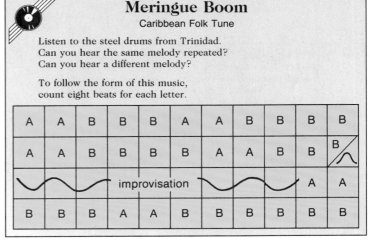

Meringue Boom
Caribbean Folk Tune

Listen to the steel drums from Trinidad.
Can you hear the same melody repeated?
Can you hear a different melody?

To follow the form of this music,
count eight beats for each letter.

A	A	B	B	B	A	A	B	B	B	B
A	A	B	B	B	B	A	A	B	B	B
∼	∼	improvisation			∼	∼	∼		A	A
B	B	B	A	A	B	B	B	B	B	B

36

Introducing the Lesson

Play short excerpts from "Meringue Boom" and *"Jesusita en Chihuahua"* ("Little Jesus in Chihuahua"). Explain that they are both examples of music from Latin American countries—Mexico and the island of Trinidad. One of the groups plays traditional instruments, which you may recognize. The other group plays instruments that were created from materials they found in their own environment. Play *"Jesusita en Chihuahua."* Help the class identify instruments such as guitar, trumpets, and violin. Then play "Meringue Boom." **Can you figure out what these instruments are made from?**

After they have made suggestions, have the class open their books to page 36. Explain to the students that the steel drums of Trinidad date from the time around World War II—a time when their grandparents were young. **During the war years wood and metal were scarce. The people of Trin-**idad began making music on anything they could find. They discovered that by "dimpling" the end of oil drums, they could create a pitched instrument sounding much like a xylophone.

Developing the Lesson

1. Discover more about the music of Trinidad by discovering the way in which two melodic ideas are repeated. Have the students silently count eight beats as they follow each letter on the grid. **Can you hear when the improvisation is performed?**

2. Compare the sound of the steel drum ensemble from Trinidad with the Mexican music of the mariachis (a strolling musical group). Invite the students to follow the call chart on pupil page 37. Students will immediately recognize more familiar instruments such as

Jesusita en Chihuahua

Mexican Folk Tune

How many different melodies do you hear mariachis from Mexico playing?

Each section gets 32 counts.

Call **Introduction**

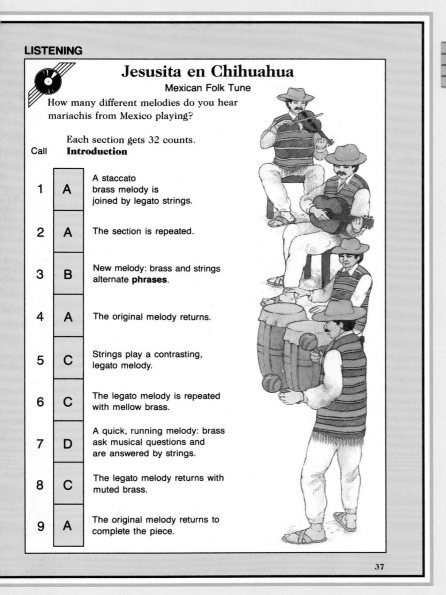

1	A	A staccato brass melody is joined by legato strings.
2	A	The section is repeated.
3	B	New melody: brass and strings alternate **phrases**.
4	A	The original melody returns.
5	C	Strings play a contrasting, legato melody.
6	C	The legato melody is repeated with mellow brass.
7	D	A quick, running melody: brass ask musical questions and are answered by strings.
8	C	The legato melody returns with muted brass.
9	A	The original melody returns to complete the piece.

37

brass and strings. The class will also notice that this piece uses more melodic variety than did "Meringue Boom."

Closing the Lesson

Return to "Meringue Boom." This time ask the class to listen for the harmonic changes. They will discover that the harmony is very simple and repetitious: Beats 1, 2, 3, and 4 use the I chord, Beats 5 and 6 use the V7 chord, and Beats 7 and 8 use the I chord. (Some students may hear a more subtle chord change: the II chord on beats 3 and 4.) This pattern continues throughout the piece.

LESSON 17

Lesson Focus

Expression: The expressiveness of music is affected by the way timbre, rhythm, and melody contribute to the musical whole. *(D–I)*

Materials

○ **No Piano Accompaniment**
○ **Record Information:**
  • Are You Sleeping?
    Record 2 Side B Band 3
    Voices: woman, man
    Accompaniment: oboe, harp, chimes
  • *Symphony No. 1 in D Major,* Third Movement (excerpt)
    by Gustav Mahler (**mah**-ler), 1860–1911
    Record 2 Side B Band 4
    The Columbia Symphony Orchestra
    Bruno Walter, conductor
○ **Instruments:** nine percussion instruments of different timbral qualities (3 woods, 3 that ring, and 3 with drumlike sounds); appropriate mallets and strikers; piano or timpani; alto metallophone; soprano glockenspiel
○ **Teacher's Resource Binder:**
  • Optional—
    Kodaly Activity 6, page K10
    Mainstreaming Suggestion 13, page M22

(continued on next page)

Are You Sleeping?

Traditional Words   French Folk Tune

Sing this song in unison, then as a round.

Use the rhythm pattern of the words to create a percussion piece.

Some people may hold instruments while three players perform.

| Group I
wood sounds | Group II
ringing sounds | Group III
drumlike sounds |

Perform the percussion piece as a three-part round.

38

Introducing the Lesson OPTIONAL

With the class, sing the familiar round, "Are You Sleeping?" After singing, clap the melodic rhythm of the first measure and ask the students to echo your clapping in Measure 2. Point out that you and the class clapped the same pattern, and together you have performed a complete phrase. Complete the song in this manner.

Developing the Lesson

1. To play the melodic rhythm of the song as a percussion piece, organize the class into three groups of four students each. Distribute three percussion instruments, each with different sound qualities, to each group. Give the first group wood sounds, the second ringing sounds, and the third thudding sounds. Select one student from each group to be the soloist. The remaining three students hold the instruments in playing position.

2. Each soloist may play any of the three instruments to perform the melodic rhythm of "Are You Sleeping?" The soloists begin by playing the rhythm of the first measure of each line and, using the same instrumental combination, repeat it for the second measure. **Be sure you remember how you perform each pattern.** Continue in this manner and perform the song in its entirety.

3. Allow each group to perform the piece alone. Then ask the groups to play it as a three-part round.

4. Play the melody for the class as notated on pupil page 39. Some students will notice that it sounds different. Ask them to sing it on "loo." When the students are familiar with this version of the melody, have them sing it as a round. Comment that the melody has been changed from major to minor.

Sing "Are You Sleeping?" in the following way.

Loo loo loo _ loo . . .

How many different ways is the melody varied?

Perform the following parts as you sing.

INTRODUCTION (2 meas.) AND ACCOMPANIMENT
Piano or Timpani

Alto Metallophone

Soprano Glockenspiel

LISTENING

Symphony No. 1 in D Major [excerpt]

by Gustav Mahler

Listen to this music.
What do you hear that is the same, almost the same, or different from the way you performed "Are You Sleeping?" the first time?

39

Materials (continued)
○ **For additional experience with harmony:** Special Times 13, page 226

For Your Information
The excerpt from the third movement of *Symphony No. 1 in D Major* by Mahler:
• The timpani plays a pattern on the first and fifth steps of the scale.
• The double bass enters with a melody based on "*Frère Jacques.*"
• Bassoon, cello, and tuba perform the theme in canon.
• The tuba plays a countermelody (repeated later).
• More instruments repeat the theme, building up the dynamic level.
• The excerpt ends quietly on a sustained chord.

5. Help the students learn to play the instrumental parts on page 39. The piano or timpani part should enter very softly. Voices enter next, singing the melody first in unison then as a round. The metallophone and glockenspiel parts should be played only occasionally as the group sings.

Closing the Lesson

Play the recording of the third movement from the *Symphony No. 1 in D Major* by Mahler. Help the students realize that this music is based on the same melody they just performed. The drum parts were the same; both melodies were in minor and were performed both in unison and in canon. The metallophone and glockenspiel parts are similar to the woodwind parts on the recording.

Lesson Focus

Harmony: Chords and melody may move simultaneously in relation to each other. *(D–I)*

Materials

○ **No Piano Accompaniment**

○ **Record Information:**
   • Allelujah
   Record 2 Side B Band 5
   Voices: boys' choir
   Accompaniment: bells
   • Sing Together
   Record 2 Side B Band 6
   Voices: children's choir
   Accompaniment: bells

○ **Instruments:** resonator bells C, F, G, A, B♭, C', and E (all octaves); seven bell mallets

○ **Teacher's Resource Binder:**
   • Optional—
   Enrichment Activity 5, page E8
   Kodaly Activity 9, page K13
   Mainstreaming Suggestion 15, page M24

○ **For additional experience with harmony:** Perform 12, page 148

Chords not shown on pupil page

Allelujah

Round by E. B.

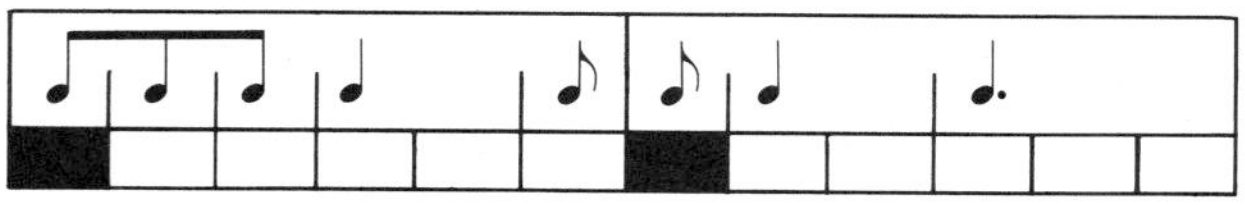

Which bell is Step 1?

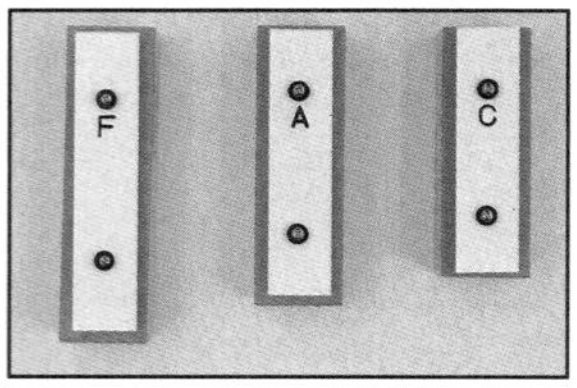

Tune up.

1 3 5 3 1

Melody   F

Al - le - lu - jah; al - le - lu - jah.

Al - le - lu - jah; al - le - lu - jah.

Al - le - lu - jah!

Chord

I

40

Introducing the Lesson

Ask the class to open their books and study the rhythm ruler at the top of pupil page 40. **Can you read the rhythm? How long should you make the last note?** (equal to three short sounds) **The quarter note usually lasts for two short sounds. What clue might tell you that this note will be longer?** (the dot following the note) Establish the shortest sound. Ask the class to read the words of "Allelujah" in rhythm.

Developing the Lesson

1. Draw attention to the box shown below the rhythm ruler. Agree that the lowest resonator bell, F, will be Step 1. Ask one student to play the bells while the class sings the tune-up pattern on the right.

2. **What can you tell me about the melody of the first phrase of "Allelujah"?** (stays on 1) **the second phrase?** (stays on 3) **Phrase 3?** (stays on 5) Ask the class to sing the song.

3. When the class can sing the melody accurately, draw attention to the numbers above the three phrases. **These numbers tell us that this song is a round.** (Recall "Are You Sleeping?")

   Organize the class into three groups. Challenge each group to sing the melody independently. Then perform it as a round. (Group 2 begins when Group 1 starts Phrase 2; Group 3 begins when Group 1 starts Phrase 3.)

4. **What nice harmony you've created. When three pitches are sounded at the same time, a chord is produced. You've performed the I chord. Why do you suppose it's called that?** (Because the lowest sound is scale step 1.)

   Draw attention to the chords shown on the right side of the page. Perform the round

40

Sing Together

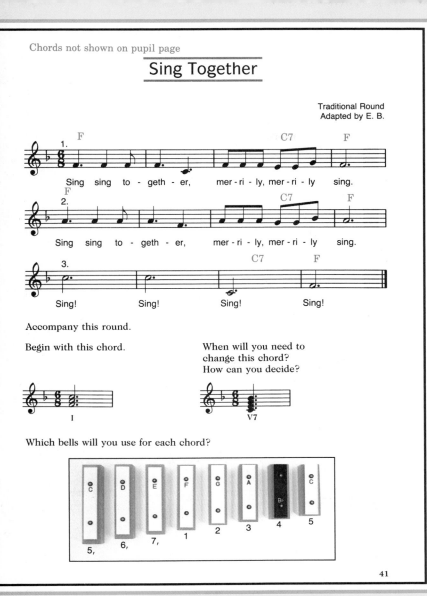

Traditional Round
Adapted by E. B.

F ... C7 ... F

1.
Sing   sing   to - geth - er,   mer - ri - ly, mer - ri - ly   sing.

F ... C7 ... F

2.
Sing   sing   to - geth - er,   mer - ri - ly, mer - ri - ly   sing.

C7 ... F

3.
Sing!   Sing!   Sing!   Sing!

Accompany this round.

Begin with this chord.

When will you need to
change this chord?
How can you decide?

I

V7

Which bells will you use for each chord?

41

---

again. This time choose three students to accompany the song with bells F, A, and C'. They should tap their bells very rapidly and "nervously" in order to create a sustained sound.

Closing the Lesson

Follow a similar procedure to help the class learn "Sing Together" on pupil page 41. Read the words in rhythm after determining that the dotted half notes must last for six short sounds.

This song begins on "1." Can you learn the melody by reading the scale numbers? Look at the bottom of the page. Help the class figure out, by determining the scale step for each chord, that bells F, A, and C' make up the I chord and bells C, E, G, and B♭ make up the V7 chord.

Distribute all seven bells and mallets to seven students. **I will sing the melody; the I chord bell**

players will accompany me. When you think the V7 chord players should begin, raise your hands. Help the class conclude that the V7 chord should occur on the fourth pulse of Measures 3, 7, and 11.

Organize the class into three groups and perform the song as a round with bell accompaniment.

Lesson Focus

Harmony: Chords and melody may move simultaneously in relation to each other. *(D—I)*

Materials

○ **Piano Accompaniment:** page 260

○ **Record Information:**
  • *Acadian Songs and Dances* (excerpt) by Virgil Thomson, 1896—
  Record 2 Side B Band 7
  Cleveland Pops Orchestra
  Louis Lane, conductor
  • Polly Wolly Doodle
  Record 2 Side B Band 8
  Voices: children's choir
  Accompaniment: fiddle, harmonica, banjo, guitar, double bass, percussion

○ **Instrument:** autoharp

○ **Teacher's Resource Binder:**
  Activity Sheets
  • **Activity Sheet 8,** pages A11–A12 (Prepare copies for students.)
  • Optional—
  Biography 3, page B5
  Curriculum Correlation 6, page C8
  Enrichment Activity 6, page E8
  Mainstreaming Suggestion 8, page M16
  Orff Activity 13, page O19

○ **For additional experience with harmony:** Special Times 6, page 218

LISTENING

Acadian Songs and Dances (excerpt)

by Virgil Thomson

The songs on these pages may be accompanied by two chords.
When will you use each?

Voor-hies fam-'ly pass-ing by, Going to town, to St. Mar-tin.

Oh, I fear they will wear out the road to St. Mar-tin.

Polly Wolly Doodle

Traditional

F   Chords not shown on pupil page

1. Oh, I went down South to see my Sal,
2. Oh, my Sal - ly is a maid - en fair,
3. Be - hind the barn, down on my knees,
4. He ___ sneezed so hard with whoop - ing cough,

42

Introducing the Lesson

Review "Sing Together" (page 41). Invite a student to find the chords on the autoharp. **What chord will you play for I?** (F chord) **for V7?** (C7) As the autoharp accompanist strums twice in each measure, ask the class to sing the song first in unison then as a round.

Developing the Lesson

1. **We can accompany the tune at the top of page 42 with the same chords that we used to accompany "Sing Together."** Play the autoharp and sing the melody. Ask the students to raise their hands when the chord should change to V7 (second beat of Measure 7) and when it should return to I (second beat of Measure 8). Invite the class to sing the melody as you accompany them.

2. **This little tune was used by a composer in a** composition for an orchestra. **Listen. Did he use the same chords? Is the melody exactly the same?** Play the first statement of *Acadian Songs and Dances.* Agree that the chord changes are the same. Note a slight change in the melodic rhythm of Measure 7.

3. Distribute Activity Sheet 8 *(Acadian Songs and Dances).* Read the instructions with the class. Play the recording and guide the students to complete their "music map." Boxes 1, 2, 3, 5, 6, and 15 have been completed for them. Replay Sections 1, 3, and 5 of the recording until the students are familiar with the melodies. Then help them complete the remaining boxes by writing the letter name of the theme (A, B, or C) in each small box, drawing the shape of the new melody and circling the answers to the questions. (See **For Your Information** for details on each section.) Replay the recording as often as necessary.

Sing Pol - ly wol - ly doo - dle all the day.

My ___ Sal - ly is a spunk - y gal,
With ___ curl - y eyes and laugh - ing hair,
I ___ thought I heard a chick - en sneeze,
He ___ sneezed his head and tail right off,

Sing Pol - ly wol - ly doo - dle all the day.

Refrain

Fare thee well, fare thee well, Fare thee

well, my fair - y fay. For I'm

going to Loui - si - an - a, for to see my Su - sy - an - na,

Sing Pol - ly wol - ly doo - dle all the day.

43

For Your Information

All numbers correspond to those on Activity Sheet 8:

1. **A**—bassoons in F
2. **A**—violins in G
3. **B**—xylophone plays tune twice
4. **A**—oboe in F♯
5. **C**—strings in B♭; answers will vary
6. **Bridge**—based on chromatic scale
7. **A**—oboe in C; different accompaniment
8. **A**—muted trumpet in D
9. **B**—flute in G
10. **B**—xylophone in A
11. **A**—trumpet in E
12. **C**—violins, flutes, oboe
13. **A**—flutes, clarinets; new accompaniment
14. **C**—same instruments as in 12.
15. **D**—French horns; accompaniment material for **B**
16. **B**—trumpets, one half step apart

Closing the Lesson

End the class with "Polly Wolly Doodle." Learn the song by singing the melody with scale numbers. Add an accompaniment, using the I and the V7 chords.

F
Oh, I went down South to see my Sal,

F   **C7**
Sing Polly wolly doodle all the day;

C7
My Sally is a spunky gal,

 C7   **F**
Sing Polly wolly doodle all the day.

  F
Fare thee well, fare thee well,

     C7
Fare thee well, my fairy fay,

  C7
For I'm going to Louisiana for to see my Susyanna,

 C7   **F**
Sing Polly wolly doodle all the day.

LESSON 20

Lesson Focus

Melody: Each pitch within a melody moves in relation to a home tone. *(P–S)*

Materials

○ **Piano Accompaniment:** page 262
○ **Record Information:**
  • One Cold and Frosty Morning
  Record 2 Side B Band 9
  Voice: man
  Accompaniment: harmonica, hammered dulcimer, banjo, guitar, double bass
○ **Instruments:** resonator bells C, D, E, F, G, A, and B in all octaves; bell mallets
○ **Teacher's Resource Binder:**
  • Optional—
  Mainstreaming Suggestion 14, page M24
○ **For additional experience with texture and harmony:** Create 7, page 200; Create 10, page 203; Special Times 8, page 220.

Chords not shown on pupil page

One Cold and Frosty Morning

Alabama Folk Song

Use your knowledge of the major scale to learn this melody.
It uses the pitches of the C scale.

1 2 3 4 5 6 7 1'

Brightly   C   G

One   cold and frost-y   morn-ing,   just   as   the sun did   rise,

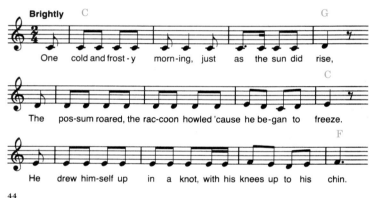

The   pos-sum roared, the rac-coon howled 'cause he be-gan to   freeze.

He   drew him-self up   in   a knot, with his knees up to his   chin.

44

Introducing the Lesson [OPTIONAL]

Warm up with the body scale. (See page xxvii.) Play the C resonator bell. Then, ask the class to perform the scale up (1 2 3 4 5 6 7 1') and down (1' 7 6 5 4 3 2 1).

Developing the Lesson

1. Have the class turn to page 44 and read the instructions at the top of the page together. Look at the whole song. Name the scale number for the first pitch in Measures 1–14 and each note of Measures 15 and 16. As students name the pitches, write them on the chalkboard:

1 1 1   2 2 2   3 3 3 3   4 4 4 4   5 5   6   7   1'

Ask the class to then sing the pattern they have discovered. **What do you hear?** (a major scale)

2. **You can sing the "outline" of the song. Can you follow the notes and "fill in" the rest of the melody by singing all the scale numbers?** Note that Measures 17–20 "stretch out" the melodic rhythm of Measures 15 and 16.

3. After the students have sung the complete melody, examine the rhythm, noting that most of the time it moves evenly with the eighth note as the short sound. Identify places where there are "shorter" sounds. ("as the," "with his," "had to") **What happens to the rhythm at the end of the song?** (It is stretched out; it imitates the meaning of the words.)

4. Invite the students to sing the complete song. Then play the recording so that they can be sure they learned the melody correctly.

And ev-ery-thing had to clear the track when he stretched out a - gain;

When he stretched out a - gain.

Use your knowledge of **chords** to add harmony to this song.

You will need to use three chords.

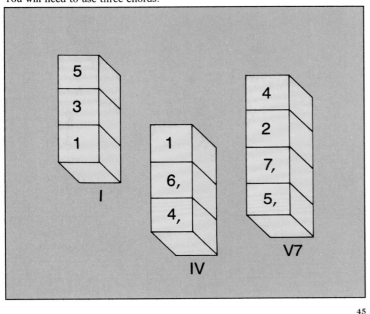

45

5. Read the instructions at the middle of pupil page 45. Focus attention on the "chord boxes." Examine the numbers in the three boxes. **What do you get if you put all the different numbers used, in a row?** (a scale) **How will you decide when you should play each chord to add harmony to the melody?** Guide the students to conclude that they can locate the scale number that begins each measure; then identify the chord(s) that uses the scale number. **What will we need to do if the same scale number is used in two chords?** (You will need to use your ears to decide which sounds best.)

Ask the class to study the chord pictures and decide which chord should be used to accompany each measure. Write the chord numbers below each scale step as shown. (The chords in parentheses are possible answers but do not "sound right" in this context.)

```
                                          1′
                                          I (IV)
                                     7
                                     V7
                                 6
                                 IV
                            5  5
                            I (V7)
                    4  4  4  4
                    V7    (IV)
              3  3  3  3
              I
        2  2  2
        V7
  1  1  1
  I (IV)
```

Closing the Lesson

Hand out resonator bells C, D, E, F, G, A, and B (in all octaves available) and mallets. Give one to every student if possible. **Be sure you know which chord uses your bell!** Sing the song slowly as students play the appropriate bells. (Tap bells lightly and continuously to create a sustained sound.) When two chords have been suggested, experiment with both until the class agrees on the correct chord for that measure.

Lesson Focus

Expression: Musical elements are combined into a whole to express a musical or extramusical idea. *(P—I)*

Materials

○ **Piano Accompaniment:** page 259

○ **Record Information:**
   • The Colorado Trail
   Record 2 Side B Band 10
   Voices: children's choir
   Accompaniment: guitar, accordion, double bass, percussion

○ **Teacher's Resource Binder:**
   • Optional—
   Curriculum Correlation 5, page C8
   Enrichment Activity 9, page E16
   Kodaly Activity 7, page K10

○ **For additional experience with harmony:** Perform 9, page 145

The Colorado Trail

Cowboy Song
Arranged by Kurt Miller

Cowboy Meditation, polychromed bronze, 22" X 20" X 9", © 1964. © Harry Jackson, artist, © Wyoming Foundry Studios, Inc., 1964.

Chords not shown on pupil page

Eyes like the morn-ing star, Cheek like a rose,

Lau-ra was a pret-ty girl, ev-ery-bod-y knows.

46

Introducing the Lesson

Begin by chanting the following patterns:

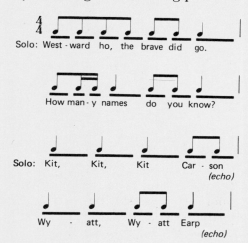

Solo: West-ward ho, the brave did go.

How man-y names do you know?

Solo: Kit, Kit, Kit Car-son
(echo)

Wy - att, Wy - att Earp
(echo)

After the students have practiced and come to understand how the chant is to be performed, divide them into two teams in order to perform the chant as a game. Members of each team take turns adding new names to the list of heroes of the Old West for the other team to echo. Each new name must be chanted so that it lasts for four beats. The game continues until one team cannot think of a new name. Provide planning time for the class before beginning the game.

Developing the Lesson

1. Ask the class to look carefully at the song on pages 46–47. **What kind of song do you think this is?** (lonesome cowboy song) **How would you arrange this song if you were asked to record it? What instruments would you use? How could you make it sound like a cowboy song?** Students may offer a variety of answers: Use a guitar; add a sound to suggest horses' hooves throughout; use a male vocalist singing in a "western" style. **Should the song be fast or slow? loud or soft?**

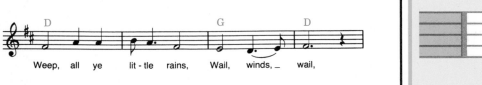

LESSON 21

Weep, all ye lit-tle rains, Wail, winds, _ wail,

All a-long, a-long, a-long the Col-o-ra-do Trail.

Listen for this **descant**.
Can some people sing it while others sing the melody?

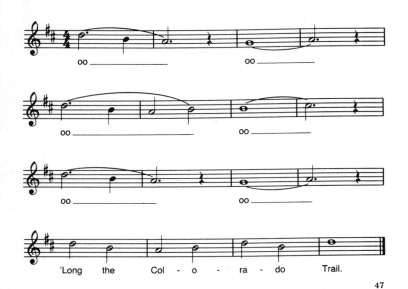

oo _____ oo _____

oo _____ oo _____

oo _____ oo _____

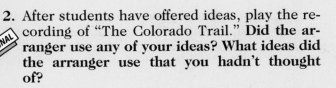

'Long the Col-o-ra-do Trail.

47

2. After students have offered ideas, play the recording of "The Colorado Trail." **Did the arranger use any of your ideas? What ideas did the arranger use that you hadn't thought of?**

OPTIONAL

3. Help the students learn to sing and perform the melody expressively. The song should be sung with smooth phrasing in a moderately soft voice. Students should breathe only at the end of phrases.

Closing the Lesson

Look at the melody written at the bottom of page 47. This is the special descant, or melody, we heard on the recording. Choose a few students who are independent singers to perform this part while the rest of the class sings the song. **Performing two different melodies at the same time is another way to add harmony.**

Lesson Focus

Expression: Musical elements are combined into a whole to express a musical or extramusical idea. *(P–E)*

Materials

○ **Piano Accompaniment:** page 264

○ **Record Information:**
  • Woke Up This Morning
    Record 2 Side B Band 11
    Voice: man
    Accompaniment: guitar, electric bass, electric organ, percussion
  • On the Mall
    by Edwin Franko Goldman, 1878–1956
    Record 3 Side A Band 1
    The Regimental Band of the British Guards
    Major Hillary Wilkenson, conductor

○ **Teacher's Resource Binder:**
  • Optional—
    Mainstreaming Suggestion 7, page M13

○ **For additional experience with expression:** Describe 3, page 164 and Special Times 17, page 234

Woke Up This Morning

1960s Civil Rights Anthem

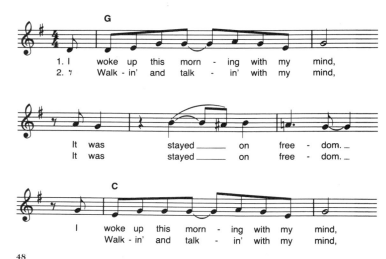

G

1. I woke up this morn - ing with my mind,
2. Walk - in' and talk - in' with my mind,

It was stayed _____ on free - dom. _
It was stayed _____ on free - dom. _

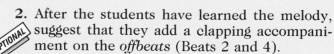

C

I woke up this morn - ing with my mind,
Walk - in' and talk - in' with my mind,

48

Introducing the Lesson

Discuss "freedom" with the class. **What does the word mean to you? How many different kinds of freedom can you name?** (freedom to play, freedom to make decisions, freedom to live where you wish, freedom to go where you wish, freedom to think as you choose, and so on)

Listen to a song that expresses one person's ideas about freedom. Play the recording of "Woke Up This Morning." Ask students to offer their ideas about the freedom described in the song.

Developing the Lesson

1. **Look at page 48. Why will the words of this song be easy to learn?** (Phrases are repeated.) **Will the melody be as easy to learn?** (It may be a little harder. Although Phrases 1 and 3 are the same, Phrase 2 is a little different.)

2. After the students have learned the melody, **OPTIONAL** suggest that they add a clapping accompaniment on the *offbeats* (Beats 2 and 4).

3. Show the class a special way of clapping by having them hold their left hands, palm down, over their right hands. The right hand taps the upper leg on Beat 1, then "bounces back" to hit the left palm on Beat 2, down on Beat 3, and up on Beat 4. After the students can do this easily, suggest that they strike "empty space" rather than their legs on Beats 1 and 3 so that the sound is heard only on Beats 2 and 4.

Closing the Lesson

Play the recording of "On the Mall." **Where are we likely to hear this kind of music?** (parades, patriotic events, at summer band concerts in a park) Play the recording again and invite stu-

It was stayed _____ on free - dom. ___
It was stayed _____ on free - dom. ___

G

D7 G

I woke up this morn - ing with my mind,
Walk - in' and talk - in' with my mind,

G7 **Em**

It was stayed _____ on free - dom. ___
It was stayed _____ on free - dom. ___

G **Em** **A7**

Hal - le - lu, _____ Hal - le - lu, _____
Hal - le - lu, _____ Hal - le - lu, _____

G D7 G

Hal - le - lu - jah! ____
Hal - le - lu - jah! ____

LISTENING

On the Mall

by Edwin Franko Goldman

Where might you hear this kind of music?

Listen. How many different melodies do you hear?

49

For Your Information

The form of "On the Mall":
Introduction (very brief)
Section A: a bright tune played by woodwinds
Section A: similar to first **A** section, but with an altered ending
Section B: a new melody; snare drum and cymbals frequently heard
Section B: same as first **B** section
Bridge: a brief musical idea that connects one section to the next
Section C: this is the trio; the melody is whistled with a low brass accompaniment
Bridge
Section C': melody repeated, now with full band

dents to try to whistle the melody of the trio section. (See **For Your Information**.)

Invite students to move to the music. They are free to choose the kind of movement as long as it reflects something they hear, such as the underlying beat, the melodic rhythm, the instrumentation, and so on. Play the recording again and ask students to show various marching ideas, such as marching in place, stepping forward and backward, and pivoting.

Ask students to identify the form of the music for you. Write the labels for each section on the chalkboard.

A   A   B   B   Bridge   C   Bridge   C'

Invite the class to move again to the recording. This time they should change the way they march as each new section begins.

Lesson Focus

Time and Place: The way musical elements are combined into a whole reflects the origin of the music. *(D—S)*

Materials

○ **No Piano Accompaniment**

○ **Record Information:**
  • Sioux Grass Dance
    Record 3 Side A Band 2
    St. Michael's Singers
  • Face-Dance Song
    Record 3 Side A Band 3
    Voice: man
    Accompaniment: water drum

○ **Instruments:** high and low drums; sticks

○ **Teacher's Resource Binder:**
  • Optional—
    Kodaly Activity 4, page K5

○ **For additional experience with time and place:** Perform 14, page 150 and Describe 15, page 185

Face-Dance Song

Transcribed and Arranged
by Louis W. Ballard

As you learn this song,
can you find clues that help you decide when and where
it was first sung?

   Look at the words. Can you **see** any clues?
   Listen to the music. Can you **hear** any clues?

Ha - na t'si wah, Ha - na＿＿ t'si wah, ＿＿

Ha - na＿＿ t'si wah, Ha - na t'si wah.

Yo - ho wa - ni na - ah yo - ha hey,

Yo - ho wa - ni na yo - ha hey,

Yo - ho wa - ni na - ah yo - ha hey.

50

Introducing the Lesson

Open your books to page 50. Help the students decide where and when this song was first sung. **Look at the words. Can you see any clues?** The students may recognize the sound of American Indian words. (The words are called "vocables" and function similarly to the English words "tra-la-la.")

To help the students understand how vocables can work, say the phrase "doo-bee-doo-bee-doo" in different ways. Point out that the *way* one speaks is often more important than the *words* one speaks.

Developing the Lesson

1. **Listen to the music.** Play the recording of "Face-Dance Song." **Are there any clues that tell you this is American Indian music?** The students should recognize the steady beat of the drum and the vocal quality that is typical of American Indian music. The generally descending melodic line based on a pentatonic scale is also a clue.

2. **This is a song from the Quapaw Indian tribe.** Play the recording again. Then ask the students to sing the song. Practice the syncopated rhythm. Write these patterns on the chalkboard:

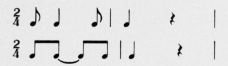

Clap the patterns. **Which pattern am I clapping?** Guide the students to realize that it is impossible to decide because both sound exactly the same.

Sioux Grass Dance

51

For Your Information

The Sioux are a confederacy of tribes who originally lived in the upper-Midwest. The Quapaw tribe lives in northeastern Oklahoma. Only a few songs and dances from their culture remain with us today. The name Quapaw means downriver people. They are cousins to the Omaha Indians—upriver people. This "Sioux Grass Dance" may be enjoyed by young and old together.

Review the function of the tie: It "ties" two tones together so that they sound like a single tone.

$$\quarter \smile \quarter = \half$$
$$\eighth\eighth = \half$$

3. Find the pattern in the music. It can be found throughout the song. It is first heard in Measure 1.

4. Add an accompaniment on high and low drums, following the pattern heard on the recording. Play the steady beat. The low drum should begin first and end first.

OPTIONAL

Closing the Lesson

Listen to "Sioux Grass Dance." How is this piece similar to the "Face-Dance Song"? (Both use

drums.) Students may dance with the "Sioux Grass Dance" recording. Have them stand in a circle with their hands joined. The dancers should move clockwise by stepping with their left feet first, in a shuffle style. (Step to the left with the left foot; then slide the right foot to meet the left.)

LESSON 24

Lesson Focus

Form: A musical whole may be made up of same, varied, or contrasting segments. *(D–I)*

Materials

○ **Record Information:**
- Tinikling
  Record 3 Side A Band 4
- *La Raspa*
  Record 3 Side A Band 5

○ **Other:** two bamboo poles about nine feet long; two boards about two inches thick and three feet long (Poles lie on boards about a foot from each end.)

○ **Teacher's Resource Binder:**
- Optional—
  Mainstreaming Suggestion 9, page M16

○ **For additional experience with time and place:** Describe 12–13, pages 180, 182

La Raspa
Mexican Folk Dance

How well can you follow dance instructions?
Learn the movements for this Mexican dance.

Dance with a partner.

Step I
L-hop; right heel out

Step II
R-hop; left heel out

A-section of the music

Step   L   R   L (pause)   R   L   R (pause) | repeat

B-section of the music

Step
Clap   repeat

How many times will you dance each section?

52

Introducing the Lesson

Listen to the recording of *"La Raspa"* ("The File"). Explain that it is a Mexican folk dance. It is performed with a shuffling step, which suggests the rasping sound of a file. **Listen to the music again. How does it move?** (in twos) **How many different sections do you hear in this music?** (Two: Each is eight measures long.) Play the recording again. **How many times do you hear each section?** (five times: A B A B A B A B A B) Help the students hear that the music changes key: It moves up to a new home tone at the beginning of the third, fourth, and fifth statements. During the fourth statement of **B**, a different melody is heard.

Developing the Lesson

1. Help the class learn the dance by following the instructions on pupil page 52. This is a partner dance. Dancers may move freely around the room or perform the dance in a circle. (See **For Your Information** for complete instructions.)

2. Play the recording of "Tinikling." **How is this music different from *"La Raspa"*?** Students may comment on various aspects of the music. Help them also notice that it moves in threes rather than in twos, as does "La Raspa." "Tinikling" is from the Philippines. The dance is named for a bird, the tinikling, that looks like a crane or heron. The dance imitates the way the bird moves as it steps over branches in the forest.

3. Listen to the recording and identify the form. The introduction is seven and a half measures. Section **A** is made up of a 16-measure melody that is repeated. Section **B** also consists of a 16-measure melody that is repeated. The entire dance is then played in a new key.

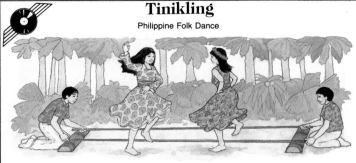

Tinikling
Philippine Folk Dance

PLAYERS

Two players sit on the floor and hold the ends of two bamboo poles.

Introduction:
Begin when the music begins. Slide poles together on Beat 1. Lift the poles apart and tap the boards on Beats 2 and 3.

Sections A and B:
Continue playing the "pole rhythm."

click tap tap click tap tap

DANCERS

Two dancers on either side of the poles face each other.

Introduction:
Listen for 4 measures. Then tap right toes between the poles:

rest tap tap rest tap tap

Section A:
Measure 1: Start with left foot.
1 Hop on left foot outside of poles.
2 Step between poles with right foot.
3 Step between poles with left foot.
   Repeat, starting with *right* foot.

Section B:
Start with left foot.
Walk outside the poles: left, right, left, right.
Leap inside the poles: right foot, then left foot.
Repeat, starting with *right* foot.

53

For Your Information

Dance instructions for *"La Raspa"*:

Section A: Partners face each other, extend arms forward at shoulder level, and join hands. The sequence takes four beats to complete.

On Beat 1, hop with the left foot while sliding the right foot out and touching the heel to the floor.

On Beat 2, hop with the right foot while sliding the left foot out. Beat 3 is the same as Beat 1. Pause on Beat 4. Repeat the pattern, starting with the right foot. Perform the pattern four more times for each **A** section.

Section B: Partners hook right elbows and hold left hands high. Swing clockwise for Beats 1 and 2 while snapping left-hand fingers on the beat. On the third beat, release partners. Clap hands on Beat 4. Repeat the pattern, joining left elbows. Perform the pattern four more times for each **B** section.

Closing the Lesson [OPTIONAL]

Read the instructions on pupil page 53 and help the students learn to perform "Tinikling."

LESSON 25

Lesson Focus

Rhythm: A series of beats may be organized into regular or irregular groupings by stressing certain beats. *(P–S)*

Materials

○ **Piano Accompaniment:** page 266
○ **Record Information:**
  • Songmaker
  ▭ **Record 3 Side A Band 6**
  Voices: man, children's choir
  Accompaniment: flute, guitar, electric piano, electric bass, percussion
○ **Instruments:** hand drum or snare drum and brushes; resonator bells F, G, B♭, C, and D' or xylophone; mallets
○ **Other:** overhead projector
○ **Teacher's Resource Binder:**

  Activity Sheets • **Activity Sheet 9,** page A13 (Prepare a transparency from the activity sheet.)

  Evaluation • Optional—
  Enrichment Activity 3, page E6
  Checkpoint 2, page Ev6
○ **For additional experience with expression:** Special Times 2, page 212

Songmaker

Words and Music by
Fred Willman

1. Make a song for you and me.
2. What if your voice is - n't beau - ti - ful?

Sing it so the world can hear. _____
What if your voice is - n't clear? _____

Sing with a voice that has force - ful - ness,
Sing it the best that you can, my friend. If it's

One that has no fear. _____
right, then the whole world will hear. _____

Song - mak - er, song - mak - er,

Tell what you have to say.

54

Introducing the Lesson

Review "Wells Fargo Wagon" (page 28). Use a hand drum or snare drum and brushes to add this pattern to the song. (If no brushes are available, students can play the pattern using left and right hands on the drum surface.)

$\frac{4}{4}$

tap / slide / tap / slide
left / right / left / right
brush / brush / brush / brush
(hand) / (hand) / (hand) / (hand)

Developing the Lesson

1. Play the recording of "Songmaker." **How would you need to change the drum pattern for "Wells Fargo Wagon" to fit this song?** Agree that it must now move in threes instead of fours. One way to play in threes would be:

$\frac{3}{4}$

tap / slide / slide
left / right / right
brush / brush / brush
(hand) / (hand) / (hand)

Students may add this pattern as they listen to the recording again.

2. **This song has many repeated patterns, so it should be very easy to learn. Can you find the phrases that are alike, almost alike, and different?** (Each phrase is 8 measures long.) Help the students use letters to describe the form **A A' A B A B'.**

3. Help the class practice Phrases 1 and 4. Then invite them to sing the entire song. When they know it, some students may add the drum pattern as others sing.

B♭m

Dm7

Tell it in a way that the whole wide world will

Gm   C7   F

Soon sing it and say: _____

Gm

Song - mak - er, song - mak - er,

C   C7   F

Make it hap - py or sad. _____

B♭m   Dm7

Tell of the times that are good, my friend, but

Gm   C7   F

Don't be a - fraid of the bad. _____

55

4. Display the transparency prepared from Activity Sheet 9 *(Accompany Songmaker)*. **How often will the accompanists play a sound?** (once per measure; always on the first, accented beat) Choose one or more students to add this part on bells or xylophone as the rest of the class sings the melody.

Closing the Lesson [OPTIONAL]

Discuss the words with the students and emphasize the importance of always taking a deep breath before singing in order to sing the best that one can. Comment on how movement in threes helps create an expressive, flowing melody. **Can you sing in a way that adds to that expressiveness?**

LESSON 26

Lesson Focus

Timbre: The total sound is affected by the number and qualities of sounds occurring at the same time. *(P—I)*

Materials

○ **Piano Accompaniment:** page 270

○ **Record Information:**
• I Bought Me a Cat
  by Aaron Copland, 1900—
  Record 3 Side A Band 7
  William Warfield, baritone
  Columbia Symphony Orchestra
  Aaron Copland, conductor
• The Cat Came Back
  Record 3 Side A Band 8
  Voices: solo child, children's choir
  Accompaniment: bass clarinet, saxophone, double bass, piano, percussion

○ **Instruments:** bass xylophone; alto xylophone; soprano glockenspiel; drum; cymbal; and a variety of small percussion instruments

○ **For additional experience with expression:** Describe 5, page 168

Introducing the Lesson

Expressively speak the following verse, allowing time for the students to echo each phrase.

> I had a cat, the cat was fat! (echo)
> He mrrr-owed and phsssstttt (echo)
> And that's that! (echo)

Individuals may create new words to replace the second line for others to echo. Encourage students to use their most expressive voices, changing from high to low, loud to soft, and long to short.

Improvise an instrumental piece based on the rhythmic ideas that emerge from the spoken poem. Distribute a variety of classroom percussion instruments to the students. They should select one sound (such as a drum) to play the rhythm of the words "I had a cat, the cat was. . . ." They should choose a different sound

to play on "fat." Have one student improvise a rhythm for the second phrase using any instrument. Another student may play cymbals in the rhythm of "And that's that!" Repeat the activity several times so that different students may play on the second phrase.

Developing the Lesson

1. Have the class open their books to page 56, "The Cat Came Back." **Will this song be hard or easy to learn?** (probably harder than usual because there is very little repetition) **How many times do you think you will need to listen before you will be able to sing the song without the recording?** Play the recording the number of times the students suggest, as they follow the notation. Then ask them to sing it without the recording. If necessary, repeat the activity.

Refrain

Dm   C   Dm   C

But the cat came back _ the ver-y next day! _

Dm   C   Dm   C

The cat came back! _ Thought he was a gon-er.

Dm   Dm   C

But the cat came back! _ He just would-n't stay a-way. _

Dm   1.   2.

He

Add these ostinatos as an accompaniment.

Bass Xylophone

Alto Xylophone

Soprano Glockenspiel

57

LESSON 26

For Your Information

While listening to William Warfield's imaginative rendition of "I Bought Me a Cat," point out the ways in which Aaron Copland, the great American composer, selected certain orchestral sounds to represent different animal voices. Help the class to understand how the instrumental texture thickens as the song progresses.

2. **Stand beside your seat. This time listen carefully to the accompaniment. Each time the chord changes, turn a quarter turn.** Students will quickly decide that they must turn every two beats. **Listen again as you follow the music in your book. How many different chords do you hear?** (Two: The pattern alternates between Dm and C.)

3. **Because of this chord-pattern repetition, we can add an ostinato accompaniment to our song.** Help the class learn each part on pupil page 57. Add each part, one at a time, to create a full, rich-sounding ensemble.

4. Add the fun of cat sounds by asking a small group of students to supply a "mrrow" sound during the refrain after the words "the cat came back (mrr-ow)." OPTIONAL

Closing the Lesson

Play the recording of "I Bought Me a Cat," another American folk song arranged by Aaron Copland. Ask the class to listen for the interesting ways the performer uses his voice to help tell the story.

57

LESSON *27*

Lesson Focus

Timbre: The quality of a sound is determined by the sound source. *(D—I)*

Materials

- **Piano Accompaniment:** page 237
- **Record Information:**
  - My Momma Told Me
  - **Record 3 Side A Band 9**
    Voices: children's choir
    Accompaniment: synthesizer, electric guitar, piano, percussion
- **Instruments:** a variety of percussion instruments
- **Teacher's Resource Binder:**

Activity Sheets

  - **Activity Sheet 10,** page A14 (Prepare one copy for each student.)
  - Optional—
    Curriculum Correlation 7, page C11
- **For additional experience with timbre:** Describe 19, page 190

My Momma Told Me

Traditional Song Game

1. My mom-ma told me, mm,_____ if I was good-ie, mm,_____ that she would
2. My aunt-ie told her, mm,_____ I kicked a boul-der, mm. _____ Now she won't

buy me, oh, _____ a rub-ber dol-ly, mm. _____
buy me, oh, _____ a rub-ber dol-ly, mm. _____

Perform a dance: Make a circle.
Walk counterclockwise.

Verse I

My mom-ma...   Stand still.

Step forward right; left.   Touch right heel forward.   Touch right toe back.

Beats   1 2 3 4   1   2   3   4

Repeat this pattern throughout Verse I.

58

Introducing the Lesson

Ask the class to look at the music symbols above the first three notes of the song on pupil page 58. **Listen to the recording. Can you figure out what these symbols tell us to do?** Play the recording of "My Momma Told Me." Students will quickly determine that each of these notes has been held longer than usual. **That is the purpose of this symbol, called a "fermata." The note must be held much longer than usual.** Help the students learn to sing the song observing the fermatas as each verse is sung.

Developing the Lesson

1. Divide the class into three groups. Assign Group 1 to Verse 1, Group 2 to Verse 2, and Group 3 to the interlude. Each group is to read the instructions for its part of the song-game, practice the dance, and prepare to teach its part to the rest of the class. Group 3 will also need to collect the instruments and arrange them in a circle.

2. Provide time for each of the groups to work out its part of the dance. After a few minutes, ask the groups to demonstrate and then to teach their part of the song-game to the rest of the class. Perform the entire song and include the interlude between the two verses.

3. Alter the song-game. Speak the interlude chant to the students, changing the last words. Ask for a different sound (clicking, thudding, ringing, swishing) while pointing to one student. That improvisor must then select an instrument and play an appropriate sound while the rest of the class repeats the chant. Students may then take turns speaking the interlude chant, calling for the sound of their choice.

Verse II

Stand still.

My aunt - ie...

Turn in a circle, shaking hands on:
"...told her, mm,
I kicked a boulder, mm.
Now she won't..."

"Buy me, oh, a rub-ber dol-ly, mm"

Side step and
point direction.

Point heels and
fingers up.

then down
to end.

Interlude

Clap beat and chant:

Rub - ber dol - ly,   danc-ing all a-round.

Shake a   lit - tle, shake a   lit - tle,   show me your   sound.

Choose one person to move to
the center, dance, and find
an instrument to play.
All others keep clapping the beat.

59

4. Define the word timbre—the distinctive quality of a sound. Distribute Activity Sheet 10 (*Tricky Timbres*). Explain that this is a blank "score" for a composition the class is to compose. Begin by identifying the instruments that the students may use in their composition (shown at the bottom of the page). Determine the category (listed in the first column of the score) to which each belongs.

5. Ask the class to create a "tricky timbre" piece. They should decide when each instrument is to be played and should write the letter code of the instrument in the correct box on the activity sheet. **Will you want a sound in every box?** (No, silence will add interest.)

Closing the Lesson

When the piece is planned, choose students to be responsible for specific sounds; then perform the piece. Establish a slow tempo and count one beat for each box (a total of 16 beats). Each performer should play the correct sound on the appropriate beat as shown in the score.

Lesson Focus

Timbre: The quality of a sound is affected by the material, shape, and size of the source.

Timbre: The quality of a sound is affected by the way the sound is produced. *(D–I)*

Materials

○ **No Piano Accompaniment**

○ **Record Information:**
- *Rondo* (excerpt) from *Eine Kleine Nachtmusik*
  by Wolfgang Amadeus Mozart (**moet**-sahrt), 1756–1791
  Record 3 Side B Band 1
  The Cleveland Symphony Orchestra
  George Szell, conductor
- *Concerto in G Minor,* Third Movement
  by Antonio Vivaldi (vih-**vahl**-dee), 1675–1741
  Record 3 Side B Band 2
  Murray Panitz, Flute
  John de Lancie, oboe
  Bernard Garfield, bassoon
- *Almand*
  by William Brade, 1560–1630
  Record 4 Side A Band 3
  The Philadelphia Brass Ensemble
- *Allegro* from *Percussion Music*
  by Michael Colgrass
  Record 3 Side B Band 4
  Paul Price, percussion

(continued on next page)

Instruments of the Orchestra

The instruments of the orchestra are grouped into families. Each family has at least one instrument in every range:

low,   middle,   and high.

Listen to the sound of each family of instruments as you look at the pictures on pages 60, 61, 62, and 63.

String Family

Viola

Violin

Double Bass

Cello

60

Introducing the Lesson

Review "My Momma Told Me" (page 58). Perform the song-game and the interlude. Discuss ways the timbre of an instrument can be predicted and how an instrument can be assigned to a specific category by the way the sound is produced, by the instrument's shape, by the material of which it is made, and by its size. Students may enjoy suggesting new categories such as blowing, scraping, tapping, and so on, to add to those identified in Activity Sheet 10 (Lesson 27).

Developing the Lesson

1. **There is another way to organize instruments into categories, or families.** Ask the class to turn to pupil pages 60–63 and examine the pictures of instruments commonly found in the symphony orchestra. Draw attention to the way the various instruments have been grouped into families.

Discuss the family "resemblance" of each of the members. Agree that members of instrument families (like real families) often look like each other. They usually have similar shapes, although they may be of different sizes, and are made of similar or the same materials. They are usually played in much the same way, but some may sound lower or higher in pitch than others.

2. Play the four orchestral selections. (See **Materials.**) After each is played, guide the students to identify each featured instrument as being from either the string, woodwind, brass, or percussion family. (See **Glossary,** for additional information on each instrument.)

(continued on page 64)

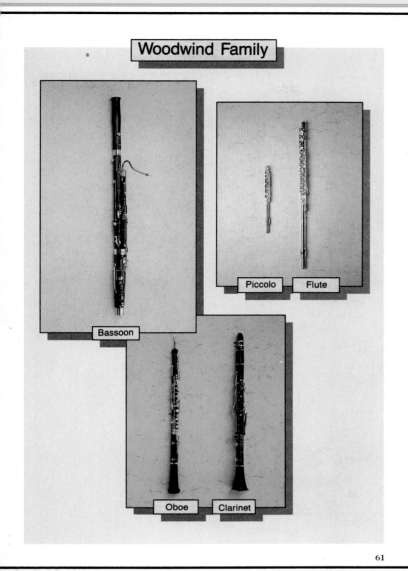

Woodwind Family

Bassoon

Piccolo | Flute

Oboe | Clarinet

61

Materials *(continued)*
- The Instruments
  Record 3 Side B Band 5
  Voices: children's choir
  Accompaniment: accordion, clarinet, flute, French horn, trumpet, violin, double bass, drum
- ○ **Instruments:** several autoharps; set of resonator bells
- ○ **Other:** Activity Sheet 10, prepared for Lesson 27
- ○ **Teacher's Resource Binder:**
  Activity Sheets
  - **Activity Sheet 11,** page A15 (Prepare one copy for each student.)
  - Optional—
    Enrichment Activity 10, page E16
- ○ **For additional experience with timbre and expression:** Create 4–5, pages 195, 196 and Create 12, page 208

For Your Information
See pupil pages 60–63 for illustrations of orchestral instruments.

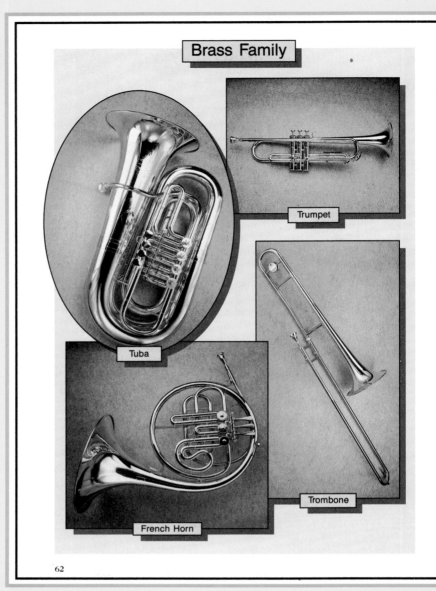

Brass Family

Trumpet

Tuba

Trombone

French Horn

62

Percussion Family

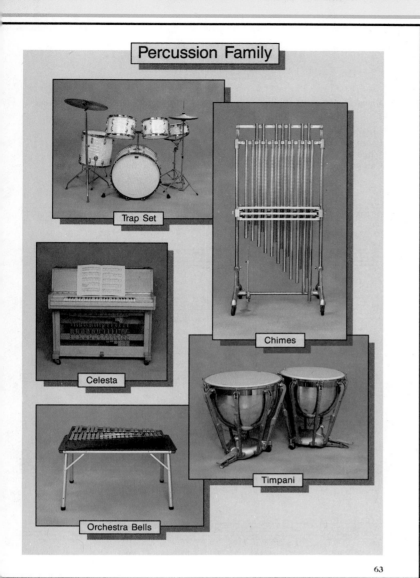

Trap Set

Chimes

Celesta

Timpani

Orchestra Bells

63

The Instruments

Arranged by Julius G. Herford

Words and Music by Willy Geisler

Choose your favorite instrument.
Learn its song.
When all know their parts, sing them together.
Can you make your voice sound like the instrument you chose?

1

The vi - o - lin's ring - ing like love ly ___ sing - ing. The vi - o - lin's ring - ing like love - ly ___ song.

2

The clar - i - net, the clar - i - net, makes dood - le, dood - le, dood - le, dood - le det. The clar - i - net, the clar - i - net, makes dood - le, dood - le, dood - le det.

3

The trum - pet is bray - ing ta - ta - ta

64

(continued from page 60)

3. Turn to page 64 and look at the song "The Instruments." **What is your favorite instrument?** Suggest to the class that they form groups, so each may sing the melody related to a favorite instrument.

4. **First we must all learn the melodies.** Draw attention to the part performed by the drum. **This instrument has just two tones—scale steps 1 and 5. The rest of the parts sing melodies based on chords built on those two scale steps.** Recall Lessons 18–20, pages 41–44 where the class learned melodies based on the I and V7 chords. **In this song the I chord is on C and the V7 chord begins on G. Name the chord to be used for each measure.** (C G7 G7 C C G7 G7 C) The same chords are used to accompany each measure of each instrument's melody.

5. Organize the class into groups based on their choice of instruments. If possible, provide each group with an autoharp and a set of resonator bells. Have one student play the accompaniment on the autoharp, a second student play the patterns on the bells, and the other students practice the melody.

6. Invite each group to perform its part for the other students. **Can you make your voices suggest the sound quality of your instrument?** Sing the sections in the order shown in the pupil book.

Closing the Lesson

Distribute Activity Sheet 11 (*Make an Instrument*). This is a homework assignment. Students are to select one of the orchestral families studied and create a new member for that family. They may

ta - ta - te - ta, ta - ta - ta ta - ta - te - ta. The trum - pet is

bray - ing ta - ta - ta ta - ta - te - ta, ta - ta - ta - ta.

4

The horn, the horn, a -

wakes me at morn. The horn, the

horn, a - wakes me at morn.

5

The drum's play - ing two tones and

al - ways the same tones: Five, one, one,

five, five, five, five, five, one.

If you chose the flute, sing its song while the others hold their last pitch.

The flute's play - ing sweet - ly with tone ___ so clear.

65

use the suggestions on the activity sheet, or they can invent a different instrument. The instrument must be able to produce a sound, and the student must be able to name the family to which the instrument belongs and explain why it belongs to that family. The completion of this activity forms part of the evaluation lesson (Lesson 30).

LESSON 29

Lesson Focus

Timbre: The quality of a sound is affected by the material, shape, and size of the source.

Timbre: The quality of a sound is affected by the way the sound is produced. *(D–I)*

Materials

○ **Record Information:**
  • *Concerto for Orchestra,* Second Movement by Béla Bartók, 1881–1945
    Record 4 Side A Band 1
    The Cleveland Orchestra
    George Szell, conductor

○ **Instruments:** piano; resonator bells

○ **For additional experience with timbre:** Create 6, page 198

LISTENING

Concerto for Orchestra, Second Movement

by Béla Bartók

Béla Bartók composed music for different pairs of instruments in the orchestra. Can you name each pair?

1

2

3

4

5

This music is sometimes called "A Game of Pairs."
Why is this a good title?

66

Introducing the Lesson *(OPTIONAL)*

Review "The Instruments" on pages 64–65. Each group should perform the part it learned during the previous lesson. After each group has demonstrated that it can sing its part independently, perform the song as a round.

Developing the Lesson

1. Ask the class to turn to page 66 of their books and answer the question at the top of the page. After each pair of instruments has been named, play the recording as far as the chorale section. (See **For Your Information.**) Stop the recording and discuss the music. **This music is sometimes called "A Game of Pairs." Why do you think the music was given this title?** (Instruments in this composition always perform in family pairs, with one pitched higher and the other lower.)

2. Play the first section of the music again, this time through the chorale. Identify the instruments that perform this section. (trumpets, trombones, tuba)

3. Play the last section. **Do you hear the same instruments? Are they playing the same music?** (yes)

Closing the Lesson

Explain that the paired instruments play duets by playing the same melody, always at the same interval. Write the following pattern on the chalkboard. Help the students discover the size of each interval by calling the bottom note "1," then counting lines and spaces until the top number is reached. Label each interval as shown below:

second   third   fourth   fifth   sixth   seventh

66

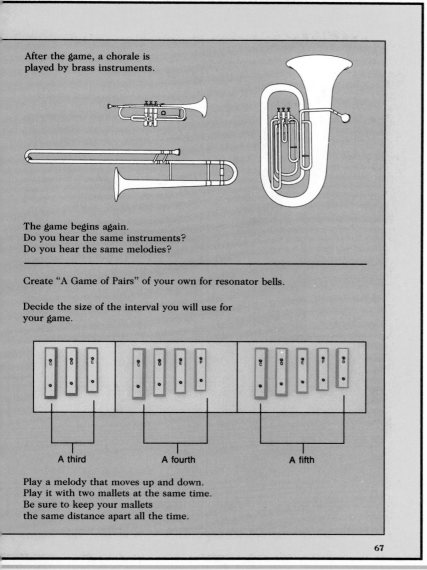

After the game, a chorale is played by brass instruments.

The game begins again.
Do you hear the same instruments?
Do you hear the same melodies?

Create "A Game of Pairs" of your own for resonator bells.

Decide the size of the interval you will use for your game.

A third   A fourth   A fifth

Play a melody that moves up and down.
Play it with two mallets at the same time.
Be sure to keep your mallets
the same distance apart all the time.

67

For Your Information

The structure of *Concerto for Orchestra,* Second Movement:
A Section:
- Bassoon duet in **minor sixths**; pizzicato strings
- Oboes a **third** apart; strings continue soft accompaniment
- Clarinets a **minor seventh** apart
- Flutes a **perfect fifth** apart (Their delicate melody is sometimes answered by strings.)
- Muted trumpet duet a **major second** apart

B Section: The middle section is a chorale, a hymnlike composition with a simple melody.

A Section: The main melodies for each duet are basically the same; the accompaniment is usually altered.

Identify the size of the interval played by each pair of instruments. (See **For Your Information**.) Play the composition again as the students locate the intervals on page 66. Invite individuals to follow the suggestions at the bottom of page 67 and create their own composition, "A Game of Pairs." They may use the white keys of the piano, resonator bells (white bells only), or any other mallet instrument.

LESSON 30

Lesson Focus

Evaluation: Review and test concepts and skills studied in the Second Quarter. *(D–S)*

Materials

○ **Piano Accompaniment:** page 272

○ **Record Information:**
  • Sing Along

⊡ **Record 4 Side A Band 2**
  Voices: solo man, children's choir
  Accompaniment: piccolo, flute, clarinet, flügelhorn, euphonium, trombone, tuba, double bass, piano, percussion

○ **Instruments:** students' own inventions (See Lesson 28, page 60.)

○ **Other:** a pencil for each student

○ **Teacher's Resource Binder**

| **Evaluation** | • **Review 2,** page Ev8 (Prepare one copy for each student.) |

  • **Musical Progress Report 2,** page Ev9

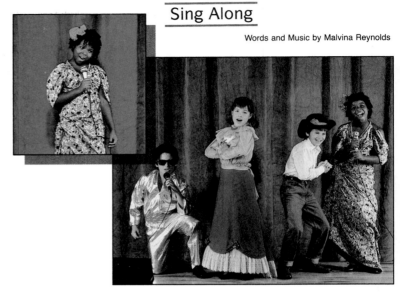

Review 2

Sing Along

Words and Music by Malvina Reynolds

Verse

D   G   D

1. I get but-ter-flies in my stom-ach when-ev-er I start to sing.

G   D   E7   A

And when I'm at a mi-cro-phone, I shake like an-y-thing.

D   G   D

But if you'll sing a-long with me, I'll hol-ler right out loud.

68

Introducing the Lesson

Ask the students to hold up the instruments that they invented and invite all to look around and see the variety. **Are there any the same?** (Answers will vary.)

Administer the evaluation for the Second Quarter. Distribute Review 2 (*Hurdle 2*) and a pencil to each student. Explain that one of the tasks will be to group the instruments into families. Review the information from Lesson 28.

Developing the Lesson

1. Instruct the class to fill in the information about their inventions on the Review Sheet.

2. Invite each student to hold up his or her instrument, demonstrate how it is played, and tell its name (if one was chosen). The students should complete Step 2 of the Review sheet by writing their classmates' names in the appropriate "family" box.

3. Correct the Review sheets by asking all the students who made percussion instruments to stand, all students who made string instruments to stand, and so on. Give the students an opportunity to check their answers.

4. Divide the class into groups of three or four. Explain that for this part of the Review, the students are to create an accompaniment for the song of their choice using their invented instruments. Each group should choose a song learned earlier in the quarter, complete the Review sheet (Step 3), and then create their accompaniment. Before beginning, briefly review information from Lessons 16–29 that may be important in creating an accompaniment: meter (movement in twos or threes), form (same and different sections), expression

Cause I'm aw-ful-ly ner-vous, lone-some. But I'm swell when I'm a crowd.

Refrain G   D

Sing a - long. _____ Sing a - long. _____

And just sing "la la   la la la" if you don't know the song.

You'll quick-ly learn the mu - sic, you'll find your-self a word.

'Cause when we sing to - geth - er, we'll be heard! _____

2. Oh when I need a raise in pay and have to ask my boss,
   If I go to see him by myself I'm just a total loss.
   But if we go together, I'll do my part right pretty.
   Cause I'm awfully nervous, lonesome. But I
   Make a fine committee. (Refrain)

3. My congressman's important: he hobnobs with big biz.
   He soon forgets the guys and gals who
   Put him where he is.
   I'll just write him a letter to tell him what I need.
   With a hundred thousand signatures,
   Why even he can read! (Refrain)

69

For Your Information

The students were instructed in Lesson 28 to choose one of the orchestral families studied (string, woodwind, brass, percussion) and create a new instrument for that family.

(mood), and rhythm (relationship of shortest sounds within the rhythm line).

5. Give the students approximately 10 minutes to work with their instruments. Circulate among the groups, observing their application of all they have learned up to now. Invite each group to perform as the class sings the chosen song.

Closing the Lesson

Direct attention to "Sing Along" on pages 68–69. **This is a great song to use with our instruments. It's a fun song!** Learn the song. Ask the students to decide which of their homemade instruments will accompany the refrain each time it is sung.

Use the information gained from this lesson, as well as from observations made throughout the quarter, to complete a copy of Musical Progress

Report 2 for each student. This may be used as a report to parents, as well as a permanent record for your files.

The Third Quarter

Be a Song Leader 1

Set the starting pitch.

Have you ever gone camping or
on a field trip with your friends?
Everyone wants to sing.
Someone has to be the leader and get everyone started.
Can you be the leader while the class
sings "She'll Be Coming 'Round the Mountain"?
Hum a pitch you think is right for the starting pitch.
Lead everyone in singing the song.
Was the melody too high? too low? Try again!

She'll Be Coming 'Round the Mountain

Traditional

5,   6, 1 1 1   1 6, 5, 3,   5, 1
She'll be com-ing round the moun-tain when she comes. (toot toot)

1   2 3 3 3   3 5   3 2   1 2
She'll be com-ing round the moun-tain when she comes. (toot toot)

70

Lesson Focus

Melody: Each pitch within a melody moves in relation to a home tone. *(P–I)*

Materials

○ **Piano Accompaniment:** page 274

○ **Record Information:**
  • On Top of Old Smoky
  📼 **Record 4 Side A Band 3**
  Voice: children's choir
  Accompaniment: pedal steel guitar, acoustic guitar, electric guitar, electric bass, electric piano, percussion

○ **Instruments:** a complete set of resonator bells; bell mallets

○ **For additional experience with expression:** Special Times 1, page 210

Introducing the Lesson

Read the discussion at the top of page 70 with the class. Ask individuals to share songs they have sung at camp or at other club outings. **Who can be a song leader and get us started?** Ask for a volunteer to start the song "She'll Be Coming 'Round the Mountain" by "thinking" a pitch, humming it aloud, and then giving the class a signal to start singing. (See page 84 for complete song.) Give several students the opportunity to be the leader. After each performance discuss the questions in the pupil book. **Was the starting pitch too high? too low? just right?**

Developing the Lesson

1. Turn to page 71 and look at "On Top of Old Smoky." Read the directions at the top of the page. Locate the lowest scale number (1) and the highest scale number (1'). Agree that the home tone will be a low tone.

2. Ask a student to play a bell that he or she has chosen from the complete box of resonator bells. The student should then hum that pitch and signal the class to start singing. If the class is not familiar with the melody, they should first sing it with scale numbers. Discuss whether or not the choice for a starting pitch was a good one. If not, ask another student to find a different pitch and repeat the song.

Closing the Lesson

Ask the students to think of other songs they have learned this year. Without looking at the musical notation, ask the class to "think" the melody and identify the tone in the song that is scale step 1, the tonal center. **Do you think it**

```
5    4  3   3   3    3  2    1
She'll be com-ing round the moun-tain,

1    1  6,  6,  6,   6, 2    1
She'll be com-ing round the moun-tain,

7,   6, 5,  5,  5,   5, 3    2  6,  7,  1
She'll be com-ing round the moun-tain when she comes.
```

You can set the pitch by "thinking" a sound.
If you have an instrument handy,
you can play the starting pitch.

Set the starting pitch for "On Top of Old Smoky" on the bells.
To do this:

1. Find the lowest scale number in the song.
Find the highest.
Find the tonal center.

2. Where is the tonal center? Is it low? high? in the middle?

3. Find a bell you think will be a good pitch for the tonal center.

4. Play the bell. Hum the pitch. Lead the class.

On Top of Old Smoky

Kentucky Folk Song

```
1  1  3  5  1'  6  6 4  5      6  5
On top of Old Smo-ky all cov-ered with snow,
11    3  5    5 2 3 4    3 2    1
I lost my true lov-er by court-ing too slow.
```

should be a high, low, or middle pitch? Ask a volunteer to select a bell and play it. Sing the song; discuss whether or not the pitch was a good choice. Some songs that might be used for this activity are: "Sweetly Sings the Donkey" (page 15), "Pop Goes the Weasel" (page 23), "Kookaburra" (page 16), and "My Momma Told Me" (page 58).

On Top of Old Smokey

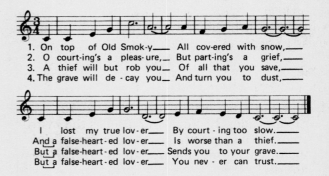

```
1. On top    of Old Smok-y___ All cov-ered with snow,
2. O court-ing's a pleas-ure,__ But part-ing's a   grief,___
3. A thief will but rob you___ Of all that you save,___
4. The grave will de-cay you___ And turn you to dust,___

I    lost   my true lov-er___ By court-ing too slow.___
And a false-heart-ed lov-er___ Is worse than a   thief.___
But a false-heart-ed lov-er___ Sends you  to your grave.___
But a false-heart-ed lov-er___ You nev-er can trust.___
```

LESSON 32

Lesson Focus

Rhythm: A series of beats may be organized into regular or irregular groupings by stressing certain beats. *(P–I)*

Materials

○ **Teacher's Resource Binder:**
  Activity Sheets • **Activity Sheets 12a–b,** pages A16–A17 (Prepare one copy for each student.)

○ **For additional experience with texture:** Describe 4, page 166

Be a Song Leader 2

Set the beat.
You know how to set the starting pitch for a song.
To be a good song leader, you also need to know how to set the beat.
To set the beat, you need to know whether beats are grouped in twos, threes, or fours.
How are the beats in "On Top of Old Smoky" grouped?
"Think" the melody and tap the heavy and light beats.
Which picture below matches your tapping pattern?

Show the singers how the beats are grouped by using one of these conducting patterns.

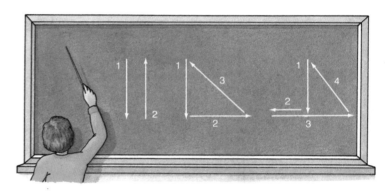

Be sure to hum the starting pitch before you signal the group to begin singing.
What about "She'll Be Coming 'Round the Mountain"?
How will you conduct that song? In twos? threes? fours?

72

Introducing the Lesson *OPTIONAL*

Invite some students to again take the role of song leader. Volunteers may choose a favorite song, establish the starting pitch, and signal the class to begin singing.

Developing the Lesson

1. Ask the students to turn to page 72, "Be A Song Leader 2." Read and discuss the instructions at the top of the page. **Can you "think" a melody without singing out loud? Tap heavy and light beats as you sing. Let's all start together. Rea-dy "think."** Think the melody while silently clapping heavy–light–light, heavy–light–light.

   After "thinking" the first verse, ask the class to offer ideas. **Did you find yourself clapping in twos?** (Show heavy–light–heavy–light.) **in threes?** (Show heavy–light–light.) **in fours?**

(Show heavy–light–light–light.) Agree that this song moves in threes.

2. Draw attention to the conducting patterns shown in the box in the middle of page 72. Help the students practice each pattern.

Twos: Beat 1— Move hand down and slightly "out" to the right.
Beat 2— Move hand back up to its original position.

Threes: Beat 1— Move hand down.
Beat 2— Move hand to the right.
Beat 3— Move hand diagonally back to its original position.

Fours: Beat 1— Move hand down.
Beat 2— Move hand across body to the left.
Beat 3— Move hand far to the right.
Beat 4— Move hand diagonally back to its original position.

Here is a list of "Favorite Songs to Sing."

Work in small groups.
Choose one of the songs.

How will you choose the starting pitch?
Review the suggestions on pages 70 and 71.

How will you decide whether the song moves
in twos, threes, or fours?
Practice the conducting pattern.

Take turns being the song leader.
Choose one person to lead the whole class.

Favorite Songs to Sing

Someone's in the Kitchen With Dinah
Kum Ba Yah
I've Been Working on the Railroad
Three Jolly Fishermen
Are You Sleeping?
Who Did?

73

LESSON 32

For Your Information
Songs included on the activity sheets:
"The Old Gray Mare"
"Someone's in the Kitchen With Dinah"
"Kum Bah Yah"
"I've Been Working on the Railroad"
"Three Jolly Fishermen," page 22
"Who Did?," page 85

3. Remind the students that they need to use the conducting pattern in threes for "On Top of Old Smoky." **Let's all conduct this time.** Ask one student to hum a starting pitch. Sing the song as everyone practices the conducting pattern. Then choose a volunteer to be the leader.

4. Follow the same procedure to discover that "She'll Be Coming 'Round the Mountain" moves in fours.

Closing the Lesson

Follow the instructions on the top of page 73. Organize the class into groups of five or six. Distribute Activity Sheets 12a–b (*Favorite Songs for Singing*). Allow each group to choose a song it wishes to prepare (or assign a different one to each group). Most of the melodies will probably be familiar. You may wish to review them as a class before working in small groups. (See **For Your Information**.) Give each group five minutes to practice its song and to decide who will be the class song leader. Each leader may then lead the entire class.

73

LESSON 33

Lesson Focus
Rhythm: A series of beats may be organized into regular or irregular groupings by stressing certain beats. *(D–S)*

Materials
○ **Piano Accompaniment:** page 282
○ **Record Information:**
• Some People
Record 4 Side A Band 4
Voices: children's choir
Accompaniment: crumhorn, shawm, sackbut, percussion
• Unsquare Dance
by Dave Brubeck 1920–
Record 4 Side A Band 5
The Dave Brubeck Quartet
○ **Other:** overhead projector
○ **Teacher's Resource Binder:**
• Optional—
Biography 4, page B7
Orff Activity 8, page O13

Review these songs. Who will be the song leader?

She'll Be Coming 'Round the Mountain
Traditional

1. She'll be com-ing round the moun-tain when she comes.

On Top of Old Smoky
Kentucky Folk Song

On top of Old Smok - y _____

You know how the beats are grouped in these two songs.
Look at the first phrase of each song.
Can you find a musical symbol that is a
clue for this information?

The clue is the $\frac{3}{4}$ **meter signature**.

The top number tells you to count the beats in groups.
The bottom number tells you the note that
moves with the beat.

74

Introducing the Lesson
Write the poem shown in **For Your Information** on the chalkboard or on a transparency. Establish a steady beat in threes and ask the students to chant the poem. Repeat the poem, adding the stamp—clap accompaniment. Help the students discover that they were stamping on the heavy beat at the beginning of each measure and clapping on all other beats. Discuss how the heavy beats helped them know when the grouping of the beats was to be changed within the chant.

Developing the Lesson
1. Ask the students to turn to page 74. Review the songs as suggested at the top of the page. After the class has sung "She'll Be Coming 'Round the Mountain" and "On Top of Old Smoky," read and discuss the information at the bottom of the page. **This is a "short-cut" way to find out how beats in a song will be grouped.**

2. Guide the students to use their new information to determine how the beats will be grouped for "Some People" on page 75. Agree that the meter signature tells us that the beats will be grouped in fours.

3. **The bottom number in all three meter signatures (for "On Top of Old Smoky," "She'll Be Coming 'Round the Mountain," and "Some People") is a four. That number tells us which note will move with the beat. Which note will that be?** If the students are not sure, ask them to sing the first two songs again, while tapping the beat. Discover that the quarter note moves with the beat.

Chords not shown on pupil page

Some People

Traditional

1 F ... 2 ...

Some peo-ple talk a lot and don't say a thing,

C7 F

So it's bet-ter yet to let them sing!

LISTENING

Unsquare Dance

by Dave Brubeck

Listen to an unsquare dance.
Why is this a good title?
Listen for the patterns below:

2/4 ... 3/4 ...

fid - dle   fid - dle   bass fid - dle

2/4 ... 3/4 ...

(hand) clap   (hand) clap   (hand) clap - ping

75

For Your Information

Stamp on the first beat of each measure.
Clap on the other beats.

3/4

Oh!   Oh!   What hit my   toe?

'Twas noth-ing dear, just a   fif - ty pound crow.

2/4 ... 3/4 ... 2/4

Oh!   No!   That can't be   so.

3/4 ... 2/4

Nev-er was there such a   hu - mon - gous   crow.

3/4

No.   No.   Then what hit your toes? 'Twas

2/4

one mixed-up but-ter-fly who thought them a   rose!

4. Help the students learn the melody by singing it with numbers or listening to the recording.

Closing the Lesson

Look at the title of the composition listed at the bottom of page 75. **Listen. Is "Unsquare Dance" a good title? Why?** Play the recording and invite students to respond. Ask them to chant and clap the patterns shown at the bottom of the page. For the second pattern, chant the word "hand"; clap and chant on the word "clap." Play the recording again and help the class identify the two patterns. Agree that the music is "unsquare" because the beats, which are not always grouped the same way, alternate between threes and fours.

LESSON 34

Lesson Focus

Rhythm: A series of beats may be organized into regular or irregular groupings by stressing certain beats. *(C–I)*

Materials

- **Piano Accompaniment:** page 276
- **Record Information:**
  - Some People
    (Record 4 Side A Band 4)
  - Hurdy-gurdy Man
    Record 4 Side A Band 6
    Voices: children's choir
    Accompaniment: piano
- **Instruments:** autoharp; resonator bells D, E♭, F♯, G, and A; bass xylophone C and F; soprano glockenspiel F, G, A, and C; mallets
- **Teacher's Resource Binder:**
  - Optional—
    Enrichment Activity 7, page E12
    Mainstreaming Suggestion 11, page M18
- **For additional experience with harmony:** Perform 10 and 11, pages 146 and 147

Hurdy-gurdy Man

Translation by Merritt Wheeler   Music by Franz Schubert

What is the meter signature of this song?
What does the top number tell you? the bottom number?

Play a drone autoharp accompaniment by pressing two keys at the same time.

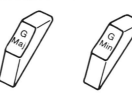

Use this rhythm throughout the song.

In the vil-lage stands a   hur-dy-gur-dy man,   *(improvise on bells)*

Play-ing fro-zen-fin-gered, when and where he can.   *(improvise on bells)*

On bare feet he wan-ders through the ice and snow,   *(improvise on bells)*

And his lit-tle cup swings emp-ty, to and fro.   *(improvise on bells)*

76

From GROWING WITH MUSIC SERIES, Book 4, Wilson, et al (Englewood Cliffs, NJ: Prentice-Hall, Inc. © 1966)

Introducing the Lesson *(OPTIONAL)*

Review "Some People" on page 75. Choose two students to learn an instrumental accompaniment for the song. (See **For Your Information.**) Remind students to accent the first beat of each measure to provide a sense of beat grouping in the music.

Developing the Lesson

1. Ask students to open their books to page 76, "Hurdy-gurdy Man." Explain that a hurdy-gurdy man is a musicmaker that one might have seen long ago in a park or village. Hurdy-gurdy men are still seen in some parts of the world. **The hurdy-gurdy is a music box that can make sounds similar to those we just played. The hurdy-gurdy player turns a crank located on the side of the box to make the hurdy-gurdy play its tune.**

Sing the melody or play the recording for the class as they follow the notation. They will discover that there are times when the drone accompaniment is all that is heard.

2. Guide the students to discover that Phrases 1 and 2 are the same, as are Phrases 3 and 4. Play the recording again and invite the students to sing along.

3. When the class knows the melody, answer the questions on the pupil page. (The meter signature is ¾; the meter is in threes; the quarter note will move with the beat.) Choose a student to add an autoharp accompaniment as suggested in the pupil book. Be sure that both chord buttons are pressed down firmly to create the open-fifth sound of the drone.

4. Follow the instructions at the end of the song on page 77 and begin to fill in the "empty spaces." Decide that each measure includes 3

And his lit-tle cup swings emp-ty, to and fro. *(improvise on bells*

mf

Play, old man, keep play-ing,　and I'll go with you;

mp

Play your hur-dy gur-dy　till my songs are through. ___

There are many measures in this song
when a voice does not sing.
How many beats will you count for each of these measures?
Use these bells to create a melody.
Play it during the measures when the voice is resting.

Listen to "Hurdy-gurdy Man" with Schubert's
piano accompaniment.
Compare the accompaniment he created with
those you made up.

77

For Your Information

The instrumental accompaniment for
"Some People":
Bass Xylophone:

Soprano Glockenspiel:

beats. Guide the students to determine how
many beats of rest occur at the end of each
vocal phrase. One student may use the resonator bells to fill in these measures. Sing the
song several times, giving different students
the opportunity to provide improvised melodies during these "resting" measures.

Closing the Lesson

Listen to the recording of "Hurdy-gurdy Man"
again. Ask the class to listen especially to the accompaniment written by Franz Schubert. Compare Schubert's ideas with those improvised by
the students (different instrumentation, different
melodies, rhythm, and so on). Turn the balance
on the phonograph so that the class may sing
with Schubert's accompaniment.

Lesson Focus

Rhythm: Individual sounds and silences within a rhythmic line may be longer than, shorter than, or the same as the underlying steady beat. *(P–S)*

Materials

○ **Piano Accompaniment:** page 261
○ **Record Information:**
　• Sing Together
　　(Record 2 Side B Band 6)
　• Whether the Weather
　　Record 4 Side B Band 1
　　Voices: children's choir
　　Accompaniment: strings
○ **Teacher's Resource Binder:**
　• Optional—
　　Enrichment Activity 8, page E12
○ **For additional experience with rhythm:**
　Describe 8, page 175

Introducing the Lesson

Review "Sing Together" on page 41 with books closed. Ask the students to tap the shortest sound on their upper legs as they sing, stressing the heavy beats. **Which syllables were the same length as the short sounds we tapped?** ("merrily, merrily") **three times as long?** ("geth-er") **How are the beats grouped?** Some students may suggest that the beats move in twos; others may say threes. Ask the students to open their books to page 41 and find the meter signature, $\frac{6}{8}$. Explain that sometimes songs can be sensed in either twos or threes. **Sometimes we can feel the beats as moving in twos:**

Chant:	Mer – ri – ly,	mer – ri – ly,
Clap:	■ ☐ ☐	■ ☐ ☐
Chant:	1 du du,	2 du du
Clap:	■ ☐ ☐	■ ☐ ☐

Sometimes we can feel the beats as moving in two groups of three:

Chant:	Mer – ri – ly,	mer – ri – ly,
Clap:	■ ▨ ▨	■ ▨ ▨
Chant:	1 2 3	4 5 6
Clap:	■ ▨ ▨	■ ▨ ▨

When music moves like this, it is sometimes notated with a meter signature of $\frac{6}{8}$. The beats are grouped in sixes with the eighth note moving with the beat.

Developing the Lesson

1. Invite the class to learn the rhythm of the chant, "Whether the Weather" on page 78. Discover that its meter signature is the same

C

Chords not shown on pupil page

Weth - er the weath - er be cold _____

G

Or wheth - er the weath - er be hot

Or wheth - er the weath - er be fair _____

C

Or wheth - er the weath - er be not,

We'll weath-er the weath-er what - ev - er the weath-er,

G   C

Wheth - er we like it or not!

79

as "Sing Together." **Which notes in the melodic rhythm will be the same length as the short sound?** (eighth notes, as in the first measure) **Are there any notes that are twice as long?** (yes; "er" in "weath-er") **three times as long?** (yes; "hot" and "not") **longer?** (yes; "cold" and "fair")

2. When the class can readily perform the rhythm, read the chant again, this time following the staff notation on page 79.

3. Establish tonality in C and help the students learn to sing the song with scale numbers.

Closing the Lesson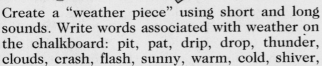

Create a "weather piece" using short and long sounds. Write words associated with weather on the chalkboard: pit, pat, drip, drop, thunder, clouds, crash, flash, sunny, warm, cold, shiver,

shake, ice, and so on. Determine which words best fit into the categories of short or long sounds. Perform the piece in **A B A** form:

A	**B**	**A**
short sounds	long sounds	short sounds

Appoint one student to be the "conductor" who points at short words and slowly moves a finger under long words so that the class can perform them at approximately the same time.

79

LESSON 36

Lesson Focus

Rhythm: Individual sounds and silences within a rhythmic line may be longer than, shorter than, or the same as the underlying steady beat. *(P–S)*

Materials

- **Piano Accompaniment:** page 275
- **Record Information:**
  - Sweetly Sings the Donkey
    (Record 1 Side A Band 7)
  - My Name Is Yon Yonson
    Record 4 Side B Band 2
    Voices: man, solo child, children's choir
    Accompaniment: barrel organ, percussion
- **Other:** overhead projector; pencil for each student
- **Teacher's Resource Binder:**
  - **Activity Sheet 13a–b,** pages A18–A19
    (Prepare a copy for each student, and prepare as a transparency.)
  - Optional—
    Enrichment Activity 11, page E20
- **For additional experience with rhythm:** Describe 10, page 177; Create 3, page 194

My Name Is Yon Yonson

Traditional

Longer sounds may be shown by adding together shorter notes:

The "+" is not a music symbol.
To add notes together we use a "musical plus sign" called a **tie**.
It looks like this:

Find the musical addition symbols as you speak the rhythm of this song.

My name is Yon Yon - son. I come from Wis-con-sin.

I work in the lum - ber-yards there. _____

When I walk down the street, all the peo-ple I meet Say,

"Hel - lo. What's your name?" And I say: _____

When [notes] are added together
they may also look like this: [note]

80

Introducing the Lesson *OPTIONAL*

Begin with a rhythmic chanting game. Students should keep a steady beat with a patschen-clap pattern while individuals take turns chanting the "Bragging Chant":

My name is (insert name) the best you can get.
My name is great, and I'm worth it!

Move down the row, giving all the students a chance to brag about their names.

Developing the Lesson

1. Invite the students to turn to page 80. Introduce "musical addition" by reading the discussion at the top of the page. Ask the class to examine the chant and determine the length of the long sounds created by the use of the tie. Read the chant in rhythm, making sure to sus-

tain the long words for the correct number of short sounds.

2. Discuss the information at the bottom of the page. Help the students realize that it is more efficient to write the longer sounds in another way than to have to tie many notes together.

3. Turn to page 81. Have the class tap the short sounds as they sing the song with scale numbers.

4. Help the students practice adding short sounds together to make longer sounds. Distribute Activity Sheet 13a *(Short Sounds— Quarter Notes)*. Sing "Sweetly Sings the Donkey" (page 15). As you sing and tap the underlying short sound, the class should begin with the first note on the first line of the activ-

Chords not shown on pupil page

Tap the short sounds (♪) as you sing this song.

Notice how the long sounds are now written.

My name is Yon Yon-son. I come from Wis-con-sin.

I work in the lum-ber-yards there.____

When I walk down the street, all the peo-ple I meet say,

"Hel-lo. What's your name?" And I say:____

For Your Information

The correct completion of "Sweetly Sings the Donkey" shown with the "musical plus sign":

Short Sounds: Quarter Notes

Short Sounds: Eighth Notes

ity sheet and touch each quarter note in time with the short sounds.

5. When they think two short sounds should be added together to make a long sound, have the students pretend to draw a tie between the two quarter notes. They should sense sounds that last for two short sounds on the syllables "don-key" and "feed him" and for four short sounds on the word "day." Distribute pencils and sing the song again. This time students should draw the ties in the appropriate places.

6. Project a transparency of the activity sheet and ask a student to show the correct placement of the "musical plus signs." Invite the class to write the pattern in traditional notation, "translating" the tied notes into the appropriate note, as necessary. (See correct answers in **For Your Information**.)

Closing the Lesson

Distribute Activity Sheet 13b *(Short Sounds— Eighth Notes)*. Follow the same procedure as for Steps 5 and 6 as you sing "Sweetly Sings the Donkey" again. Ask the class to compare the two notational examples they have drawn. Help them realize that the rhythm patterns sound the same, even though the shortest sound is represented by a different note in each example. This is because the relationships between the notes remain the same.

Lesson Focus

Melody: Each pitch within a melody moves in relation to a home tone.

Melody: A series of pitches bounded by the octave "belong together," forming a tonal set. *(D–S)*

Materials

○ **Piano Accompaniment:** page 280

○ **Record Information:**
- Follow Me
  Record 4 Side B Band 3
  Voices: children's choir
  Accompaniment: clarinet

○ **Instruments:** resonator bells C,, D,, E,, F, G, A, B♭, C, D, E, and F' or xylophone; mallets

○ **Teacher's Resource Binder:**

Evaluation • Optional—
Checkpoint 3, page EV10
Enrichment Activity 12, page E20
Kodaly Activity 14, page K22

Follow Me

Traditional Carol

Learn to sing and play this two-part song. Begin by learning to play Part 2 on the bells.

Which bells will you need to use?

Do you know how to choose the right bells?
Each bell has a letter name.
Each line and space on the staff has a letter name.
Can you match the bells with the staff?

C, D, E, F G A B♭ C D E F'

Part 1
Come a - long,   sing a   song,

Part 2
Come a - long,   sing a

82

Introducing the Lesson *(OPTIONAL)*

Ask a volunteer to be a song leader. The volunteer should set the pitch by "thinking" then humming scale step "1," the tonal center, and should then lead the class in singing "On Top of Old Smoky." **One way to set the tonal center for a song is to "think" the pitch. Another way is to look at a song written on a staff, find the tonal center, and then play the pitch on an instrument.** Ask the students to turn to page 82, so they can begin to learn how to do this.

Developing the Lesson

1. Invite the class's responses to each question on page 82. **Which bells will you need to use?** (Some students may already know how to associate the letter names of the resonator bells with the lines and spaces of the staff.)

2. **Can you match the bells with the staff?** Help the class realize that each line or space represents a pitch, which is named with a letter of the alphabet. **These are the same letter names given to the pitches one plays on the bells, or on any other instrument.** Ask a student to locate the bells and place them in order, as the class identifies the letter name of each line and space. The lines and spaces are shown on the staff in the middle of page 82.

3. Focus attention on Part 2 of "Follow Me." Ask the class to identify the letter name of each note in the melody. As each is named, ask a student to locate the correct bell. The first pitch is F. The player will discover that there are two F bells. **Which one do we need?** Play both. Agree that the lower F will be needed since the note is placed low on the staff.

Fol-low me. It is eas-y, you can

song, Fol-low me. It is

see. Ev-ery day, in this way,

eas-y, you can see. Ev-ery day, in this

Just re - peat till the tune's com - plete.

way, Just re - peat, com - plete.

Learn Part 1 by singing the scale numbers.
Can you decide which note is the tonal center?
If you know which note on the staff is "1," can you name the
scale numbers for the other notes in the song?

83

For Your Information
Tints on part music throughout HOLT MUSIC assist the student who is inexperienced in reading music from multiple staves.

4. Ask the bell player to locate the other bells. Comment that one of the bells has a small symbol after the letter. Point out that this symbol, called a flat, is found on the "B" line at the beginning of the song. **This tells us that we must play B♭ instead of B.**

5. When all the pitches have been named, give several students the opportunity to practice this pattern on xylophones or bells while the rest of the class learns to sing Part 1. **Take a nice, deep breath before singing.**

6. Read the discussion at the end of the song on page 83. **Can you decide which note is the tonal center?** Remind the class that it is often the first and last pitch of a song. **Look at Part 1. What is the letter name of the first and last note?** (F) Play F. Ask the students to sing the melody and observe the rests.

Closing the Lesson

Help the class learn to perform the two-part song with voices and bells. Invite some independent singers to sing Part 2 while others play the bells. The rest of the class continues to sing Part 1.

LESSON 38

Lesson Focus

Melody: Each pitch within a melody moves in relation to a home tone.
Melody: A series of pitches bounded by the octave ''belong together,'' forming a tonal set. *(P–S)*

Materials

○ **Piano Accompaniment:** pages 281 and 258

○ **Record Information:**
  • She'll Be Coming 'Round the Mountain
  Record 4 Side B Band 4
  Voices: children's choir
  Accompaniment: fiddle, 5-string banjo, guitar, double bass, harmonica
  • Who Did?
  Record 4 Side B Band 5
  Voices: children's choir
  Accompaniment: guitar, electric bass, electric organ, percussion

○ **Instruments:** multiple sets of resonator bells or chromatic xylophones; mallets

○ **Other:** overhead projector and transparency pen; pencil for each student

○ **Teacher's Resource Binder:**
  Activity Sheets
  • **Activity Sheet 14,** page A20 (Prepare a copy for each student and prepare as a transparency.)
  • Optional—
  Orff Activity 12, page O21

(continued on next page)

Chords not shown on pupil page

She'll Be Coming 'Round the Mountain

Traditional

Find a Pitch

Can you sing the songs on this page and the next by using scale numbers?
1. Locate the tonal center, scale step 1.
2. Figure out the scale step numbers for all the other notes.
3. Locate the bell you need to give the sound of the first pitch.
The "Pitch Facts Guide" sheet will help you learn how to do this.

84

Introducing the Lesson OPTIONAL

Review "Follow Me" on pages 82–83. **How will we find the bell we need to play to give us the sound of "1"?** (Locate "1"on the staff; determine its letter name; find the correct resonator bell.) Divide the class into two groups and sing in canon.

Developing the Lesson

1. Distribute a copy of Activity Sheet 14 *(Pitch Facts)* and a pencil to each student. Guide the class to fill in the blanks below the first staff. Project a transparency of the activity sheet and write the correct answers on the transparency. Follow the same procedure to complete the blanks below the second and third staffs.

2. Ask the students to compare the three staffs and their answers for each one. Conclude that the letter names remained the same and were in the same order. The order of the scale numbers changed. Explain that each staff has a "key signature." **It is the "key" to discovering which pitch is to be called "1."**

3. Locate the resonator bells needed to play the pitches shown on each staff. While finishing them, the class will notice that there are two bells named "B." **Which will we use?** (the one with the lower sound, which has the flat symbol after its name) When locating the bells for the third staff, decide that the F bell with the higher sound, shown by a ♯ after the F, must be used.

4. Ask the class to fill in the blanks below the fourth staff. Help them realize that (a) the letter name of a line or space is always the same; (b) only seven letters are used (one for each step of the scale); (c) when we "run out" of letters, we begin again.

Who Did?

Traditional

1. Who did, who did, who did, who did,
2. Whale did, whale did, whale did, whale did,

Who did swal-low Jo, Jo, Jo, Jo?
Whale did swal-low Jo, Jo, Jo, Jo.

Who did, who did, who did, who did,
Whale did, whale did, whale did, whale did,

Who did swal-low Jo, Jo, Jo, Jo?
Whale did swal-low Jo, Jo, Jo. Jo.

Who did, who did, who did, who did,
Whale did, whale did, whale did, whale did,

Who did swal-low Jo, Jo, Jo, Jo?
Whale did swal-low Jo, Jo, Jo. Jo.

three times, each verse

Who did swal-low Jo - nah down.
Whale did swal-low Jo - nah

3. Gabriel, blow your trumpet loud!
4. Daniel in the lion's den.

85

Materials *(continued)*
○ **For additional experience with melody:**
Describe 9, page 176

5. **Open your books to pages 84 and 85. Using the information you discovered, can you learn to play these songs on the bells?** Divide the class into as many small groups as you have sets of bells or chromatic xylophones. Each group is to select one of the songs and:

• Locate the tonal center by comparing the key signature of the song with the signatures on Activity Sheet 14.
• Identify by letter name each pitch used.
• Locate the necessary bells and arrange them from lowest to highest pitch.
• Identify a leader to play bells while other members of the group sing with letter names.

Closing the Lesson

Allow ten minutes to complete the task. Ask each group to perform its song for the class.

Lesson Focus

Melody: Individual pitches, when compared to each other, may be higher, lower, or the same. *(P–S)*

Materials

○ **Piano Accompaniment:** page 284

○ **Record Information:**
  • Bye Bye Blues

🔲 **Record 4 Side B Band 6**
   Voices: children's choir
   Accompaniment: electric guitars, double bass, vibraphone, piano, percussion

○ **Instruments:** complete, multiple sets of resonator bells or chromatic xylophones; mallets

○ **Other:** overhead projector; pencils

○ **Teacher's Resource Binder:**

Activity Sheets • **Activity Sheet 15,** pages A21–A22 (Prepare one copy for each student, and prepare as a transparency.)

○ **For additional experience with harmony:** Perform 15, page 152

Chords not shown on pupil page

Bye Bye Blues

Words and Music by Fred Hamm, Dave Bennett, Bert Lown, and Chauncey Gray

Bye   bye   blues. _____

Bye   bye   blues. _____

Bells   ring,   birds   sing.

Sun   is   shin - ing,   No   more   pin - ing.

86

Introducing the Lesson

Organize the class into as many small groups as you have complete sets of resonator bells or chromatic xylophones. Distribute Activity Sheet 15 *(Higher or Lower?)* and a pencil to each group. Explain to the class that they are to read the instructions carefully and complete the activity sheet through Step 6. When the groups have finished, project a transparency of the activity sheet. Ask representatives from each group to announce their answers. Discuss each group's responses and put the correct ones on the transparency.

Developing the Lesson

1. **Before you complete Steps 7 and 8, let's look at the song on pages 86–87 together.** Discuss the rhythm of the song. **Which note is the shortest sound?** (half note) Discuss how un-

usual this is. More frequently the shortest sound is the quarter or eighth note. **Which note is twice as long as the shortest sound?** (whole note) **Are there any notes in this song that are held longer than the whole note?** (Tied notes, as in measures 3–4, will be four times as long as the half note.)

2. **Look at the meter signature. How will the rhythm move?** (in twos) **Which note will move with the beat?** (half note—the shortest sound) Ask a student to establish the meter in twos and invite the class to read the words of the song in rhythm.

3. Invite the groups to complete Steps 7 and 8 on the activity sheet. Instruct them to choose one person to be the bell player and one to be the conductor. The others should sing the melody.

Just we two, _____

Smil - ing through. _____

Don't sigh, don't cry.

Bye bye blues. _____

87

Closing the Lesson

After the groups have worked on the activity for about ten minutes, call the class together. Challenge the students to sing the song. Listen to the recording (first statement of the verse). **Did you perform the melody and rhythm correctly?** If students feel mistakes were made, help them correct the errors independently.

Lesson Focus

Rhythm: Music may be comparatively fast or slow depending on the speed of the underlying pulse. *(D—S)*

Materials

○ **Piano Accompaniment:** page 286
○ **Record Information:**
  • Bye Bye Blues
    (Record 4 Side B Band 6)
  • Chickery Chick
    Record 4 Side B Band 7
    Voices: man
    Accompaniment: clarinet, double bass, celesta, harpsichord, electric organ, positive organ, percussion
○ **Other:** metronome
○ **Teacher's Resource Binder:**
  • Optional—
    Orff Activity 4, page O4
○ **For additional experience with rhythm:**
  Describe 7, page 172

Musical Decisions

Tempo
After a performer has learned to sing a song, there are still many musical decisions to be made.

One of them is choosing the best speed, or *tempo,* for a song.
Listen to "Chickery Chick."
What tempo decision did this performer make?

Chords not shown on pupil page

Chickery Chick

Words by Sylvia Dee   Music by Sidney Lippman

88

Introducing the Lesson

As class begins, play the complete recording of "Bye Bye Blues" (pages 86–87) without comment or interruption. After they have listened, ask the students to comment on differences they noticed between the two versions. They may notice a variety of differences. After listening to their ideas, focus on the difference in speed, or *tempo.* Write the following terms on the chalkboard:

Adagio   *Allegro*   *Andante*

The performer first sings the song *adagio* and then sings it *allegro.* **Listen to the recording again. Can you define each tempo term?** After listening to the recording, accept the class's ideas. Conclude that *adagio* is a fairly slow tempo and that *allegro* is quite fast. *Andante,* a "walking" tempo, is somewhere between *adagio* and *allegro.* Invite the students to sing the song at the tempo of their choice.

Developing the Lesson

1. Ask the students to open their books to page 88. Read the discussion at the top of the page. Play the recording as the class follows the notation. Agree that this performer could not seem to make a musical decision about the right tempo. So he sang it five times, each time at a different speed! Invite the students to offer their comments as to the best tempo. (no correct answer)

2. **Can you sing the song? Which tempo do you think would be a good one to use when you are first learning the song?** (probably a moderate one) Establish the tempo by tapping the beat. Challenge the class to sing the song independently.

3. Draw attention to the discussion and to the pictures at the end of the song. Explain that *largo* means very slow and *presto* means very

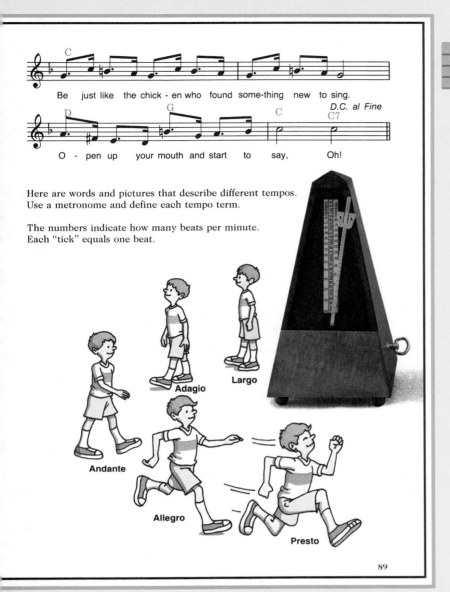

Be just like the chick-en who found some-thing new to sing.

O - pen up your mouth and start to say, Oh!

D.C. al Fine

Here are words and pictures that describe different tempos. Use a metronome and define each tempo term.

The numbers indicate how many beats per minute. Each "tick" equals one beat.

Adagio

Largo

Andante

Allegro

Presto

89

For Your Information

Tempos and metronome markings:

English	Italian	Metronome Setting
very slow	*largo*	about 50
moderately slow	*adagio*	about 70
moderate	*andante*	about 106
fast	*allegro*	about 132
very fast	*presto*	about 164 or more

Pronunciation of Italian terms:
lahr-go
ah-**dodge**-ee-oh
ahn-**dahn**-tay
uh-**leg**-ro
pray-sto

fast. Show the class a metronome and how to set it.

Focus attention on the figures, each of which has a tempo term beneath it. Explain that these terms are Italian words, describing different tempos. **In written music the tempo is usually described in Italian rather than in English.** (See **For Your Information**.)

4. Observe the figure above the word *adagio*. **How do you think this tempo will move?** After the class has offered ideas, ask a student to set the metronome for an *adagio* tempo. Invite the class to sing "Chickery Chick" at that speed.

5. Follow the same procedure until each term has been discussed and the class has attempted to perform the song at each of the five tempos shown.

6. Adjust the balance on the record player so that only the accompaniment is heard. Invite the class to sing the song. **Remember! You will have to sing at a new tempo each time the song is repeated.**

Closing the Lesson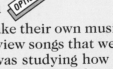

Invite the students to make their own musical decisions about tempo. Review songs that were performed when the class was studying how to be a song leader (pages 70–74). Individuals may take turns choosing a song, announcing the tempo at which it is to be sung, setting the metronome, establishing the tonal center, and conducting the class as they sing.

LESSON 41

Lesson Focus

Dynamics: Music may be comparatively loud or soft.
Articulation: A series of sounds may move from one to the next in either a smoothly connected or a detached manner. *(P–S)*

Materials

○ **No Piano Accompaniment**
○ **Record Information:**
  • French Cathedrals
    Record 4 Side B Band 8
    Voices: boys' choir
    Accompaniment: oboe, French horn, harp, chimes
○ **Instruments:** resonator bells G♯, B, C♯, and D; bell mallets
○ **Teacher's Resource Binder:**
  • Optional—
    Mainstreaming Suggestion 12, page M22
○ **For additional experience with dynamics:** Describe 17, page 187

Introducing the Lesson

Ask the class to open their books to page 90 and perform the number chant shown at the top of the page. **What will you change each time you chant a different number?** Because of the different size and thickness of the numbers, students will probably suggest that each successive group of numbers should be spoken a little louder than the previous group.

Developing the Lesson

1. Write the following Italian terms on the chalkboard, as they appear below:

   piano   mezzoforte   **forte**

   Ask the class to define each of the terms by looking at the way you have written them. Decide that *piano* means soft, *mezzoforte* means

medium loud, and *forte* means loud. Draw attention to the letters above the sets of numbers shown in the pupil book. Help the students decide that *ppp* will be the softest, *fff* will be the loudest, and *mf* or *mp* will be medium loud or medium soft.

2. Help the class learn "French Cathedrals" by identifying the letter names of each pitch, locating the appropriate resonator bells, playing them, and singing the melody. Have them sing it first with "loo." When the students know the melody, help them learn to pronounce the French words. (See **For Your Information.**) Explain that the words are the names of famous cathedrals in French cities.

3. Follow the instructions above the song and sing it, observing the dynamic markings shown above each name.

Articulation

Experiment with different ways
of singing "French Cathedrals."

How will you start and stop the sounds?

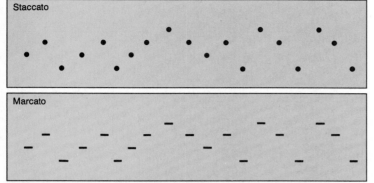

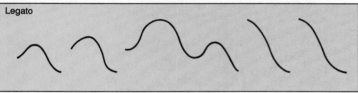

The musical term "articulation" describes how
sounds start and stop.

There are different ways to articulate sounds.

Can you decide what each term means?

91

For Your Information
The pronunciation of the cathedral names:

Orléans: **or**-lay-ahn
Beaugency: **bow**-john-see
Notre Dame de Cléry: **no**-truh dahm
                                     deh **clay**-ree
Vendôme: **vahn**-dome

4. Turn to page 91. Invite the class to sing
   "French Cathedrals" in ways that match the
   three pictures. Draw ideas suggested by the
   students as they plan each performance:
   • Each pitch should be short and detached.
     (staccato)
   • Each pitch should be slightly stressed and
     sustained for its full value. *(marcato)*
   • Pitches should move smoothly from one to
     the next. *(legato)*
   Associate the three ways of singing with the
   appropriate Italian terms on the pupil page.

Closing the Lesson [OPTIONAL]

Write the cathedral names on the chalkboard.
Students may experiment with different ways of
singing the song by taking turns writing different
articulation markings above the names. The
writer may then become the conductor and point
at the words as the class sings.

Lesson Focus

Form: A musical whole may be made up of same, varied, or contrasting segments.
Expression: The expressiveness of music is affected by the way tempo, dynamics, and articulation contribute to the musical whole. *(D–S)*

Materials

o **Piano Accompaniment:** page 288

o **Record Information:**
  • Variations on Hot Cross Buns by F. Wayne Scott
  Record 4 Side B Band 9
  Janet Pummill, piano
  • Schnitzelbank
  Record 4 Side B Band 10
  Voices: man, children's choir
  Accompaniment: clarinet, trumpet, trombone, tuba, guitar, double bass, accordion, percussion

o **Instruments:** resonator bells C, D, E♭, E, F, G, A♭, A, B♭, B, and C; bell mallets; kazoos

o **Other:** overhead projector

o **Teacher's Resource Binder:**
  | Activity Sheets | • **Activity Sheets 16a–c,** pages A23–A25 (Prepare a transparency from each page of the activity sheet.) |

(continued on next page)

LISTENING

Variations on Hot Cross Buns
by F. Wayne Scott

Hot cross buns, hot cross buns.

One a pen-ny, two a pen-ny, hot cross buns.

A composer makes musical decisions about:

Melody	Tempo
Rhythm	Dynamics
Harmony	Articulation
Form and Style	

What decisions did the composer make in his "Variations on Hot Cross Buns"?

92

Introducing the Lesson *OPTIONAL*

Ask the students to browse through the lessons they have recently completed that focus on making musical decisions (Lesson 40, pages 88–89; Lesson 41, pages 90–91). Ask them to identify the following things about which performers need to make decisions: tempo, dynamics, and articulation. **These musical decisions affect the feeling, or expression, of a song. What would happen to the feeling of "Are You Sleeping?" if you performed it in different ways?** Invite individuals to suggest ways of combining different tempos, dynamics, and articulations to express a feeling.

Developing the Lesson

1. **Composers must make musical decisions too. Not only must they decide about the melodies, rhythms, and harmonies they are going to use, but they also have to make decisions about tempo, dynamics, and articulation.**

2. Examine the list of decisions given on page 92. Review the melody of "Hot Cross Buns." **Composer F. Wayne Scott chose to create a composition by taking this familiar melody and varying it. Each variation is based on a different dance style. As you listen figure out what other musical decisions he made each time to create a series of interesting variations.**

3. Play the recording of "Variations on Hot Cross Buns." Display the appropriate transparencies prepared from Activity Sheets 16a–c *(Variations on Hot Cross Buns)* as each variation is heard. Pause after each variation and invite the students to identify the musical decisions the composer made. Focus on the following:

   • **Waltz:** The change to $\frac{3}{4}$ meter makes this familiar tune sound unusual. The melody is *legato,* the tempo *presto.*

   • **Square Dance:** The meter is in two. The mel-

Chords not shown on pupil page

Schnitzelbank

German-American Song

Ist das nicht ein
1. Schnit - zel - bank?
2. Bü - cher - schrank?
3. Jun - ger Herr?

Ja, das ist ein
1. Schnit - zel - bank. (to Refrain,
2. Bü - cher - schrank. 1st time
3. Jun - ger Herr. only)

2. Bü - cher - schrank, Schnit - zel - bank?

3. Junger Herr   7. Stolzer Hahn

4. Schwarzer Bär   8. Wasserfall

5. Blaues Meer   9. Gummiball

6. Eisenbahn   10. Fledermaus

Refrain

Lie - be Leut' in die - sem Land

Ja, das ist ein Schnit - zel - bank.

93

LESSON 42

Materials (continued)
- **Activity Sheet 17,** page A26 (Prepare a transparency from the activity sheet.)
- **For additional experience with form:** Create 9, page 202

For Your Information
Translation for "Schnitzelbank":

Is this not a (1) cutting bench?
Yes, this is a cutting bench.
Beloved people in this place,
Yes, this is a cutting bench.

2. bookcase   7. proud rooster
3. young man   8. waterfall
4. black bear   9. rubber ball
5. blue sea   10. bat
6. train

ody is *staccato,* with added tones, and the tempo is *allegro.*
- **Tango:** Notice the tango rhythm. The tempo is moderate.
- **Blues:** The meter is in two. The added melody tones are typical of the blues style.
- **Minuet:** The meter signature is $\frac{3}{4}$. Extra tones "blur" the melody. The accompaniment is *legato,* the tempo *allegro.*
- **Sarabande:** The meter signature is still $\frac{3}{4}$. Notice the added, moving bass line. The melody is *legato,* the tempo moderate.
- **Gavotte:** The melody and rhythm are altered again by added tones. The meter is in four, the tempo *lento.*
- **Gigue:** The uneven rhythm is written in $\frac{6}{8}$, with the melody now in the bass. The upper voice is *staccato* at times.

4. After each variation has been discussed, play the complete composition without pausing be-tween variations. Continue to show the appropriate transparency as the music progresses.

5. Challenge the class to use their information about rhythm and melody to learn "Schnitzelbank." After learning the melody, project the transparency of Activity Sheet 17 *(Schnitzelbank)* as the class sings all the verses.

Closing the Lesson

Invite the class to play resonator bell or kazoo variations on "Schnitzelbank," using some of the ideas Scott used when composing "Variations on Hot Cross Buns."

Lesson Focus

Expression: Musical elements are combined into a whole to express a musical or extramusical idea. *(C–S)*

Materials

○ **No Piano Accompaniment**

○ **Instrument:** piano

○ **Teacher's Resource Binder:**
  • Optional—
    Enrichment Activity 13, page E20

○ **For additional experience with expression:** Perform 16 and 17, pages 154–159

Lacadel Was a Ponderous Bear
B.A.

Perform this poem with music.
Choose two performers to play the piano ostinato throughout the piece.
Choose three performers to create a black-key improvisation after each verse.

Piano ostinato

Player 1

Player 2

Lacadel was a ponderous bear,
A ponderous bear who lived in a lair.
He consumed six months rations,
Slept the rest in great fashion,
And didn't pay bills for a "yair."
Nope, didn't pay bills for a "yair."

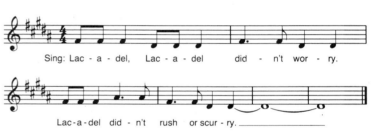

Sing: Lac - a - del, Lac - a - del did - n't wor - ry.

Lac-a-del did - n't rush or scur - ry. _____

He merely rolled over
And slept like a loafer.

Improvisation 1

94

Introducing the Lesson

Read the poem "Lacadel Was a Ponderous Bear" to the students as they follow the narration on pages 94–95 of their books.

Developing the Lesson

1. Invite the class to perform the poem as a vocal composition by following the instructions in their books. Choose two performers to play the piano ostinato throughout the piece. Students will find that these dissonant harmonies add to the expressiveness of the poem. The other class members should recite the poem, except for the phrase "Lacadel, Lacadel didn't worry . . . ," which is to be sung. Direct the students to begin this phrase each time on the first beat of the measure so that it fits with the piano accompaniment figure. The class should alternate between singing and speaking to complete the poem.

2. After performing the composition once, add the improvisations. Select a volunteer to be soloist for Improvisation 1. This improvisation should suggest the sound of a lazy bear. The soloist will need to decide whether to improvise in the upper or lower register of the piano (in an area of the keyboard not being used by the accompanists). When the register is chosen, the soloist will have to make decisions regarding tempo, dynamics, and articulation.

3. Invite two more students to create Improvisations 2 and 3. To perform the complete poem, the class should alternate between singing and speaking and should pause for each improvisation. End by repeating the "Lacadel, Lacadel didn't worry. . . ." phrase, gradually slowing the tempo and softening the dynamics.

4. Evaluate the performance. **Did we speak and play expressively? Did we communicate the**

Rising up ravenous one early spring day,
Lacadel hurried to the honey-pot tray.
In great disbelief and emitting a growl,
Lacadel read with a furrowed brow:
"Borrowed your honey just for the day,
Hope you don't mind, it was right on my way!"

Lac - a - del, Lac - a - del did - n't wor - ry.

Lac - a - del did - n't rush or scur - ry. _____

He calmly sat down in a group of one
and had himself a bear tan-trum.

Improvisation 2

Lacadel roared and Lacadel simpered,
His lower lip quivered, and he pitifully whimpered.
He took his loss but was really chagrined,
"I'll grind this thief in a pretzel bend!"
The thief came sneakin', honey pot in hand,
Tiptoeing back to where this began.

Lac - a - del, Lac - a - del did - n't wor - ry.

Lac - a - del did - n't rush or scur - ry. _____

"Gotcha thief! Oh, pardon me.
Such a lovely, fair bear . . . . Do stay for tea!"

Improvisation 3

95

personalities of the characters? Did we make the best possible choices for dynamics, tempo, articulation, register, and rhythm? Would other choices make the poem more exciting? Invite the students to make suggestions, select a new group of improvisers, and perform again.

Closing the Lesson

Make plans to invite another class (perhaps a Kindergarten or first grade) to a performance of "Lacadel Was a Ponderous Bear."

The class can make this a more sophisticated production by preparing costumes and selecting characters to pantomime the action while others perform the tale.

LESSON 44

Lesson Focus

Expression: Musical elements are combined into a whole to express a musical or extramusical idea. *(D—I)*

Materials

○ **Record Information:**
- Little Train of the Caipira, from *Bachianas Brasileiras No. 2,* by Heitor Villa-Lobos (vee-lah **loe-boess**), 1887–1959
  Record 5 Side A Bands 1a—b
  The London Symphony Orchestra, Sir Eugene Goosens, conductor
  Band 1c: The Winter Consort

○ **Teacher's Resource Binder:**
- Optional—
  Biography 5, page B9

○ **For additional experience with expression:** Describe 1, page 160

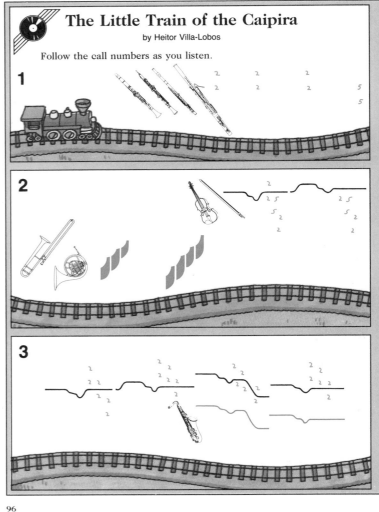

Introducing the Lesson

Invite the class to imagine that they are taking a trip through the countryside on an old-fashioned train. **This trip might have occurred many years ago, when trains were powered by steam and went through many little towns. What kinds of sounds might you have heard? What events might you have seen along the way?**

Developing the Lesson

1. After the students have offered ideas, ask them to open their books to page 96. **The pictures on these pages suggest some of the musical sounds that the composer Heitor Villa-Lobos used to describe a trip on a little steam train through the Brazilian countryside.** Ask the class to follow the "music map" as they listen. Explain that they will hear the numbers in each box called out on the recording. This will help them "stay on the train"!

2. Guide the students to move from box to box as the numbers are called out. After listening to the complete recording you may wish to listen to each section again, pausing to discuss the kinds of musical decisions made by the composer.

Box 1: The train moves slowly out of the station. The woodwinds suggest the sound of a cheerful whistle as the train gets under way. The timpani imitate the sound of the accelerating engine. The clicking-wheel sounds are produced by several instruments:

- the *ganza* (a metal tube filled with gravel)
- the *chocalhos* (a rattle containing gourd seeds or covered with netted gourd seeds)
- the *reco-reco* (a notched stick)
- the *ranganella* (a ratchet)
- the *tamburello* (a tambourine)

Box 2: The trombone and French horns play *glissandos,* as shown by the curved shapes.

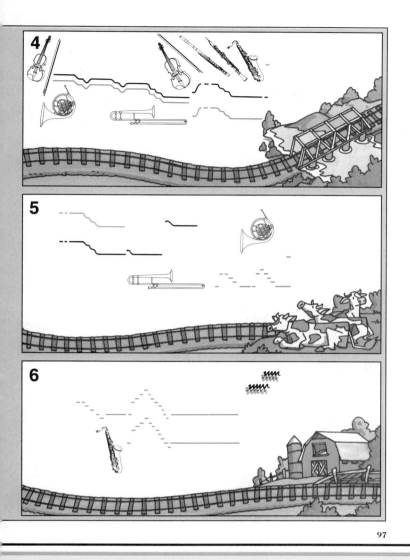

97

The violins enter with this eight-measure theme:

Box 3: The violins restate the first melody one step higher. Then, joined by the saxophone, they continue with this new melody:

Draw attention to the perky melodic fragments played by the woodwinds and the sustained chords played by the French horns and the trombone.

Box 4: The French horn, followed by the trombone, joins the high strings in a variation of the theme as the lower strings and percussion continue the clicking-wheel rhythm. The flute, oboe, and saxophone join the strings.

Box 5: The entrance of the trombone at the end of the music is represented in this box. The French horn then begins a melody that is joined by the saxophone. Each note of this melody is played *marcato*.

Box 6: The entrance of the flutes and oboes, continuing in Box 7 and followed by the entrance of the full orchestra in two sustained, trilled chords, signals a momentary pause in the trip.

Box 7: The trip resumes as the woodwinds and high strings play a rapidly descending line, while French horns, saxophone, trombone, piano, and low strings play a series of ascending chords. The chords suggest the sounds of the train as it builds up steam for the trip ahead. Preceded by a sustained clarinet note, the theme returns, now played by the flute and oboe. The trombone and French horns provide variety with a brief pattern.

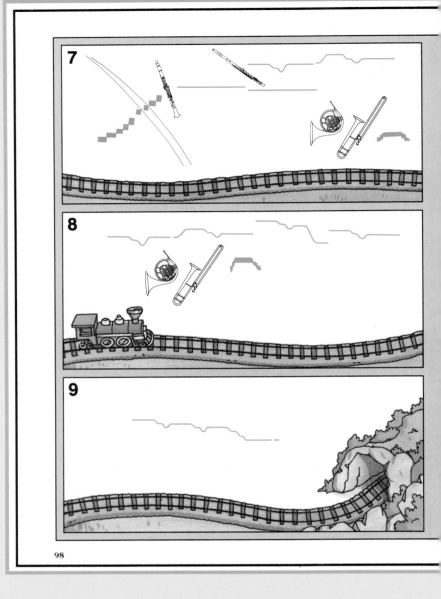

98

Box 8: The flute and oboe duet continues, as the other instruments accompany with various patterns. The trombone and French horns, on different pitches, repeat the brief pattern heard during Box 7.

Box 9: The woodwinds continue the theme, accompanied by other instruments, as the train makes its way through the mountains.

Box 10: The woodwinds, accompanied by other instruments, continue and come to the end of the melody.

Box 11: The bassoon, French horns, and trombone enter with a new, accented figure. The other instruments continue the sound of the clicking wheels. The woodwinds begin a trill. The music begins a gradual *ritardando,* signaling that the end of the trip is near.

Box 12: The flute and oboe continue the trill. The tempo becomes slower, and the sounds become softer until the train, giving one last puff of steam, finally pulls into the station.

Closing the Lesson

When the children have enjoyed the composition by Villa-Lobos, play the arrangement performed by The Winter Consort. **Is this the same music?** (Not exactly; it is based on the same musical ideas and uses the same main theme.) Encourage the students to comment on the similarities and differences between the two versions. Some distinctive characteristics of the second version are:

- The accompaniment is different, instrumentally and rhythmically.
- The main melody is usually played by the saxophone, in a more syncopated rhythm.
- The high woodwinds play a different pattern when punctuating the theme.

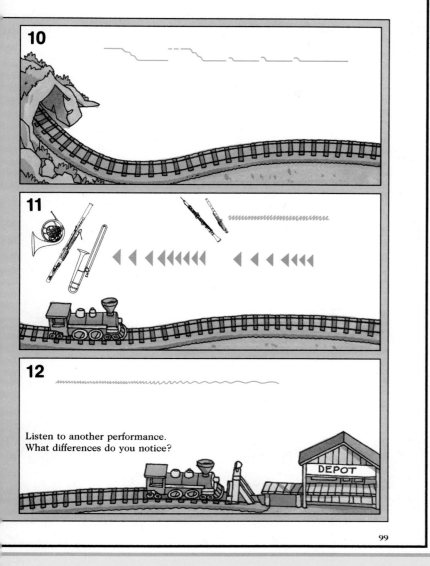

10

11

12

Listen to another performance.
What differences do you notice?

DEPOT

99

Does the train ever pause? (only momentarily)
What else is different about the two performances? (The trip is much shorter in the second version.)

Lesson Focus

Evaluation: Review and test concepts studied in the Third Quarter. *(D–S)*

Materials

○ **Piano Accompaniment:** page 283

○ **Record Information:**
  • You Can't Make a Turtle Come Out
    Record 5 Side A Band 2
    Voices: solo child, children's choir
    Accompaniment: English horn, baritone saxophone, bass clarinet, contrabassoon, percussion

○ **Other:** a pencil for each student

○ **Teacher's Resource Binder:**

  Evaluation • **Review 3,** pages Ev13–Ev14 (Prepare one copy for each student.)
  • **Musical Progress Report 3,** page Ev15

Review 3

Chords not shown on pupil page

You Can't Make a Turtle Come Out

Words and Music by Malvina Reynolds

100

Introducing the Lesson

Explain that the class time will be divided into two sections: reviewing and testing. Begin by reviewing songs and activities from Lessons 31 and 32. Observe how effective the students are as Song Leaders.

Developing the Lesson

1. Review the following songs: "Some People" (page 75), "Whether the Weather" (page 78), "My Name Is Yon Yonson" (page 80), and "Follow Me" (page 82). Encourage the students to describe what they learned about music when they first learned each of the songs. Use the chalkboard to illustrate ideas as needed to review concepts such as meter, tonal center, rhythm, etc. (See Lessons 31–44.)

2. Distribute a pencil and Review 3 (*Hurdle 3*) to each student and administer the evaluation

for the Third Quarter. Read the first instruction to the class. Play the recording of "You Can't Make a Turtle Come Out" as the students tap the shortest sound.

To help the students follow the second instruction, play or sing the song as many times as needed while they "add the notes together," using the "musical plus sign" (the tie). They are to show which words are held longer than the shortest sound. Review this activity by drawing an example on the chalkboard.

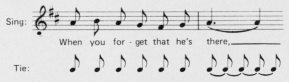

3. Read the remaining instructions to the students. After you have read each question, give

2. If he wants to stay in his shell,
   If he wants to stay in his shell,
   You can knock on the door but you can't ring the bell.
   And you can't make a turtle come out, come out.
   You can't make a turtle come out.

3. Be kind to your four-footed friends.
   Be kind to your four-footed friends.
   A poke makes a turtle retreat at both ends.
   And you can't make a turtle come out, come out.
   You can't make a turtle come out.

4. So you'll have to patiently wait.
   So you'll have to patiently wait.
   And when he gets ready, he'll open the gate.
   But you can't make a turtle come out, come out.
   You can't make a turtle come out.

5. And when you forget that he's there,
   And when you forget that he's there,
   He'll be walking around with his head in the air.
   But you can't make a turtle come out, come out.
   You can't make a turtle come out.

101

For Your Information

Answers to Review 3:

1. Students should tap eighth-note beat.

2.

3a. $\frac{3}{8}$; **3b.** 3; **3c.** eighth; **3d.** 1 and 2; **3e.** raise it; **3f.** moderately

4. Numbers: 5–5–6–5–4–3–4–5;
   5–5–6–5–4–3–4–5;
   5–5–6–4–6–1'–7–6–5–6–5–3;
   4–4–5–6–5–4–3–2–3–4–5;
   5–6–7–6–5–3–2–1
   Letters: A–A–B–A–G–F♯–G–A;
   A–A–B–A–G–F♯–G–A;
   A–A–B–G–B–D–C♯–B–A–B–A–F♯;
   G–G♯–A–B–A–G–F♯–E–F♯–G–A;
   A–B–C♯–B–A–F♯–E–D

them time to study the music and circle the answer before reading the next question. (Correct answers are in **For Your Information**.)

Closing the Lesson

Turn to pages 100–101. Enjoy singing all five verses of the song.

Use information gained from this lesson, as well as from observations made throughout the quarter, to complete Musical Progress Report 3 for each student. This may be used as a report to parents, as well as a permanent record for your files.

Lesson Focus

Form: A musical whole may be made up of same, varied, or contrasting segments. *(D–I)*

Materials

- **Piano Accompaniment:** page 290
- **Record Information:**
  - Give a Little Whistle
- **Record 5 Side B Band 1**
  Voices: children's choir
  Accompaniment: small show orchestra
- **Instruments:** extended resonator bells or piano with marked keys
- **Other:** Prepare a classroom set of Form Cards by using different-colored pieces of construction paper for each letter and different shades of the same color for prime (') letters.
- **Teacher's Resource Binder:**
  - **Activity Sheet 18,** page A27 (Prepare several sets of Form Cards for each student.)

  Activity Sheets
- **For additional experience with form:** Special Times 15, page 230

The Fourth Quarter

A Memory Game

How well do you remember what you hear?
Play a game to find out!

Listen to two phrases.
Are they . . .

the same,   similar,   or different?

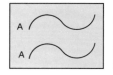   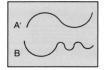

102

Introducing the Lesson

Have the students open their books and read the discussion at the bottom of page 102. Play the following examples on resonator bells or piano.

Example 1: (A A) Play the first two phrases, four measures each, of "Silver Birch" (page 19).
Example 2: (A B) Play the first two phrases, four measures each, of "School Days" (page 21).
Example 3: (A A′) Play the first two phrases, four measures each, of "Wells Fargo Wagon" (page 28).
After playing each example, ask the students to choose the box that shows what they have heard.

Developing the Lesson

1. Continue the game with books closed. Prepare several sets of Form Cards from Activity Sheet 18 for each student and distribute them. Explain the rules: As you play two phrases, the students are to listen. They should then locate the appropriate cards to show whether the two phrases are the same, similar, or different. The first card will always be **A.** Play a variety of examples. (A list of songs is suggested in **For Your Information.**) After the students have chosen their cards, identify the correct letters.

2. When the students show that they can readily identify the form of two phrases, challenge them to expand their memory skills by listening to three or four phrases. **You will need to compare each additional phrase you hear with all the phrases you've already heard.** Continue to use the songs listed in **For Your Information.** Pause briefly after each phrase. Replay each phrase group two or three times if necessary.

Give a Little Whistle

by Ned Washington and Leigh Harline

When you get in trou-ble and you don't know right from wrong,
When you meet temp-ta-tion and the urge is ve-ry strong,

Give a lit-tle whis-tle! (*whistle*)__ Give a lit-tle whis-tle! (*whistle*)__

Not just a lit-tle squeak, Puck-er up and blow.

And if your whis-tle's weak, yell "Ji-mi-ny Crick-et"!

Take the straight and nar-row path, and if you start to slide,

Give a lit-tle whis-tle! (*whistle*)__ Give a lit-tle whis-tle! (*whistle*)__

And al-ways let your con-science be your guide.__

103

For Your Information

Songs and Form:
''Do Your Ears Hang Low?'' (page 31): **A B A' B' Coda**
''Woke Up This Morning'' (page 48): **A A' A B**
''Sweetly Sings the Donkey'' (page 15): **A A' B**
''Kookaburra'' (page 16): **A A' B C**
''Silver Birch'' (page 19): **A A B B**
''Wells Fargo Wagon'' (page 28): **A A' B B'**
''Janišek the Highwayman'' (page 26): **A A**
''Bye Bye, Blackbird'' (page 24): **A B A' B' C C' A' D (or coda)**
''Chickery Chick'' (page 88): **A A B B' (or C) A**

3. **This time I'm going to really challenge you. I'm going to play a whole song, phrase by phrase.** Play the seven phrases that make up "Give a Little Whistle," pausing after each phrase to give each student time to find the appropriate card. Be sure to follow the repeat sign and play the first two phrases again.

4. When the students have chosen the nine cards, ask them to reopen their books to page 103. **This is the song I just played. Look at the notation to see if your answers were correct.** Guide the class through the song, phrase by phrase. Agree, by comparing each successive phrase to the first, that the Form Cards should be in the following order: **A B A B C D (or C') A B' E.** (Be sure the class understands that even though Phrases 1 and 2 are only shown once, they are repeated. There will be a card to show each phrase they heard.)

Closing the Lesson *OPTIONAL*

Play the recording of "Give a Little Whistle" as the class follows the notation. Adjust the balance on the phonograph so that only the accompaniment is heard. Challenge the students to sing the entire song with the recording. Remind them to take a deep breath before singing.

LESSON 47

Lesson Focus

Form: A musical whole may be made up of same, varied, or contrasting segments. **(D–I)**

Materials

○ **Record Information:**
  • Papa's Tune from *Acadian Songs and Dances* by Virgil Thomson, 1896—
  Record 5 Side B Band 2
  The Cleveland Pops Orchestra
  Louis Lane, conductor
  • Chorale from *The Louisiana Story* (Suite) by Virgil Thomson
  Record 5 Side B Band 3
  The Westphalian Symphony Orchestra
  Siegfried Landau, conductor

○ **Instruments:** resonator bells C, D, E, F, G, A, and B♭; bell mallets; autoharp

○ **Other:** Form Cards prepared from Activity Sheet 18, Lesson 46

○ **Teacher's Resource Binder:**
  • Optional—
  Enrichment Activity 16, page E28

○ **For additional experience with form:** Special Times 3, page 214

You can remember sections of a song.
Can you now remember a longer form?

Can you stretch your musical memory?
Can you remember the **A** section
when you hear a longer composition?

LISTENING

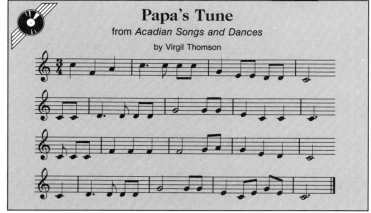

Papa's Tune
from *Acadian Songs and Dances*
by Virgil Thomson

LISTENING

Chorale
excerpt from *The Louisiana Story* (Suite)
by Virgil Thomson

104

Introducing the Lesson

Read the discussion on page 104 together. Remind the students of the game they played during the previous lesson (page 102). **Do you think you can play the memory game as well when the sections are longer and there are no words?** Distribute the Form Cards. Play the recording for the first section of "Papa's Tune" as the class follows the theme in their books. Agree that this is section A.

Now listen to the complete composition. Decide how many sections you hear. Select one Form Card for each section. Play the complete recording. Agree that there are only two sections.

Some students may feel that the changes in key and instrumentation justify calling the second section **A′**. Others may feel that it is really the same and call it **A**. Either answer is acceptable. (See **For Your Information** for the form of "Papa's Tune.")

Developing the Lesson

1. Follow the same procedure to determine the form of "Chorale." Play the recording as the class follows the first theme in their books. Then play the complete recording as many times as necessary for the students to select the appropriate Form Cards.

2. Turn to page 105. Follow the instructions to create a four-section composition. Begin by helping the students learn to sing and play the A-section melody. Ask one student to add an autoharp accompaniment, strumming this rhythm:

$$\frac{2}{2} \quad \text{♩} \qquad \text{♩} \quad \text{:} \|$$

3. Invite students to take turns demonstrating ways the melody might be changed slightly to

Creating Form

1. Create a 4-section composition.

Use this melody to play the **A** section.
Play it on these resonator bells: C, D, E, F, G, and A.
Play this autoharp chord:

Use a chord built on the first step of
the song's scale, the **I** chord.

Jump Down, Turn Around   Southern Folk Song

Goin' to   jump down, turn a - round,   pick a bale of cot - ton.

Goin' to   jump down, turn a - round,   pick a bale a day.

2. Now plan an **A'** section. You might want to
- Change the end of the melody.
- Change the rhythm of the melody.
- Play in a new **key**.

Use these resonator bells: G, A, B♭, C, D, and E.
Use this autoharp chord:

3. Plan a **B** section.
Use the C chord for the accompaniment.
Create a new melody using these resonator bells: C, D, E,
F, G, and A.
The melody must be the same length as the **A** melody.

4. Repeat the **A** section to complete your composition.

105

For Your Information
Form of "Papa's Tune":
A—theme in pupil book
A or **A'**—altered instrumentation and accompaniment
B—new melody
A or **A'**— same melody, similar instrumentation
C or **A"**—melody derived from **A**
A or **A'**—different instrumentation

create an **A'** section. Some possible alterations might be:

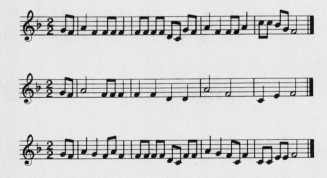

4. Ask one student to use the resonator bells listed in the book to create a completely new melody. An accompanist should play the F chord for eight strokes to help the composer feel the rhythmic flow and determine the length of the section.

Closing the Lesson

Invite one student to use the Form Cards to show a particular form the composition should take. The class should perform in the order selected. Discuss the effectiveness of the decisions. Invite others to suggest different formal arrangements for the four sections.

LESSON 48

Lesson Focus

Form: A musical whole may be made up of same, varied, or contrasting segments. *(D–I)*

Materials

○ **Piano Accompaniment:** page 292
○ **Record Information:**
  • Sally Don't You Grieve
  Record 5 Side B Band 4
  Voices: children's choir
  Accompaniment: electric guitar, electric bass, electric organ, piano, percussion
○ **Instruments:** two sets of resonator bells G, A, B, C, D, E, F♯, and G'; bell mallets
○ **For additional experience with harmony:** Perform 8, page 144

Chords not shown on pupil page

Sally Don't You Grieve

Spiritual

1. Oh, I want to go to hea-ven, — Echo

And I want to go right, — Echo

I want to go to hea-ven, — Echo

All dressed in white. — Echo

106

Introducing the Lesson

Recall the memory games previously played. (See Lessons 46 and 47.) **Let's change our game today. Instead of listening to two phrases and telling me whether they are the same or different, can you listen to a phrase and play it back to me on bells?** Direct the class's attention to the "echoes" on page 106. Invite one student to echo. Explain that while the student echoes, the rest of the class should decide if the player's echo was the same as, similar to, or different from the phrase you played.

Put out two sets of bells. Play simple patterns drawn from the melody of "Sally Don't You Grieve." Give several students an opportunity to play back the pattern you presented. They may echo the pattern, or they may alter it. Ask the class to determine whether the performer played it exactly the same, almost the same, or changed it completely.

Developing the Lesson

1. **This time, I'd like everyone to echo my singing.** Sing the four patterns shown at the bottom of the pupil page. Establish a steady eighth-note pulse and guide the students to echo you without interrupting the rhythmic flow.

2. Repeat the same four phrases. This time sustain the last sound of each phrase while the students perform the echo. **What have we added to the song?** (harmony)

3. Direct the students' attention to the remainder of the song shown on page 107. **We have started to learn this song using our ears and our memories. Can we finish learning it by reading the notation? It begins on the tonal center, scale step 1.** Ask the students to identify each different pitch used in the melody

2. Oh, you can't go to heaven in a rockin' chair,
   Get down on your knees and say a prayer.
   Oh, you can't go to heaven in a rockin' chair,
   Get down on your knees and say a prayer.
   Oh, Sally don't you grieve,
   Don't you grieve no more.

3. Oh, you can't go to heaven on roller skates,
   You'll roll right by those pearly gates.
   Oh, you can't go to heaven on roller skates,
   You'll roll right by those pearly gates.
   Oh, Sally don't you grieve,
   Don't you grieve no more.

4. "That's all there is, there isn't any more,"
   Saint Peter said, as he closed the door.
   "That's all there is, there isn't any more,"
   Saint Peter said, as he closed the door.
   Oh, Sally don't you grieve,
   Don't you grieve no more.

107

LESSON 48

For Your Information

Descant part for last four measures of "Sally Don't You Grieve":

Sing on a neutral syllable.

---

by scale number. Write them on the chalkboard.

1–1–2–2–3–3–4–4–4–4–4–4–4–4
4–1–1–2–2–3–3–3–3–3–3
3–5–5–3–3–2
7,–7,–3–2–1

Challenge the students to sing the complete melody first with scale numbers and then with words.

4. **Do you think we performed the melody correctly? Listen and decide if our melody was the same, similar, or different!** Play the recording through the first verse so that the students may check their reading accuracy. Enjoy singing the rest of the verses.

Closing the Lesson

Divide the class in half. Designate one half as the leaders and the other half the echo. Remind the leaders to sustain the last note of each phrase. Volunteer soloists may lead each verse.

LESSON 49

Lesson Focus

Melody: A series of pitches bounded by the octave "belong together," forming a tonal set. **(D—S)**

Materials

○ **No Piano Accompaniment**

○ **Record Information:**
  • Allelujah, Amen
    Record 5 Side B Band 5
    Voices: boys' choir
    Accompaniment: bells

○ **Instruments:** extended set of chromatic resonator bells, from A,-G'; bell mallets

○ **Teacher's Resource Binder:**
  • Optional—
    Kodaly Activity 17, page K25

○ **For additional experience with melody:** Describe 9, page 176

Allelujah, Amen

Traditional

Learn to sing and play "Allelujah, Amen."

What scale steps are used?
What pitches are used?
Which bells will you use to play the melody?

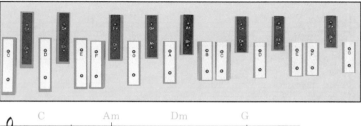

Al - le - lu - jah, al - le - lu - jah.

A - men, a - men.

"Allelujah, Amen" is written in three different ways on page 109.

Compare the three ways.

How are they the same?
How are they different?

108

Introducing the Lesson

Turn to page 108 and help the class answer the questions. **First we will have to decide which note is the home tone, scale step 1.** Remind the class that songs usually begin and end on the home tone. Determine the numbers of all the scale steps used in the song: 1', 7, 6, 5, 4, 3, 2, 1. If necessary, review Lesson 38, page 84 to help the class determine the letter names of the pitches used.

Draw the C scale on the chalkboard. (See **For Your Information**.) Arrange the resonator bells in the order shown in the pupil book. Ask a student to locate the appropriate bells and play the melody. Invite the class to sing it.

Developing the Lesson

1. Read the discussion at the bottom of the page. Follow the procedure used in the lesson intro-duction and determine the pitches for the other versions of "Allelujah, Amen" on page 109. Put the G, D, and A scales on the chalkboard, below the C scale as the discussion proceeds. (See **For Your Information**.)

2. Ask the class to compare the four versions. Help the students conclude that:
   • The melody is always the same.
   • The scale steps used are always the same.
   • The pitches (letter names) are different.
   • The placement of the home tone differs.

3. **What do we hear when we play each set of bells from low to high?** (a major scale) **Each scale is given the name of its first pitch. Can you name the four scales** (C, G, D, A)

4. Melodies are made up of tones that belong to a particular scale. The first pitch of the scale is the home tone. Ask the class to examine the

For Your Information

The C, G, D, and A major scales:

symbols following the treble clef at the beginning of each melody. **These symbols, called sharps, make up what is known as the key signature. It is the "key" to discovering the home tone. Let's turn that key in the lock and figure out how to find the home tone.** Ask the class to count from the home tone to determine the scale number of the last sharp (the one that is farthest to the right). Discover that it is always scale step 7. **If you know how to find scale step 7, can you find the home tone?** (yes, by counting down seven lines and spaces to "1")

Closing the Lesson

End the class by trying to sing each version of the song. **Which is the easiest to sing?** (the version in C or D) **Which is the easiest to play?** All four versions are equally easy after you have found the bells to make up the correct scale.)

Lesson Focus

Melody: A series of pitches bounded by the octave "belong together," forming a tonal set. *(D–S)*

Materials

○ **Piano Accompaniment:** page 278
○ **Record Information:**
 • Buffalo Gals
  Record 5 Side B Band 6
  Voices: children's choir
  Accompaniment: violin, tenor banjo, double bass, accordion, piano, fiddlesticks, jew's harp
○ **Instruments:** as many sets of resonator bells as are available; bell mallets
○ **For additional experience with harmony:** Special Times 6 page 218

Chords not shown on pupil page

Buffalo Gals

American Folk Song

Learn to sing and play "Buffalo Gals."

What scale steps are used?
What pitches are used?
Which resonator bells will you use to play the melody?

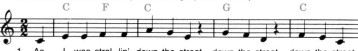

1. As I was strol - lin' down the street, down the street, down the street,
2. I'd like to make this gal my wife, gal my wife all my life.

A pret - ty lit - tle gal I chanced to meet.
I'd like to make her hap - py all her life.

Oh she was sweet to see!
If she would just have me!

Refrain

Buf - fa - lo gals won't you come out to - night, won't you
come out to - night, why not come out to - night?

Buf-fa - lo gals won't you come out to-night and dance in the light of the moon?

110

Introducing the Lesson

Ask the class to turn to page 106. **Who can find the resonator bell we need to give us the sound of the home tone?** Remind the class of the rule they discovered in Lesson 49 for determining the home tone. (The last sharp in the key signature is scale step 7. Count down to find the name of the home tone.) Agree that the home tone for this song is G. Ask a student to play the G bell. Invite the class to sing the song.

Developing the Lesson

1. Challenge the students to recall the procedures they used when learning "Allelujah, Amen" (page 108) and ask them to follow the same steps to learn "Buffalo Gals" on page 110. They should determine that the first pitch is the home tone and that the melody includes scale steps 1, 2, 3, 4, 5, 6, 7, and 1'.

The pitch names are C, D, E, F, G, A, B, and C'.

2. After the class has learned the verse, guide them to realize that the refrain is the same melody; only the rhythm has been changed. Help them learn to sing the complete song.

 OPTIONAL

3. Turn to page 111. Ask the students to examine the three melodies. They should quickly realize that each melody is the verse of "Buffalo Gals." **All three versions use the same scale steps. How are they different?** (They each use the pitches of a different scale.)

4. Ask students to name the pitches used in Example 1. As each pitch is named, write it on the chalkboard. (See **For Your Information.**) Ask a student to locate the necessary bells and play the pattern you have shown. **What do you hear?** (a major scale)

Look at these three melodies.

How are they the same?
How are they different?

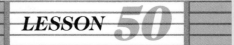
For Your Information

The F, B♭, and E♭ major scales:

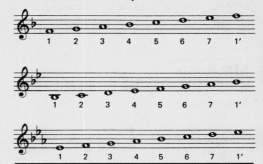

5. Follow the procedure outlined in Step 4 and determine the pitches in Examples 2 and 3. Compare the three scales drawn on the chalkboard and name each scale. (F, B♭, E♭) Ask the class to examine the symbols that make up the key signature for each scale. Count up from the home tone and determine the scale number of the last flat (scale step 4). **If you know how to find scale step 4, can you find the home tone?** (Yes, count down four lines and spaces to "1.")

Closing the Lesson

Organize the class into as many groups as you have sets of resonator bells. Each group is to choose one version of "Buffalo Gals," locate the bells they will need, and learn to play and sing the song. Ask each group to perform for the class. **Which versions are the easiest to sing?** (Depending on the comfortable vocal range of the students, they may conclude that the C and B♭ versions are the easiest to sing.)

LESSON 51

Lesson Focus

Melody: A series of pitches bounded by the octave "belong together," forming a tonal set. *(D–S)*

Materials

○ **Piano Accompaniment:** page 294
○ **Record Information:**
  • Allelujah, Amen
    (Record 5 Side B Band 5)
  • Brethren in Peace Together
    Record 5 Side B Band 7
    Voices: children's choir
    Accompaniment: clarinet, violin, harp
○ **Instruments:** chromatic resonator bells, from E to E'; 13 bell mallets; piano (optional)
○ **Teacher's Resource Binder:**
  • Optional—
    Orff Activity 7, page O11
○ **For additional experience with melody:**
  Special Times 12, page 224

Brethren in Peace Together

Jewish Folk Song

Look at the **key signature**.
On what scale is this song based?

Name the pitches used in the song.
Play them on the resonator bells, from low to high.

Does the pattern sound like the scale you named?

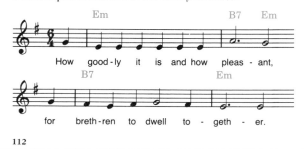

How good-ly it is and how pleas - ant,

for breth-ren to dwell to - geth - er.

112

Introducing the Lesson

Put the following key signatures on the chalkboard. (Do not draw the notes.)

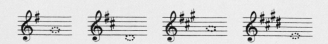

Ask the class to recall the rule for determining the home tone when looking at a key signature that uses sharps. (See Lesson 49. The last sharp is on the 7th step of the scale. Count down from its position on the staff to locate the home tone.) Apply the rule to the four key signatures shown and invite a student to draw the home tone on the correct line or in the correct space for each signature.

Let's sing "Allelujah, Amen." (page 109). Which key has the most comfortable singing range for us? Students may experiment. Depending on the class, either D or E should be the most comfortable key.

Developing the Lesson

1. **Turn to page 112 in your books. On what scale is this song built?** (G) Follow the instructions at the top of the page. As the students name the pitches used in the song, draw them on the chalkboard.

2. Distribute chromatic resonator bells from E to E' and bell mallets to thirteen students. Ask them to stand in a row across the front of the room. The students who have the bells identified by the letter names shown on the chalk-

How good-ly it is and how pleas-ant,

for breth-ren to dwell to-geth-er.

Good-ly, pleas-ant, breth-ren in peace to-geth-er.

How good-ly it is and how pleas-ant

for breth-ren to dwell to-geth-er.

Someone may play this on the bells.
Others may sing it while the class sings the melody.

It is good to dwell in peace.

113

board should play their bells in order from low to high. **When we've arranged the bells from low to high at other times, what have we heard?** (a major scale) **Does this sound like a major scale?** (no) Explain that the sounds heard were those of the E minor scale. **It uses the same pitches as the G major scale but in a different order.**

3. Ask the class to listen as the bell players play the scale again. **Raise your hand when you hear a pitch that is different from what you expected.** Students should raise their hands on Steps 3, 6, and 7. Ask the performers to play the scale again. This time those who are standing to the right of the players whose steps sounded "wrong" should play their bells (G♯, C♯, and D♯). **Does it sound like a major scale now?** (yes) **In a minor scale, Steps 3, 6, and sometimes 7 are lower than in a major scale. Can you sing this scale with numbers?**

Remember to sing those three steps a little lower than usual.

4. Focus the students' attention on page 112 and guide them to learn the melody. Sing it with numbers, remembering to sing scale steps 3, 6, and 7 "a little lower."

OPTIONAL

Closing the Lesson

Invite a few students to take turns playing and singing the ostinato shown on page 113 while the rest of the class sings the melody. To perform the song as a canon, divide the class into two groups. All should sing Phrases 1 and 2 together. Group 1 then continues alone with Phrases 3 and 4. When Group 1 begins Phrase 5, Group 2 should begin to sing Phrase 3.

LESSON 52

Lesson Focus

Melody: A series of pitches bounded by the octave "belong together," forming a tonal set. *(D–S)*

Materials

○ **Piano Accompaniment:** page 296

○ **Record Information:**
 • Lady From Baltimore
  Record 5 Side B Band 8
  Voices: solo child, children's choir
  Accompaniment: electric guitar, acoustic guitar, electric bass, double bass, synthesizer, piano, percussion

○ **Instruments:** chromatic resonator bells, from C to G'; bell mallets; piano

○ **Other:** overhead projector

○ **Teacher's Resource Binder:**
 Activity Sheets
 • **Activity Sheet 19,** page A28 (Prepare as a transparency.)
 • Optional—
  Enrichment Activity 15, page E24
  Orff Activity 11, page O17

○ **For additional experience with melody:** Describe 16, page 186

Chords not shown on pupil page

Lady From Baltimore

Southern Folk Song

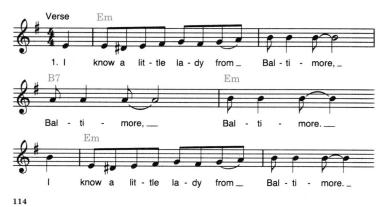

Verse   Em
1. I know a lit-tle la-dy from _ Bal-ti-more, _

B7   Em
Bal-ti - more, _   Bal-ti - more. _

Em
I know a lit-tle la-dy from _ Bal-ti - more. _

114

Introducing the Lesson

Project Activity Sheet 19 *(Major or Minor?)*. Point out the staffs at the top of the transparency. Put the resonator bells in chromatic order, as shown on page 108. Ask a student to locate the bells and play each scale. Label the first G major and the second E minor.

Draw attention to "Mary Had a Little Lamb." **Can you find the key of this song? Is it based on G major or E minor?** Explain that melodies of songs frequently center around 1–3–5. **If this song is in G major, then the pitches G, B, and D will occur at the beginnings and ends of phrases.** Ask the class to sing "Mary Had a Little Lamb" while focusing on the circled pitches. Agree that this melody does indeed center around the first, third, and fifth steps of the G scale. Follow the same procedure and discover that since the melody of "Joshua Fought the Battle of Jericho" centers around E, G, and B, it is in E minor. If the stu-

dents are not familiar with the melody, play it on the bells or sing it as they follow the notation. Then ask the students to sing the melody.

Developing the Lesson

1. Have the class open their books to page 114. **Listen to the recording of another song. As you listen see if you can recognize the two songs we just sang.** Guide the class to realize that the first half of "Lady From Baltimore" is the same as "Joshua Fought the Battle of Jericho." The second half is similar to "Mary Had a Little Lamb." although the rhythm has been changed. It is now syncopated.

2. Invite the students to listen again to "Lady From Baltimore" and identify the different kinds of dances that the "lady" can't do (samba, lindy, rhumba, ickaboga). Ask the students to give the names of dances they know.

Let's ___ see what she can do.

Refrain
Oh, she can't dance;___ I know she can't, ___

Know she can't, ___ Know she can't. ___

Oh, she can't dance;___ I know she can't. ___

Let's ___ see what she can do.

2. Oh, she can't do the Samba;
   I know she can't,
   Know she can't,
   Know she can't.
   Oh, she can't do the Samba;
   I know she can't.
   Let's see what she can do.

3. Oh, she can't do the Lindy; etc.

4. Oh, she can't do the Rhumba; etc.

5. Oh, she can't Ickaboga; etc.

115

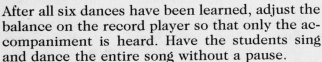

LESSON 52

3. **If we wanted to make up a dance for each large section of the song, how many parts should there be to the dance?** (two; one for the refrain and one for each verse)

4. **Divide the class into six groups. Groups 1 through 5 are each to devise a dance to fit one of the five verses, as assigned. Group 6 is to make up a dance for the refrain. Give the groups a few minutes to plan and practice their dances. The groups may then teach their dances to one another.**

Closing the Lesson *OPTIONAL*

After all six dances have been learned, adjust the balance on the record player so that only the accompaniment is heard. Have the students sing and dance the entire song without a pause.

Lesson Focus

Form: A musical whole may be made up of same, varied, or contrasting segments. *(D–S)*

Materials

○ **Piano Accompaniment:** page 298

○ **Record Information:**
  - March of the Kings
    Record 6 Side A Band 1
    Voice: man
    Accompaniment: woodwind quartet, percussion
  - Farandole
    from *Suite L'Arlesienne No. 2*
    by Georges Bizet (bee-**zay**), 1838–1875
    Record 6 Side A Band 2
    The Silesian Philharmonica
    Karoi Stryja, conductor

○ **Other:** Form Cards prepared from Activity Sheet 18, Lesson 46 (Prepare a transparency from the Activity Sheet); lined paper and a pencil for each student; overhead projector; overhead pen

○ **For additional experience with form:** Special Times 9, page 221

Chords not shown on pupil page

March of the Kings

Translated by Satis Coleman

French Folk Melody

Three great kings_ I met at ear-ly morn,_ With all their
Ce ma - tin, __ J'ai ren-con-tré le train__ De trois grands

ret - i - nue were slow - ly march - ing. Three great
Rois qui al - laient en voy - a - ge, Ce ma -

kings ___ I met at ear - ly morn, ___ Were on their
tin, ___ J'ai ren - con - tré le train ___ De trois grands

116

Introducing the Lesson

Ask the students to listen as you play the recording of "March of the Kings." Discuss the mood the composition creates. Students may have a variety of ideas. After accepting their suggestions, comment that to you the song suggests the feeling of a dignified hymn or processional.

Developing the Lesson

1. Ask the students to open their books to pages 116–117. **Can you decide what scale this melody is based on by studying the key signature and looking at the pitches in the melody?** Guide the students to decide that the key signature suggests that this song might be based on the major scale of A♭. Examine the song more thoroughly and discover that the melody centers around F, A♭, and C. Agree that the song is in F minor.

2. Distribute a set of Form Cards (see **Materials**) to each student. With books closed, play the recording as often as necessary to help the students arrange the cards in this order: **A A' B B'** (Each phrase is four measures long.)

3. Invite the students to sing the song. Encourage them to take a nice deep breath before singing. When they know the song well, write the following on the chalkboard:
What do you hear?
A. "March of the Kings"? a different melody?
B. Is it major or minor?
C. Is it performed as a canon?
D. Are two melodies heard as partner songs?

Distribute lined paper and a pencil to each student. They are to number the lines down the left side of the page as follows (one letter for each line): 1A-1D, 2A-2D, 3A-3D, 4A-4D, and 5A-5D. Explain that the composer, Bizet,

way to meet the new - ly born. With gifts of
Rois des - sus le grand che - min. Tout char - gés

gold brought from far a - way____ And val - iant
d'or les sui - vaient d'a - bord____ De grands guer -

war - riors to guard the king - ly treas - ure, With gifts of
riers et les gar - des du tré - sor,____ Tout char - gés

gold brought from far a - way____ And shields all
d'or les sui - vaient d'a - bord____ De grands guer -

shin - ing in their bright ar - ray.
riers a - vec leurs bou - cli - ers.

LISTENING

Farandole
by Georges Bizet

Listen to this piece of music.
Is it based on "March of the Kings"?
Is the melody played in major or minor?

Is it played as a **canon**?
Is it played with another melody?

117

LESSON 53

For Your Information

The correct answers regarding the five sections of "Farandole" heard in Step 3:

1. "March of the Kings," in minor
2. "March of the Kings" in canon
3. a different melody, in major
4. partner songs
5. "March of the Kings" in major, performed as a partner song with the melody heard in 3

used the melody they just learned in a piece called "Farandole" as part of *L'Arlesienne Suite No. 2.* **You will hear five sections: The music is varied each time. As you listen, be prepared to answer the four questions I've written on the chalkboard five times, one for each section of the music!**

Play the recording as often as necessary to allow students time to answer the questions.

4. Discuss the correct answers with the students. Ask them to review the answers as you play the recording again. (See **For Your Information**.)

Closing the Lesson

Invite the class to perform the song as a canon, as they heard it performed by the members of the Silesian Philharmonica in the instrumental composition.

117

LESSON 54

Lesson Focus

Harmony: Chords and melody may move simultaneously in relation to each other. *(P–I)*

Materials

- **No Piano Accompaniment**
- **Record Information:**
  - *Zum Gali Gali*
- **Record 6 Side A Band 3**
  Voices: man, children's choir
  Accompaniment: tambourine
- **Instruments:** as many autoharps as are available; kazoos; tambourine
- **Other:** oaktag strip
- **Teacher's Resource Binder:**

  Activity Sheets
  - **Activity Sheet 20,** page A29 (Prepare one copy. Cut page lengthwise and paste the two strips on oaktag.)
- **For additional experience with expression:** Special Times 7, page 219

Chords not shown on pupil page

Zum Gali Gali

Israeli Work Song

Fm
Melody

1. He - cha - lutz   l' - maan a - vo - dah;_____
2. A - vo - dah   l' - maan he - cha - lutz;_____
3. He - cha - lutz   l' - maan ha - b'tu - lah;_____
4. Ha - sha - lom   l' - maan ha - 'a - mim;_____

Chant

Zum ga - li ga - li ga - li, Zum ga - li ga - li ga - li,

___ A - vo - dah   l' - maan he - cha - lutz.
___ He - cha - lutz   l' - maan a - vo - dah.
___ Ha - b'tu - lah   l' - maan he - cha - lutz.
___ Ha - 'a - mim   l' - maan ha - sha - lom.

Zum ga - li ga - li ga - li, Zum ga - li ga - li.

118

Introducing the Lesson

Using Activity Sheet 20 (*Scale Play*), challenge the students to sing scales, intervals, and simple songs by following your directions. Sing the beginning pitch and point to a disc on the Scale Strip as the class sings the corresponding pitch. Begin by singing patterns based on 1–3–5–1. Sing "Hot Cross Buns" by pointing to the following pitches.

| 3 | 2 | 1 | | 3 | 2 | 1 |

| 1 | 1 | 1 | 1 | 2 | 2 | 2 | 2 | 3 | 2 | 1 |

Developing the Lesson

1. Play the recording of *"Zum Gali Gali"* as the class follows the music on page 118 of their books. **On what scale is this song based? It has the same key signature as "March of the Kings." Is it based on the same F minor scale?** (yes) Help the class learn the chant part of the song.

2. Use the home tone, F, to create a drone for the chant. Point to "1" on the Scale Strip and ask the class to sing the chant on that tone.

3. Divide the class into two groups. As one group sings the notated chant, have the other sing the drone.

4. Play the recording again as the students follow the notation for the melody part. Help the class learn to pronounce the Hebrew words. Organize the class into three groups. Group 1 will sing the melody part. Group 2 will sing the chant part, and Group 3 will sing the drone.

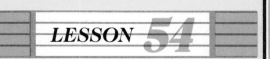

Sing "Zum Gali Gali" in a new key.
Change the home tone from F to G.
Add an accompaniment.

①' ⑦ ⑥ ⑤ ④ ③ ② ① [G]

Use a chord built on the first step of
the song's scale, the I chord.

G maj   G min

The I Chord

Press both buttons at the same time.
Strum on the first beat of each measure.

Use kazoos to play the melody
for introductions, interludes, and codas.

Add a tambourine for rhythm.

119

Closing the Lesson

Read the instructions on page 119. **If we sing the
song in G minor what will be different?** (It will
now sound one step higher.) Develop an accompaniment,
introduction, interlude and a coda.

- **Accompaniment:** Distribute as many autoharps
  as are available. The performers must press
  both the G maj and G min chord buttons at the
  same time to create a drone. They should strum
  once per measure throughout the song.

  Invite one student to improvise rhythm patterns
  on the tambourine. Some students may
  continue to sing the one-pitch accompaniment.
  Others may sing the melody while pointing at
  the correct numbers on the Scale Strip shown
  on the upper left side of page 119.

- **Introduction, Interlude, Coda:** Ask the class to
  decide whether to use parts of the melody or

the chant for the introduction. Perform it by
humming into the kazoo. Make similar decisions
with the students to devise an interlude
and a coda.

Lesson Focus

Harmony: Chords and melody may move simultaneously in relation to each other. *(P–I)*

Materials

- ○ **Piano Accompaniment:** page 254
- ○ **Record Information:**
  - • Down by the Riverside
    Record 6 Side A Band 4
    Voices: children's choir
    Accompaniment: electric guitar, electric bass, electric organ, piano, percussion
- ○ **Instruments:** autoharp
- ○ **Other:** scale play strip, prepared from Activity Sheet 20
- ○ **For additional experience with time and place:** Describe 18, page 188 and Special Times 4, page 216

Down by the Riverside

Spiritual

1. Gon-na lay down my sword and shield, ⎤
2. Gon-na put on my long, white robe, ⎦

(Clap, clap) Down by the riv-er - side, ⎤

(Clap, clap) Down by the riv-er - side, ⎤

(Clap, clap) Down by the riv-er - side, ⎤

Gon - na lay down my sword and shield, ⎤
Gon - na put on my long, white robe, ⎦

(Clap, clap) Down by the riv-er - side, ⎤

Oh, down by the riv - er - side.

120

Introducing the Lesson

Use the scale-play strip to review the scale, interval, and song activity from the previous lesson (page 118). This time, invite the students to go on a search for the special sound of the interval between scale steps 5, and 1. Point to the numbers on the scale-play strip to indicate that the students should sing this interval several times. Then ask them to raise their hands when they hear the sound of 5,–1 or 1–5, as you slowly sing phrases from well-known songs that use this interval. (See **For Your Information.**)

Developing the Lesson

1. Ask the students to turn to page 120. Play the recording of "Down by the Riverside" and then invite the students to study the key signature to find the home tone. Determine that the song is based on the F major scale. Ask the students to tune up in this key in preparation for singing the song. Point to the scale-play strip: 1–3–5–3–1, as the class sings the intervals. **On which number of the scale will this song begin?** (3) Play the recording again as the students sing along.

2. Direct the students' attention to the special harmony part on page 121. Tell them that they are to use the home tone, F, as one of the pitches in this part. **Which other scale step will we need in order to sing this harmony part?** (low 5) **Where else have we heard these two pitches sung?** (in the examples sung earlier) Guide the class to sing the harmony part several times. The students will notice that with the exception of the last phrase, the harmony part is sung during the hand-clap parts. Divide the class into two groups. Have one group sing the melody while the other sings the harmony part.

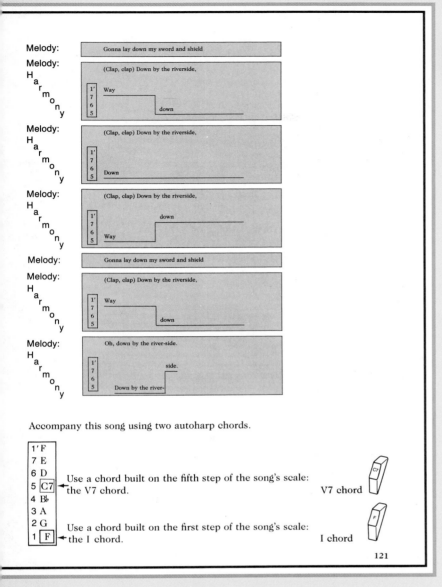

Melody: Gonna lay down my sword and shield

Melody:
Harmony:
(Clap, clap) Down by the riverside,
1' / 7 / 6 / 5 — Way ... down

Melody:
Harmony:
(Clap, clap) Down by the riverside,
1' / 7 / 6 / 5 — Down

Melody:
Harmony:
(Clap, clap) Down by the riverside,
1' / 7 / 6 / 5 — Way ... down

Melody: Gonna lay down my sword and shield

Melody:
Harmony:
(Clap, clap) Down by the riverside,
1' / 7 / 6 / 5 — Way ... down

Melody:
Harmony:
Oh, down by the river-side.
1' / 7 / 6 / 5 — Down by the river- ... side.

Accompany this song using two autoharp chords.

1' F
7 E
6 D
5 C7 ← Use a chord built on the fifth step of the song's scale: the V7 chord.   V7 chord
4 B♭
3 A
2 G
1 F ← Use a chord built on the first step of the song's scale: the I chord.   I chord

121

For Your Information

Excerpts from songs that use the 5–1 interval follow:

(C)
5, 1   5, 2 7,
Here comes the bride,   la - la - la - la

(C)
5,   1   3
Day is done,   gone the sun...

(F)
1 5,   2 3   5
Three great kings_ I met at ear-ly morn_

Closing the Lesson

Invite the students to add an autoharp accompaniment to this song. Focus their attention again on the harmony part and on the vertical arrangement of the scale steps shown on page 121. Explain that the first pitches of the accompaniment they sang can be also used as the first pitch, or root, of an accompanying chord. **What is the difference between hearing one pitch at a time, as in the accompaniment we just sang, and hearing the sound of a chord?** (The chord is made up of several pitches sounding together.) While the class sings, one student may play an autoharp accompaniment by following the chord changes indicated above the melody.

Lesson Focus

Harmony: Chords and melody may move simultaneously in relation to each other. *(P–S)*

Materials

○ **Piano Accompaniment:** page 300
○ **Record Information:**
  • The Caravan
    Record 6 Side A Band 5
    Voices: woman, men's ensemble
    Accompaniment: tar, santour, cymbal
○ **Instruments:** high-pitched drum; finger cymbals; bass metallophone; mallets; piano or autoharp (optional)
○ **For additional experience with harmony:** Perform 13, page 149

Chords not shown on pupil page

The Caravan

Syrian Folk Song

Group 1 sings the **melody** while **Group 2** sings an **ostinato.**

Tramp, tramp, heav-y go the cam-els, Tramp, tramp,

Tramp, tramp, heav - y, Tramp, tramp,

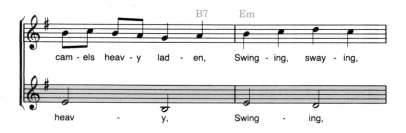

cam-els heav-y lad - en, Swing-ing, sway-ing,

heav - y, Swing - ing,

122

Introducing the Lesson

Turn to page 120 and review "Down by the Riverside". **How many pitches do we need to add a vocal harmony part to this melody?** (two pitches—1 and 5) Sing this song with its vocal accompaniment.

Developing the Lesson

1. Turn to page 122. **Does this song include harmony or does it just have a melody?** Decide that it includes harmony because each pair of staffs is connected, indicating that the two parts are to be performed at the same time.

2. **Can you decide by studying the notation which part will usually move on the beat? What will help you decide?** (Looking at the meter signature; the lower "2" tells us that the half note moves with the beat.) Agree that the lower part usually moves with the beat.

3. Divide the class into two groups. Group 1 will perform the upper part while Group 2 performs the lower part. Establish the shortest sound by lightly tapping eighth notes. Guide the students to practice chanting the rhythm of the two parts.

4. Read the instructions at the top of page 122. **Who recalls the meaning of the word ostinato?** (a repeated pattern) Discover that Group 2 repeats the same two-measure pattern throughout. Call on a student to locate on the resonator bells or piano, the three pitches used in the ostinato (E, D, and B). As the student plays the pattern, Group 2 should practice its part.

5. Draw attention to the upper staff. **Is there any repetition in this part?** (Yes, Measures 1 and 3 are the same; Measures 2, 4, 6, and 7 are the same; Measure 9 is nearly the same.) Put out

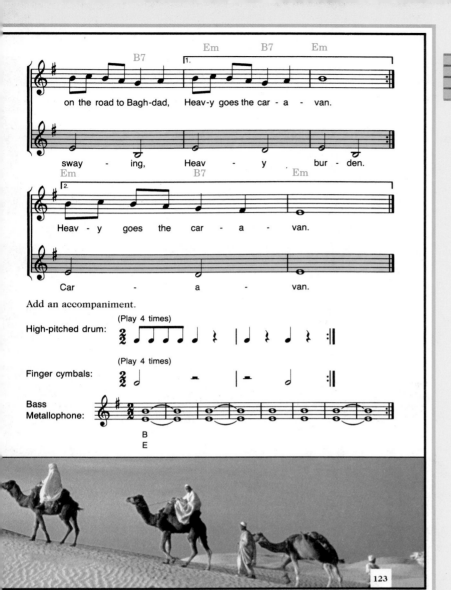

on the road to Bagh-dad, Heav-y goes the car - a - van.

sway - ing, Heav - y bur - den.

Heav - y goes the car - a - van.

Car - a - van.

Add an accompaniment.

High-pitched drum: (Play 4 times)

Finger cymbals: (Play 4 times)

Bass Metallophone:

B
E

123

bells G, A, B, and C. One student may play Measures 1 and 2. Group 1 should then sing that pattern. **Can you sing the whole song?**

6. When both groups have practiced their parts, challenge them to perform the melody and harmony together.

OPTIONAL

Closing the Lesson

When the class can perform the two-part song, add the accompaniments as suggested at the bottom of page 123. The bass metallophone drone may also be played on the piano, or the E and B strings of the autoharp could be plucked.

Lesson Focus

Expression: Musical elements are combined into a whole to express a musical or extramusical idea. *(D–S)*

Materials

○ **Piano Accompaniments:** pages 301, 302, and 374

○ **Record Information:**
  • Get Along, Little Dogies
    Record 6 Side A Band 6
    Voices: children's choir
    Accompaniment: harmonica, bass harmonica, two acoustic guitars, double bass
  • I Ride an Old Paint
    Record 6 Side A Band 7
    Voices: children's choir
    Accompaniment: marimba, accordion, two acoustic guitars, double bass
  • My Home's in Montana
    Record 6 Side A Band 8
    Voices: children's choir
    Accompaniment: whistler, harmonium, banjo, acoustic guitar, double bass
  • Cattle
    by Virgil Thomson, 1896–
    Record 6 Side A Band 9
    The Symphony of the Air
    Leopold Stokowski, conductor

○ **Instruments:** resonator bells C, D, E♭, E, F♯, G, A, and B♭; bell mallets; autoharp
(continued on next page)

Get Along, Little Dogies

Cowboy Song

Use the information you have learned this year.
Learn the three western songs on pages 124 through 127.
  1. Describe the form.
  2. Study the rhythm.
  3. Learn the melody.

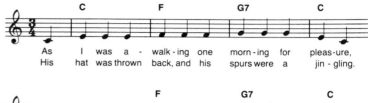

As I was a - walk-ing one morn-ing for pleas-ure,
His hat was thrown back, and his spurs were a jin - gling.

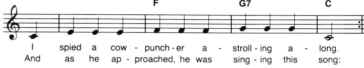

I spied a cow - punch-er a - stroll-ing a - long.
And as he ap - proached, he was sing-ing this song:

124

Introducing the Lesson

Read the discussion at the top of page 124 with the class. **Can you demonstrate how well you can perform as independent musicians by learning to sing these three songs?** Begin by asking the class to compare the three songs to discover similarities and differences. By focusing their attention on various aspects of the musical score, guide them to conclude that:

• All three songs move in threes with the quarter note moving with the beat.
• Each song is based on a different scale: "Get Along, Little Dogies" in C; "I Ride an Old Paint" in G; and "My Home's in Montana" in D.

Developing the Lesson

1. This portion of the lesson may be completed by small groups working independently or by the entire class working together. Determine the phrase form for each song by studying the notation. The students' description should be as follows:

"Get Along, Little Dogies"–A A (or A') A A' B B C (or A') A "I Ride an Old Paint"–A A' A' B (or A") A' (same as Phrase 2) B (same as Phrase 4) "My Home's in Montana"–A B A B'

2. One student should establish the beat in threes, in a moderate tempo. The groups may then practice reading the words in rhythm. Review duration relationships between notes. (The dotted quarter note, for example, is equal to three eighth notes.)

3. Another student should establish tonality by locating scale steps 1, 3, and 5 on the resonator bells or by playing the appropriate I chord on the autoharp. The groups may then sing the melody with scale numbers.

124

Refrain

C7 — Whoop-ee ti - yi - yo, get a - long, lit - tle do - gies. **F**

C7 — It's your___ mis - for - tune and none of my own. **F**

C — Whoop-ee ti - yi - yo, get a - long, lit - tle do - gies. **G7** **C**

F — You know that Wy - o - ming will be your new home. **G7** **C**

125

Materials *(continued)*

o **Other:** scissors, paper and paste for each student
o **Teacher's Resource Binder:**

Activity Sheets
  • **Activity Sheet 21,** page A30
  • Optional—
    Curriculum Correlation 6, page C8
    Kodaly Activity 6, page K10
    Orff Activity 14, page O25

o **For additional experience with expression:** Create 8, page 201

For Your Information

The Form of "Cattle":

A ("I Ride an Old Paint"): oboe melody; "um-pah-pah" guitar accompaniment

B ("My Home's in Montana"): clarinet melody; same style accompaniment as in the preceding A section.

A ("I Ride an Old Paint"): solos by the oboe, the clarinet, and then the oboe again; same accompaniment

C ("Get Along, Little Dogies"): flute, banjo, clarinet, and oboe; string arpeggios provide the accompaniment

A ("I Ride an Old Paint"): strings, horns, guitar, and banjo supplement chordal accompaniment by full orchestra.

B ("My Home's in Montana"): Strings are featured; same style accompaniment as the previous section.

A ("I Ride an Old Paint"): trumpet melody; guitar and banjo accompaniment.

(continued on next page)

4. Play the recording of each song to help the students evaluate their success at analyzing the phrase form.

5. Read the discussion at the bottom of Pupil page 127. **Listen. Raise your hand as soon as you hear the melody for one of the songs you've just learned to sing.** Play the recording and ask students to identify the song ("I Ride an Old Paint"). Discuss any differences the students noted in the melody or rhythm.

6. Distribute Activity Sheet 21 (*Cattle*), scissors, paper, and paste to each student. Ask the students to divide their blank papers into six boxes, and number them from one to six. Read the instructions at the top of the Activity Sheet. Give the students a few minutes to cut the pictures apart and arrange them in stacks of like words or pictures, so that they can easily find the one they need. Play the recording

of "Cattle." On the first listening the students should paste the picture (hat, boot, saddle) that matches the melody heard in each of the six sections. They can identify the picture that represents each melody because it is also seen beside the title of each song in their books.

When the students have completed this task, ask them to listen to the recording again. This time, they are to paste the pictures of the instruments they hear in the correct boxes. (See **For Your Information.**)

7. **Listen carefully to the instruments that play** *OPTIONAL* **the melody. Place the picture of the instrument you hear in each box. Don't paste it in yet!** Play the recording as often as needed.

Closing the Lesson

Play the recording again. This time invite students to identify the pictures of instruments that provide harmony.

LESSON 57

For Your Information *(continued)*

C ("Get Along, Little Dogies"): bassoon, full orchestra, flute and then oboe melody; guitar accompaniment.

I Ride an Old Paint

American Folk Song

G
I ride an old Paint. I lead an old Dan.

D7   G   G
I'm going to Mon - tan - a to throw the Hou - li - han.

D7   D7   G
They feed in the cou - lees, they wa - ter in the draw.

D7   D7   G
Their tails are all mat - ted, their backs are all raw.

Refrain   D7   G
Ride a - round, lit - tle do - gies, ride a - round them slow.

D7   G
For the fier - y and snuf - fy are rar - in' to go.

126

126

My Home's in Montana

Cowboy Song

D   G

1. My home's in Mon - tan - a; I wear a ban - dan - na.
2. When far from the ranch - es, I chop the pine branch - es

D   A

My spurs are of sil - ver; my po - ny is gray.
To heap on my camp - fire, as day - light grows pale.

D   G

When rid - ing the rang - es, my luck nev - er chang - es.
When I have par - tak - en of beans and of ba - con,

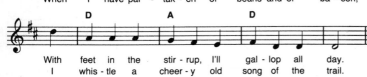

D   A   D

With feet in the stir - rup, I'll gal - lop all day.
I whis - tle a cheer - y old song of the trail.

LISTENING

Cattle

by Virgil Thomson

The composer used these three songs
of the West as the themes for a composition.
Listen to "Cattle."

Can you find each song?
Are the melodies exactly the same as you sang them?

127

LESSON 58

Lesson Focus

Review: Review all concepts learned during this quarter. *(D–S)*

Materials

○ **Piano Accompaniment:** page 304

○ **Record Information:**
  • So Long, Farewell
  📼 **Record 6 Side A Band 10**
    Voices: solo child, children's choir
    Accompaniment: small show orchestra

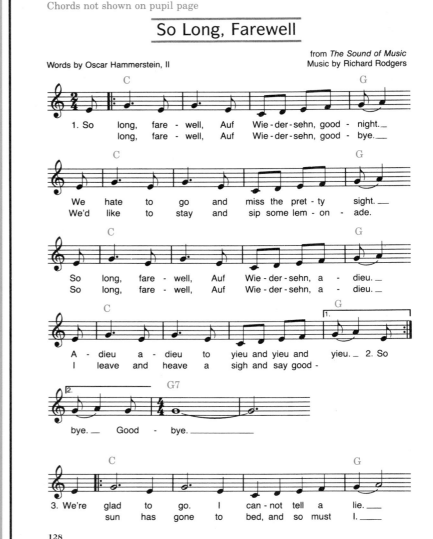

Chords not shown on pupil page

So Long, Farewell

Words by Oscar Hammerstein, II

from *The Sound of Music*
Music by Richard Rodgers

1. So long, fare-well, Auf Wie-der-sehn, good-night.
   long, fare-well, Auf Wie-der-sehn, good-bye.

We hate to go and miss the pret-ty sight.
We'd like to stay and sip some lem-on-ade.

So long, fare-well, Auf Wie-der-sehn, a-dieu.
So long, fare-well, Auf Wie-der-sehn, a-dieu.

A-dieu a-dieu to yieu and yieu and yieu. 2. So
I leave and heave a sigh and say good-

bye. Good-bye.

3. We're glad to go. I can-not tell a lie.
   sun has gone to bed, and so must I.

128

Introducing the Lesson

Many students may have seen either a stage presentation or the movie version of the musical *The Sound of Music*. Ask them to identify the point in the story where the song is heard. If they are not sure, give the answer. (See **For Your Information**.)

Ask the class to turn to page 128 and study the song. **What can you discover about the song by looking at it? What will make it easier to learn?** (Answers will vary. Focus the students' attention on the melodic repetition, the limited range, and the lyrics.)

Developing the Lesson

1. Begin by establishing tonality in C. Ask the class to sing the scale while they do the body scale motions. (See page xxvii.) **Can you find patterns in the melody of the song that move by scale steps?** ("Wiedersehn, goodnight," "miss the pretty sight," etc.)

2. **Look over the first verse of the song. How many different rhythm patterns can you find?** (two)

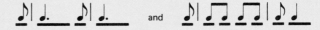 and

Tap the shortest sound, represented by the eighth note, as the students chant the first verse.

3. **Where is Verse 2 found?** Help the class find the repeat signs and the first and second ending brackets.

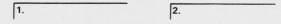

The first verse ends with the "first ending." We must then return to the beginning to sing

128

We flit, we float, we fleet-ly flee, we fly. __ 4. The
So long, fare-well, Auf Wie-der-sehn, a-

dieu. __ Good - bye, __ good - bye, __

good - bye. __

129

For Your Information

"So Long, Farewell" comes from the musical *The Sound of Music.* It was sung by the children when they had to leave their parents' party to go to bed. Various phrases were sung by different children.

Verse 2. Where is the end of Verse 2? (under the second ending bracket)

4. **What happens after the second ending?** (A new meter signature tells us that the meter in Verses 3 and 4 will change from moving in twos to moving in fours.) Help the class realize that the time-value relationships between the notes remain the same, but the rhythm is "stretched out." Each note in the third verse is twice as long as the corresponding note in Verse 1.

Does the shape of the melody change? (No, it is the same as for the first two verses.)

5. **Look at the ending. Why do you think the composer chose to add some extra "good-byes"? Why do you think he made each one so long?** (Sometimes when people say good-bye, they do not really want to. In the musical the children actually got to stay a little longer by singing more goodbyes. It also makes the song sound more complete.)

Closing the Lesson OPTIONAL

Enjoy singing the song together. Invite the students to sing duets or solos on each phrase as the children in the musical did when they sang the song.

LESSON 59

Lesson Focus

Evaluation: Review concepts and skills studied in Lessons 46–58. **(D–S)**

Materials

- ○ **Piano Accompaniment:** page 306
- ○ **Record Information:**
  - Concerto in D by Johann Altenburg, 1734–1801
    Record 6 Side B Band 1
    New York Trumpet Ensemble and the "Y" Chamber Orchestra of New York
    Gerald Schwartz, trumpet and conductor
  - There Was an Old Woman
    Record 6 Side B Band 2
    Voices: man, children's choir
    Accompaniment: synthesizer, percussion, sound effects
- ○ **Instruments:** resonator bells C, D, E, and F; bell mallets
- ○ **Teacher's Resource Binder:**

Evaluation
- **Checkpoint 4,** page Ev16 (Prepare a copy for each student.)
- Optional—
  Orff Activity 14, page O25

To sing "Row Your Boat," which key is more comfortable?

There Was an Old Woman

American Folk Song

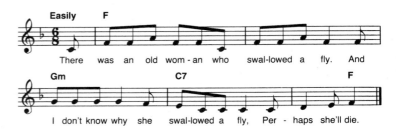

There was an old wom-an who swal-lowed a fly. And
I don't know why she swal-lowed a fly, Per - haps she'll die.

p 2. There was an old woman who swallowed a spider that
wiggled and jiggled inside her!
She swallowed the spider to swallow the fly, and I
don't know why she swallowed the fly. Perhaps she'll
die!

130

Introducing the Lesson

Remind the students of the story of "Goldilocks and the Three Bears." **Papa bear's porridge was too _ _ _, mama bear's porridge was too _ _ _ _, and baby bear's porridge was just _ _ _ _ _.** (hot, cold, right) **Papa bear's bed was too _ _ _ _ and mama bear's bed was too _ _ _ _. But baby bear's bed was just _ _ _ _ _.** (hard, soft, right) **Perhaps if Goldilocks had tried to sing papa bear's song it would have been too _ _ _ and mama bear's song would have been too _ _ _ _. But baby bear's song would have been just _ _ _ _ _!** (low, high, right)

Developing the Lesson

1. Comment that sometimes a song is uncomfortable to sing because it is too high or too low. **When that happens we need to move the home tone. When we move the home tone, the other pitches change as well so that they all "fit" together.**

2. Direct the class's attention to the first scale on page 130. Review the rule for finding the key. (Locate the last sharp to the right and count down 7 steps.) Ask the class to sing the vocal warm-up 1–3–5 (G–B–D). Ask the class to sing "Row Your Boat." **Is it too low, too high, or just right?** (too high)

3. Look at the second staff. Again determine the key. Guide the class to sing the warm-up 1–3–5 (D–F♯–A) and then sing "Row Your Boat" in the new key. **Was it too high? too low? just right?** (probably just about right)

4. Find the key and tonal center of the song on page 130 after reviewing the rule for flats. (Count down 4 scale steps from the last flat to

f   3. There was an old woman who swallowed a bird! How absurd to swallow a bird! She swallowed the bird to swallow the spider to swallow the fly, and I don't know why she swallowed the fly. Perhaps she'll die!

p   4. There was an old woman who swallowed a cat! Imagine that to swallow a cat! She swallowed the cat to swallow the bird to swallow the spider to swallow the fly, and I don't know why she swallowed the fly. Perhaps she'll die!

mf   5. There was an old woman who swallowed a dog! What a hog to swallow a dog! She swallowed the dog to swallow the cat to swallow the bird to swallow the spider to swallow the fly, and I don't know why she swallowed the fly. Perhaps she'll die!

f   6. There was an old woman who swallowed a goat! Just opened her throat and swallowed a goat! She swallowed the goat to swallow the dog to swallow the cat to swallow the bird to swallow the spider to swallow the fly, and I don't know why she swallowed the fly. Perhaps she'll die!

p   7. There was an old woman who swallowed a cow! I don't know how she swallowed a cow! She swallowed the cow to swallow the goat to swallow the dog to swallow the cat to swallow the bird to swallow the spider to swallow the fly, and I don't know why she swallowed the fly. Perhaps she'll die!

ff   8. There was an old woman who swallowed a horse! SHE'S DEAD, OF COURSE!

LISTENING

Concerto in D

Johann Altenburg

The trumpet concerto has three short movements identified by tempo markings. Listen to the composition. Which movement is *Andante*? *Allegro*? *Vivace*? Can you hear dynamic changes?

131

LESSON 59

For Your Information
Answers for Checkpoint 4 *(Concerto in D)*
1. key of D; key of E♭
2. A.4 B.1 C.2 D.3 E.5
3. Movement 1: Allegro, Loud, Yes, $<$
   Movement 2: Andante, Soft, No, Soft
   Movement 3: Vivace, Loud, No, Very loud

---

the right.) Sing the vocal warm-up (F–A–C). **This song does not begin on the home tone. It begins on low 5.** Help the students read the song with numbers.

5. Read over the rest of the verses in the pupil book. Determine the dynamic levels to be used for each verse. This humorous song will probably become a favorite of the class.

6. Place resonator bells C, D, E, and F in a row. For each verse choose one student to play them on the words "Perhaps she'll die". The rest of the class should sing.

OPTIONAL

7. Distribute Checkpoint 4 *(Concerto in D).* Read the instructions for Question 1 with the class. Give them time to complete the question. Then proceed to Question 2. Ask the students

to write the number accompanying each musical symbol in the blank next to the term that describes that symbol.

8. Refer to Question 3 and play the complete recording of the *Concerto in D* (three movements). **After each movement circle the correct tempo.** Play the recording again, and ask the students to circle the correct dynamics. A third hearing will enable the students to verify their answers.

Closing the Lesson

After the students' papers are collected, ask the class to listen again to the *Concerto in D*, this time concentrating on the instrumentation.

Lesson Focus

Evaluation: Review concepts and skills studied in the Fourth Quarter. *(D–S)*

Materials

- **Piano Accompaniments:** pages 308 and 310
- **Record Information:**
  - Lament for a Donkey
    Record 6 Side B Band 3
    Voices: man, children's choir
    Accompaniment: violin, 3 acoustic guitars, percussion
  - Gypsy Rover
    Record 6 Side B Band 4
    Voices: man, children's choir
    Accompaniment: flute, harpsichord, lute
- **Instruments:** resonator bells C, D, E, G, A, B♭, C′, and D′; bell mallets
- **Other:** a pencil for each student
- **Teacher's Resource Binder:**
  Evaluation • **Review 4,** pages Ev 18–19 (Prepare one copy for each student.)
  - **Musical Progress Report 4,** page Ev20
  - Optional—
    Orff Activities 5, 14, pages O4, O25

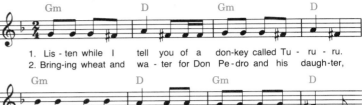

Review 4

Chords not shown on pupil page

Lament for a Donkey

Spanish Folk Tune

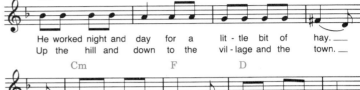

1. Lis-ten while I tell you of a don-key called Tu-ru-ru.
2. Bring-ing wheat and wa-ter for Don Pe-dro and his daugh-ter,

He worked night and day for a lit-tle bit of hay.
Up the hill and down to the vil-lage and the town.

He worked all night and day, just for a lit-tle hay.
He went up hill and down to the vil-lage and the town.

He worked all night and day, just for a lit-tle hay.
He went up hill and down to the vil-lage and the town.

3. One hot summer day, though
   Poor Tururu passed away, oh.
   He breathed weary sighs
   And forever closed his eyes.
   He breathed such weary sighs
   And forever closed his eyes.
   He breathed such weary sighs
   And forever closed his eyes.

4. All the village people
   came together round the steeple.
   Said, "We'll ring the bell
   For the donkey worked so well."
   They said "We'll ring the bell
   For the donkey worked so well."
   They said "We'll ring the bell
   For the donkey worked so well."

132

From GROWING WITH MUSIC SERIES, Book 4, Wilson, et al (Englewood Cliffs, NJ: Prentice-Hall, Inc. © 1966)

Introducing the Lesson

Distribute Review 4 and a pencil to each student. **This is our "final hurdle" for this year! How much have you learned in a year's time? Are you an independent musician? Can you look at new songs that you have not heard and make decisions as to how they will sound?**

Developing the Lesson

1. Explain that the students are to look at the music for "Lament for a Donkey" and "Gypsy Rover" on pages 132–133 as they answer the questions on review sheets. All the questions refer to those two songs.

2. Read the instructions with the class, question by question. Remind the students that they must compare the music in the book to the pictures on the sheet in order to answer the questions. (See **For Your Information** for answers.)

3. Explain to the students that to complete Question 3, they must draw the key signature and meter signature on the appropriate staff for each song.

4. Give students time to answer Question 4 after being sure they understand the question.

5. Play the introductions of the recordings of the two songs so that the students may answer Question 5. Then provide time for them to complete Questions 6 and 7 independently.

6. Explain to the students that for Question 8 they are to write scale numbers in the first row of blanks below each staff and the letter names of the resonator bells in the second row of blanks below each staff.

Chords not shown on pupil page

Gypsy Rover

English Ballad

Verse 1

G   D7   G   D7

1. The gyp-sy ro-ver came o-ver the hill,

G   D7   G   D7

Bound through the val-ley so sha-dy.

G   D7   G   Em

He whist-led and he sang till the green woods rang.

G   Am   G   C   G

And he won the heart of a la - dy.

Refrain   D7   G   D7   G   D7   G   D7

Ah - di - do ah - di - do - da - day. Ah - di - do ah - di - day - dee;

G   D7   G   Em

He whist-led and he sang till the green woods rang.

G   Am   G   C   G

And he won the heart of a la - dy.

133

For Your Information

Answers to Review 4:
1. Lament for a Donkey; Gypsy Rover
2. Gypsy Rover; Lament for a Donkey

3.

4. Answers May Vary:

slowly	fast
sad	happy
soft	medium—loud

5. violin; flute
6. **ABCC**
7. **AA**
8. 4–3–2–5–4–3
C–B♭–A–D–C–B♭
1–5,–1–5,–1–5,–1–5,–1–5,–1–6,–
1–2–1–4,–1
G–D–G–D–G–D–G–D–G–D–G–E–G–
A–G–C–G

---

7. Help the class use the information they gained when answering the questions on the Review sheets to learn to sing each song.

OPTIONAL

Closing the Lesson

Choose a few students to add the harmony parts that were given in Question 8 of the Review while the class sings.

Lament for a Donkey

Gypsy Rover

Use the information gained from this lesson, as

well as from observations made throughout the quarter, to complete a copy of Musical Progress Report 4 for each student. It may be used as a report to the parents, as well as a permanent record for your files.

Extra Verses for Gypsy Rover

2. She left her father's castle gate;
She left her own true lover.
She left her servants and her estate
To follow the gypsy rover.

3. Her father saddled his fastest steed;
He roamed the valley all over.
He sought his daughter at great speed
And the whistling gypsy rover.

4. He came at last to a mansion fine
Down by the river Clayde.
There was music and bright sunshine
For the gypsy and his lady.

5. He's no gypsy, my father, said she,
My lord of free lands all over.
And I will stay till my dying day
With my whistling gypsy rover.

133

Unit 2

Unit Overview

Unit 2, More Music to Explore, provides songs, activities, and recorded listening selections to extend the core material. Musical concepts are expanded upon and performance, descriptive, and creative skills are further developed. The lessons function independently of Unit I, but each has been cross-referenced with the core lessons.

Perform Music provides an opportunity for the students to develop solo and ensemble performance skills. Autoharps and classroom instruments are used to build confidence and skill in performing songs and playing correct chordal accompaniments.

In Describe Music students observe how music relates to their everyday lives, and they learn to

More Music To Explore

define music according to form, rhythm, harmony, melody, and other musical concepts. At the end of this chapter, students comment on the instruments and theme and variations used in the Rustic Symphony by Carl Goldmark.

Create Music gives students suggestions for creating their own musical compositions. They explore different forms, rhythms, and melodic possibilities and learn to rely on their own creative abilities. They produce a radio show and plan their own script, dialogue, songs, and commercials.

Special Times focuses on seasonal events and holidays that occur throughout the year. The students explore, experience, and participate in the music and holiday traditions of various cultures.

Lesson Focus

Expression: Musical elements are combined into a whole to express a musical or extramusical idea. **(P–I)**

Materials

- ○ **Instruments:** as many autoharps as are available
- ○ **Teacher's Resource Binder:**
  Activity Sheets • **Activity Sheets 22a–b,** pages A31–A32
  - ○ Optional—
    Enrichment Activity 14, page E24
    Mainstreaming Suggestion 16, Page M27
- ○ **Extends Lesson 4,** page 12

Perform Music

Learn to Play the Autoharp

It's as easy as "one, two, three!"
Easy as "one . . ."

- Play an expressive accompaniment as you speak these words.
- Use only:

I am the wind
I blow and I roar
I stir the low waters
And hurl them ashore.

I whirl o'er the dunes
Then settle on flowers
I lift each soft petal
Then rise to chase showers.

136

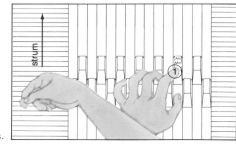

The Lesson

1. Distribute as many autoharps as are available. Give other students practice autoharps prepared from Activity Sheets 22a–b *(Practice Autoharp)*. Students should take turns using real and practice autoharps.

2. Demonstrate the proper playing position:
   - Place the autoharp on a table or on your lap, with the straight side of the harp nearest your body.
   - Place the fingers of your left hand over the chord buttons.
   - Hold the pick between the thumb and index finger of the right hand.
   - Cross the right hand over the left forearm and strum the strings away from your body—from low to high.

3. **OPTIONAL** When the students are comfortable with the correct position, invite them to explore what happens when different chord buttons are pressed as they strum.

4. Have the students open their books to page 136. **Autoharp playing can be as easy as "one, two, three."** Explore the use of finger "one," the left-hand index finger.

5. Ask the class to expressively read the poem at the bottom of the page. Autoharp players may accompany the reading by pressing the A minor chord button with the "one" finger and rhythmically strumming the chord while the rest of the class reads. Or they may play string sounds after one or two lines of the poem. For example, they may strum the A minor chord with the words "I blow and I roar," gradually releasing the button so that a blur of dissonant sounds grows from soft to loud.

Three Blind Mice

Traditional Round

- Find the [C Maj] chord button.

Press it down firmly with your left index finger.
- Use your right hand to strum the chord while you sing.

Three blind mice,___ three blind mice,___ See how they run,___

see how they run!___ They all ran af-ter the farm-er's wife,

She cut off their tails with a carv-ing knife;

Did ev-er you see such a sight in your life As three blind mice?

Sing "Three Blind Mice" several times.
Each time, choose a different **major**
chord and change the
beginning pitch of the melody.

Play these chords:
Begin singing on these pitches:

What was different about your singing when you repeated the
round in each of the **major** keys?

Which was your best **key** for singing?

137

Lesson Focus

Melody: A melody may be relatively high or low. *(P–I)*

Materials

○ **No Piano Accompaniment**
○ **Record Information:**
  • Three Blind Mice
    Record 6 Side B Band 5
    Voices: solo child, children's choir
    Accompaniment: flutes, oboes, clarinets, bassoon, French horn, percussion
○ **Instruments:** resonator bells E, F♯, A, and B; bell mallets; as many autoharps as are available
○ **Other:** practice autoharps prepared from Activity Sheets 22a–b, pages A31–A32
○ **Extends Lesson 4,** page 12

The Lesson

1. Distribute as many autoharps as are available and give other students practice autoharps. (See **Materials.**) Tell the class to follow the instructions on page 137. **Find the C major chord button. Press it down firmly and strum from low to high.** Ask a student to play the starting pitch on a resonator bell (E). Then those with real autoharps may strum on the first beat of each measure.

2. Introduce the class to transposition by playing and singing the same melody in different keys. **We just accompanied "Three Blind Mice" with the C major chord. We sang the song in the key of C. What will happen if we accompany it with a different major chord?** Ask the students to strum a different major chord on their autoharps while they sing "Three Blind Mice." They will need to begin singing the melody on a different pitch each time they change

to a new chord. Ask one student to find the correct starting pitch on the resonator bells:

• D major chord—Begin on F♯.

• F major chord—Begin on A.

• G major chord—Begin on B.

3. **What was different about your singing each time you repeated the song in a different key?** (Students' responses may vary. Conclude that the melody was higher or lower—sometimes uncomfortably so!)

4. Help the students realize the advantage of being able to sing in different keys. *OPTIONAL* **Can you sing in the range that is most comfortable for your own voice?** Some singers may be comfortable singing in a higher range while others may prefer to sing in a lower one. The key of C major will probably be the most comfortable for the entire class to sing "Three Blind Mice."

137

Lesson Focus

Melody: A melody may be relatively high or low. *(P–I)*

Materials

○ **No Piano Accompaniment**

○ **Record Information:**
  • Hey, Ho! Anybody Home?
  Record 6 Side B Band 6
  Voices: children's choir
  Accompaniment: clarinet, bassoon, xylophone

○ **Instruments:** as many autoharps as are available

○ **Other:** practice autoharps prepared from Activity Sheets 22a–b, pages A31–A32

○ **Extends Lesson 4,** page 12

Hey, Ho! Anybody Home?

English Round

Hey, ho! An-y-bod-y home?

Meat and drink and mon-ey have I none;

Still I will be ver-y mer-ry!

Sing and accompany "Hey, Ho! Anybody Home?"

Use one **minor** chord:

Repeat the song in different **minor keys,** changing the first pitch.

Play these chords:

Begin singing on these pitches:

Which was your best **key** for singing?

138

The Lesson

1. Continue to explore "Easy as one . . . " by using one finger to play minor chords. Begin by reviewing the poem on page 136.

2. Ask the class to turn to page 138. Help the students learn to sing "Hey, Ho! Anybody Home?" without autoharp accompaniment. **This song begins on the first step of the minor scale. Can you find the other scale steps?** Guide the students to sing with numbers, reminding them to sing step 3 lower than when singing in a major key.

3. Ask the students to locate the minor chords on their autoharps. To decide which key is the most comfortable for individual voices, play and sing in different keys as follows:

   • E minor—Begin on E.

   • D minor—Begin on D.

   • G minor—Begin on G.

   • A minor—Begin on A.

   The key of E minor or D minor will probably be the most comfortable. A minor and G minor should be either too high or too low, depending on the register in which the song is sung.

Groundhog

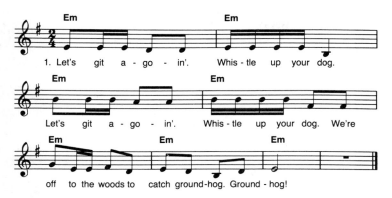

Traditional

1. Let's git a-go-in'. Whis-tle up your dog.
Let's git a-go-in'. Whis-tle up your dog. We're
off to the woods to catch ground-hog. Ground-hog!

2. Everybody ready and everybody set.
Everybody ready and everybody set.
We'll catch a groundhog, you can bet. Groundhog!

3. Too many rocks and too many logs.
Too many rocks and too many logs.
Too much trouble to catch groundhogs. Groundhog!

Lesson Focus
Harmony: Chords and melody may move simultaneously in relation to each other. *(P–S)*

Materials
- ○ **Piano Accompaniment:** page 312
- ○ **Record Information:**
  - Groundhog
    Record 6 Side B Band 7
    Voice: children's choir
    Accompaniment: kazoo, bass harmonica, autoharp, mountain dulcimer, psaltery, jug, washboard
- ○ **Instruments:** as many autoharps as are available
- ○ **Other:** practice autoharps prepared from Activity Sheets 22a–b, pages A31–A32
- ○ **Extends Lesson 4,** page 12

The Lesson

1. Ask the students to open their books to page 139 and help them learn to sing "Groundhog." Draw attention to the chord names written above the staff. **How many different chords will you use?** (only one) Give several students the opportunity to strum the chord while the rest of the class sings. Strum only on the first beat of each measure.

2. Have the students learn a play-party game. One or more people can be the autoharp accompanists, and the other students should stand in a circle. Choose one student to be the groundhog who stands in the center. The game is as follows:

Introduction: Accompanists strum four times while others "whistle up" the dog.

Verse 1: Everyone pantomimes getting ready to catch a groundhog in the woods. Students should walk counterclockwise around the circle on the words "We're off to the woods to catch a groundhog . . ."

Verse 2: Continuing to walk in a circle, students should step rhythmically toward the center, roll up their sleeves, and step back to place in the circle.

Verse 3: The groundhog should come running from the center and weave in and out among the students in the circle. At the end of the song, the groundhog should capture one person and return to the center with the captive.

(The fun of this game is that the tables are turned. Instead of the catcher catching the groundhog, the groundhog catches the catcher!)

139

Lesson Focus

Harmony: Chords and melody may move simultaneously in relation to each other. *(P–S)*

Materials

○ **Piano Accompaniment:** page 313
○ **Record Information:**
  • Found a Peanut
  Record 7 Side A Band 1
  Voices: solo child, children's choir
  Accompaniment: synthesizer, percussion
○ **Instruments:** as many autoharps as are available
○ **Other:** practice autoharps prepared from Activity Sheets 22a–b, pages A31–A32
○ **Extends Lesson 4,** page 12

Found a Peanut

Nonsense Song

1. Found a pea - nut, found a pea - nut, Found a
2. It was rot - ten, it was rot - ten, It was
3. Ate it a-ny - way, ate it a-ny - way, Ate it

pea - nut last __ night. Last __ night I found a
rot - ten last __ night. Last __ night it was
a-ny - way last __ night. Last __ night I ate it

pea - nut, Found a pea - nut last __ night.
rot - ten, It was rot - ten last __ night.
a-ny - way, Ate it a-ny - way last __ night.

4. Got sick . . .   6. Had an operation . . .   8. Went to heaven . . .
5. Called the doctor . . . 7. I died anyway . . .   9. Woke up . . .

What other verses can you make up to finish this song?

140

The Lesson

1. Turn to page 140 and have the students learn to sing the nonsense song "Found a Peanut." **On what scale step will the song begin?** Point out the face with the letter *F* for a mouth above the first staff. Explain that this is the starting pitch.

2. When the students know the song, ask them to determine which chord should be used to accompany it. They will discover that they need two chords, F and C7.

3. Explain to the class that, since they can perform well using one chord, they are now ready to proceed to "Easy as one, two . . ." Direct their attention to the illustration at the top of page 140. Explain that once they have found the position for the first (index) finger, the other chord will be directly under the second (middle) finger. Ask the students to locate the F major chord button and place their first finger over it; then they should place their middle finger over the C7 chord button.

4. Give the students time to practice moving back and forth between these chords in the following sequence: **F F F C7 C7 F C7 F.** Then invite them to take turns accompanying the class as all sing the song.

5. Invite the students to add other verses to complete the song. Some students may be aware of traditional ones such as "wouldn't take me" (after Verse 8), and so on. Encourage them to be inventive in devising extra verses.

OPTIONAL

A Sailor Went to Sea

Traditional

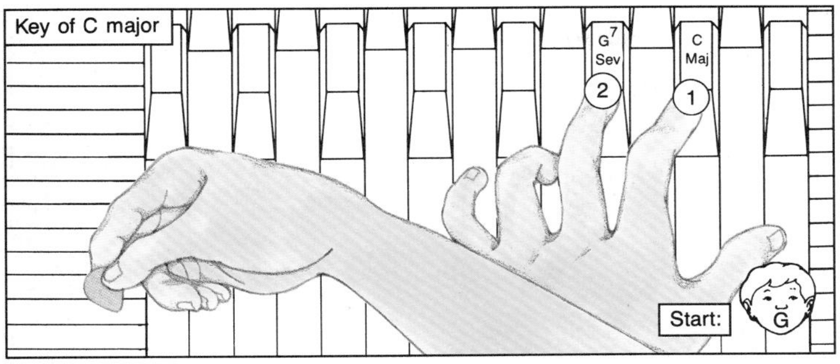

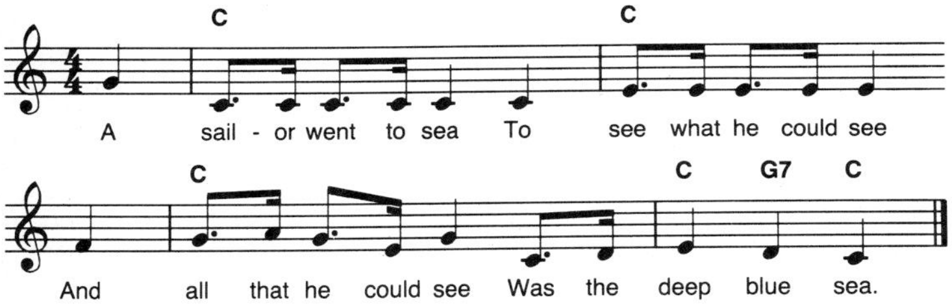

Key of C major

Start: G

| C | | C |

A sail - or went to sea To see what he could see

| C | | C | G7 | C |

And all that he could see Was the deep blue sea.

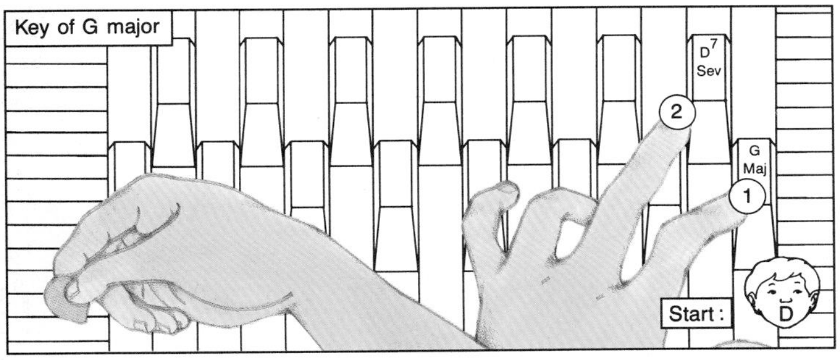

Key of G major

Start: D

141

Lesson Focus

Harmony: Chords and melody may move simultaneously in relation to each other. *(P–S)*

Materials

○ **Piano Accompaniment:** page 282
○ **Record Information:**
  • A Sailor Went to Sea
  Record 7 Side A Band 2
  Voices: children's choir
  Accompaniment: ocarina, concertina, ukelele, guitar, double bass, percussion
○ **Instruments:** as many autoharps as are available
○ **Other:** practice autoharps prepared from Activity Sheet 22a–b, pages A31–A32
○ **Extends Lesson 4,** page 12

The Lesson

1. Have the students turn to page 141 and discover that this song may also be accompanied with two chords. Before the class practices the accompaniment, help them learn the song. **On what pitch does the song begin?** (G, as shown by the face above the first staff) **This is scale step 5. Can you sing the rest of the song?** Help the students discover that it is almost entirely made up of scale steps 1–3–5 (steps which make up the I chord).

2. Establish a procedure for singing a song with autoharp accompaniment. Have the students locate the correct chords and place their fingers over them as shown in the diagram at the top of the page. Establish tonality and the starting pitch as follows:

   • Strum C–G7–C in the tempo of the song.

   • Pluck G, the starting pitch of the melody.

   • Resume strumming and begin to sing.

3. Remind the students of their experience singing a melody with higher and lower pitch levels (page 137). Follow the same procedure used in Step 2. This time perform the song in the key of G, using the chords G and D7.

4. Ask the class to decide which key seems most comfortable. (Most students will probably feel that the key of C is best.)

141

Lesson Focus

Harmony: Chords and melody may move simultaneously in relation to each other. **(P–S)**

Materials

○ **Piano Accompaniment:** page 316
○ **Record Information:**
  • So Long It's Been Good to Know You
    Record 7 Side A Band 3
    Voices: childrens's choir
    Accompaniment: whistler, harmonium, 2 acoustic guitars, double bass, knee slaps
○ **Instruments:** as many autoharps as are available
○ **Other:** practice autoharp prepared from Activity Sheets 22a–b, pages A31–A32
○ **Extends Lesson 4,** page 12

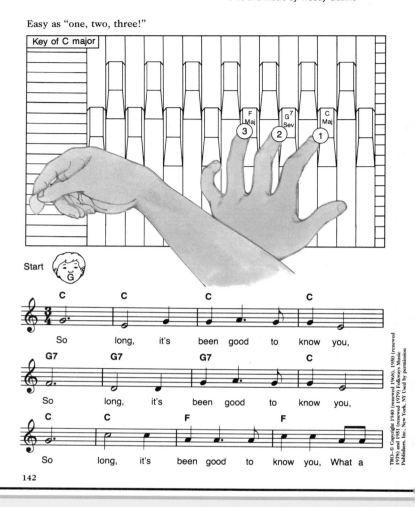

So Long It's Been Good to Know You

Words and Music by Woody Guthrie

Easy as "one, two, three!"

Key of C major

Start

| C | C | C | C |
So long, it's been good to know you,

| G7 | G7 | G7 | C |
So long, it's been good to know you,

| C | C | F | F |
So long, it's been good to know you, What a

TRO—© Copyright 1940 (renewed 1968), 1950 (renewed 1978) and 1951 (renewed 1979) Folkways Music Publishers, Inc., New York, NY Used by permission

142

The Lesson

1. Help the students learn to play songs that use three different chords. Begin by learning to sing "So Long It's Been Good to Know You" on page 142.

2. When the class knows the song and can sing it easily, draw attention to the illustration at the top of the page. **This means you're now ready for "Easy as one, two, three!"** The students will need to use three fingers to press down the necessary chord buttons. **By keeping your hand in this position, with your fingers curved over the three chord buttons, you will be able to move easily from one chord to the next.**

   Remind the students that the index finger always plays the I chord (in this case, C), the middle finger always plays the V7 chord (G7), and the ring finger always plays the IV chord (F). **If you can remember this, you won't need to look at the buttons in order to find the right chord.**

3. Ask the students to position their right-hand fingers over the C, G7, and F chords. Challenge them to play the following chord sequence, without looking at the buttons: C–G7–C–F–G7–C.

4. Ask the class to look at the notation for "So Long It's Been Good to Know You" and determine when and where the three chords are used (always on the heavy, first beat of a measure). Remind the students of the procedure learned in the previous lesson (page 141). Help them to play an introduction. Then sing the song as some class members play the accompaniment.

142

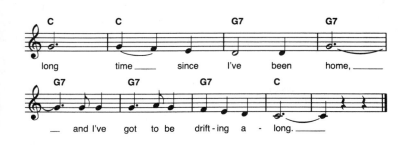

long   time ____ since   I've   been   home, ____

____ and I've   got   to be   drift-ing   a   -   long. ____

5. Plan a special ending for the song. **How could you use changes in dynamics to show that the singer is going on down the road?** (by getting gradually softer) Suggest that the students create a coda by strumming the autoharp, more softly each time, until they feel the song should end.

OPTIONAL

Lesson Focus

Harmony: Chords and melody may move simultaneously in relation to each other. *(P–S)*

Materials

○ **Piano Accompaniment:** page 314
○ **Record Information:**
  • Down by the Bay
    Record 7 Side A Band 4
    Voices: solo man, children's choir
    Accompaniment: clarinet, tenor banjo, piano, acoustic bass, percussion
○ **Extends Lesson 48,** page 106

For Your Information

The songs on this and the succeeding pages are planned to introduce your students to part singing. The sequence includes
• echo songs ("Down By the Bay," "Old Texas")
• drone accompaniments ("Grizzly Bear")
• two-pitch harmony ("Portland Town")

The Lesson

1. Challenge the class to learn to sing "Down by the Bay" on page 144. Begin by examining the song and discovering that it is to be sung by two groups, with each Group 1 pattern echoed by Group 2. Ask everyone to practice the Group 1 patterns. Establish tonality in the key of G. Tell the class to warm up by following your body scale motions (See page xxvii). Sing the following scale-step patterns on "loo":

   • 5,–6,–5,–1 ("Down by the Bay")("I dare not go")

   • 5,–6,–5,–7, ("Where the watermelons grow") ("Back to my home")

   • 1–7,–6,–5, ("My mother will say")

   Challenge the students to locate the words that match each pattern (as shown above). **Which pattern haven't we practiced?** ("For if I do") Sing this pattern on "loo." **What does the** symbol in front of the note above "I" do? (makes the note a little lower)

2. Divide the class into two groups and challenge each group to sing its part to perform the entire song. Play the recording. Ask the class to listen carefully as they follow the notation. **Did you make any mistakes?** If mistakes were made, play the recording again. Then ask the class to sing the complete song and have the two groups trade parts.

3. Encourage students to create other silly words for Measures 12–14. Write several sentences on the chalkboard for students to complete. For example:
   "Did you ever see a bat . . . "
   "Did you ever see a crow . . . "
   "Did you ever see a pig . . . "
   Have the students sing the new verses, continuing to sing in two parts.

Old Texas

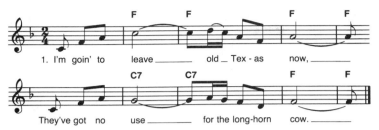

F   F   F   F

1. I'm goin' to leave_____ old_ Tex-as now,_____

C7   C7   F   F

They've got no use_____ for the long-horn cow._____

2. They've plowed and fenced my cattle range,
   And the people there are all so strange.

3. I'll take my horse, I'll take my rope,
   And hit the trail upon a lope.

4. Say *adios* to the Alamo,
   And turn my head toward Mexico.

5. I'll make my home on the wide wide range,
   For the people there are not so strange.

6. The hard hard ground shall be my bed,
   And my saddle seat shall hold my head.

Divide into two groups.
Perform this song singing
two special parts.
When do you hear
only a melody?
When do you hear harmony?

145

Lesson Focus

Harmony: Chords and melody may move simultaneously in relation to each other. *(P–S)*

Materials

○ **Piano Accompaniment:** page 318
○ **Record Information:**
   • Down by the Bay
     (Record 7 Side A Band 4)
   • Old Texas
     Record 7 Side A Band 5
     Voice: baritone
     Accompaniment: harmonica, guitar, double bass
○ **Instruments:** as many autoharps as are available
○ **Extends Lesson 21,** page 46

The Lesson

1. Review "Down by the Bay," page 144. Then invite the class to learn another echo song on page 145. Learn "Old Texas" in unison, as notated and then divide the class into two groups. Group 2 will echo Group 1. Sing the complete song in this manner.

I'm   goin'   to   leave_____

                     I'm   goin'   to

old Tex-as   now,

leave_____   old_ Tex-as   now,

2. Expand the students' awareness of harmony. **When we perform "Old Texas," we sometimes hear only melody. At other times, we hear melody and harmony.** Ask the students to again perform the song in groups. **This time, raise your hand when you think you hear melody and harmony at the same time.** (Students should raise their hands when Group 1 is sustaining the long sound and Group 2 is singing the echo.) **When did you hear only melody?** (at the beginning of each phrase, when Group 1 was singing alone, before Group 2 began)

3. Invite some students to play the autoharp accompaniment while the rest of the class sings. **What chords will you use?** (F and C7) **On which chord button will you place your index finger?** (F— so that the C7 chord button is directly under the middle finger)

OPTIONAL

145

Lesson Focus

Harmony: Chords and melody may move simultaneously in relation to each other. *(P–S)*

Materials

○ **Piano Accompaniment:** page 319

○ **Record Information:**
- I'm on My Way
  Record 7 Side A Band 6
  Voices: children's choir
  Accompaniment: electric guitar, electric bass, electric organ, piano, percussion

○ **Instrument:** autoharp

○ **Extends Lesson 34,** page 76

I'm on My Way

Traditional

Look at this song.
How many ways can you find to add special parts?

I'm on my way, _____ and I won't turn back.

I'm on my way, _____ and I won't turn back.

I'm on my way, _____ and I won't turn back.

I'm on my way, oh yes, I'm on my way! _____

146

The Lesson

1. Ask the class to turn to page 146. Learn the song by sight-reading the rhythm and melody in relation to the underlying harmony. Play the chords on the autoharp as the class reads the song. (Strum twice per measure.)

2. Invite the students to follow the suggestion on the pupil page and plan different ways to add harmony. Some ideas might be

   - Divide the class into two groups and perform the song in echo style.

   - Repeat the words and music of each phrase, but now sustain the last pitch.

I'm on my way, _____

I'm on my way

- Group 2 (or one student) might change the words and vary the melodic rhythm, as well as the pitch. For example:

I'm on my way, _____

Yeh yeh yeh yeh yeh

- Invite a student to improvise an echo, using any pitches. (Accept the students' improvisation, even if it is "out of tune.")

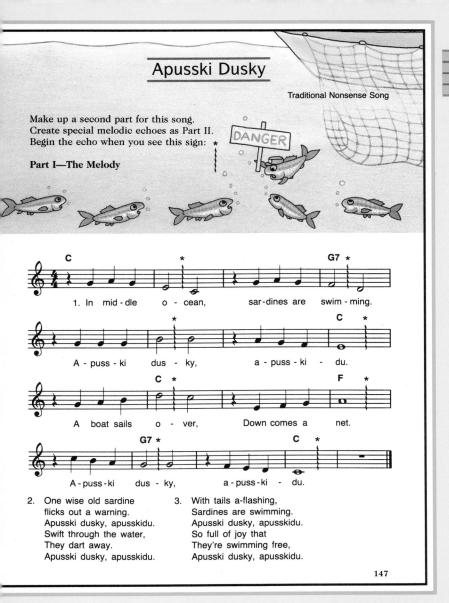

Apusski Dusky

Traditional Nonsense Song

Make up a second part for this song.
Create special melodic echoes as Part II.
Begin the echo when you see this sign: ★

Part I—The Melody

DANGER

C ★ G7 ★

1. In mid-dle o-cean, sar-dines are swim-ming.

★ C ★

A-puss-ki dus-ky, a-puss-ki-du.

C ★ F ★

A boat sails o-ver, Down comes a net.

G7 ★ C ★

A-puss-ki dus-ky, a-puss-ki-du.

2. One wise old sardine
flicks out a warning.
Apusski dusky, apusskidu.
Swift through the water,
They dart away.
Apusski dusky, apusskidu.

3. With tails a-flashing,
Sardines are swimming.
Apusski dusky, apusskidu.
So full of joy that
They're swimming free,
Apusski dusky, apusskidu.

147

Lesson Focus
Harmony: Chords and melody may move simultaneously in relation to each other. *(P–S)*

Materials
○ **Piano Accompaniment:** page 322
○ **Record Information:**
 • Apusski Dusky
  Record 7 Side A Band 7
  Voices: children's choir
  Accompaniment: mandolin, acoustic bass, synthesizer, accordion, percussion
○ **Extends Lesson 34,** page 76

The Lesson

1. Review "I'm on My Way" on page 146. Then introduce "Apusski Dusky" on page 147 by playing the recording as the students listen. Play it a second time, inviting the class to sing the melody.

2. After the students are familiar with the melody, ask them to look for rhythmic similarities between the two songs. (Both have long sounds at the end of every phrase.)

3. Suggest that a harmony part for this new song may be created in the same style that was used in "I'm on My Way." Ask the students to read the instructions on the pupil page. Then perform the song, following the signs indicating when to begin the echo part (Beat 2 of every other measure). Have them first chant their echo idea, then sing it. They may wish to

remain on the same pitch they used for Beat 1 or make up a melodic pattern. Ask individuals to share their echo while the class softly sings the melody.

Lesson Focus

Harmony: Chords and melody may move simultaneously in relation to each other. *(P–S)*

Materials

- **Piano Accompaniment:** page 320
- **Record Information:**
  - Grizzly Bear
    Record 7 Side A Band 8
    Voices: man, children's choir
    Accompaniment: tenor banjo, bass harmonica, double bass
- **Instruments:** resonator bells D and A; two bell mallets
- **Extends Lesson 18,** page 40

Chords not shown on pupil page

Grizzly Bear

Southern Work Song

Verse

1. I'm gon-na tell ___ you a sto-ry 'bout griz-zl-y bear, ___
2. He had ___ great ___ long ___ teeth ___ like a griz-zl-y bear, ___
   3. Tell me who ___ was ___ the griz-zl-y bear, ___

Jack ___ o' Dia-monds was-n't noth-ing but a griz-zl-y bear. ___
He made a track ___ in the bot-tom like a griz-zl-y bear. ___
Tell me who ___ was ___ the griz-zl-y bear. ___

Refrain

Oh, ___ the griz-zl-y, ___ griz-zl-y, ___ griz-zl-y bear, ___

Oh, ___ the griz-zl-y, ___ griz-zl-y, ___ griz-zl-y bear. ___

Take turns being the leader.
Improvise your own "grizzly bear" story using this melody.
Be sure to keep the phrase lengths the same so that the chorus knows when to respond.

148

The Lesson

1. Ask the class to follow the notation for "Grizzly Bear" on page 148 as they listen to the recording. **When do you hear voices sing in harmony?** (on the words "grizzly bear") **Listen again. Is the harmony part the same or different each time it is repeated?** (always the same)

2. Ask the students to examine the way the song is placed on the page. Notice that the leader's call contains different words, rhythms, and pitches, but that the chorus' response contains words, rhythm, and pitches that don't change. Divide the chorus into two groups. Tell Group 1 to sing the lower pitch (D) and Group 2 to sing the upper pitch (A). After the class has practiced the response, sing the leader's part. The students will answer you at the end of each phrase.

3. Comment that hearing the pitches one is to sing is sometimes difficult when singing in harmony. Ask each group to stand in a close circle looking toward the center. Choose one student in each group to stand in the middle of the circle and play the appropriate resonator bell (D or A). Members of each group are to sing toward each other. Perform the song as in Step 2. Ask the students to decide if this careful listening approach helps improve their ability to sing in harmony.

4. Divide the class into three groups. Group 1 should sing the leader's part, Group 2 the lower response part, and Group 3 the upper response part.

OPTIONAL

Happiness Runs

Words and Music by Donovan Leitch

Hap - pi - ness runs in a cir - cu - lar mo - tion,

Thought is like a lit - tle boat up - on the sea.

You can have ev - ery - thing if you let your - self be,

You can have ev - ery - thing if you let your - self be.

Sing a special **ostinato** part with the melody.

Dum dum dum dum

Lesson Focus
Harmony: Chords and melody may move simultaneously in relation to each other. *(P–I)*

Materials
○ **Piano Accompaniment:** page 321
○ **Record Information:**
 • Happiness Runs
  Record 7 Side B Band 1
  Voices: children's choir
  Accompaniment: guitar, electric bass, piano, percussion
○ **Instruments:** soprano glockenspiel; alto xylophone; bass xylophone; alto metallophone; bell mallets
○ **Teacher's Resource Binder:**
 • Optional—
  Orff Activity 9, page O15
○ **Extends Lesson 56,** page 122

The Lesson

1. Invite the class to look at page 149 and learn to sing "Happiness Runs." Begin by examining the words "Happiness runs in a circular motion." **Look carefully at the notation. How did the composer express the idea of circular motion?** (The same few pitches are used over and over.) Guide the class to learn the melody.

2. When the students can sing the song easily, reinforce the idea of circular motion by adding a harmony part. **Look at the notation for the ostinato, which is shown at the bottom of the page. On which step of the scale does this part begin?** (Step 4) **Then what happens?** (moves down by steps to 1) Have the students practice the descending scale pattern. Then divide the class into two groups. Ask Group 2 to sing the ostinato while Group 1 sings the melody.

3. Add other harmonic ostinatos on the instruments. Choose students to play each part below. Challenge them to learn to perform their parts on the designated instruments while reading the notation. Ask them to perform the ostinatos as the class sings.

Soprano glockenspiel

Alto xylophone

Alto metallophone

Bass xylophone

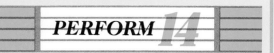

Lesson Focus

Harmony: Two or more musical lines may occur simultaneously. *(P–I)*

Materials

○ **Piano Accompaniment:** page 323
○ **Record Information:**
  • Portland Town
    Record 7 Side B Band 2
    Voices: man, woman, children's choir
    Accompaniment: pan pipes, mountain dulcimer, celtic harp, harmonium
○ **Instruments:** resonator bells C and D; bell mallets
○ **Extends Lesson 23,** page 50

Portland Town

Words Adapted by B. A.   Music by Derroll Adams

Can you sing these two pitches?

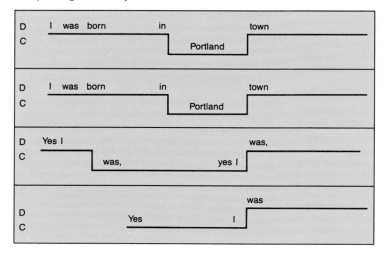

Look at Part 2.
On what pitch does it begin?
How is it the same or different from the part you have just sung?

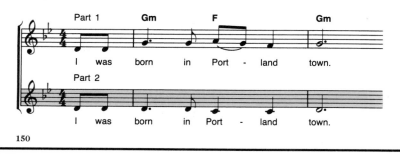

150

The Lesson

1. Listen to the recording of "Portland Town." Discuss the idea of the song: a grandparent's thoughts about a long, happy life in Portland Town. **A song that tells a story like this is called a ballad.**

2. Ask the class to turn to page 150. **Can you learn this special harmony part by following the picture?** Follow this procedure:

   • Determine the number of pitches to be sung and their letter names (two: C and D).

   • Locate the resonator bells for the pitches and play them.

   • Ask the students to sing the contour on "loo." Indicate with hand gestures when they are to change pitches.

   • Guide them to sing Part 2 of the song on pages 150-151 in the correct rhythm.

3. Compare the contour picture on page 150 with the traditionally notated Part 2 below it. Using information from both, ask the students to answer these questions:

   • **What is the same about both types?** (melodic contour)

   • **What is different?** (Contour picture does not give the rhythm.)

   • **On what pitch does this part begin?** (D)

   • **Which picture gives us more accurate information?** (Part 2)

4. Focus attention on Part 1. Ask the class to compare it with Part 2, the harmony part that they have just learned. Conclude that the rhythm is almost the same in both parts. Notice that in both parts Phrases 1 and 2 begin on the same pitch. Part 1 then skips up. Guide the class to learn the melody for Part 1.

150

I was born in Port - land town.

I was born in Port - land town.

Yes I was, yes I was.

Yes I was, yes I was.

Yes I was.

Yes I was.

2. I got married in Portland town,
   Me and my gal (guy),
   We settled down.
   Yes we did, yes we did,
   Yes we did.

3. Had children, one, two, three,
   They grew up and soon left me.
   Yes they did, yes they did,
   Yes they did.

4. I grew old in Portland town,
   Had a good life
   In Portland town.
   Yes I did, yes I did,
   Yes I did.

5. I was born in Portland town,
   I was born in Portland town.
   Yes I was, yes I was,
   Yes I was.

151

5. When the students can independently sing the melody, divide them into two groups and perform the two-part song. **Listen carefully to your own voice and to the voices of those who are singing the other part so that you are sure your musical line makes pleasing harmony with the other line.** Select two small groups (four or five for each group) to perform the song for the class so that all can hear how the two musical lines are combined to create harmony.

PERFORM 15

Lesson Focus

Harmony: Two or more musical lines may occur simultaneously. *(P–I)*

Materials

○ **Piano Accompaniment:** page 330

○ **Record Information:**
  • Sing a Little
    Record 7 Side B Band 3
    Voices: children's choir
    Accompaniment: flute, oboe, clarinet, bassoon, clavinet, double bass, percussion

○ **Instruments:** piano; xylophone or resonator bells for C scale; bell mallets

○ **Other:** scale strip, prepared from Activity Sheet 20, Lesson 54

○ **Teacher's Resource Binder:**
  • Optional—
    Kodaly Activity 15, page K22

○ **Extends Lesson 39,** page 86

The Lesson

1. Use the scale strip (see **Materials**) to help the students become proficient at singing steps and skips. Establish tonality in the key of C. Point to the scale numbers on the scale strip. The students should then respond by singing the correct pitch. Sing patterns such as:

1–2–3–4–5–6–7–1'   1'–7–6–5–4–3–2–1

1–2–3–5–6–5–3–2–1   1'–7–1'–6–4–2–5–1

1–3–5–3–4–5–4–3–1   1–3–5–6–7–6–5–3–1

2. Teach the students to sing the poem below as a scale song. Start with the bottom line of words. Sing it on scale step 1. Sing the line above it on scale step 2. Move up one step for each new phrase. Sing it for the class phrase by phrase. Have them echo you until they have learned all the words of the poem.

To snap and sniff at the moon!
You are not equipped to croon.
"Can't you see we're quite agreed,
Stop it, stop it!" they would plead,
They would say "You're out of tune!"
Just when I would start to croon,
They used to snap and sniff at the moon.
I had an alligator and a raccoon.

3. Ask the students to open their books to pages 152–153. Follow the instructions on the page and learn the scale song. **How does the melody move?** (up by steps; then down by steps—except at the end of each section, where the melody skips back and forth between 1 and 1') Tell the students to look carefully at the notation and figure out when they will have to move to the next step of the scale (usually at the beginning of each measure).

Sing a lit - tle, sing a lit - tle, la, la, la.

Sing a lit - tle, sing a lit - tle, la, la, la.

Sing a lit - tle, sing a lit - tle, la, la, la.

Sing a lit - tle, sing a lit - tle, la, la, la.

La, la, la, la, la, la, la, la, la, la.

What is the mystery tune played on the scale?

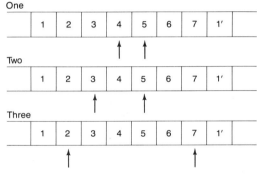

153

4. Before singing, examine the rhythmic notation. **Does the rhythm pattern begin with a short sound or a long sound?** (with the shortest sound, the sixteenth note) Establish the shortest sound and ask the class to chant the first two measures. Discover that most of the song repeats this pattern. **Where does it change?** (in Measures 9 and 19)

5. Divide the class into two groups. Challenge them to learn to sing the song in harmony. Explain that Group 2 will begin at the beginning at the same time that Group 1 starts to sing Measure 3. Have the students sing slowly so that they can hear the sound of thirds that results when the two lines are combined. When they can accurately sing the song in two parts, increase the tempo.

6. Introduce another scale idea that uses harmony. Follow the steps shown on page 153 to discover the name of the mystery tune. It begins in the middle of the scale. Choose a student to play piano with two fingers or xylophone or bells (set up for C scale) with two mallets. Explain that the student is to play only the pitches marked with an arrow. Each pair of pitches is to be played simultaneously six times (moving in threes). Notice that each pair of pitches creates a new interval to provide harmony. They are to end by playing the two octave pitches, 1 and 1′. Students may recognize "Chopsticks." They may add rhythmic ideas to the playing of this familiar tune.

Lesson Focus

Expression: Musical elements are combined into a whole to express a musical or extramusical idea. *(C–I)*

Materials

- ○ **Piano Accompaniments:** pages 324, 325, 326, 328
- ○ **Record Information:**
  - • We're Off to See the Wizard
  - 🔲 **Record 7 Side B Band 4**
    Voices: children's choir
    Accompaniment: small show orchestra
  - • If I Only Had a Brain
    Record 7 Side B Band 5
    Voices: children's choir
    Accompaniment: small show orchestra
  - • The Merry Old Land of Oz
  - 🔲 **Record 7 Side B Band 6**
    Voices: children's choir
    Accompaniment: small show orchestra
  - • Ding-Dong, the Witch Is Dead
  - 🔲 **Record 7 Side B Band 7**
    Voices: children's choir
    Accompaniment: small show orchestra
  - • Somewhere Over the Rainbow
  - 🔲 **Record 7 Side B Band 8**
    Voices: solo child, children's choir
    Accompaniment: small show orchestra

(continued on next page)

The Wizard of Oz

Once upon a time, a little girl named Dorothy and her dog, Toto, had an exciting adventure. A great wind came and blew them out of their farmhouse in Kansas. They needed help in finding their way home again. Who could help?

Chords not shown on pupil page

We're Off to See the Wizard

Words by E. Y. Harburg   Music by Harold Arlen

154

The Lesson

1. **Once upon a time there was a little girl named Dorothy who lived on a farm in Kansas with her Auntie Em and Uncle Henry. She had a little dog named Toto. One day a terrible cyclone swept through the farm . . . How many of you have heard this story?** Students will probably know that you have begun the story of *The Wizard of Oz.* Invite the students to continue the story, telling their own version of Dorothy's adventures in Oz.

The Story: Dorothy and her dog Toto live on a Kansas farm with Auntie Em and Uncle Henry. A terrible cyclone blows Dorothy and Toto into another land called Oz. They journey through Oz meeting many characters, as they search for the Wizard, who is supposed to help them return to Kansas. Along the way, Dorothy and Toto meet the Straw Man, who wants a brain: the Tin Man, who wants a heart and the Cowardly Lion, who wants courage.

They meet both good and bad witches. The Wicked Witch of the West tries to do them harm. However, when Dorothy accidentally spills water on her, she dissolves, freeing them all to pursue their search for the Wizard. It turns out that the Wizard hasn't any powers to help Dorothy and Toto return to Kansas, but he does have the wisdom to help the Straw Man understand that he really has a brain, the Tin Man a heart, and the Cowardly Lion courage. The Good Witch of the North tells Dorothy how to return to Kansas. By tapping the heels of her magic shoes, Dorothy can make a wish come true. She and Toto are whisked safely back to Kansas.

2. Ask the class to open their books to page 154. Tell them that *The Wizard of Oz* has been told

We're off to see the Wiz - ard, ___ the won-der-ful Wiz-ard of Oz!

Along the way Dorothy met friends who had their own special reasons for wanting to see the Wizard of Oz.

If I Only Had a Brain

Words by E. Y. Harburg

The Straw Man

I could while away the hours
Conferrin' with the flow'rs
Consultin' with the rain

And my head, I'd be scratchin'
While my thoughts were busy hatchin'
If I only had a brain.

The Tin Man

When a man's an empty kettle
He should be on his mettle
And yet I'm torn apart

Just because I'm presumin'
That I could be kind-a human
If I only had a heart.

The Cowardly Lion

Life is sad believe my missy
When you're born to be a sissy,
Without the vim and verve

But I could change my habits,
Never more be scared of rabbits
If I only had the nerve.

Chords not shown on pupil page

The Merry Old Land of Oz

Words by E. Y. Harburg

Music by Harold Arlen

Ha - ha - ha! Ho - ho - ho! and a coup-le of tra - la - las, That's how we laugh the day a - way, In the mer-ry old land of Oz.

155

Materials *(continued)*

○ **Instruments:** cymbals; glockenspiel, xylophone, or resonator bells C, F, and G; bell mallets; two different-sized drums; drum mallets

○ **Teacher's Resource Binder:**
  • Optional—
  Biography 6, page B11
  Curriculum Correlation 9, page C15
  Kodaly Activity 8, page K13

○ **Extends Lesson 43,** page 94

as a musical story. Many students have probably seen the film on television. Read the story line in the pupil book. Listen to the recordings to learn the songs. Follow the suggestions beginning in Step 3 to develop an enjoyable "mini-performance."

3. **"We're Off to See the Wizard":** Sing the song. Whistle the descending scale (or play it on the bells). Create a "follow-the-leader" skipping dance for some to perform while others sing the song. The leader may skip low or high and may make silly motions for the followers to copy.

4. **The Straw Man:** Encourage the children to speak this verse dramatically as the recorded accompaniment is played. Create an accompaniment to simulate the sounds of the Straw Man's movements by swishing paper back and forth in a steady beat. Rhythmically speak the verse with the paper sound accompaniment.

5. **The Tin Man:** As with the Straw Man, invite students to dramatically speak this verse as you play the recorded accompaniment. **In what way will the Tin Man sound different from the Straw Man?** Create an accompaniment to simulate the sounds of the Tin Man's movements by rhythmically rubbing cymbals together. Rhythmically speak the verse with these accompanying sounds.

6. **The Cowardly Lion:** As with the other sections, the students should plan to speak this verse while hearing the recorded accompaniment. **In what way will the Cowardly Lion sound different from the other characters?** Create an accompaniment to simulate the sounds of the lion's movements by softly playing steady beats on two drums of different

sizes, alternating between high and low pitches. Speak the verse with the sound of the drum accompaniment.

7. **"The Merry Old Land of Oz"**: Sing this bright tune. Play a jolly bell or glockenspiel accompaniment by following this pitch sequence in a steady half-note rhythm:

C G F G C C F G
C G F F C G C C

8. **"Ding Dong, the Witch Is Dead"**: Help the class learn to sing the song by listening to the recording. They may play G on all available bells each time the phrases "ding dong" or "wake up" are sung.

9. **"Somewhere Over the Rainbow"**: This is one of the loveliest melodies in *The Wizard of Oz*. Encourage the students to expressively sing

the song after they have listened to the recording and learned the melody. Prepare students to sing these phrases in a smooth, sustained manner by suggesting that they make "tonal rainbows" with their voice. Use your hand to draw the rainbow in the sky, one motion or "color" per phrase. Accompany the slow movement of the hand by singing the first "color" of the rainbow on "loo." Help the students to plan a long breath to support this "rainbow strip" by showing them how long the rainbow will be. Add other colors to the rainbow by singing different syllables such as "lie," "low," "lae," and so on.

Ask the class to sing the song, "spinning out" each phrase in the way they have just been practicing.

Somewhere Over the Rainbow

Words by E. Y. Harburg
Music by Harold Arlen

PERFORM 16

With the help of all her good friends, Dorothy and Toto find their way back to Auntie Em and Uncle Henry and live happily ever after on their Kansas farm.

1. Some-where O - ver the Rain-bow way up high,
2. Some-where O - ver the Rain-bow skies are blue,
3. Some-where O - ver the Rain-bow blue - birds fly,

There's a land that I heard of once in a lull - a -
And the dreams that you dare to dream real - ly do come
Birds fly o - ver the Rain - bow, why then, oh why can't

by. true. Some - day I'll wish up - on a star and

wake up where the clouds are far be - hind me, _____ Where

trou - bles melt like lem - on drops, a - way, a - bove the chim - ney tops that's

where you'll find me. I?

157

Lesson Focus

Expression: Musical elements are combined into a whole to express a musical or extramusical idea. *(C–I)*

Materials

○ **Instruments:** harmonica
○ **Extends Lesson 43,** page 94

Meeting the Musicker

Adapted from *The Road to Oz* by L. Frank Baum

Create a musical theater piece from further adventures with Dorothy.

Storyteller: Dorothy and some new friends again traveled down the road to Oz. Presently, they saw a little man dressed in red, sitting on a bench before a door. The musical sounds they heard seemed to come from inside the man himself, for he was playing no instrument nor was any to be seen near him. Dorothy and her friends came up and stood in a row listening while the queer sounds came from the little man.

Instrumentalist: Breathe out on the heavy beat.

All (Class): Chant this poem in a rhythmic singsong:

$\frac{3}{4}$
Tiddle-iddle-widdle, **oom** pom-pom,
Oom pom-pom, **oom** pom-pom,
Tiddle-iddle-widdle, **oom** pom-pom,
Oom pom-pom-**pah**!

Storyteller: One of Dorothy's friends said, "Why I do believe this little man is a musicker!"

Dorothy: "How funny, when he speaks his breath makes the music."

Storyteller: "That's nonsense," said her friend, but the music began again and they all listened.

158

The Lesson

1. Invite the class to create their own musical theater piece. Continue the fun of Dorothy and her adventures in the Land of Oz. Tell the students that the story of the Wizard was so well received that the author, L. Frank Baum, wrote many other books about the land of Oz. In the stories, Dorothy continues to meet the most unusual people. One of the characters in the book *The Road to Oz* is the Musicker, a very strange fellow who cannot talk or breathe without making music.

2. Ask the students to open their books to pages 158–159 and take turns reading aloud portions of the story from the original text. After reading the story, assign parts. To dramatize, there will need to be a Storyteller, an Instrumentalist, and Dorothy. Perform the story following the suggestions on the pupil page.

The harmonica represents the breathing in and out of the Musicker. The instrumentalist who is chosen to play the harmonica should select a "spot" on the instrument and always breathe in and out in the same position. This way, the sounds will remain the same, creating an ostinato. This harmonica ostinato should continue throughout the performance, while the class is either singsonging or chanting the Musicker's words.

3. Dramatize this strange encounter for other classes or for parents. Choose students to be the Storyteller and Dorothy. The remainder of the class should chant the Musicker's words in a singsong fashion. They do not all need to be on the same pitch because the Musicker's voice was supposed to sound very strange.

4. Encourage students to seek out the many *Oz* books written by L. Frank Baum. They will

158

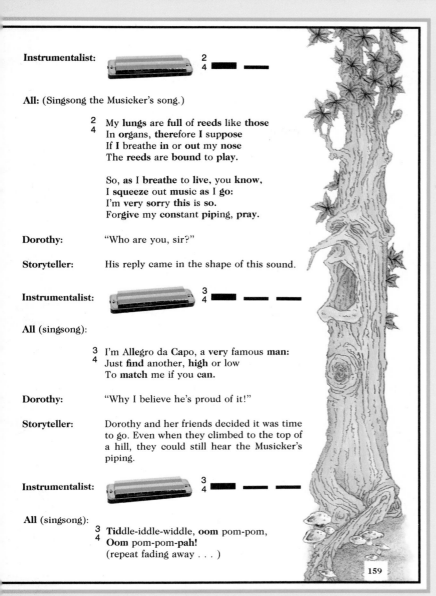

Instrumentalist:
$\frac{2}{4}$

All: (Singsong the Musicker's song.)

$\frac{2}{4}$ My **lungs** are **full** of **reeds** like **those**
In **organs, therefore I** suppose
If **I** breathe **in** or **out** my **nose**
The **reeds** are **bound** to **play.**

So, **as I breathe** to **live,** you **know,**
I **squeeze** out **music** as I **go:**
I'm **very sorry this** is **so.**
For**give** my **constant piping, pray.**

Dorothy: "Who are you, sir?"

Storyteller: His reply came in the shape of this sound.

Instrumentalist:
$\frac{3}{4}$

All (singsong):

$\frac{3}{4}$ I'm Allegro da Capo, a **very** famous **man:**
Just **find** another, **high** or low
To **match** me if you **can.**

Dorothy: "Why I believe he's proud of it!"

Storyteller: Dorothy and her friends decided it was time to go. Even when they climbed to the top of a hill, they could still hear the Musicker's piping.

Instrumentalist:
$\frac{3}{4}$

All (singsong):
$\frac{3}{4}$ **Tiddle-iddle-widdle, oom** pom-pom,
Oom pom-pom-**pah!**
(repeat fading away . . .)

159

become acquainted with many delightful characters and become involved in a most fantastic world! These books are readily available in most school and public libraries.

Lesson Focus

Expression: Musical elements are combined into a whole to express a musical or extramusical idea. *(D–I)*

Materials

o **Record Information:**
  • Nuages from *Nocturnes* by Claude Debussy (deh-byoo-**see**), 1862–1918
    Record 8 Side A Band 1
    New Philharmonia Orchestra
    Pierre Boulez, conductor

o **Other:** large sheets of paper and crayons for each student

o **Extends Lesson 44,** page 96

Describe Music

LISTENING

Nuages
from *Nocturnes*
by Claude Debussy

Have you ever watched the clouds float overhead and imagined that you saw people or animals or strange shapes? Listen to "Nuages." This is the French word for "clouds." Does the music suggest cloud shapes?
Listen for the melodies played by the English horn, the flute, and the viola as the rest of the instruments create "floating" music.

160

The Lesson

1. Begin the class quietly by playing the recording of *"Nuages."* Signal the students to sit comfortably and listen. After the music has continued for about two minutes, begin to speak softly (so that the class must pay attention) while the music continues. **Did you ever lie on the grass or sit on the steps on a sunny afternoon and watch the clouds float overhead? Did you see shapes that you imagined were animals or people?** Suggest that music can help one imagine things too. Listen quietly until the recording ends.

2. Ask the students to open their books and read the questions at the bottom of page 160. Invite their responses, reassuring them that there are no "right" answers. Enjoy the photograph of the boy sitting on the grass, perhaps also thinking about shapes in the clouds.

3. Distribute large pieces of paper and crayons of different colors to each student. If space is available, allow the students to sit on the floor where they can use large arm motions while drawing. Explain that you are going to play the recording again. They are to choose a crayon and draw lines, loops, and shapes as they listen to the music. They may use different colors as the music continues. **Don't try to draw anything specific. Just let your crayon "follow" the music. It doesn't matter if your lines cross over each other; just keep drawing.** Play the recording as the students draw.

4. **I wonder if we can find any shapes that look like people or animals or things in your drawings!** Play the recording a third time and signal to each student in turn to display his or her drawings. After they have listened, give the students time to make comments about what they saw.

Clouds

Words by Christina Rossetti

White sheep, white sheep
On a blue hill,
When the wind stops
You all stand still.
When the wind blows
You walk away slow,
White sheep, white sheep
Where do you go?

161

Lesson Focus

Expression: Musical elements are combined into a whole to express a musical or extramusical idea. *(D–I)*

Materials

○ **Piano Accompaniments:** pages 331, 332, and 333
○ **Record Information:**
   • Nuages from *Nocturnes*
     (Record 8 Side A Band 1)
   • Clouds
   Record 8 Side A Band 2a
   Voices: children's choir
   Accompaniment: English horn, harp, percussion
   Record 8 Side A Band 2b
   Voices: children's choir
   Accompaniment: rubbed glasses, bowed piano, synthesizer
   Record 8 Side A Band 2c
   Voices: solo woman
   Accompaniment: piano
○ **Extends Lesson 3,** page 10

The Lesson

1. Begin by listening to the recording of *"Nuages"* that the students heard during the previous lesson. Ask the class to read the poem on page 161. Help the students realize that this poem is also about imagining things in the clouds. **What did the poet see?** (sheep)

2. **If you were going to set these words to music, what kind of music would you want to use to help express the poem's ideas? What decisions would you need to make?** Guide the students to conclude that they need to think about kinds of rhythm (whether to move in twos or threes, to use long, short, even, or uneven sounds); the melody (whether to use major or minor, high or low pitches, or to move mostly with big skips or mostly by steps); the tempo (fast or slow); dynamics (loud or soft); and articulation (whether to se-

lect sounds that are separate and detached or smoothly connected). Encourage the students to make suggestions. Assure them that there are no right answers; every composer may have his or her own ideas.

3. **Many composers have set this poem to music. Let's listen to settings by three of them and see if they agreed with your ideas!** Tell the students to follow the notation on pages 162–163 as they listen to the recordings. After they have heard all three, guide them to compare similarities and differences. As discussion proceeds, some of the following differences and similarities might be noted.

Rhythm: Each song is in a different meter. (The Malin and Frackenpohl choices are perhaps more appropriate since they suggest a rocking, floating feeling.) Malin and Frackenpohl use melodic rhythms that reinforce the

161

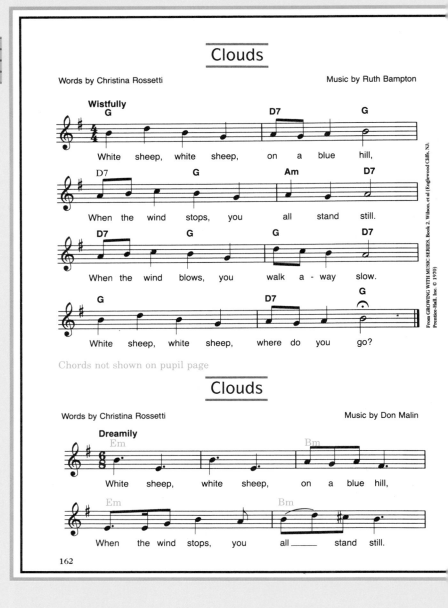

Clouds

Words by Christina Rossetti

Music by Ruth Bampton

Wistfully

White sheep, white sheep, on a blue hill,

When the wind stops, you all stand still.

When the wind blows, you walk a - way slow.

White sheep, white sheep, where do you go?

From GROWING WITH MUSIC SERIES, Book 2. Wilson, et al (Englewood Cliffs, NJ: Prentice-Hall, Inc. © 1970)

Chords not shown on pupil page

Clouds

Words by Christina Rossetti

Music by Don Malin

Dreamily

White sheep, white sheep, on a blue hill,

When the wind stops, you all _____ stand still.

162

floating feeling by occasionally using uneven rhythms; the Bampton rhythm always moves evenly. Note how the Frackenpohl rhythm stops on the word "stops." The importance of the question at the end of the song is stressed by lengthening the word "where."

Melody: The Bampton melody is in major, has the narrowest range (five notes), and moves with a rocking motion, back and forth. The largest skip is to the word "walk." Note how the song ends on the third, suggesting a questioning feeling. Malin's song also ends on a pitch other than the tonal center. The Malin and Frackenpohl versions are each in minor; both have ranges of seven steps and begin with descending intervals. Frackenpohl uses melody to support the word ideas as illustrated by his use of slurred pitches and his placement of the highest pitch in the melody over the word "blows." Malin's melody moves around the

most, combining steps and skips, and frequently changing direction.

Form: Bampton—A B B' A
Malin—A B C A'
Frackenpohl—A A' B B' A"
Notice that Frackenpohl expands his song by repeating the first line of words. Of the three composers, Malin uses the least repetition.

4. **Which do you like the best?** (Preferences will vary; taste is a personal thing!) Invite the students to decide which of the three settings they would like to learn to sing. Help them learn the song of their choice by reading the notation and/or listening to the recording.

When the wind blows, you walk a-way slow.

White sheep, white sheep, where did you go?

Clouds

Words by Christina Rossetti

Music by Arthur Frackenpohl

Wistfully

White sheep, white sheep, on a___ blue___ hill,

White sheep, white sheep, on a___ blue___ hill,

When the wind stops, You all___ stand still.

When the wind blows,___ You walk a - way slow.

White sheep, white sheep, Where do___ you go?___

163

Lesson Focus

Expression: Musical elements are combined into a whole to express a musical or extramusical idea. **(D–I)**

Materials

- ○ **Piano Accompaniment:** page 334
- ○ **Record Information:**
  - Me and My Shadow
  - **Record 8 Side A Band 3**
- ○ **Other:** paper and pencil or crayon for each student
- ○ **Extends Lesson 22,** page 48

Describe What You Hear

1. Show what you hear:

   instruments?   mood?

   melody?   form?

   rhythm?

2. Draw what you hear:

   melody?   form?

   rhythm? instruments?

   other?

3. Talk about what you hear:

   form?   rhythm?

   instruments?   melody?

   other?

164

The Lesson

1. Ask the students to read the first instruction on page 164. **Before you show what you hear, listen to this music.** Without identifying the title, play the first (instrumental) statement of "Me and My Shadow". Then invite the students to find spaces where they can "show what they hear" without bothering anyone else. *(OPTIONAL)*

2. Without discussing their movements, ask the students to return to their seats and read the second instruction. Distribute blank paper and a pencil or crayon to each student and play the recording again. Students may ask that you play it a third time so they can complete their drawings.

3. Ask the class to read the third instruction. Guide the students to tell what they heard in relation to:
   - **Form** (Three sections: **A B A**)

- **Rhythm** (Moves evenly in twos.)
- **Instruments** (Tenor saxophone, muted trumpet, guitar, double bass, and percussion may be identified.)
- **Melody** (In major; most phrases move gradually upward.)
- **Mood** (Sad, wistful, quiet, etc.)

4. **Listen. Do the words describe the mood you thought the music suggested?** Play the second statement (vocal) while the students follow the words on page 165. After some discussion, invite them to sing the song.

5. Play the third statement of the song. Students will quickly realize that the shadow is now heard in the music. End the class by having pairs of students describe the music. As they stand facing each other, one student is "Me" and moves during the first statement of the phrase. The second student moves during its repetition, "shadowing" the first person's movement.

Me and My Shadow

Words and Music by Billy Rose,
Al Jolson, and Dave Dreyer

Me and my Shadow,

Strolling down the avenue.

Me and my Shadow,

Not a soul to tell our troubles to.

And when it's twelve o'clock,

We climb the stair.

We never knock,

For nobody's there.

Just me and my Shadow,

All alone and feeling blue.

165

Me and my sha - dow,

Stroll - ing down the av - e - nue.

Me and my sha - dow, Not a soul to

tell our trou - bles to. And when it's

twelve o' - clock, We climb the stair. We

nev - er knock, For no - bod - y's there. Just

me and my sha - dow,

All a - lone and feel - ing blue.

Lesson Focus

Texture: Musical quality is affected by the number of and degree of contrast between musical lines occurring simultaneously. *(D–I)*

Materials

○ **Record Information:**
  • Cantata No. 147 (excerpt)
    by Johann Sebastian Bach (**bahk**),
    1685–1750
    Record 8 Side B Band 1
    The Columbia Chamber Orchestra
    Zoltan Rozsynai, conductor
    E. Power Biggs, organist

○ **Other:** paper and pencil for each student

○ **Extends Lesson 32,** page 72

LISTENING

Cantata No. 147
(Excerpt)

by Johann Sebastian Bach

Describe what you hear.
Show the shape of the melodies played by the trumpet.

How many times did you hear each melody?

166

The Lesson

1. Discuss the need for careful listening before describing the music. Ask the class to take a sheet of paper and follow the instruction at the top of page 166. As they listen to the recording, they should try to draw the shape of the trumpet melody (shown in their books) each time it is heard. Play the complete recording. Agree that the **A** melody is heard three times; the **B** melody is heard once.

2. **Before we follow the instructions on page 167, let's listen for the parts that each group is to show with their movements.** Ask the students to lightly tap the slow, steady beat frequently heard in the low strings as they hear the recording.

3. Draw attention to the constantly moving pattern in the high strings and woodwinds. Help

the class sense that this pattern usually moves in a three-to-one relationship with the underlying steady beat.

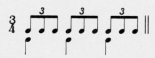

4. **Now we are ready to use movement to show what we hear. We need three groups. Should they all be the same size?** (Perhaps the trumpet group should be smallest because only one instrument plays that part.) Discuss ways that the dancers can show:
   • **Rhythm** (by the size of steps taken)
   • **Melody** (by up-down movements of arms and upper body)
   • **Form** (by changing direction at ends of phrases and sections)
   Draw the students' attention to:
   • **Articulation** (Trumpet and upper strings

OPTIONAL

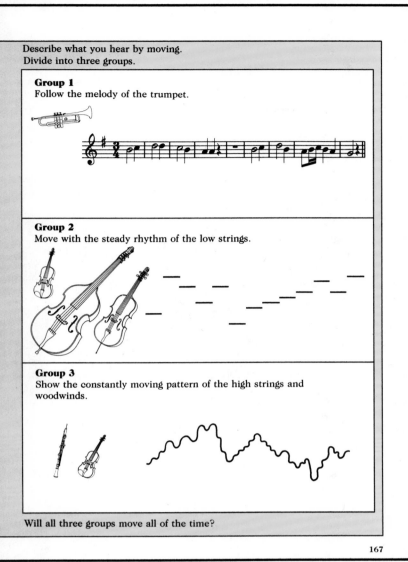

Describe what you hear by moving.
Divide into three groups.

Group 1
Follow the melody of the trumpet.

Group 2
Move with the steady rhythm of the low strings.

Group 3
Show the constantly moving pattern of the high strings and woodwinds.

Will all three groups move all of the time?

For Your Information

The excerpt from Bach's "Cantata No. 147" was originally written for organ and choir. There are two main ideas in the composition. The first (**O**) is made up of constantly moving patterns played by strings and woodwinds. The same rhythmic and melodic ideas are continued as an accompaniment for the second idea (**T**), a chorale melody played by the trumpet. This melody, in two sections, is shown on the pupil page. The structure of this arrangement is shown below. "**T**" stands for the trumpet melody, and "**O**" represents the rest of the orchestra.

O T O T O T O T O

move smoothly; lower strings are somewhat detached.)
- **Dynamics** (Volume changes slightly.)
- **Tempo** (Note slight *ritard* at end.)

5. Provide a few minutes for each group to plan its movements as you play the recording several times. Then invite each group to move for the other two before combining the three groups into a final performance.

Lesson Focus

Expression: Musical elements are combined into a whole to express a musical or extramusical idea. *(D–I)*

Materials

○ **Record Information:**
- Cantata No. 147 (excerpt) **(Record 8 Side B Band 1)**
- *Six Pieces for Orchestra* (Third Piece and First Piece) by Anton Webern (**vay-burn**), 1883–1945
  Record 8 Side B Bands 2a–b
  Band a: Third Piece
  Band b: First Piece
  Columbia Symphony Orchestra
  Robert Craft, conductor

○ **Other:** large sheets of paper; crayons, watercolors, or colored chalk

○ **Teacher's Resource Binder:**
- Optional—
  Biography 7, page B13

○ **Extends Lesson 26,** page 56

Six Pieces for Orchestra
Third Piece/First Piece
by Anton Webern

An artist described what she heard by making this design. Listen to the music she heard. What did she do to describe these sounds?

168

The Lesson

1. Begin class by listening again to "Cantata No. 147" (page 166). Recall how the students used movement to describe what they heard.

2. **Turn to page 168. Here is a design created by an artist to show what she heard in this music. What do you think she heard?** Play the recording of "Third Piece" (Band a). Encourage the students to share their ideas, basing their comments on specific aspects of the design—the color, the shapes, the lines, and so on. **Will you hear any sounds or patterns repeated? Do you think the music will be mostly smooth or jerky? fast or slow? high or low? even or uneven?** (Any answer is appropriate.)

3. After the students have shared their ideas, ask them to listen and try to follow the design. **Can you tell when each part of the picture is represented in the music?** Play the brief composition several times. The students should listen in order to identify specific aspects of the illustration and associate each with a specific segment of the music. (See **For Your Information.**)

4. When the students have enjoyed the music and the design, read the suggestion at the bottom of page 169. **Here is another short piece by the same composer. Can you draw a design to show what you hear?** Play the recording of "First Piece" (Band b). Ask the students to comment about specific things they heard, such as the sounds of contrasting instruments, when different instruments enter, the shapes of distinctive melodies, and the long and short sounds of rhythm patterns.

5. Distribute large sheets of paper and crayons, watercolors, or colored chalk. Suggest that the

Describe what you hear by drawing.
Listen to another piece of music.
Draw a design to show what you hear.

169

For Your Information

Structure of "Third Piece" from *Six Pieces for Orchestra* (scored for winds, brass, strings, harp, celesta, and percussion):
- Solo viola begins, followed by brass.
- Clarinet enters with a descending figure.
- Low strings play sustained chords.
- Flute, horn, and glockenspiel enter.
- Bassoon plays an ascending figure; violin plays a descending figure.
- Harp plays two repeated tones.
- Celesta plays a descending figure.
- Harp plays a series of repeated tones; a trumpet solo ends the piece.

Structure of "First Piece" (scored for winds, brass, celeste, harp, and strings):
- Flute begins.
- Clarinet and trumpet play a duet, accompanied by strings.
- Starting with a string tremolo, full orchestra builds to a *forte* climax.
- Gradual *diminuendo*.
- Harp *glissando* (slide).
- Trumpet figure, played twice, and single note on harp end the piece.

students listen quietly several times before beginning to draw their designs. Play the recording many times as the class works.

6. When all the students have completed their drawings, make a display around the room. Play the recording one more time as the students observe the many ways they described music with color, shape, and line.

Lesson Focus

Expression: Musical elements are combined into a whole to express a musical or extramusical idea. **(D–I)**

Materials

○ **Piano Accompaniment:** page 356

○ **Record Information:**
  • The Music Is You
    Record 8 Side B Band 3
    Voices: children's choir
    Accompaniment: guitar, electric bass, electric piano, percussion

○ **Instruments:** autoharp; bass xylophone C and D; glockenspiel or resonator bells C, E, G, F, A, and C′; bell mallets

○ **Teacher's Resource Binder:**
  • Optional—
    Biography 8, page B15

○ **Extends Lesson 10,** page 24

Describe What You Hear by Talking

Listen to "The Music Is You."

1. Describe what the song is about.

2. Describe how the composer made the music match the words.

3. Describe how the melody moves.

4. Describe how the rhythm moves.

5. Describe the harmony.

Perform "The Music Is You."

Add an accompaniment:

Bass xylophone

Glockenspiel or bells

170

The Lesson

1. Begin by asking the class the meaning of the word "definition." **The words of this song "define" music. Listen and tell me what this poet's definitions were.** Play the recording of "The Music Is You" as often as necessary until the students can tell you most of the words for the first verse. Write the "key" word from each idea on the chalkboard:

pictures	pictures
stories	stories
magic	magic
true	you

2. Comment that most of the key words are used twice. **Listen carefully to the melody. Did the composer follow this same pattern of repetition in the music?** Help the students realize that the music is divided into two sections; each section is made up of four motives. The first three motives in the first section are almost the same as the first three motives in the second section. **What happens to the fourth motives?** (They are different.) **Why do you suppose the composer changed the music there?** (The word idea is different.) Play the recording as often as needed for the students to hear this structure.

3. Ask the students to turn to page 170. **You've already completed the first two instructions. Can you follow the third instruction and describe how the melody moves? How can we describe with words the way a melody moves?** (We can say whether it moves up, down, stays the same, or moves by steps or skips. We can identify the scale steps: For example, the first pattern moves 3–5–3–2–1.) Invite the students to use any words they choose·to describe the melody of the first section.

The Music Is You

Words and Music by John Denver

Mu - sic makes__ pic - tures and of - ten tells__ sto -

- ries, All of it__ mag - ic and all of it__ true.

__ And all of the pic - tures and all__

__ of the sto - ries And all of__ the

mag - ic, the mu - sic is__ you. __

171

4. Help the students describe how the rhythm moves. Agree that it moves in threes; that the melodic rhythm sometimes moves with the underlying beat; that it sometimes occurs before the beat (as on the syllables pic-, of-, sto-, mag-, and true). Introduce the term "syncopation" as another way of describing this kind of melodic rhythm.

5. Help the students sense that the harmony goes back and forth between two chords (C and Dm). Sing the song and play the autoharp, so that the students can hear the harmony more clearly.

6. **Can you now follow the next instructions and perform this song?** Help students sing the melody without the accompaniment as they follow the notation on page 171.

7. When the class can sing the melody accurately, choose two students to add the bass xylophone and glockenspiel parts.

OPTIONAL

Lesson Focus

Rhythm: Music may be comparatively fast or slow, depending on the speed of the underlying pulse.

Rhythm: Music may become faster or slower by changing the speed of the underlying pulse. *(D–S)*

Materials

○ **Piano Accompaniment:** page 336

○ **Record Information:**
  • The Unicorn
    Record 8 Side B Band 4
    Voices: solo man
    Accompaniment: saxophone quartet, clavinet, sound effects

○ **Extends Lesson 40,** page 88

The Lesson

1. Read the instructions at the top of page 172. Review the meaning of the word tempo (the speed of the underlying beat). **Can you define the terms just by looking at the design following each word?** Pronounce each word for the students. Then invite them to offer a definition using terms such as very fast, fast, medium, slow, very slow, etc.

2. Ask the students to look over the song to find the tempo instructions. **How will the song begin?** (*Andante,* medium) **When will it change?** (at the beginning of the refrain) **Will the beat become faster or slower?** (faster) Play the first verse of the recording of "The Unicorn." Suggest that the students lightly tap the underlying beat as they listen. After they have heard the first verse, ask the students to decide if their definitions were correct.

3. Play the complete recording as the students follow the many verses of this amusing song. Discuss the musical terms found before each verse. Invite the students to describe the tempo of each as faster or slower than the preceding one. **Can you describe the tempo for the last two verses and refrains?** Play this section of the recording again. The correct answers are
   Verse 5: *Adagio;* Refrain: *Presto*
   Verse 6: *Andante;* Refrain: *Accelerando Ritardando*

4. Ask the students to demonstrate that they learned the melody while they were listening to the tempo changes. Challenge them to sing the first verse and refrain without the recording. When they know the melody well, they may sing with the recording. **Be sure you remember to change tempo!**

Humpback camels and chimpanzees, ___
Cats and rats and elephants but sure as you're born, ___
the loveliest of all was the Unicorn. Unicorn.

Allegro   Verse 2

But the Lord seen some sinnin' and it caused him pain,
He says, "Stand back, I'm gonna make it rain.
So hey, Brother Noah, I'll tell you what to do.
Go and build me a floating zoo."

Ritardando   Refrain

And you take two alligators and a couple of geese,
Two humpback camels and two chimpanzees,
Two cats, two rats, two elephants but sure as you're born,
Noah, don't you forget my unicorns.

Andante   Verse 3

Now Noah was there and he answered the callin',
And he finished up the ark as the rain started fallin',
Then he marched in the animals two by two,
And he sung out as they went through.

Largo   Refrain

Hey Lord, I got you two alligators and a couple of geese,
Two humpback camels and two chimpanzees,
Two cats, two rats, two elephants but sure as you're born,
I sure don't see your unicorns.

Adagio   Verse 4

Well, Noah looked out through the drivin' rain,
But the unicorns was hidin'– playin' silly games.
They were kickin' and a-splashin' while the rain was pourin'
Oh them foolish unicorns.

173

Accelerando   Refrain

And you take two alligators and a couple of geese,
Two humpback camels and two chimpanzees,
Two cats, two rats, two elephants but sure as you're born,
Noah, don't you forget my unicorns.

        ?   Verse 5

Then the ducks started duckin' and the snakes started snakin',
And the elephants started elephantin' and the boat started shakin',
The mice started squeakin' and the lions started roarin',
And everyone's aboard but them unicorns.

        ?   Refrain

I mean the two alligators and a couple of geese,
The humpback camels and the chimpanzees,
Noah cried, "Close the door 'cause the rain is pourin',
And we just can't wait for them unicorns."

        ?   Verse 6

And then the ark started movin' and it drifted with the tide,
And the unicorns looked up from the rock and cried,
And the water came up and sort of floated them away,
That's why you've never seen a unicorn to this day.

        ?   Refrain

You'll see a lot of alligators and a whole mess of geese,
You'll see humpback camels and chimpanzees,
You'll see cats and rats and elephants but sure as you're born,
You're never gonna see no unicorn.

174

Once

Israeli Folk Song

Describe what you see by moving.

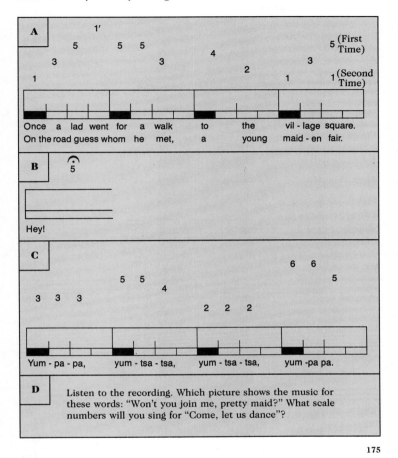

Lesson Focus

Rhythm: Individual sounds and silences within a rhythmic line may be longer than, shorter than, or the same as the underlying shortest pulse.

Melody: A series of pitches may move up or down by steps or skips. (*D–I*)

Materials

○ **Piano Accompaniment:** page 338

○ **Record Information:**
  • Once
    Record 8 Side B Band 5
    Voices: man, children's choir
    Accompaniment: French horn, trumpet, tuba, percussion

○ **Teacher's Resource Binder:**
  • Optional—
    Curriculum Correlation 12, page C26

○ **Extends Lesson 35,** page 78; **Lesson 6,** page 16; **Lesson 14,** page 32

175

The Lesson

1. Help the students follow the instruction on page 175 and use movement to describe the rhythm and melody of "Once." To show the rhythm, ask the class to clap the melodic rhythm while you tap the shortest sound.

2. As they sing the scale numbers, ask the class to move their hands up and down to show the contour of the melody.

3. After the class has described the patterns shown in Boxes A, B, and C, play the recording. Help them decide that the first part of Box A shows the music for "Won't you join me, pretty maid?" The scale numbers for "Come, let us dance" are 4–4–2–1. The open-ended box (Box B) means that they can hold the word "Hey" for as long as they like!

4. Guide the class to sing the complete song.

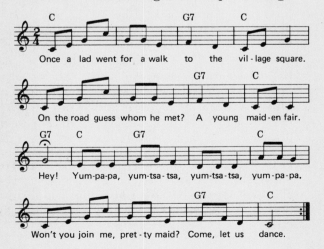

Lesson Focus

Rhythm: Individual sounds and silences within a rhythmic line may be longer than, shorter than, or the same as the underlying shortest pulse.
Melody: A series of pitches may move up or down by steps or skips. *(D–I)*

Materials

○ **Piano Accompaniment:** page 317
○ **Record Information:**
  • My Hat
    Record 8 Side B Band 6
    Voice: man
    Accompaniment: French horn, trumpet, tuba, percussion
○ **Other:** copy of *Measure a Rhythm,* prepared from Activity Sheet 4; a pencil for each student
○ **Extends Lesson 5,** page 14; **Lesson 38,** page 84; **Lesson 49,** page 108

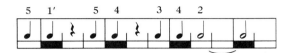

Chords not shown on pupil page

My Hat

German Folk Song

Describe what you see by drawing.

Here is Phrase 1.

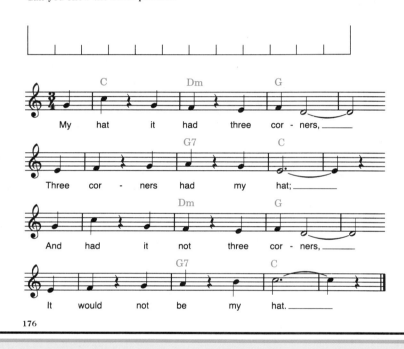

Can you show the other phrases?

My hat it had three cor-ners, _____
Three cor-ners had my hat; _____
And had it not three cor-ners, _____
It would not be my hat.

176

The Lesson

1. Review the activity on page 175 in which students described the picture of sounds that were shown with rhythm bars and numbers. Turn to page 176 and explain to the class that this time they need to turn the process around. They will need to look at a picture of music written in notation and "draw" it with rhythm bars. The first phrase has already been drawn for them at the top of the page.

2. **How will you know where to draw the lines to show the rhythm?** (The quarter note is the shortest sound—equals one short sound; the half note equals two short sounds, and so on.)

3. **How will you know which scale number to write above each sound?** (First note in the song is 5; count lines and spaces up or down to find the scale numbers for other notes.)

4. Distribute a copy of *Measure a Rhythm* (see **Materials**) and a pencil to each student. Ask them to draw Phrase 2. **Do you need to draw Phrase 3?** (No, it's the same as Phrase 1.) **Phrase 4?** (Yes, it starts like Phrase 2, but ends differently.)

   OPTIONAL

5. After their pictures have been drawn and checked, ask the students to sing the song with numbers, observing the melodic rhythm. **Now can you sing it with words?**

The Smoke Went Up the Chimney

American Camp Song

F   Gm

Oh, we pushed the damp-er in and we pulled the damp-er out,

G7   F

And the smoke went up the chim - ney just the same.

C7   F

Just the same, just the same,

C7   F

And the smoke went up the chim - ney just the same.

177

Lesson Focus
Rhythm: Individual sounds and silences within a rhythmic line may be longer than, shorter than, or the same as the underlying shortest pulse. *(D–S)*

Materials
o **Piano Accompaniment:** page 340
o **Record Information:**
   • The Smoke Went Up the Chimney
   Record 8 Side B Bands 7a–c
   Voices: children's choir
   Accompaniment: synthesizer, sound effects, percussion
o **Other:** a pencil for each student
o **Teacher's Resource Binder:**
   [Activity Sheets] • **Activity Sheet 23,** page 33 (Prepare a copy for each student.)
o **Extends Lesson 36,** page 80

For Your Information
Correct responses for the activity sheet are:

The Lesson

1. [OPTIONAL] Play the recording of "The Smoke Went Up the Chimney" (first statement only). With books closed, ask the students to lightly tap the underlying shortest sound (the sixteenth note).

2. Divide the class into two groups. Ask one group to continue to tap the shortest pulse while the other group claps the rhythm of the melody. Play the first statement of the recording again. Guide the students to observe that the rhythm is frequently uneven, with a long sound followed by a short one.

3. Draw four sixteenth notes on the chalkboard. **How many short sounds are needed to show the length of the first word of the song?** (3) Draw the "musical plus sign" under the notes. (See musical examples in **For Your Information.**) Review the fact that this curved line is called a tie.

4. Distribute Activity Sheet 23 *(Short Sounds)* and pencils. Have the class "add" short sounds together to show the rhythm of the melody. Play the first statement of the recording. When finished the students may open their books to page 177 and check their work.

5. Invite the class to sing the song. Play the remainder of the recording and help the students identify each tempo.
   Statement 1: *Largo* (quarter note = 60)
   Statement 2: *Adagio* (quarter note = 88)
   Statement 3: *Andante* (quarter note = 116)
   Invite them to sing the song in each of the three ways.

6. Add body motions to the song on key words.
   (1) *Pushed:* Push down with right hand.
   (2) *Pulled:* Pull up with right hand.
   (3) *Smoke:* Make circular motion with hand while moving it upward.
   (4) *Same:* Toss hands outward.

DESCRIBE 11

Lesson Focus

Form: A musical whole may be made up of same, varied, or contrasting segments. *(D–I)*

Materials

- **Piano Accompaniment:** page 342
- **Record Information:**
  - I'm Looking Over a Four-Leaf Clover
    Record 8 Side B Band 8
    Voices: children's choir
    Accompaniment: tenor saxophone, trumpet, trombone, tenor banjo, double bass, piano, percussion
- **Instrument:** tambourine
- **Other:** Form Cards prepared from Activity Sheet 18; Rhythm Ruler transparency prepared from Activity Sheet 3; overhead projector; overhead pen
- **Extends Lesson 12,** page 28

I'm Looking Over a Four-Leaf Clover

Words by Mort Dixon   Music by Harry Woods

- Find the shortest sound in the song.
- Find the sound that will move with the beat.
- Tap the beat. Chant the words.
- Can you find the places where the accents of the words come before the accent of the beat, making a **syncopated** rhythm?

178

The Lesson

1. With books closed, ask the class to listen to "I'm Looking Over a Four-Leaf Clover," and decide how many musical ideas they hear. Play the recording; call for responses. There will be disagreement. Play the recording again. This time, instruct the students to raise their hands when they think one idea is ending and a new one beginning. Help the class sense that each idea is four measures (8 beats) long.

2. **Can you decide which phrases are the same, which are similar, and which are different?** Distribute a set of Form Cards to each student. (See **Materials.**) To show the similarities and differences in the form, play the recording (first statement only) several times to give the students the opportunity to listen and arrange the cards in order. If they feel they do not have the required letters, they may use blank cards.

3. **Keep your cards in order and open your books to page 178. Compare the notation for each phrase. Decide whether or not you arranged your cards correctly.** Through listening and looking, guide the students to decide that the form of the four-measure patterns should be: **a b c c'** (some students may call this **a b c d, a b c″ d,** or **a b c″ e**).

4. Play the recording one more time as the students follow the notation. **Can you now sing the melody?** Establish tonality in C major. Challenge the class to sing the song without the recording. **Did you make any mistakes? Do you need to listen again?**

5. Some students may have trouble with the rhythm where the tied notes occur. Display the rhythm ruler transparency. (See **Materials.**) Fill it in for Phrase 1 as follows:

D
-ing is some- bod- y I a-

Dm
dore. _____ I'm look- ing

F   Em   A7
o- ver a four- leaf clo- ver that

Dm   G7   C
I o- ver- looked be- fore.

179

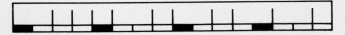

Ask the class to tap the shortest sound (represented by the quarter note in this song). They should stress the accented sounds (the dark bars) while they chant the rhythm pattern with the words of the first phrase, "I'm looking over a four-leaf clover." **Listen carefully!**

What do you notice about the relationship between the accents in the rhythm you are chanting and the accents you are clapping? Help the students realize that they do not always occur at the same time. On the syllable *-ver*, the accent is delayed, occurring after the accent of the short sound. On the syllable *clo-*, the accent is anticipatory, occurring before the accent of the underlying short sound. When the rhythms of the melody and the un-

derlying pulse occur at different times we say that the rhythm is syncopated.

6. Ask the class to sing the song again. Invite one person to lightly tap the underlying shortest sound on the tambourine, accenting the first of every four pulses. The singers should lightly stress the syncopated words.

OPTIONAL

Lesson Focus

Time and Place: The way musical elements are combined into a whole reflects the origin of the music. *(D–I)*

Materials

○ **Record Information:**
 • One of These Does Not Belong
 Record 9 Side A Bands 1 a–f
 (See Describe 13, Step 2, for record contents.)

○ **Other:** paper and pencil for each student

○ **Extends Lesson 24,** page 52

Listen to the music.

• You will hear four pieces of music in each set.
• Three of the pieces are the same kind of music.
• One is different!
• Can you pick the one that does not belong?

A

Peach Tree, Peonies and Cranes, Shen Ch'uan (1682-1758), The Metropolitan Museum of Art.

180

The Lesson

1. Ask the class to examine the pictures on pages 180–183. **Do you think that each was created in the same place? at the same time? Or do they come from different times and places?** (Answers will vary.) After the students have offered their ideas, direct their attention to the instructions at the top of page 180. **Can you decide by listening which pieces "belong together"?** Explain that "belonging together" relates to when or where the music was first performed or composed. For example, the pieces might come from the same country or time period as one of the works of art on pages 180 and 181.

2. Distribute blank paper and pencils to the students. Show them how to prepare their answer sheet so that it looks like this:
   a. 1 2 3 4   b. 1 2 3 4   c. 1 2 3 4
   d. 1 2 3 4   e. 1 2 3 4   f. 1 2 3 4

3. Explain that you will play four short examples. **Listen to all four examples. Three of them "belong together." One does not. Listen carefully. Then circle the letter that matches the example that does not belong with the others.** To be sure the students understand the instructions, do the first set together. Play Band a of the recording. **Can you choose the example that sounds different from the others? Listen again before circling your answer.** Play Band a again. After the students have circled a letter, have them compare answers. (The correct answer is "2.")

4. Play the remaining bands without further discussion. Play each band at least twice so that students have time to listen to all four examples and compare them before circling a letter.

5. After all examples have been played, play each band again and engage the class in a discus-

181

sion. **Why do you think these three belonged together and this one did not?** (Answers will vary.) Encourage the students to offer reasons based on choice of instruments, kinds of melody or harmony, or type of rhythm. Correct answers are: Band b: Example 4; Band c: Example 1; Band d: Example 3; Band e: Example 3; Band f: Example 4

Lesson Focus

Time and Place: The way musical elements are combined into a whole reflects the origin of the music. *(D–I)*

Materials

○ **Record Information:**
  • One of These Does Not Belong **(Record 9 Side A Bands 1a–f)**
○ **Teacher's Resource Binder:**
  • Optional—
  Curriculum Correlation 6, page C8
○ **Extends Lesson 24**, page 52

Music of Different Times and Places

Listen to the musical examples you heard when studying pages 180 and 181.
This time look at the pictures on pages 180, 181, 182, and 183 as you listen.
Can you pick the picture that comes from the same time or place as the music you hear?

182

The Lesson

1. Continue the lesson begun when studying pages 180 and 181. Discuss each of the pictures on pages 180–183 in greater detail (see **For Your Information**) and identify the time or place that each represents.

2. Play each band of the recording while the students look at the pictures. After they hear each band, ask the students to name the time or place of each selection and give reasons for their choices. (See **For Your Information**.) "Out of place" items are marked with an asterisk:

Band a—Mexico:
1. "Male Rosa," Tarascan Indian folk song, recorded in the State of Michoacán by Henrietta Yurchenco.
*2. "Praeludium" *Lute Suite* by J.S. Bach (1685–1750), John Williams, guitar.
3. "Jarabe Tapatio," played by a mariachi band (Mariachi "Jalisco" de Pepe Villa).
4. "Scherzino Mexicano" by Manuel Ponce (1882–1948), John Williams, guitar.

Band b—Renaissance:
1. "Providebam Dominum" by Roland de Lassus (1532–1594), The Philadelphia Brass Ensemble.
2. "Fata la Parte" by Juan del Enciña (1468–1530), Spanish composer; The Krainis Consort and Baroque Ensemble.
3. "Ballo Milanese", sixteenth century, anonymous; Lionel Rogg, positif organ; Ancient Instrument Ensemble of Zurich.
*4. "Eons Ago Blues" (1962) by Robert Dorough, The Krainis Consort and Baroque Ensemble.

Band c—Contemporary:
*1. "Jesu, Joy of Man's Desiring" from *Cantata No. 147* by J.S. Bach, The Columbia Chamber Orchestra.

E

F

183

For Your Information

Band a: Picture B, *Rug/Tapestry* (Mexico)
Band b: Picture C (Renaissance country scene)
Band c: Picture F, *Region of Brooklyn Bridge Fantasy* (1932) by John Marin (contemporary)
Band d: Picture A, *Peach Tree, Peonies and Cranes,* Shen Chu'uan (Japan)
Band e: Picture E, *Pictorial Quilt* (1883) by Grandma Hanchett (Appalachia, USA)
Band f: Picture D, *Kwele tribal mask* (Africa)

2. "Jesu, Joy of Man's Desiring" by J.S. Bach. Realized and performed by Walter Carlos with the Assistance of Benjamin Folkman on the Moog Synthesizer.
3. "Star Trek," created by John Keating in 1972, featuring the E.M.S. Synthi VCS3.
4. Excerpt from "Silver Apples of the Moon" by Morton Subotnick (born 1933), electronic music synthesizer.

Band d—Japan:
1. "Edo Lullaby," traditional Japanese folk lullaby. The Ensemble Nipponia.
2. "Mushi no Aikata" ("Insect Interlude"), shamisen solo. The Ensemble Nipponia.
*3. "Talkin' Blues," American banjo solo.
4. "Azuma Jishi" ("Azuma Lion Dance") from late eighteenth-century Japanese composition. The Ensemble Nipponia.

Band e—Appalachia (U.S.A.):
1. "Cripple Creek," played on five-string banjo. Bookmiller Shannon, banjo.
2. "Arkansas Traveller," famous fiddling tune. Buddy Lancaster, Walter Grosser, Mike Hill, and Dean Hinesley.
*3. "La Visita" ("The Visit"), Tarascan Indian tune, probably eighteenth century. Recorded in the State of Michoacán by Henrietta Yurchenco.
4. "Harrison Town," Ozark outlaw ballad, Elliot Hancock, mountain dulcimer and vocal.

Band f—Africa:
1. "Tuta Jara," Mandingo song, the Basse area in The Gambia and Senegal, West Africa.
2. "Mandingo Street Drumming," recorded at a street festival in Banjul, The Gambia.
3. "Jola Dance," a village dance, West Africa.
*4. "Hand-Game Songs" from the Cree (Canadian) Indians. William Peaychew and Group. Recorded by Ken Peacock.

Lesson Focus

Time and Place: A particular use of rhythm and harmony reflects the origin of the musical whole. **(D–I)**

Materials

○ **Piano Accompaniment:** page 344
○ **Record Information:**
  • One of These Does Not Belong
    (Record 9 Side A Bands 1a-f)
  • *La Jesusita*
    Record 9 Side A Band 2
    Voices: man, childrens's choir
    Accompaniment: 2 trumpets, violin, guitar, double bass, marimba
○ **Teacher's Resource Binder:**
  • Optional—
    Orff Activity 6, Page O8
○ **Extends Lesson 1,** page 6

The Lesson

1. Review Describe 12 by playing three of the selections in that lesson that reflect specific cultures (Band a 1, Mexico; Band d 1, Japan; Band f 1, Africa). **Listen to this song. To which of these three cultures does it belong?** Play *"La Jesusita"* with books closed.

2. Ask the students to open their books and identify the origin of the song. Students may identify *Jesusita* as a Mexican name or may recognize the Mexican mariachi accompaniment.

3. **Let's study the notation. Perhaps we can discover other characteristics of Mexican music. Does the melody move by steps or by skips?** (usually by skips) Write a I chord (G–B–D) and a V7 chord (D–F♯–A–C) on the chalkboard. Point out that in Phrases 1 and 3, Measures 1–3 outline the I chord; Measure 4 is

based on the V7 chord. In Phrases 2 and 4, Measures 1–3 outline the V7 chord; Measure 4 is based on the I chord. In the last two phrases, the first pitch in each measure alternates between the I and V7 chords.

4. Ask students to read the words of the first four phrases in rhythm. Notice that there are two short sounds to the beat. Draw attention to the numeral 3 above the staff (Measures 18, 20, 22, and 24). This is called a "triplet"; it tells us that the rhythm must now move with three short sounds to the beat instead of two. Play the recording and invite students to tap the short sounds. The shift from two short sounds to a beat to three short sounds to a beat is another characteristic of Mexican music.

5. Ask the students to sing the pitches of the I and V7 chords as you accompany them on the autoharp.

OPTIONAL

The Purple Bamboo

Chinese Folk Song

1. See I bring to you pur-ple bam-boo shoot,
2. You must try and grow like the bam-boo tall,

Now 'twill make a love - ly flute;
Then those part - ing lips so small

But those lips so small Can - not play at all
Soon will play the flute Made from bam-boo shoot;

On a love - ly gold - en ___ flute.
Sil - very tunes will gent - ly ___ fall.

Refrain

Ee - tee - tee, Soon will come the hap - py

1. day. 2. day. My son the flute will play.

Add the percussion accompaniments. Someone may improvise a recorder part. Use these pitches: D, E, F♯, A, and B.

Reprinted by permission of G. Schirmer, Inc.

185

Lesson Focus

Time and Place: The way musical elements are combined into a whole reflects the origin of the music. *(P—I)*

Materials

- **Piano Accompaniment:** page 341
- **Record Information:**
  - The Purple Bamboo
    Record 9 Side B Band 1
    Voice: woman
    Accompaniment: *ch'in,* recorder, percussion
- **Instruments:** suspended cymbal or small gong; woodblock; tom-tom; temple blocks; mallets; flute or recorder
- **Other:** overhead projector
- **Teacher's Resource Binder:**
  - **Activity Sheets 24 a–b,** pages A34–A35 (Prepare as a transparency, or make 5 copies—one for each accompanist.)
  - Optional—
    Enrichment Activity 17, page E28
- **Extends Lesson 23,** page 50

The Lesson

1. Help the students decide when and where "The Purple Bamboo" was first sung. **Look at the words. Can you see any clues?** (Phrases such as "bamboo shoot" might give some students a clue that this is music from either China or Japan.)

2. **Listen to the music. Can you hear any clues?** The recorded accompaniment for the song includes the *ch'in,* a unique sounding instrument that reflects the music's Chinese origin.

3. Help the students learn to sing the song. It is based on a pentatonic scale, D–E–F♯–A–B. (Pentatonic scales are often used in Chinese folk music.) Practice singing up and down the scale until the students feel comfortable with its sound. Then sing the song.

OPTIONAL

4. Project the transparencies made from Activity Sheets 24 a–b *(Accompany "The Purple Bamboo").* Assign students to each part. Choose a student who has studied flute or recorder to improvise a "bamboo flute" part. Give the students time to practice their parts and then have them accompany the class.

185

Lesson Focus

Melody: A series of pitches bounded by the octave "belong together," forming a tonal set. *(D–S)*

Materials

○ **Piano Accompaniment:** page 249
○ **Record Information:**
  • The Riddle Song
  Record 9 Side B Band 2
  Voice: woman
  Accompaniment: English horn, guitar
○ **Instruments:** resonator bells; soprano glockenspiel; bass xylophone D, E, G, A, and B; bell mallets
○ **Extends Lesson 52,** page 114

The Riddle Song

American Folk Song

1. I gave my love a cher-ry that has no stone;
2. How can there be a cher-ry that has no stone?
3. A cher-ry when it's bloom-ing, it has no stone;

I gave my love a chick-en that has no ___ bone;
How can there be a chick-en that has no ___ bone?
A chick-en when it's pip-ping, it has no ___ bone;

I gave my love a ring ___ that has no ___ end;
How can there be a ring ___ that has no ___ end?
A ring ___ when it's roll-ing, it has no ___ end;

I gave my love a ba-by, there's no cry - in'.
How can there be a ba-by, there's no cry - in'?
A ba - by when it's sleep-ing, there's no cry - in'.

186

The Lesson

1. Ask the students to turn to page 186 and follow the notation as they listen to "The Riddle Song." **What scale do you think was used for this melody? Was it major? minor? Was it another kind of scale?** Play the recording.

2. After the students have offered their ideas, ask them to locate all the different pitches used in the song. As the students identify them (by letter name) draw them on a staff, from low to high, on the chalkboard:

D E G A B D′ E′

3. Ask one student to locate the bells needed to play the scale. **How many different pitches are in this new scale?** (five) **This is called a pentatonic scale.** *Penta* **is a Latin word for five;** *tonic* **means tone. This scale has five tones.**

4. Play the recording again as the students draw the contour of the melody in the air. Ask them to sing the song.

5. Invite two students to improvise an accompaniment in the rhythms shown below, using any of the pitches found in the song.

OPTIONAL

Soprano glockenspiel

Bass xylophone

Sweet and Low

Words by Alfred Lord Tennyson

Music by Joseph Barnaby

Sweet and low, sweet and low, Wind of the west-ern sea, ___

Low, low, breathe and blow, Wind of the west-ern sea, ___

O - ver the roll - ing wa - ters go, Come from the dy - ing

moon ___ and blow, Blow him a - gain to me, ___

While my lit - tle one, While my pret - ty one sleeps. ___

After you know the song well, you might want to add this
harmonizing part to the last phrase:

While my lit - tle one, While my pret - ty one sleeps. ___

Lesson Focus

Dynamics: Music may be comparatively loud or soft.
Dynamics: Music may become louder or softer. **(D–S)**

Materials

○ **Piano Accompaniment:** page 376
○ **Record Information:**
 • Sweet and Low
▭ **Record 9 Side B Band 3**
  Voice: woman
  Accompaniment: string quartet
○ **Extends Lesson 41**, page 90

The Lesson

1. Ask the students to read the words of the song on page 187 silently to themselves. **What kind of a song do you think this is?** There may be various responses. Explain that it is a lullaby that was written and sung nearly a hundred years ago. The words may have been sung by a mother as she rocked her baby and waited for her sailor-husband to return home.

2. Ask the class what kind of music they would expect to hear for these words (soft, smooth, "rocking," and so on). Play the recording to see if the students' predictions were correct. Help them observe how the melody "rocks" by frequently changing direction—up and down, up and down. The ⁶/₈ meter is felt in twos, with three short sounds to every beat. It also adds to the "rocking" feeling.

3. Draw attention to the letters (*p, mp, mf*) and other dynamic markings above the staff. **Listen to the song again. Pay careful attention to the changes in loud and soft, the dynamics. Be ready to tell me what each letter or mark means.** Play the recording. Guide the class to conclude that *"p"* means soft, *"pp"* means very soft, *"ppp"* means very, very, soft, *"mp"* means medium soft, and *"mf"* means medium loud. Point out that the crescendo marking above Measures 9 and 10 means to get gradually louder; the decrescendo marking in Measures 12 and 14 shows a gradual decrease in loudness.

4. **Can you sing the song, following the dynamic markings?**

Lesson Focus

Time and Place: The way musical elements are combined into a whole reflects the origin of the music. *(D–I)*

Materials

○ **Piano Accompaniment:** page 346
○ **Record Information:**
- Sir Eglamore
  Record 9 Side B Band 4
  Voices: two baritones, two sopranos
  Accompaniment: rauschpfeife, cornett, regal organ, viola da gamba
- Two Ductiae
  Record 9 Side B Bands 5a–b
  The Ancient Instrument Ensemble of Zurich
  Lionel Riggs, positif organ
○ **Extends Lesson 55,** page 120

Old English Ballad

1. Sir Eg - la - more, that val - iant knight, Fa la
2. There starts a huge drag - on out of his den, Fa la

lank - y down dil - ly, He took up his sword and he
lank - y down dil - ly, Which had killed I know not

went for to fight; Fa la lank - y down dil - ly.
how man - y men; Fa la lank - y down dil - ly.

And as he rode o'er hill and dale, All
But when he saw Sir Eg - la - more, If

arm - èd with a coat of mail,
you'd but heard how the dra-gon did roar!

188

The Lesson

1. While the class keeps their books closed, play the recording of "Sir Eglamore." **When do you think this song might have been sung? What helps you decide?** After the students listen, remind them of other music they heard from the Renaissance period (Describe 13, Band b). Clues students might use to determine this include the words (i.e., knight, dragon) and the instrumental sounds. (See **For Your Information** for description of instruments used in the accompaniment.)

Some students may sense that the melody and harmonies seem "different." The way in which these elements are organized indicates that this song is based on an ancient mode rather than a modern major scale, even though the pitches are the same.

2. Guide students to look at pupil page 188 and determine the design of the song. Agree that knowing which sections are repeated makes it possible to learn the osng more quickly. The design is:

A: There are four measures, made up of two two-measure patterns.
A: The second phrase is the same as the first, except for slight rhythmic changes.
B: Phrase 3 is also made up of two patterns; both use the same rhythm.
C: Phrase 4 is the refrain. Draw attention to the similarity between the first and second measures of this phrase.

3. Ask the students to sing the song in a way that shows the design. Divide the class into three groups. Groups 1 and 2 are each subdivided into two more groups, A and B. Sing in this fashion:

Phrases 1 and 2: Group 1A sings the first pat-

Refrain

Fa lank-y down, la lank-y down, Fa la lank-y down dil - ly.

3. This dragon had a plaguey hard hide,
Fa la lanky down dilly,
Which could the strongest steel abide;
Fa la lanky down dilly.
But as the dragon yawning did fall,
He thrust his sword down hilt and all. (*Refrain*)

4. The dragon laid him down and roared,
Fa la lanky down dilly,
The knight was sorry for his sword;
Fa la lanky down dilly.
The sword it was a right good blade,
As ever Turk or Spaniard made. (*Refrain*)

LISTENING

Two Ductiae
Anonymous

Listen to music of long ago.
Then learn to dance as knights and ladies did.

189

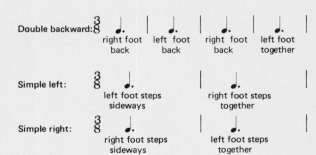

For Your Information

Three of the instruments on the recording of ''Sir Eglamore'' were popular during the Renaissance.

The **rauschpfeife** is a capped double-reed wind instrument with a somewhat nasal tone.

The **cornett** is a type of wooden trumpet with a mellow sound. It is curved in shape and covered in leather.

The **regal organ** is a small reed organ with a characteristic reedy tone.

The instruments are heard in the introduction in the following order: cornett, viola da gamba rauschpfeife, regal organ.

tern; Group 1B sings the second.
Phrase 3: Group 2A sings the first pattern; Group 2B sings the second.
Phrase 4: Group 3 sings the entire refrain.

4. Play the recording of "Two Ductiae." **This is music from long ago, like "Sir Eglamore." What do you think this music was for?** (dancing) Help the students learn the dance:

Formation: Make a double circle of partners.

Introduction: Face partners, bow or curtsey.

3/8 step back | bend knees | straighten knees | feet together |

Dance: Partners join hands and step around the circle using these patterns:

Double forward: **3/8** left foot forward | right foot forward | left foot forward | right foot together |

Double backward: **3/8** right foot back | left foot back | right foot back | left foot together |

Simple left: **3/8** left foot steps sideways | right foot steps together |

Simple right: **3/8** right foot steps sideways | left foot steps together |

Repeat the dance several times.

Lesson Focus

Timbre: The quality of a sound is determined by the sound source.
Form: A series of sounds may form a distinct musical idea within the musical whole.
(D–I)

Materials

○ **Record Information:**
  • Wedding March from *Rustic Wedding Symphony*
    by Carl Goldmark (1830–1915)
    Record 9 Side B Band 6
    The New York Philharmonic
    Leonard Bernstein, conductor
○ **Other:** overhead projector
○ **Teacher's Resource Binder:**
  Activity Sheets • **Activity Sheet 25,** page A36
    (Prepare as a transparency.)
○ **Extends Lesson 27,** page 58

LISTENING

Wedding March
from *Rustic Wedding Symphony*
by Carl Goldmark

Goldmark composed thirteen variations of his wedding march theme. Listen to five of them.

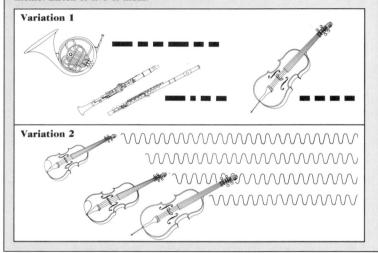

Variation 1

Variation 2

190

The Lesson

1. Ask the students if they have ever been to a wedding. **What kind of music did you hear? What instruments were played?** (Answers will vary.) Discuss the wedding march. Many students will be familiar with "Here Comes the Bride" usually played on the organ. Tell them that they will hear a wedding march but that it might not be familiar, nor will it be played on the organ. **Your first task will be to identify the instruments.** Play the theme.

2. Display the transparency prepared from Activity Sheet 25 (*Theme of "Rustic Wedding Symphony"*). Point out that the class has the skill to follow the parts that the cello and bass play. Play the theme again as the students follow the notation.

3. Play the theme one more time before proceeding to play the variations so that the students may become familiar with the theme. The students may try softly humming the melody as they listen.

4. **Goldmark, the composer, had lots of ideas! He played the theme thirteen more times and he changed something each time so that it would not be boring!** Ask the students to look at the first box on pages 190–191 and predict what might change in Variation 1. (See **For Your Information.**) Play the theme and the first variation.

5. Explain that they will hear the theme and five of the thirteen variations. **As you listen, try to decide what has changed. Can you still hear the theme each time?** Explain that sometimes the theme is varied to the point of being difficult to recognize. This is especially true of Variation 2. Play the theme and its five variations.

OPTIONAL

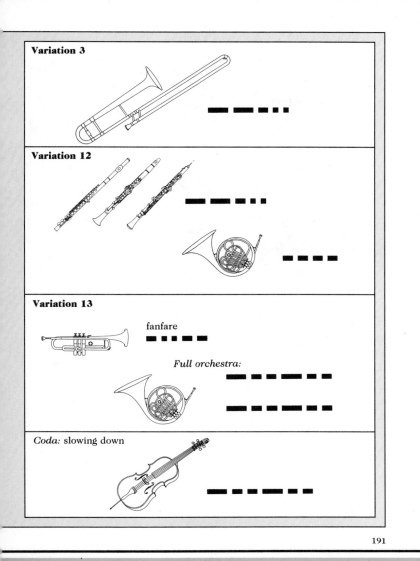

Variation 3

▬▬ ▬▬ ▬ ▬ ▬

Variation 12

▬▬ ▬▬ ▬ ▬ ▬

▬ ▬ ▬ ▬

Variation 13

fanfare

▬ ▬ ▬ ▬

Full orchestra:

▬ ▬ ▬ ▬ ▬ ▬

▬ ▬ ▬ ▬ ▬

Coda: slowing down

▬ ▬ ▬ ▬ ▬

191

For Your Information

The first movement of *Rustic Wedding Symphony* by Carl Goldmark was composed in 1876 and consists of a march and thirteen variations. Only the theme and Variations 1, 2, 3, 12, and 13 are used in this lesson.

The featured instruments are as follows:
  Theme: Cello and basses; moderate tempo
  Var. 1: horns, clarinets, and flutes
  Var. 2: violins, violas, cellos, and basses
  Var. 3: trombones, trumpets, woodwinds, and strings; fast tempo
  Var. 12: woodwinds, strings, and horns; moderate tempo
  Var. 13: entire orchestra

6. Invite the students to identify the instruments that they heard playing during each variation and to comment on other changes they notice. Replay the composition or portions of it to verify the students' answers. (See **For Your Information.**)

Create Music

Lesson Focus

Expression: Musical elements are combined into a whole to express a musical or extramusical idea. *(C–S)*

Materials

○ **Record Information:**
  • *Variations on Pop Goes the Weasel*
    (Record 4 Side B Band 9)
  • *Variations on Pop Goes the Weasel*
    (Record 2 Side A Band 1)

○ **Instruments:** a variety of classroom instruments

○ **Other:** one envelope for each group of up to five students

○ **Teacher's Resource Binder:**

Activity Sheets
  • **Activity Sheets 26a–b,** pages A37–A38 (Make copies of each page. Prepare missions for teams of up to five students by cutting the copies in half.)
  • Optional—
    Curriculum Correlation 11, page C26

○ **Extends Lesson 9,** page 22

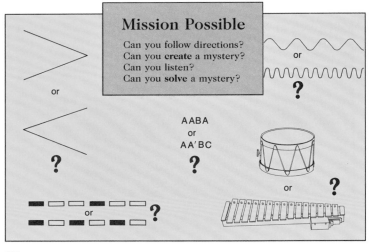

The Lesson

1. Replay *Variations on Hot Cross Buns* (page 92) or *Variations on Pop Goes the Weasel* (page 23). **What decisions did the composer make about this song?** List the students' answers on the chalkboard and review their meanings. *(OPTIONAL)*

2. Draw the students' attention to the title at the middle of page 192. Ask the students if they have ever seen the old television series called "Mission Impossible." Explain that at the beginning of each program the undercover agents received an envelope and a tape recording that described their next mission. On the tape a deep, mysterious voice began by saying, "Your mission, should you decide to accept it, is . . . " and then described the case. The tape always ended with "This tape will self-destruct in five seconds." Smoke then poured from the tape player. **Your task is not impossible! It is called "Mission Possible." Your team will receive an envelope that contains secret directions. Don't reveal them to any other team.**

3. Divide the class into teams of not more than five students. Each team will receive directions about a composition they are to create. Give each team an envelope containing a mission prepared from Activity Sheets 26a–b, *(Mission Possible).* **The secret directions will tell you the kinds of dynamics, tempo, timbre, form, rhythm, meter, melody, and instruments to use in your composition.**

4. Invite each team to perform for the rest of the class. The class should then identify the specific contents of that team's message (*i.e.,* Team 1: Instruments, Form, Dynamics).

Words and Music

Here are some words made into a poem.
Add rhythm and harmony to make a song.

How I Get Cool
by Richard J. Smith

What a hot and muggy day.
I think I'm going to roast.
What a drippy, sweaty day.
I feel like buttered toast.

These concrete steps are sizzly-hot.
They're cooking my backside.
The heat is coming through my soles.
My toes are almost fried.

On days like this, scorchy days,
Here's how I get cool.
I eat three cherry popsicles
And swim in City Pool.

My Puppy
by Richard J. Smith

My puppy can be my very best
friend.
He'll lick me and play games for
hours on end.
Sometimes he'll kiss me right on the
nose,
And try to snuggle under my clothes.

Sometimes I like my puppy a lot.
Sometimes I do and sometimes not.
I guess with my puppy it's good and
it's bad.
He makes me happy, and he makes
me mad.

Add rhythm and melody to make a song.

193

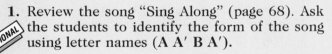

CREATE 2

Lesson Focus
Form: A musical whole may be made up of same, varied, or contrasting segments. *(C–I)*

Materials
○ **Record Information:**
  • Sing Along
    (Record 4 Side A Band 2)
○ **Instruments:** resonator bells or xylophones D,, E,, F,♯, G, A, B, C, and D; bell mallets
○ **Other:** scissors; glue; a pencil for each student
○ **Teacher's Resource Binder:**
  | Activity Sheets | • **Activity Sheet 27,** page A39 (Prepare one copy for each group of three or four students.) |
○ **Extends Lesson 13,** page 31

For Your Information
Possible song forms may include:
A A B A; A A′ B A; A A′ B A″;
A B A C; A B C D

The Lesson

1. Review the song "Sing Along" (page 68). Ask the students to identify the form of the song using letter names (A A′ B A′). *(OPTIONAL)*

2. **Why do you think a composer might repeat musical ideas?** (It gives the song unity; it makes it easier to learn.) **Why might a composer change musical ideas?** (to keep the music interesting) **The woman who wrote "Sing Along" used one form. What other forms might be used for a song?** Invite the students to suggest combinations of same, similar, and different sections. List them on the chalkboard. (See **For Your Information**.) (The first part is always "A." Each subsequent part is given a letter: B, C, D, etc. A similar part is given a prime: A′ or A″.)

3. **Today it is your turn to be a composer.** Read the poems on page 193 together until the stu-

dents sense their rhythmic flow. Explain that the class will work in groups to create a melody for the first verse of one of the poems. They will need to:
• choose a poem;
• decide the form of the song;
• create a melody they like for Phrase 1;
• write a melody with letters or scale numbers (G = 1);
• create melodies for the other phrases, following the form they have chosen.

4. Divide the class into groups of three or four. Give each group copies of Activity Sheet 27 (*Write a Melody*) and a set of bells or a xylophone. (See **Materials**.)

5. Ask each group to perform for the class. The class members are to determine the form that each team uses.

CREATE 3

Lesson Focus

Rhythm: Individual sounds and silences within a rhythmic line may be longer than, shorter than, or the same as other sounds within the line. *(C–I)*

Materials

○ **Instruments:** a variety of percussion instruments

○ **Other:** black marking pens; measuring tape or rulers; several large sheets of wrapping paper at least four feet square (Make two circles on each; include numbers as shown below.)

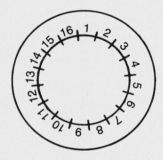

○ **Teacher's Resource Binder:**
   • Optional—
   Mainstreaming Suggestion 13, page M22

○ **Extends Lesson 36**, page 80

Percussion-A-Round

Get ready!

• Draw two circles on a large piece of wrapping paper.

• Divide the inner circle into 16 equal beats. Number them.

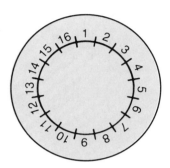

Compose

Make up a 16-count rhythm that sometimes moves

• **with** the shortest sound
• **twice as long** as the shortest sound
• **four times as long** as the shortest sound

Could you use other relationships?
Divide the outer circle into "boxes" of the correct length to show your rhythms. Draw them in.

Perform

Four people may perform this Percussion-A-Round.
Each chooses a different percussion instrument.
Player 1 begins with count 1. When that player reaches 5, **Player 2** begins.
When will **Player 3** begin?
When will **Player 4** begin?

194

The Lesson

1. Divide the class into groups of four. Give each group a large piece of paper on which circles have been drawn. (See **Materials**.)

2. Guide the students to follow the instructions on page 194 of their books and compose a rhythm pattern that lasts for sixteen counts. They should draw the pattern on the paper to show the relationship of each sound to the shortest sound. A completed rhythm might look like this:

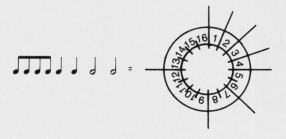

3. To answer the question "Could you use other relationships?," guide the students to conclude that they might have included sounds that were three times as long, five times as long, and so on.

4. When the students have devised their rhythms and drawn them on the circle, they may choose four percussion instruments and perform the "Percussion-A-Round" as directed in their books. Although the group could decide to have Players 3 and 4 begin at any point, in a round all performers usually begin the same number of beats apart. Therefore Player 3 would begin when Player 2 reaches Count 5. Player 4 should begin when Player 3 reaches Count 5.

5. The groups trade circles and try to perform each others' percussion rounds.

194

Make Your Own Instrument

Use ideas on these pages or ideas of your own to make new instruments. There is only one rule! You must be able to play at least two different pitches on your instrument.

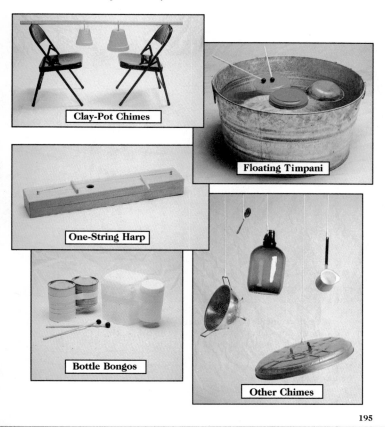

Clay-Pot Chimes

Floating Timpani

One-String Harp

Bottle Bongos

Other Chimes

195

Lesson Focus

Timbre: The quality of a sound is affected by the material, shape, and size of the source.
Timbre: The quality of a sound is affected by the way the sound is produced. *(D–I)*

Materials

○ **Other:** soft and hard mallets; materials for making instruments (See Activity Sheets 28a–c)

○ **Teacher's Resource Binder:**

[Activity Sheets] • **Activity Sheets 28a–c,** pages A40–A42 (Prepare several copies of each page.)
  • Optional—
  Curriculum Correlation 8, page C11
  Mainstreaming Suggestion 13, page M22

○ **Extends Lesson 28, page 60**

The Lesson

1. Discuss the homemade instruments shown on page 195 with the class. Ask the students to give suggestions as to how each instrument might be made and played. **Will your instrument be large or small?**

2. Allow each student to choose the instrument that he or she would like to make. (Or you may wish to make the choice, depending on the materials you have readily available.) Group the students according to the instruments they select and distribute the appropriate materials and copies of Activity Sheets 28a–c (*Make Your Own Instrument*). Remind the students that the one rule is that their instrument must be able to produce at least two different pitches. Caution the students to be especially careful when drilling and using equipment that has sharp blades or points. Supervise them carefully.

3. After each group has created an instrument, ask the members to play for the class. Discuss the difference in quality that occurs when different types of "sound starters" and mallets are used. Encourage the students to take home the activity sheets and make their own instruments, or to develop their own ideas for additional instruments not suggested in the pupil book.

Lesson Focus

Expression: The expressiveness of music is affected by the way timbre contributes to the musical whole. *(C–I)*

Materials

○ **Instruments:** homemade instruments prepared for Create 4, page 195
○ **Teacher's Resource Binder:**
  • Optional—
    Mainstreaming Suggestion 13, page M22
○ **Extends Lesson 28,** page 60

Using Your Instruments

1. Work in small groups. Create a **tone row** composition.

   • Stand side by side in a row. Take turns playing two pitches on each instrument you made to create a "tone row."
   • Can you make a "melody" out of this row? To make your melody, you may repeat pitches, use longer sounds, shorter sounds, or sometimes not play at all.
   • How do the different timbres add interest to your piece? What happens when people change places in the row?

2. Work in small groups. Create a piece using **harmony.**

   • Plan a melody.
   • Choose one or more instruments to play an **ostinato** pattern.
   • Use other instruments with the **ostinato.**
   • Will you use one or both pitches of your instrument?
   • Will you repeat any of your patterns?
   • When should certain **timbres** be heard?
   • How can you use expressive ideas, such as **dynamics, tempo,** and **articulation**?
   • Select one person to conduct the group. Perform the piece for others in the class.

196

The Lesson

1. After the students have made instruments as suggested on page 195, invite them to use their instruments in some of the ways suggested on pages 196–197.

   Organize the students into small groups, each with instruments that they have created. Each group may use the same suggestions for creating pieces, or may be assigned one of the ideas from the pupil pages. Suggestions for each of the ideas follows.

   • Create a composition based on a "tone row." The students should begin by experimenting with the pitches they can produce and deciding the order in which the performers should stand. Continue experimenting until the group is satisfied with the sound of the tone row.

   After the tone row has been agreed upon, the row members should plan their melody. They must keep the same order of tones, but may repeat tones or play them in reverse order. The group must plan the rhythm, using silence as well as sound, and decide how many times the row should be repeated.

   • The second suggestion is to create a piece using harmony. **What must you do to create harmony?** (play two or more pitches at the same time) The group should follow the instructions given in the pupil book and begin by planning a melody to be played on some of the instruments. (It could be the melody developed when following the first suggestion.) Assign other students in the group to play an *ostinato* (a repeated pattern) to produce harmony.

   • The third suggestion in the pupil book is that the students perform as an ensemble. Group at least eight students together and guide

3. Perform as a large ensemble.

- Group instruments of similar **pitch** and **timbre** together.
  Select a conductor/composer.
- Decide what signals the composer should use to tell the group which sounds to perform.

A specific performer should play.

Stop playing.

Play louder.

Everyone should play.

Play softer.

What other signals will you need?

- Perform the piece. How do you like your music?
- What in the music made you feel the way you do about the piece?
- What would you suggest to the conductor to improve or change the music?

197

them to make musical decisions by following the discussion in their books. Choose an individual to conduct who will also act as the composer. That student must make instant decisions as to which sounds should be played, for how long, and whether they should be played loudly or softly.

2. Give the groups about ten minutes to plan and rehearse their compositions. Then have a classroom concert with each group presenting its music for the remainder of the class.

Lesson Focus

Time and Place: The way musical elements are combined into a whole reflects the origin of the music. *(C–I)*

Materials

○ **Record Information:**
- *Tjarabalen*
  Record 9 Side B Band 7
  University of Wisconsin Gamelan
  Andrew Sutton, Director

○ **Instruments:** small drum; cowbell; cymbal; bass xylophone; resonator bells C, D, F♯, and G; large drum; bass metallophone; bell mallets

○ **Other:** world map

○ **Extends Lesson 29,** page 66

For Your Information

Instrumentation of *Tjarabalen* (chah-rah-**bah**-len):
- Two sets of *bonang* (**boe**-nahng), four kettle-shaped gongs suspended in a rack. (The sets are tuned an octave apart.)
- One large and one small gong.
- One *kenong* (kehn-**ong**), a kettle-shaped gong larger than a *bonang* that sits on a rack.

(continued on next page)

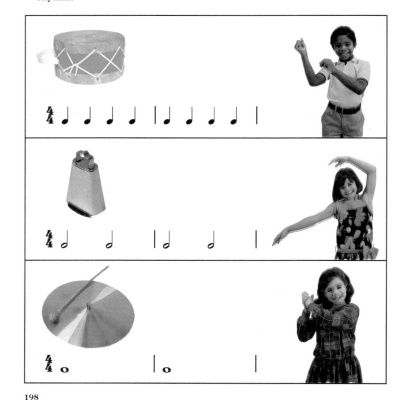

Sound Together

- Work in small groups.
- Choose one of these ideas.
- One person sets up a steady rhythm that moves in groups of four.
- The other people make up movements to match the rhythm.

198

The Lesson

1. Read the instructions on pupil page 198 together. Discuss the way each of the rhythm patterns moves in relation to the shortest sound.

   Pattern 1 (drum) twice as long
   Pattern 2 (cowbell) four times a slong
   Pattern 3 (cymbal) eight times as long
   Pattern 4 (bass xylophone) four times as long and twice as long
   Pattern 5 (resonator bells) shortest sound

   Practice chanting the rhythm of each pattern, using a different syllable for each:

   Resonator Bells: *dee*
   Drum: *buh*
   Cowbell: *ling*
   Cymbal: *shhh*
   Bass Xylophone: *pin*

2. Divide the class into five groups. Assign one of the patterns shown on pages 198–199 to each group. Give one student in each group the appropriate instrument. As they plan their parts, ask the students to think about the following:

   - How can the player play the instrument in different ways to produce different qualities of sound while still playing the correct rhythm?
   - How can the movers devise interesting movements in relation to the rhythm patterns, using different levels and different directions? (Give the movers the rule that they may move about, but they must always be within four steps of the player.)

3. When each group has prepared its pattern, choose one student to be the conductor of the entire ensemble. The conductor sets the tempo for the shortest sound and indicates to each group when it should begin and end its performance.

When each group has planned its part, put them together as an ensemble.

LISTENING

Tjarabalen
Javanese Folk Melody

Listen! Do you hear any of the patterns you played?

199

For Your Information (continued)
• *One kendang* (**kehn**-dahng), a large and small drum that rests horizontally on a stand.

Form of *Tjarabalen:*

Introduction: Played on drum (lasts four pulses).

Main Section: Three repeated sets of four *gongan.* (A *gongan* is a phrase that ends with the sound of a gong. Every fourth *gongan* ends with the sound of a large gong. In this piece, one *gongan* is eight pulses long.)

1) lower *bonang* does not play yet, ends with small gong
2) lower *bonang* is added; ends with small gong
3) ends with small gong
4) ends with large gong*
1 and 2) end with small gong
3) tempo gets faster, ends with small gong
4) faster tempo continues, ends with large gong*
1 — 3) end with small gong
4) tempo slows slightly; ends with large gong*

*(not shown in score on pupil page 200)

Ending: One *gongan*—ends with decided *ritard.*

4. **Listen to some music. Do you hear any of the patterns that you performed?** Play *Tjarabalen.* (See **For your Information.**) As the students listen, they may recognize that the melodic patterns in *Tjarabalen* are similar in shape and rhythm to the patterns they played on the xylophone and resonator bells. The rhythms of the gongs are similar to the patterns the students played on the cowbell and cymbal.

5. Explain to the students that this music is played by a *gamelan* (**gah**-muh-lahn), an orchestra from the island of Java. One of the instruments used in a gamelan, the bonang, is shown on page 199. Discuss each of the gamelan instruments with the students and identify the part that each plays. (See **For Your Information.**) Play the recording again for the class and invite them to lightly tap one of the instrument's rhythms as they listen.

OPTIONAL

CREATE 7

Create Your Own Gamelan Music

Lesson Focus

Texture: Musical quality is affected by the number and degree of contrast between musical lines occuring simultaneously. *(C–I)*

Materials

○ **Record Information:**
- *Tjarabalen*
  (Record 9 Side B Band 7)

○ **Instruments:** bass metallophone A and B; alto glockenspiel D and E; bell mallets; cymbal and soft mallet; two drums of different sizes; two gongs—one large and one small (or large metal pot lids)

○ **Other:** a pencil for each student; overhead projector; overhead pen

○ **Teacher's Resource Binder:**

[Activity Sheets] • **Activity Sheet 29,** page A43 (Prepare one transparency.)

○ **Extends Lesson 20,** page 44

Listen to *Tjarabalen* again.
This time follow the score.
After you have listened, create your own gamelan music.

The Introduction

Main Pulse	1 +	2 +	3 +	4 +	5 +	6 +	7 +	8 +
Bonang (lower)	•	•	•	•	•	•	•	$\frac{5}{1}$
Bonang (higher)	•	•	•	•	•	•	•	
Drum	•	•	•	•	H	H	H H	L H
Kenong	•	•	•	•	•	•	•	K
Gong	•	•	•	•	•	•	•	G

The Main Section is made up of eleven statements of this pattern.

	1	2	3	4	5	6	7	8
Bonang (lower)	•	$\frac{5}{1}$	2 4	$\frac{5}{1}$	2 4	$\frac{5}{1}$	2 4	$\frac{5}{1}$
Bonang (higher)	5 1 2 4	5 1 2 4	5 1 2 4	5 1 2 4	5 1 2 4	5 1 2 4	5 1 2 4	5 1 2 4
Drum	H H	H H	L H	H H	L H	H L	H H	L H
Kenong	•	K	•	K	•	K	•	K
Gong	•	•	•	•	•	•	•	g

The Ending

	1	2	3	4	5	6	7	8
Bonang (lower)	•	$\frac{5}{1}$	2 4	$\frac{5}{1}$	2 4	$\frac{5}{1}$	2 4	$\frac{5}{1}$
Bonang (higher)	5 1 2 4	5 1 2 4	5 1 2 4	5 1 2 4	5 1 2 4	5 1 2 4	5 1 2 4	$\frac{5}{1}$
Drum	H H	L H	L H	H L	H H	L	H H	•
Kenong	•	K	•	K	•	K	•	K
Gong	•	•	•	•	•	•	•	G

Key:

+ = main pulse	G = large gong	• = rest	4 = D
H = high-pitched drum	g = small gong	1 = A	5 = E
L = low-pitched drum	K = kenong	2 = B	

200

The Lesson

1. **Turn to page 200. This is a score of the music from Java we heard during our last class. Can you follow this score as we listen again? Choose one of the instruments in the left column and move your hand along its line in the score as you listen.** Play the recording. Softly count the numbered pulses as the music proceeds. Help the students realize that each pulse lasts for four short sounds. (See **For Your Information** on page 198 for guidance in following the score.)

2. **Today we will create our own music.** Display the transparency of Activity Sheet 29 (*Our Gamelan Music*). Explain to the student that they will use instruments similar to those they heard in *Tjarabalen*. (See **Materials**.) Begin by deciding how many instruments should play the introduction. Fill in the names of those instruments after each number.

3. Choose students to create melodies and/or rhythms (depending on the instrument chosen) for the introduction while another student sets the pulse by chanting the numbers. When the parts have been planned, write them in the appropriate box. A score for one instrument might look like this:

	1	2	3	4	5	6	7	8
1. Instrument (Triangle)	X		X			X		

4. Follow the same procedure to plan the main section and coda. Give other students the opportunity to play the instruments and to experiment with tempo and dynamic changes.

Create a **movement** for this suite.
Choose a title.
Make your music suggest the idea of the title.

201

Lesson Focus
Expression: The expressiveness of music is affected by the way form contributes to the musical whole. *(C–I)*

Materials
○ **Record Information:**
- *Acadian Songs and Dances* (excerpt) **(Record 2 Side B Band 7)**
- Papa's Tune from *Acadian Songs and Dances* **(Record 5 Side B Band 2)**
- Chorale from *Louisiana Story* **(Record 5 Side B Band 3)**

○ **Instruments:** a wide variety of pitched and nonpitched classroom instruments; set up pitched instruments with any combination of pitches C, D, E, F♯, G♯, and B♭ (which form a whole tone scale)

○ **Other:** tape recorder and blank tape

○ **Extends Lesson 57, page 124**

The Lesson
1. Listen again to the excerpts from *Acadian Songs and Dances* and *Chorale* by Virgil Thomson (pages 42 and 104). Explain that these are just three sections from a long work that was used as background music for a movie called *Louisiana Story.*

   Explain that a suite is a set of related pieces consisting of short sections that may suggest a story or idea. A suite may consist of a set of dances or may combine music from a stage work or musical. **When several short pieces are combined into a long work, we call it a *suite.* Each section is called a *movement.***

2. **Today, we are going to create a suite! Ours will be an "Unsweet Suite."** Discuss the title on page 201. (All snacks are not sweet.)

3. Suggest dances for the fruits and vegetables: a *march* for the ears of corn; a *waltz* for the broccoli; a peanut-butter *stomp;* a celery-stalk *samba;* an orange-juice *drip.* Discuss special musical effects that might express the idea of each dance. (a drum to keep the beat in the march; *staccato* for the drip, etc.). *[OPTIONAL]*

4. Divide the class into groups of four or five and assign each a dance movement of the suite. Provide a wide variety of instruments from which they may select. Ask the groups to write down and rehearse their movement.

5. Call the groups back together and ask each to share its movement with the rest of the class. Create a suite by performing the movements in a series, without interruption. Tape record the final performance.

CREATE 9

Lesson Focus

Form: A musical whole may be made up of same, varied, or contrasting segments. *(C–I)*

Materials

- **Instruments:** hand drum or woodblock; mallet; finger cymbals, bongo drums; resonator bells; bell mallet
- **Extends Lesson 42,** page 92

Theme and Variations on a Handshake

Greet your friend. Shake hands. Try variations on handshakes.

| Theme | Variation 1 | Variation 2 |

Create a "Theme and Variation on a Handshake for 16 Dancers."

Introduction: Two people walk toward each other.
Theme: Greet each other, shaking hands in the usual way.
Interlude: These two people walk to greet two new people.
Variation 1: These four people shake hands. Use the first variation pictured above.
Interlude: These four people greet four new people.
Variation 2: These eight people shake hands. Use the second variation pictured above.

Create two more variations. Add the interlude between each. Can you think of other ways to shake hands? Can you change the **rhythm** of your handshakes? the **tempo**?

202

The Lesson

1. To help the students further their understanding of theme and variations, invite them to explore ways that a handshake (the theme) might be varied.

2. Ask the students to follow the instructions on page 202 of their books for creating a "Theme and Variation on a Handshake for 16 Dancers."

3. Give the dancers a few minutes to plan their variations and share them with the class. Then add instruments to the performance. One student may choose a drum or woodblock to accompany the walking sounds of the introduction and interludes. The class should decide how long the walk should last and whether the rhythm pattern will move in twos, threes, or fours. This sound should be repeated for all interludes.

4. A second student may choose another instrument to accompany the handshake, such as finger cymbals, bongo drum, or two resonator bells. **What rhythm will you use? Will your pattern move the same way as the walking sound, or will it be different? How long should the handshake theme last?** (two to four measures)

5. Use a different performer and a different instrument sound for each new variation. Each performer should decide whether to play the rhythm pattern developed in Step 4 or to vary it. The players should watch the dancers closely so that their sounds express the feeling of the movement being performed.

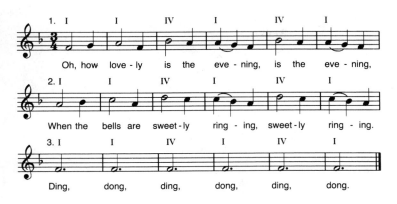

Lovely Evening

Traditional Round

1. I   I   IV   I   IV   I

Oh, how love-ly is the eve-ning, is the eve-ning,

2. I   I   IV   I   IV   I

When the bells are sweet-ly ring-ing, sweet-ly ring-ing.

3. I   I   IV   I   IV   I

Ding, dong, ding, dong, ding, dong.

Sing each "ladder." Think the missing steps.

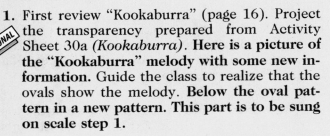

Scale   I Chord   IV Chord

Compose a harmonizing part for "Lovely Evening." When will you use the notes of the I chord? the IV chord?

203

Lesson Focus

Harmony: Chords and melody may move simultaneously in relation to each other. *(C–I)*

Materials

○ **No Piano Accompaniment**

○ **Record Information:**
  • Kookaburra
    (Record 1 Side B Band 1
  • Lovely Evening
    Record 9 Side B Band 8
    Voices: children's choir
    Accompaniment: French horn, English horn, harp, bells

○ **Instruments:** resonator bells F, A, B♭, C, and D; bell mallets; autoharp

○ **Other:** overhead projector

○ **Teacher's Resource Binder:**
  • **Activity Sheets 30a–b,** pages A44–A45 (Prepare one transparency from each page and cut transparency 31b on the dotted lines.)
  • **Activity Sheet 31,** page A46 (Prepare one copy for each student.)
  • Optional—
    Kodaly Activity 13, page K19

○ **Extends Lesson 20,** page 44

The Lesson

1. First review "Kookaburra" (page 16). Project the transparency prepared from Activity Sheet 30a *(Kookaburra)*. **Here is a picture of the "Kookaburra" melody with some new information.** Guide the class to realize that the ovals show the melody. **Below the oval pattern in a new pattern. This part is to be sung on scale step 1.**

   Divide the class into two groups. As Group 1 sings the melody, Group 2 should sing the harmony part. Add an autoharp accompaniment, strumming once per measure: **D A7 D D.** (Play the sequence four times.)

2. Leave the transparency of Activity Sheet 30a in place and overlay it with transparency 30b. **What do you now see?** (two more parts to be performed with the melody) Draw attention to the fact that the added parts sometimes include pitches from the melody. **While the parts move back and forth between only two pitches, the melody skips from part to part.**

3. Divide the class into four groups. Group 1 sings the melody, Group 2 sings Part 1, starting on scale step 5, and Group 3 sings Part 2, starting on scale step 3. Group 4 sings the drone on scale step 1 (or it could be played on a D bell).

4. Ask the students to turn to page 203 and learn the melody for "Lovely Evening." Then read the instructions at the bottom of the page and practice singing the ladder patterns.

5. Distribute Activity Sheet 31 *(Create a Harmony Part).* **Can you compose a harmony part to fit with "Lovely Evening"? Each ladder is three beats. Circle one number in each ladder to create your part.** Ask individuals to perform the part they have composed, while the class sings the melody.

203

Lesson Focus

Expression: Musical elements are combined into a whole to express a musical or extramusical idea. *(C–I)*

Materials

○ **No Piano Accompaniment**

○ **Record Information:**
  • Lovely Evening
    (Record 9 Side B Band 8)
  • The Bremen Town Musicians
    Record 9 Side B Band 9
    Voices: children's choir
    Accompaniment: electric guitar, electric bass, electric piano, percussion

○ **Instruments:** autoharp; resonator bells C, D, E, F, G, A, B, and C′; bell mallets

○ **Other:** overhead projector; overhead pen

○ **Teacher's Resource Binder:**

  Activity Sheets
  • **Activity Sheets 32a–b,** pages A47–A48 (Prepare one copy for each student and prepare as transparencies.)
  • Optional—
    Curriculum Correlation 10, page C15

○ **Extends Lesson 2, page 8**

The Bremen Town Musicians

Traditional Story

Once there was a donkey who lived on a farm. The donkey was getting too old to work anymore, so the farmer thought he would sell the donkey and buy a younger one who could help with the farm work. The old donkey was very sad and decided to run away to Bremen to become a musician. After all, he had a fine voice.

"Listen to my donkey song:
Hee-haw, hee-haw, hee!
I sing it all the whole day long,
Hee-haw, hee-haw, hee!"

As he slowly walked down the road toward Bremen, he met a very sad dog. "What's wrong?" he asked.

"I'm too old to be a watchdog;
I'm too old to hunt;
But I'm not too old to sing a song,
Bow, wow, wow!"

"Why don't you come to Bremen with me? We can sing together." So the dog and the donkey went down the road to Bremen together.

204

The Lesson

1. Read the script on pupil pages 204–207 with the class. Some students may be familiar with the story.

2. Tell the class that they are going to develop a composition based on this story. They will need to create a melody for each of the four songs identified in the story. Display the transparencies of Activity Sheets 32a–b *(The Bremen Town Musicians)* as the students listen to the story. **As you listen, think about possible melodies that would fit with the chords you hear and that would help express the ideas of the words.**

3. Remind the class of when they sang "Lovely Evening" (page 203) and created a harmonizing part to fit the melody. Explain that this time they will do just the opposite: The harmony, words, and rhythm have been given; they will need to create a melody to go with them.

Divide the class into four groups, each of which will compose a melody for one of the songs. Hand out copies of Activity Sheets 32a or 32b to each group.

4. Draw attention to the chords shown at the top of each activity sheet. Explain to the students that they must usually choose pitches for their melody from the chord, although they may also occasionally use *passing tones* (tones that do not belong to the chord). Remind the students that they must choose a pitch for every note shown in the rhythm pattern.

5. Give the students time to work on their patterns. Suggest that when they have worked out the melody, they should write the letter or scale number above each note so that they

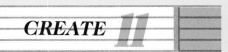
It wasn't long until they met a cat. The cat had a beautiful meow, so the donkey said, "Wouldn't you like to come to Bremen with us to become a musician?"

"I'm too old to catch mice now;
I like to sit in the sun.
I sing with a beautiful meow—
Let's go, we'll all have fun."

As the three new friends continued toward Bremen, they passed a farm. On the fence post sat a rooster. He had such a wonderful voice, they decided to ask him to join them.

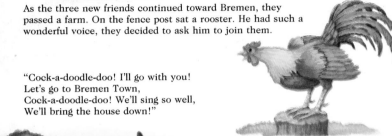

"Cock-a-doodle-doo! I'll go with you!
Let's go to Bremen Town,
Cock-a-doodle-doo! We'll sing so well,
We'll bring the house down!"

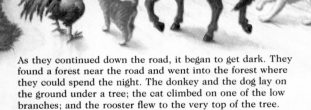

As they continued down the road, it began to get dark. They found a forest near the road and went into the forest where they could spend the night. The donkey and the dog lay on the ground under a tree; the cat climbed on one of the low branches; and the rooster flew to the very top of the tree.

205

can remember their melody. If time allows and the students know the names of the lines and spaces, they may wish to notate their melody on the staff.

6. When all have finished, invite the students to play their ideas on the resonator bells. To make sure that the melody fits the harmony, play the autoharp while members of each group play their respective melodies. The class may decide if the pitches are appropriate and fit with the accompaniment.

7. When all four melodies are complete, notate them on the transparencies. Invite the class to sing them with the recorded accompaniment.

8. Select actors for each part. Dramatize the complete story, adding the songs at appropriate places. For the finale, two or more of the

songs might be combined. (The ability of fourth graders to do this will depend on their experience as independent singers.)

OPTIONAL

Before they had gone to sleep for the night, the rooster noticed a light through the trees. The rooster flew down and said, "There must be a house on the other side of the trees; I see a light. Perhaps there will be a barn we can sleep in." The four of them set off toward the light the rooster had seen.

They went closer to the house and the rooster, the cat, and the dog all climbed on the donkey's back so they could see better. Inside the house was a band of robbers. The four friends began to make loud sounds:

"Hee-haw!"
"Bow-wow!"
"Me-ow!"
"Cock-a-doodle-doo!"

The robbers were so frightened, they ran to the woods to hide. The four friends went inside the house and found a fine dinner that the robbers had not yet eaten, and they ate until they were full. Then they all found comfortable places to sleep. The donkey lay on the floor near the door, the cat on a rug in front of the fireplace, the dog next to the cat, and the rooster on a beam near the ceiling.

After a while, the robbers came back. The donkey began to bray and kick, the dog began to bark, the cat began to hiss, and the rooster angrily flew around their heads. This time, the robbers were so frightened that they ran away and never came back.

206

The four friends lived in the house and often went to the nearby town of Bremen to give concerts in the park. They sang together in beautiful harmony. First the donkey:

"Listen to my donkey song: Hee-haw, hee-haw, hee!
I sing it all the whole day long, Hee-haw, hee-haw, hee!"
Then the dog: "I'm too old to be a watchdog;
I'm too old to hunt;
But I'm not too old to sing a song, Bow, wow, wow!"
Then the cat:
"I'm too old to catch mice now; I like to sit in the sun.
I sing with a beautiful meow—Let's go, we'll all have fun."
Then the rooster:
"Cock-a-doodle-doo! I'll go with you!
Let's go to Bremen town,
Cock-a-doodle-doo! We'll sing so well,
We'll bring the house down!"

Then they all sang together at the same time.
If you ever visit Bremen, you may be lucky enough to hear them.

207

Lesson Focus

Expression: Musical elements are combined into a whole to express a musical or extramusical idea. *(C–I)*

Materials

○ **Instruments:** a variety of percussion instruments; resonator bells; bell mallets; autoharp

○ **Other:** paper and a pencil for each student; radio (or ten-minute tape recording of a radio program); tape recorder; blank tape

○ **Extends Lesson 28,** page 60

Create Your Own Radio Program

208

The Lesson

1. **Can you imagine life without a radio? Name some times when you listen to a radio.** After students have responded, ask them to turn to pages 208–209 and identify the various types of broadcasting activities that might be taking place. Invite them to name some things that they hear on a radio (music, commercials, news, sports, weather, traffic reports, etc.). List the answers on the chalkboard.

2. **Let's listen to the radio!** Distribute paper and a pencil to each student. **Check the chalkboard list. Write what you hear in the order that you hear it.** Play approximately ten minutes.

3. Divide the class into groups of four. **We're going to put together a radio show!** Write the following subjects on the chalkboard. Each group should choose from among them.

- Rehearse a song to sing.
- Rehearse a piece of music to play on bells or autoharp.
- Write a commercial about an imaginary product. Create the script and the musical sound effects (for example, a waterproof wig).
- Create a report about a composer.
- Create a piece of music entitled "Baseball in the Summer" or another chosen topic.
- Write a traffic report for a busy day. Create background music.
- Write a mystery segment. (Students should check topics with the teacher.)
- Plan the order of the radio broadcast and create dialogue that will connect the segments.

4. Give the groups ample time to plan and experiment. **We may not finish today. Write down your ideas so that we can pick up at the be-**

209

For Your Information

Although the students listen to the radio for hours, they may not be attentive to the details of a broadcast. Arrange to tape record a portion of a radio program, or bring in a radio and play a ten-minute broadcast segment for the class.

ginning of the next class where we left off today. We'll tape record the program when you're ready. What will our call letters be?

Lesson Focus

Expression: Musical elements are combined into a whole to express a musical or extramusical idea. *(P–S)*

Materials

- **Piano Accompaniment:** page 348
- **Record Information:**
  - This Is My Country
  - **Record 10 Side A Band 1**
    Voices: children's choir
    Accompaniment: small show orchestra
- **Extends Lesson 31,** page 70

For Your Information
Old Glory

from *This Is My Country*
by Don Raye

What diff'rence if I hail from North or South,
or from the East or West?
My heart is filled with love for all of these.
I only know I swell with pride and deep within my breast,
I thrill to see "Old Glory" paint the breeze.

Chords not shown on pupil page

Special Times

This Is My Country

Words by Don Raye   Music by Al Jacobs

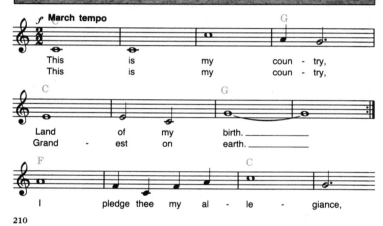

This   is   my   coun - try,
This   is   my   coun - try,

Land   of   my   birth. _____
Grand - est   on   earth. _____

I   pledge thee my   al - le -   giance,

210

The Lesson

1. Perform a patriotic chant. Invite the students to join you in softly tapping a steady beat on their knees. Ask them to take turns rhythmically chanting the names of as many states as they can, while all continue to tap the beat.

   When no one can name any more states, speak the poem "Old Glory" for the class. (See **For Your Information.**) Then ask the students to return to their rhythmic chanting, this time saying words that relate to the flag, such as "red," "blue," "white," "stars," "stripes," "Betsy Ross," etc.

2. *(OPTIONAL)* Ask the students to follow the music for the song "This Is My Country" on pages 210–211 of their books as they listen to the recording. Be sure they remember to pay attention to the repeat sign at the end of the second phrase.

3. Draw attention to the big skip from the word *is* to *my*. **If the bottom note is scale step 1, what is the scale step for the top note?** (high 1) Identify this skip as an *octave*. Suggest to the students that they "sing the melody in their minds" as they listen again, paying particular attention to the octave skip.

4. Adjust the balance on the record player so that only the accompaniment is heard and invite the students to sing the song. Encourage the children to take a nice deep breath before singing.

A - mer - i - ca, _____ the bold. _____

For this is my coun - try,

To have and to hold. _____ *Fine*

Verse **Slower and more freely**

What dif-f'rence if I hail from North or South, or from the East or West?

My heart is filled with love for all of these.

I on - ly know I swell with pride and deep with - in my breast,

I thrill to see "Old Glo - ry" paint the breeze. Oh, *D.C. al Fine*

211

Lesson Focus

Expression: Musical elements are combined into a whole to express a musical or extramusical idea. *(P–S)*

Materials

○ **Piano Accompaniment:** page 350
○ **Record Information:**
  • Birthday Hallelujah
    Record 10 Side A Band 2
    Voices: children's choir
    Accompaniment: alto flute, harp, synthesizer, percussion
○ **Instruments:** cowbell; cymbals; hand drum; bongo drums; sand blocks; brushes
○ **Teacher's Resource Binder:**
  • Optional—
    Kodaly Activity 5, page K8
○ **Extends Lesson 25,** page 54

I'm Thankful

By Jack Prelutsky

I'm thankful for my baseball bat,
I cracked it yesterday.
I'm thankful for my checker set,
I haven't learned to play.
I'm thankful for my mittens,
One is missing in the snow.
I'm thankful for my hamsters,
They escaped a month ago.

I'm thankful for my basketball,
It's sprung another leak.
I'm thankful for my parakeet,
It bit me twice last week.
I'm thankful for my bicycle,
I crashed into a tree.
I'm thankful for my roller skates,
I fell and scraped my knee.

I'm thankful for my model plane,
It's short a dozen parts.
I'm thankful for my target game,
I'm sure I'll find the darts.
I'm thankful for my bathing suit,
It came off in the river.
I'm thankful for so many things,
Except, of course, for liver!

Birthday Hallelujah

Words and Music by Malvina Reynolds

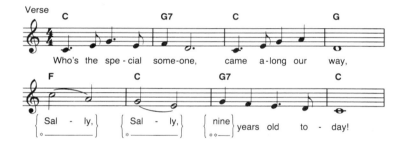

Verse

Who's the spe-cial some-one, came a-long our way,
Sal - ly, Sal - ly, nine years old to - day!

*Insert the name of the person who is celebrating a birthday.
**Insert the age of the person who is celebrating a birthday.

212

The Lesson

1. Introduce this lesson on someone's birthday. Through classroom discussion, help the students understand the importance of celebrating birthdays—not because we get presents, but because the birthday person is special. Begin the class by reading the poem "I'm Thankful" on page 212. Use this poem to reinforce the idea that birthday toys and presents may soon be broken or gone, but the important part of birthdays remains: enjoying other people and knowing that they care.

The students will enjoy the humor of the poem. You may wish to help them learn it by listening to you read it. Invite them to first join in on the "asides" (the phrases in italics), and then to speak the entire poem.

2. Play the recording of "Birthday Hallelujah" and discuss the song. Ask the following ques-

tions, replaying the recording as needed: **How many sections make up this song?** (two: verse and refrain) **How many phrases are there in each section?** (four in the verse; three in the refrain) **Are any of the phrases the same?** (Phrases 1 and 3, and Phrases 2 and 4 of the verse are the same. In the refrain, each phrase is different.) **What kind of mood does the song create? Is it the same for both the verse and the refrain?** (The mood is different; the verse is more "thoughtful"; the refrain is more "joyous.") **What helps to make the difference in mood?** (The verse is sung smoothly, *legato,* and softly, and the accompanying instruments are light and "sweet." The refrain is more detached, *staccato,* and louder, and the voices and instruments have a brighter quality.)

3. Invite the students to sing the song, inserting the appropriate person's name and age in Phrases 2, 4, and 7.

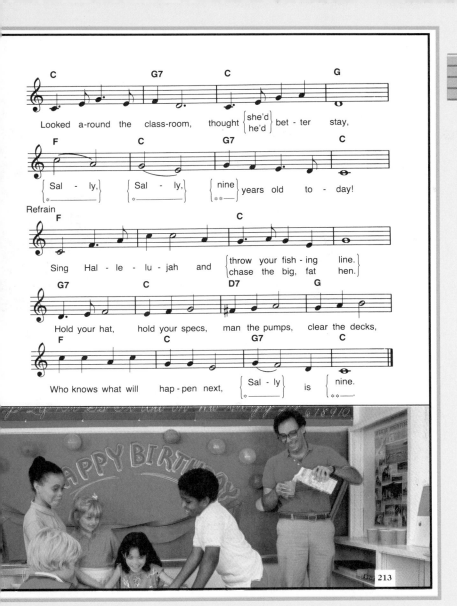

C | G7 | C | G

Looked a-round the class-room, thought {she'd/he'd} bet-ter stay,

F | C | G7 | C

{Sal - ly,} {Sal - ly,} {nine} years old to - day!

Refrain

F | C

Sing Hal - le - lu - jah and {throw your fish-ing line./chase the big, fat hen.}

G7 | C | D7 | G

Hold your hat, hold your specs, man the pumps, clear the decks,

F | C | G7 | C

Who knows what will hap - pen next, {Sal - ly} is {nine.

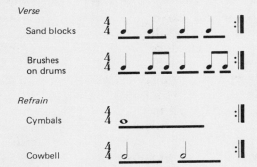

4. Several students may choose instruments to accompany each of the sections as they sing the song again. (The birthday girl or boy may have first choice.) Encourage the students to think about the mood of each section as they make their decisions. Some possible patterns are suggested below.

Verse

Sand blocks

Brushes on drums

Refrain

Cymbals

Cowbell

SPECIAL TIMES 3

Lesson Focus

Form: A musical whole may be made up of same, varied, or contrasting segments. *(D–S)*

Materials

- **Piano Accompaniment:** page 352
- **Record Information:**
  - Sing a Rainbow
  - **Record 10 Side A Band 3**
    Voices: solo child, children's choir
    Accompaniment: small show orchestra
- **Instruments:** bass metallophone or resonator bells F, G, A, B♭, C, and D; bell mallets
- **Other:** sheets of red, yellow, pink, green, purple, orange, and blue construction paper (enough for one colored sheet for each student); one sheet of white construction paper for each student
- **Extends Lesson 47,** page 104

Sing a Rainbow

Words and Music by Arthur Hamilton

Brightly

Red and yel-low and pink and green, pur-ple and o-range and blue,

I can sing a rain-bow, sing a rain-bow, sing a rain-bow, too.

Lis-ten with your eyes; lis-ten with your eyes and sing ev-ery-thing you see.

You can sing a rain-bow, sing a rain-bow, sing a-long with me.

214

The Lesson

1. Arrange one sheet of each color of construction paper in the chalk tray in random order. (See **Materials.**) Play the recording of "Sing a Rainbow." Ask the class to listen quietly without opening their books.

2. **Do you think you can put the colors in the order you heard them in the song?** Call on one or more students to recall the color sequence and arrange the sheets accordingly. Listen to the song again (still with books closed) to check the sequence.

3. Tell the class to look at the song on pages 214–215. **How many phrases do you see?** (six) **Are any of them alike or almost alike?** (The first two are almost like the last two.)

4. Distribute one sheet of any color and one sheet of white paper to each student. Have the students hold the two sheets back to back so they can flip the sheets to show either a colored sheet or a white sheet. **Have you ever seen a "card section" at a football or basketball game? Sometimes a group of people use large cards to show the rest of the audience a message. They often hold up cards to spell out words or to draw a picture. We're going to use our cards to show which parts of the song describe the colors of the rainbow and which parts describe something different.**

5. As you play the recording again, have the students hold up their colored papers as the word corresponding to their color is sung and continue to hold them up until the beginning of Phrase 3. The students should then flip their papers over to expose the white sheet. At the end of Phrase 4, indicate to the class to lower their papers and repeat the process of displaying the colors as they hear the remaining

F   Gm   Am   F7   B♭   F   Gm   C7

Red and yel-low and pink and green, pur-ple and o-range and blue. Now

F   B♭   F   Gm   F   C7   F

we can sing a rain-bow,   sing a rain-bow,   sing a rain-bow, too. __

Add this pattern on bass metallophone or resonator bells.

215

phrases. (This activity may be used during a performance for parents with the students arranged in an arc like a rainbow.)

6. Invite the class to sing the song as they continue to describe the form as well as the words with the papers.

7. Add the chord-root pattern at the bottom of page 215. Choose as many students as there are instruments available to perform the harmonizing pattern while the remainder of the class sings and continues to flip the papers to show the form.

OPTIONAL

SPECIAL TIMES 4

Lesson Focus

Expression: Musical elements are combined into a whole to express a musical or extramusical idea. *(P–I)*

Materials

○ **Piano Accompaniment:** page 367

○ **Record Information:**
  • Hallowe'en
    Record 10 Side A Band 4
    Voices: children's choir
    Accompaniment: woodwind quintet

○ **Instruments:** resonator bells for the D minor scale (D, E, F, G, A, B♭, C, and D'); bell mallets; autoharp; castanets or claves; finger cymbals, maracas or drum

○ **Extends Lesson 55,** page 120

The Lesson

1. Challenge the students to learn "Hallowe'en" by reading the music on page 216. Begin by looking for places that move by skips (the beginning of each phrase) and steps (most of the rest of the melody). Guide the students to use their knowledge of pitch letter names to identify the resonator bells needed to play this song. Ask one student to place them in a row from low to high and play the resulting pattern. Identify it as a minor scale.

2. Practice singing the skip up; 5–1', and the skip down; 5–1. Then encourage the students to sightsing as much of the song as possible. Listen to the recording to correct any errors in melody or rhythm.

3. Invite the students to add to the eerie nature of the performance. Ask them to name terms that remind them of Hallowe'en (scary ghosts, goblins, etc.). Chant the words over and over to develop an interesting rhythm pattern and then chant that pattern in a mysterious voice. Some students may chant while others sing the song.

4. Transfer the rhythm patterns to percussion instruments. Some possible patterns follow:

Funeral March of a Marionette
by Charles Gounod

A

B

C

217

Lesson Focus

Form: A musical whole may be made up of same, varied, or contrasting segments.
Form: A musical whole may include an introduction, interludes, and an ending segment. *(D–I)*

Materials

○ **Record Information:**
- Funeral March of a Marionette by Charles Gounod (goo-noh), 1818–1893
  Record 10 Side A Bands 5a–d
  The Philadelphia Orchestra
  Eugene Ormandy, conductor

○ **Other:** a pencil for each student

○ **Teacher's Resource Binder:**
  Activity Sheets • **Activity Sheet 33,** page A49 (Prepare one copy for each student.)

○ **Extends Lesson 11,** page 26

For Your Information

"Funeral March of a Marionette":
Band a: Theme A   **Band b:** Theme B
Band c: Theme C   **Band d:** Entire Piece
"Funeral March of a Marionette" form:
1. Introduction   4. Theme B   7. Interlude
2. Theme A   5. Theme A   8. Theme A
3. Interlude   6. Theme C   9. Coda

The Lesson

1. Ask the students to open their books to page 217 and follow Theme A as you play Band a of the recording. Some students may recognize it as the theme from the television program "The Alfred Hitchcock Hour."

2. Distribute a copy of Activity Sheet 33 (*Funeral March of a Marionette*) and a pencil to each student. **This time I will play the complete composition. You will hear nine numbers called out as you listen. Which of the nine sections are made up mostly of the theme you just heard, Theme A?** Tell the students to write the letter "A" in each puzzle piece that features Theme A. Play Band d of the recording. (See **For Your Information** for correct answers.)

3. Play the recording of Themes B and C (Bands b and c) as the students follow the contours in their books. **Each of these themes is heard in one of the nine sections of the piece. As you listen again, decide in which section each theme is heard. Write the letters *B* and *C* in the correct puzzle pieces on your activity sheets.**

4. Explain that the class has been identifying the *main* melodies in this composition, but sometimes there is other music that helps the piece get started, get from one section to another, or bring the composition to an end. **Listen again and write the words *introduction, interlude,* and *coda* on your activity sheets where you think they belong.**

5. Play the recording a final time to allow the students to check their answers.

217

Lesson Focus

Harmony: Two or more musical lines may occur simultaneously. *(P–S)*

Materials

○ **No Piano Accompaniment**

○ **Record Information:**
 • Praise and Thanksgiving
 Record 10 Side A Band 6
 Voices: boys' choir (*a capella*)

○ **Instruments:** resonator bells, glockenspiels, and/or xylophones (three instruments are needed) F, G, A, B, C, and D; three bell mallets

○ **Teacher's Resource Binder:**
 • Optional—
 Kodaly Activity 6, page K10

○ **Extends Lesson 50,** page 110

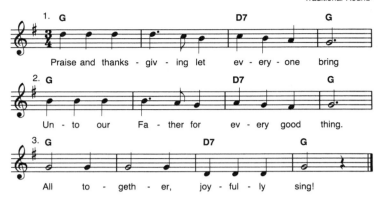

Praise and Thanksgiving

Traditional Round

1. Praise and thanks - giv - ing let ev - ery - one bring

2. Un - to our Fa - ther for ev - ery good thing.

3. All to - geth - er, joy - ful - ly sing!

218

The Lesson

1. Help the students review the way tones within a melody may move in relation to a tonal center. **In the song on page 218, the home tone is on the second line of the staff. Can you sing the melody with numbers?** Establish the tonality of the song by singing 1–2–3–4–5–3–1–5–1 in the key of G major. Ask the students to sing each phrase with numbers. Write them on the chalkboard in this order:

 5–5–5–5–4–3–4–3–2–1
 3–3–3–3–2–1–2–1–7,–1
 1– 1–1–· 1–5,–5,–5,–1

2. Discuss how each phrase of the song returns to the tonal center, scale step 1.

3. Invite the students to sing the song again, this time with words. When they know the melody well, sing the song as a three-part round.

4. Choose three students (each one should have an instrument) to play the melody on resonator bells, glockenspiel, or xylophone as the class sings. When the players have their parts securely learned, each of them may add the melody to accompany one of the three groups of singers and perform the song as a three-part accompanied round.

OPTIONAL

218

O Hanukah

Translated by Judith Eisenstein

Yiddish Folk Song

O Ha-nu-kah, O Ha-nu-kah, come light the me-no-rah,

Let's have a par-ty, we'll all dance the ho-ra.

Gath-er round the ta-ble, we'll give you a treat,

Shin-ing tops to play with and pan-cakes to eat;

And while we are play-ing, the can-dles are burn-ing low.

One for each night, they — shed a sweet light To re-

mind us of days long a - go.   mind us of days long a - go.

219

Lesson Focus

Expression: Musical elements are combined into a whole to express a musical or extramusical idea. *(P–S)*

Materials

○ **Piano Accompaniment:** page 354

○ **Record Information:**
   • O Hanukah
     Record 10 Side A Band 7
     Voices: children's choir
     Accompaniment: clarinet, trumpet, violin, accordion, double bass

○ **Instrument:** autoharp

○ **Extends Lesson 54,** page 118

For Your Information

Hanukah commemorates a victory of the Jews in their fight for religious freedom. Long ago Judas Maccabeus and his followers drove their enemies from the Holy Temple in Jerusalem. Upon their return to the temple, they found only enough oil to burn in their menorah (a kind of lamp) for one day, but miraculously the oil burned for eight days. In memory of this, Jewish families light one candle of the eight-branched menorah each evening. On the eighth day all eight candles are burning.

The Lesson

1. Ask the students to examine the rhythmic notation of the "O Hanukah" on page 219. **How does the rhythm of the melody move most of the time, especially during the first four phrases?** (with the eighth note, the shortest sound) Ask one student to lightly tap a steady pattern of short sounds while the class reads the words in rhythm.

2. Draw attention to the chord symbols above the first staff. Ask one student to play **Dm A7 Dm** on the autoharp. **Will this song be in minor or major?** (minor) Have one student (or yourself) play the chords for the song, strumming twice per measure. Ask the class to follow the notation and softly read the words to themselves. **Does the song always have a minor feeling?** (No, Phrase 3 and most of Phrase 4 sound as though they were in major.)

3. Play the autoharp accompaniment again and challenge the class to sing the melody on "loo"; repeat, singing the words.

4. Play the recording. **Did we learn the melody and rhythm correctly? Do we need to correct any errors?** If so, listen as needed until the students can perform the entire song accurately.

5. Discuss the origin of the Jewish holiday, Hanukah. (See **For Your Information.**) Discuss the qualities that make this song representative of some Jewish music (the minor tonality, the dancelike repetitive rhythms).

OPTIONAL

Lesson Focus

Harmony: Two or more musical lines may occur simultaneously. *(P—S)*

Materials

○ **Piano Accompaniment:** page 339
○ **Record Information:**
  • Sleigh Bells
    Record 10 Side A Band 8
    Voices: children's choir
    Accompaniment: mandolin, balalaika, acoustic guitar, cimbalom, accordion, double bass, percussion
○ **Instruments:** jingle bells; piano or bass xylophone G, A, B♭, C, D, E♭, F, F♯, and G'; bell mallet
○ **Other:** overhead projector
○ **Teacher's Resource Binder:**
  [Activity Sheets] • **Activity Sheet 34,** page A50
    (Prepare one transparency.)
○ **Extends Lesson 20,** page 44

Chords not shown on pupil page

Sleigh Bells

Russian Folk Song

1. Mer-ry bells go ting - a - lin-gle, Toes and fin-gers freeze and tin - gle,
2. As we ride our song goes ring-ing, Through the air its ech-oes wing-ing,

With our friends we gai-ly min-gle, While the snow-flakes fall.
Till the world seems full of sing-ing; So we speed a - long.

Boys and girls, come out to-geth-er, Clad in coats of fur and leath-er
Through the town and by the riv - er, Where the birch-es sigh and shiv-er

Made to brave the cold-est weath-er, When the sleigh bells ring.
And the birds are si - lent nev - er, Join-ing in our song.

Add this pattern during the introduction, interlude, and coda to imitate the sound of sleigh bells.

Jingle bells

220

The Lesson

1. Listen to the recording of "Sleigh Bells" as the students follow the notation on page 220 of their books. Invite one or more students to add jingle bells, using the pattern shown on the pupil page during the introduction, interlude, and coda.

2. Help the students learn to sing the song. When they know it well, display the transparency of Activity Sheet 34 (*Harmony for "Sleigh Bells"*) and sing the descant while the class sings the melody. Encourage the students to listen carefully to hear how the two lines of music fit together.

3. Encourage several students who are confident singers to join you in the descant. Gradually, as the others sense how the two parts fit to-gether, give more students the opportunity to try the descant.

4. Draw attention to the bass xylophone part shown at the bottom of the transparency. Choose a student to play the part on the bass xylophone or invite a student who plays the piano to perform the bass xylophone part on the lower register of the piano. The accompanist may add this bass line as the rest of the class sings the melody.

5. Invite the class to add the bass line and the descant at the same time. They will enjoy per-forming these parts after they have sung the song on several different days and know it very well.

220

Chords not shown on pupil page

We Wish You a Merry Christmas

English Folk Song

We wish you a mer-ry Christ-mas, We wish you a mer-ry Christ-mas,

We wish you a mer-ry Christ-mas and a hap-py New Year.

Good tid-ings we bring for you and your kin;

Good tid-ings of Christ-mas and a hap-py New Year.

1. Now bring us some fig-gy pud-ding, Now
2. We won't go un-til we get some, We

bring us some fig-gy pud-ding, Now
won't go un-til we get some, We

bring us some fig-gy pud-ding, and bring some right here.
won't go un-til we get some, so bring some right here.

(after Verse 2, D.C. al Fine)

221

SPECIAL TIMES 9

Lesson Focus
Form: A musical whole may be made up of same, varied, or contrasting segments. *(P–S)*

Materials
- **Piano Accompaniment:** page 358
- **Record Information:**
  - We Wish You a Merry Christmas
    Record 10 Side A Band 9
    Voices: children's choir
    Accompaniment: string quartet
- **Instruments:** resonator bells, glocken-spiel, or xylophone F, G, A♭, B♭, C, and D♭; bell mallets
- **Extends Lesson 53,** page 116

For Your Information
The custom of carolling comes to us from England. Discuss the words of this carol: *figgy pudding* (fig or plum pudding) is an English delicacy, traditionally served at Christmas. As the words suggest, the carol-lers refuse to leave until they have been fed or rewarded with gifts or money.

The Lesson

1. **Look at the music on page 221. How many sections do you find?** (three) **What helps you know when a section ends?** (Each ends with a double bar.)

2. **Listen to the music. How many sections do you *hear*?** (five) **Can you describe the design of the song with letters?** (A B A A A)

3. OPTIONAL **Why would it be easy to think there were only three sections when you first looked at the music? Can you find any clues that tell you that there are five?** (the repeat signs and *D.C. al Fine*)

4. **Play the recording as needed until the students can sing the song independently.**

5. **Write the two accompaniment patterns below on the chalkboard. Can you decide which**

should accompany each section of our song? Help the students discover that the notes in Pattern 1 are the first notes of each measure in the A sections (except Measures 7 and 8).

Pattern 1

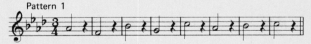

Pattern 2 serves as an accompaniment for the B section.

Pattern 2

Choose one or more students to play the patterns on resonator bells, glockenspiels, or xylophones as the rest of the class sings the song.

221

Lesson Focus

Time and Place: The way musical elements are combined into a whole reflects the origin of the music. *(P–S)*

Materials

- **Piano Accompaniment:** page 372
- **Record Information:**
  - Arruru
    Record 10 Side A Band 10
    Voices: children's choir
    Accompaniment: guitar, percussion
- **Instruments:** hand drum; finger cymbals; tambourine
- **Extends Lesson 16,** page 36

For Your Information

Versions of this Spanish carol may be found in parts of the United States and Latin America. The words of Phrase 1 mean "My lady, Mary." The refrain means "Sleep, baby Jesus," preceded by the cooing words *Arruru, arruru.*
Phonetic pronunciation for the Spanish:
Sehn-**yoh**-rah **dohn**-yah mah-**ree**-yah
ah-roo-roo **ah**-roo-roo
dwehr-meh-teh **neen**-yoh heh-**soos**

Chords not shown on pupil page

Arruru

English Words by Elena Paz

Spanish Folk Melody

1. Se - ño - ra do - ña Ma - rí - a,
2. The shep - herds are slow - ly wind - ing
3. A - blaze in the win - t'ry sky, _____

I bring you my lit - tle one.
Their way from the dis - tant hills,
The dia - mond of Beth - le - hem,

He'll help you to rock the cra - dle,
To wit - ness the new - born ba - by,
How bright is the star on high, _____

Where - in lies your new - born son.
They've braved all of win - ter's ills.
O - ver Je - ru - sa - lem.

Refrain
A - rru - ru, a - rru - ru,

Duer - me - te, Ni - ño Je - sús. sús.

222

The Lesson

1. Help the students understand that discovering the way musical elements are organized can help them identify the origin of a song. Play the recording of "Arruru." Ask the students to listen for clues that will help them recognize that this is a Spanish carol. (The "rocking rhythm" in ⁶⁄₈ is typical of Spanish music; the melodic sequences and guitar accompaniment are also typical of the music of Spanish-speaking people.)

2. Help the students learn to sing the song. Begin by practicing the following pattern, which occurs at the end of Phrases 1 and 3:

   Comment on how the pattern shifts between short-long and long-short. **This shifting rhythm is also common in the music of Spanish-speaking people.**

3. Help the students learn to perform the song with attention to melodic and rhythmic accuracy. Guide them to *expressively* perform the song, paying attention to tempo, articulation, and dynamics.

4. The students may add accompaniments based on patterns heard on the recording.

Verse
Drum
Finger Cymbals

Refrain
Tambourine (shake)

O He Did Whistle and She Did Sing

Richard Felciano

(whistle)   (whistle)

Dm   Em   Dm   Em   Dm

As I sat on a sun-ny bank, On Christ-mas Day in the morn-ing,

Em   Dm   Am   Em   Dm

I spied three ships come sail-ing by, On Christ-mas Day in the morn-ing,

Am 3   C

And who should be with those three ships but Jo-seph and his fair la - dy.

Dm   3   C   Am   Em

O he did whis-tle and she did sing And all the bells on earth did ring,

Dm   Am   Dm Am Dm

On Christ-mas day in the morn-ing. ___ (whistle)

223

SPECIAL TIMES 11

Lesson Focus
Time and Place: The way musical elements are combined into a whole reflects the origin of the music. **(P–S)**

Materials
○ **Piano Accompaniment:** page 360
○ **Record Information:**
 • O He Did Whistle and She Did Sing
 Record 10 Side B Band 1
 Voices: children's choir
 Accompaniment: string ensemble, whistler
○ **Teacher's Resource Binder:**
 • Optional—
 Enrichment Activity 10, page E16
○ **Extends Lesson 16,** page 36

For Your Information
''O He Did Whistle and She Did Sing'' was written for voice, two violins, and a cello. The string parts are written in *scordatura* notation. (The instruments are tuned to the four pitches included in each instrument's part.) This type of notation was once occasionally used for amateurs who wanted to play but had little technique. Benjamin Franklin is thought to have written a string quartet using this type of notation.

The Lesson

1. Play the recording of "O He Did Whistle and She Did Sing." **This is a Christmas carol! Do you think it is older or newer than "Arruru" (page 222)?** (much newer) **How can you tell?** (The notes in the accompaniment seem to "clash" with each other very often.) **This carol was written by a contemporary American composer, Richard Felciano.**

2. Adjust the balance on the record player so that only the melody is heard. **Let's listen again, but this time we'll hear only the melody. As you listen, follow the notation on page 223.** Draw attention to the frequent recurrence of pairs of eighth notes, and an eighth note followed by two sixteenth notes.

3. Guide the students to examine the melody. Note that for most of the song only five different pitches are used, and that the melody for the various phrases is frequently similar. Sing the five pitches up and down on "loo" (D–E–F–G–A). Observe that these are the first five pitches of a minor scale. Invite the students to try to sing the melody by following the notation. Listen to the recording again, without the accompaniment, and correct errors.

4. Adjust the record player so that only the accompaniment can be heard, and invite the class to sing with the accompaniment.

Lesson Focus

Melody: A series of pitches may move up, down, or remain the same. *(P–S)*

Materials

○ **Piano Accompaniment:** page 362

○ **Record Information:**
  • A'Soalin'
  Record 10 Side B Band 2
  Voices: solo child, children's choir
  Accompaniment: recorders, lute, viola da gamba, harpsichord, percussion

○ **Instruments:** resonator bells and xylophones B, D, E, F♯, G, A, and B; bass xylophone; piano; bell mallets

○ **Extends Lesson 8,** page 20

Chords not shown on pupil page

A'Soalin'

Words and Music by Paul Stookey,
Tracy Batteast and Elena Mezzetti

Refrain

Soal, a soal, a soal cake, Please, good mis-sus, a soal-cake, An

ap-ple, a pear, a plum, a cher-ry, An-y good thing to make us all mer-ry,

One for Pe-ter, two for Paul, Three for Him who made us all. _____

224

The Lesson

1. Write the following pitches on the chalkboard.

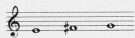

Ask a volunteer to sense and sing the three pitches. Challenge other students to determine whether the volunteer sang the correct pitches. Have other members of the class sing these pitches.

2. Explain to the students that they are going to learn a song that is built on a minor scale and that uses only the three pitches shown in the musical example. **Look at the first two measures of the song on page 224. Use the syllable "loo" to sing these measures using the pitches you just sang.** Sing the remaining phrases of the refrain in this manner. It is not necessary to focus on the exact rhythm at this time.

3. Play the recording and direct the students' attention to the rhythm. Encourage the students to softly sing along as they listen.

4. **How many new pitches are there in the verse of the song?** (none) Play the recording again. **What keeps this song from becoming monotonous?** (the variety of rhythmic ideas) Point out the syncopated patterns in the refrain. Ask the students to sing the entire song with the recording.

5. Invite a few students to take turns practicing the ostinato patterns shown at the bottom of page 225. To perform the ostinato with the song, divide the class into three groups. Group 1 sings while Group 2 plays the chordal ostinato on the xylophone or resonator bells;

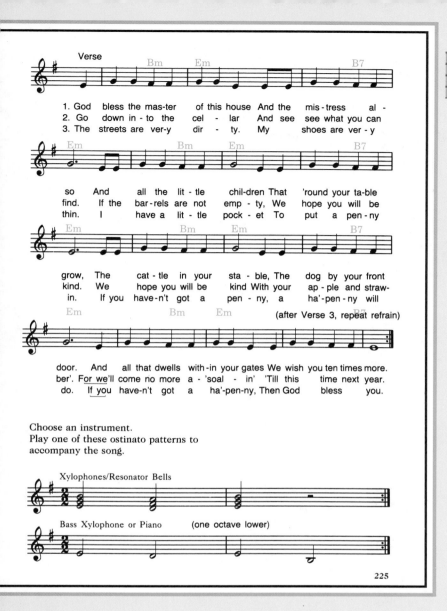

Verse

Bm   Em   B7

1. God bless the mas-ter   of this house And the   mis-tress   al -
2. Go   down in-to the   cel - lar   And see   see what you can
3. The streets are ver-y   dir - ty. My   shoes are ver-y

Em   Bm   Em   B7

so   And   all the lit-tle   chil-dren That 'round your ta-ble
find. If the bar-rels are not emp-ty, We   hope you will be
thin. I   have a lit-tle   pock-et To   put a pen-ny

Em   Bm   Em   B7

grow, The cat-tle in your   sta-ble, The dog by your front
kind. We   hope you will be kind With your ap-ple and straw-
in. If you have-n't got a   pen-ny, a   ha'-pen-ny will

Em   Bm   Em   (after Verse 3, repeat refrain)

door. And all that dwells with-in your gates We wish you ten times more.
ber'. For we'll come no more a - 'soal - in' 'Till this time next year.
do. If you have-n't got a   ha'-pen-ny, Then God   bless   you.

Choose an instrument.
Play one of these ostinato patterns to
accompany the song.

Xylophones/Resonator Bells

Bass Xylophone or Piano   (one octave lower)

225

Group 3 plays the bass ostinato on the bass
xylophone or piano. Challenge the students to
create an introduction, interlude, or coda
using only the notes E, F♯, and G.

SPECIAL TIMES 13

Lesson Focus

Harmony: Two or more musical lines may occur simultaneously. *(D–S)*

Materials

○ **Piano Accompaniment:** page 364

○ **Record Information:**
  • A Valentine Wish

 Record 10 Side B Band 3
  Voices: children's choir
  Accompaniment: harp, celesta, harpsichord, positive organ, piano, percussion

○ **Other:** five cut-out paper hearts labeled as follows: one *Introduction,* three *Interlude,* and one *Coda;* 12 cut-out paper rectangles labeled as follows: six *A,* two *B,* three *C,* and one *D* (Attach felt or magnetic tape to each shape.)

○ **Extends Lesson 17,** page 38

The Lesson

1. Help the class learn Section A of "A Valentine Wish" on page 226, through the first ending. **In this song, "1" is on the first line. On what step does the melody begin?** (5) Challenge the students to sing as much of the song as possible with scale numbers. Notice the downward skip (5–3–1) and the fact that the melody moves frequently by steps.

2. Review the first, second, and third endings. Help the students realize that they will eventually sing the same melody three times. **First we need to learn Section B of the song.** (Begin with the second ending, "Glad I'll be.") When this section has been learned by singing with numbers or by listening to the recording, ask the students to sing the entire unison section of the song, paying careful attention to when they must sing the first, second, and third endings.

3. Play the entire recording of "A Valentine Wish." **Has anything new been added?** (Yes, now voices are singing two melodies at the same time.) Explain that the second voice is singing a harmonizing part. Help the students locate this harmonizing part on page 227 of the pupil book. **What happens to the main melody?** (It is the same as in the opening section of the song.)

4. Distribute cut-out shapes, with felt or magnetic tape affixed, to several students. (Shapes may also be arranged on the chalkboard tray.) (See **Materials.**) As the class listens to the recording again, have the students arrange the shapes in order, to describe the form.

For Your Information

Form of "A Valentine Wish":
Introduction (four measures)
A
Interlude (one measure)
A
B
A
Interlude (three measures)
A and C (sung together)
Interlude (one measure)
A and C (sung together)
B and D (sung together)
A and C (sung together)
Coda (four measures)

Replay the recording as often as necessary until the students are sure of the order of the sections.

5. Sing the complete song. All students may sing Part 1 throughout or you and a few students who are strong, independent singers may add the harmony part.

OPTIONAL

227

Chords not shown on pupil page

Glad I'll be, se-cret-ly, for I can pre-tend ___

Glad you'll be, se-cret-ly, for you can pre-tend ___

It was sent by in-tent from a spe-cial friend!

It was sent by in-tent from a spe-cial friend!

game! And fails ___ to sign ___ his/her name! _____

game! For I'll ___ not sign ___ my name! _____

228

Dayenu

Jewish Folk Song

The Seder, watercolor on paper by Michael Pressman, 1950, Art Resource/The Jewish Museum, New York.

I - lu ho - tsi, ho - tsi - a - nu, ho - tsi - a - nu mi - Mits - ra - yim,

Ho - tsi - a - nu mi - Mits - ra - yim, Da - ye - nu.

Da - da - ye - nu, ___ da - da - ye - nu, ___ Da - da - ye - nu, da -

1. ye - nu, da - ye - nu, da - ye - nu 2. ye - nu, da - ye - nu.

229

Lesson Focus

Rhythm: Individual sounds and silences within a rhythmic line may be longer than, shorter than, or the same as the underlying steady beat or shortest pulse. *(P–S)*

Materials

○ **Piano Accompaniment:** page 351
○ **Record Information:**
  • Dayenu
☐ **Record 10 Side B Band 4**
  Voices: children's choir
  Accompaniment: clarinet, trumpet, trombone, tuba, violin, mandolin, cimbalom, double bass, accordion, percussion
○ **Instruments:** tambourines
○ **Extends Lesson 7,** page 18

For Your Information

"Dayenu" is a song for the Jewish feast of Passover, which commemorates the time when the Jews were liberated from slavery in Egypt. The Hebrew text means: "If He had done nothing more than take us out of Egypt, we would have been grateful." Pronunciation of Hebrew words: **ee**-lew **haw**-tsee **ah**-new mee-**mits**-rye-eem, **dye**-ay-new

The Lesson

1. Play the recording of "Dayenu" and discuss its **OPTIONAL** history. (See **For Your Information.**)

2. Put these patterns on the chalkboard:

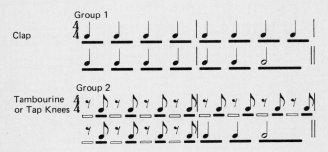

Group 1
Clap

Group 2
Tambourine
or Tap Knees

Have the class read and practice each pattern. Divide the class into two groups: Group 1 claps the first pattern while Group 2 plays the second on tambourines (or taps knees if enough tambourines are not available).

3. Play the recording. Help the students realize that the song is made up of two sections: Section A is four measures long; Section B is also four measures long, and is repeated.

4. The students may perform simple movements as they listen to the recording again. Form two lines, with partners facing each other. For Section A, all students should stand in place and clap the patterns learned in Step 2. (Line 1 claps Pattern 1, while Line 2 claps Pattern 2.) For Section B, the students may skip about, taking care not to bump into anyone else. They must plan their skipping so that they return to their original places in the line by the end of the section.

5. **Can you now sing the song?** When the students know the melody, invite them to accompany themselves with the clapping and tambourine patterns used in Step 2.

229

Lesson Focus

Form: A musical whole begins, continues, and ends. *(P–S)*

Materials

○ **Piano Accompaniment:** page 368
○ **Record Information**
  • Feed My Lambs
    Record 10 Side B Band 5
    Voices: boys' choir
    Accompaniment: two flutes, pipe organ
○ **Other:** crêpe paper or cloth streamers approximately five-feet long in a variety of bright colors
○ **Extends Lesson 46,** page 102

For Your Information

"Feed My Lambs" is based on a biblical text frequently read in Christian churches at Easter. Natalie Sleeth is a well-known contemporary American composer of anthems and songs for children and adults. This piece is dedicated to Katherine Davis, another contemporary composer best known for her song "The Little Drummer Boy."

Chords not shown on pupil page

Feed My Lambs

Words and Music by Natalie Sleeth

Feed My lambs, Tend My sheep, o - ver all a vig - il keep;

In My name, Lead them forth gent - ly as a shep - herd.

1. When they wan-der, when they stray, their pro - tec - tor be.
2. Un - to all who lose the way, hope and com - fort be.

230

The Lesson

1. Play the recording of "Feed My Lambs." Guide the students to focus their attention primarily on the instrumentation. After they have listened, help them, through discussion, to determine that the accompaniment is performed on a flute, oboe, and pipe organ

2. **Examine the notation on page 230. How long is each phrase?** (four measures) Play the recording again. Ask the students to show the shape of each vocal phrase by tracing an arc in the air with one arm, moving from left to right. Help them discover that they will need a feeling of "tension" in their arm as the arc moves uphill and a feeling of "release" as it comes back down. Play the recording until the students can predict the length of each phrase and begin and end their arcs at the appropriate times.

3. Distribute one or more streamers to each student. The students should grasp their streamers with the same hand that they used to trace the arc. Play the recording again as the students trace an arc while holding the streamers.

4. **Can you now sing the song?** (The students should be able to learn it very quickly, since the melody is repetitive and easy to learn.)

5. The students may sing the song with the recorded accompaniment as they move the streamers on each vocal phrase. (Turn the balance on the record player so that the voices are not heard.)

OPTIONAL

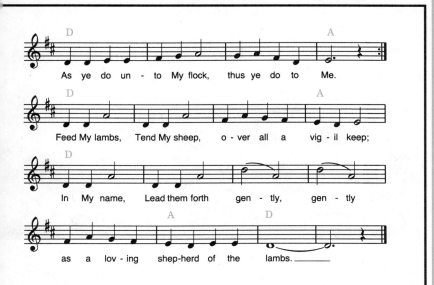

As ye do un - to My flock, thus ye do to Me.

Feed My lambs, Tend My sheep, o - ver all a vig - il keep;

In My name, Lead them forth gen - tly, gen - tly

as a lov - ing shep-herd of the lambs. _____

231

Lesson Focus

Expression: Musical elements are combined into a whole to express a musical or extramusical idea. *(P–S)*

Materials

○ **Piano Accompaniment:** page 357

○ **Record Information:**
  • America, the Beautiful
  Record 10 Side B Band 6
  Voices: children's choir
  Accompaniment: concert band

○ **Instruments:** hand drum and regulation drumsticks (to suggest sound of snare drum); tub drum and soft beater (to suggest sound of bass drum); cymbals

○ **Teacher's Resource Binder**
  • Optional—
  Kodaly Activity 5, page K8

○ **Extends Lesson 13,** page 31

The Lesson

1. Read the lyrics of America, the Beautiful" as a poem. Include the following fourth verse, which is not in the pupil's book.

   O beautiful for patriot dream
   That sees, beyond the years,
   Thine alabaster cities gleam,
   Undimmed by human tears!

   Discuss unfamiliar terms with the class. Help them learn the fourth verse.

2. **Listen to the recording. Which part of the poem do you think the composer thought was most important?** (the third phrase) **What did the composer do with his music to make this part of the poem seem so important?** The students may observe that the beginning of the phrase is the highest point in the melody. They may also notice that the performers emphasize the melodic high point with a *cre-*

scendo (the music becomes louder), and with added instruments (timpani and cymbals).

3. Help the students plan a performance. **When will you sing softly? Become louder?** Review dynamic markings and write the ones that the students select on the chalkboard, one for each phrase. The result might be like this:

   Phrase 1: *p*

   Phrase 2: *mp* ───

   Phrase 3: *ff* ───

   Phrase 4: *f* ───

   In what other ways can you help highlight the important point of your song? (We might add an accompaniment.) Begin with the snare drum (hand drum and regulation drumsticks).

   Snare Drum 4/4 ...

   Add a bass (tub) drum and cymbals at the start of Phrase 3.

232

For Your Information

The words of "America, the Beautiful" were written by Katherine Lee Bates when she visited Pike's Peak in Colorado. From the peak one can see for miles to the valleys below. The poem expresses the author's awe and admiration for the beauty that she saw.

From *Burning in the Night*
by Thomas Wolfe

So, then, to every man his chance—
To every man, regardless of his birth,
His shining, golden opportunity—
To every man the right to live,
To work, to be himself,
And to become
Whatever thing his manhood and his vision
Can combine to make him—
This, seeker,
Is the promise of America.

America, America,
America, America,
America, America,

God shed his grace on thee,
God mend thine every flaw,
May God thy gold refine,

And crown thy good with brother-hood
Con-firm thy soul in self-con-trol,
Till all suc-cess be no-ble-ness,

From sea to shin-ing sea.
Thy lib-er-ty in law.
And ev-ery gain di-vine.

233

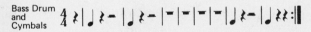

Bass Drum and Cymbals

4. Read the poem in **For Your Information** with the class. Invite them to plan a performance that combines the song "America, the Beautiful" with the Thomas Wolfe poem. They might begin by singing the first verse of "America, the Beautiful." Then as some students continue to hum the melody as a background, others may chant the poem. Suggest that they pause after each thought and fill the pauses with improvised percussion patterns such as:

To every man his chance (soft, steady beat on drums)
To every man, regardless of his birth,
His shining, golden opportunity (cymbals)

Continue in a similar fashion. End the performance by singing the last verse of "America, the Beautiful."

Lesson Focus

Expression: Musical elements are combined into a whole to express a musical or extramusical idea. *(P–I)*

Materials

○ **Piano Accompaniment:** page 370

○ **Record Information:**
  • The Star-Spangled Banner
    Record 10 Side B Band 7
    Voices: mixed chorus
    Accompaniment: concert band

○ **Extends Lesson 22,** page 48

For Your Information

The students should know the national anthem well. They may not, however, know the story behind the words or understand their meaning. They may want to research the life of Francis Scott Key and share their findings with the class.

You may also want to share the following information with the class: In 1814, a young lawyer named Francis Scott Key was determined to free his friend Dr. William Beanes, a physician. Beanes had been captured by the British in the War of 1812 and taken to Admiral Cockburn as a prisoner. *(continued on next page)*

Chords not shown on pupil page

The Star-Spangled Banner

Words by Francis Scott Key   Composer Unknown

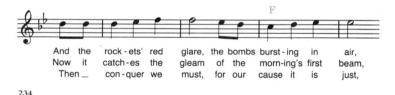

1. Oh, __ say, can you see by the dawn's ear - ly light,
2. On the shore, dim - ly seen thro' the mists of the deep,
3. Oh, __ thus be it ev - er when __ free men shall stand

What so proud - ly we hailed at the twi - light's last gleam - ing?
Where the foe's haugh - ty host in dread si - lence re - pos - es,
Be - tween their loved homes and the war's des - o - la - tion!

Whose broad stripes and bright stars, through the per - il - ous fight,
What is that which the breeze, o'er the tow - er - ing steep,
Blest with vic - t'ry and peace, may the heav'n-res-cued land

O'er the ram - parts we watched were so gal - lant - ly stream - ing?
As it fit - ful - ly blows, half con - ceals, half dis - clos - es?
Praise the Pow'r that hath made and pre - served us a na - tion.

And the rock - ets' red glare, the bombs burst - ing in air,
Now it catch - es the gleam of the morn - ing's first beam,
Then __ con - quer we must, for our cause it is just,

234

The Lesson

1. Ask the class to practice reading the words of "The Star-Spangled Banner" on pages 234–235 aloud in an expressive manner. Discuss the meaning of the words. Talk about how tempo, dynamics, phrasing, and tone quality can help express this meaning as the class sings.

2. Ask the class to analyze the form of the song. There are eight phrases, and each two phrases forms a section called a *period*. Write the form of these periods with capital letters on the chalkboard: **A A B C.** Discuss the importance of observing the form as one sings. **Each period should be sung as a complete thought. When a breath is taken at the end of the first phrase in each group it should be taken quickly so that the musical flow is not interrupted.**

3. Help the class plan meaningful, appropriate movements that will fit the $\frac{3}{4}$ meter. The movements should describe the text as much as possible and should be representative of the dignified style of this important part of the American heritage.

For Your Information *(continued)*

Hoping for a prisoner exchange, Key took a flag-of-truce boat to Chesapeake Bay where the Admiral's ship was anchored.

The Admiral agreed to make the prisoner exchange, but refused to let Beanes and Key leave until Fort McHenry, which was about to be attacked, was destroyed. He feared that the two would disclose the British plans for the attack and thus foil them.

Key watched the flag on Fort McHenry. After the constant shellings, the flag was "still there."

It was the sight of the flag still waving that inspired Key to write down his poem on the back of a letter that he had in his pocket. The poem was later printed on "handbills" and "broadsides" and distributed publicly. It was so widely accepted that a tune was chosen so it could be sung. The tune of "To Anacreon in Heaven" was used because the words easily fit the rhythm and melody of this then familiar song.

"The Star-Spangled Banner" was officially designated as our national anthem on March 3, 1931, during the administration of Herbert Hoover.

Glossary

Accelerando becoming faster, *172*

Adagio moderately slow, *89*

Allegro fast, *89*

Andante medium speed (a walking tempo), *89*

Articulation how sounds start and stop, *91*

Beat the steady pulse of the music, *72*

Brass Family wind instruments made of brass or other metal, including the trumpet, French horn, trombone, and tuba, *62*

Canon music in which a melody is imitated exactly by another voice or instrument, *117*

Chord three or more pitches occurring at the same time, *45*

Coda a short concluding section of a piece, *27*

Descant a harmony part that is played or sung above the melody, *47*

Dynamics the loud and soft changes in music, *90*

Form the design of a piece of music made up of same, similar, or different parts, *13*

Forte (*f*) loud, *12*

Fortissimo (*ff*) very loud, *90*

Harmony two or more melodies performed at the same time or one melody accompanied by chords, *196*

Interlude a section between two parts of the music, *27*

Introduction a section that comes before the main part of the music, *27*

Key Signature the sharps and flats at the beginning of the music that show where the home tone is located and the kind of scale used, *112*

Largo very slow, *89*

Legato performed in a smooth, connected way, *91*

Marcato tones that are performed heavier and "marked," *91*

Melody a series of tones arranged rhythmically to make a musical idea, *122*

Meter Signature the two numbers at the beginning of a piece of music that tell how the beats are grouped and show the kind of note that moves with the beat, *74*

Mezzo Forte (*mf*) medium loud, *12*

Mezzo Piano (*mp*) medium soft, *12*

Movement(s) the sections of a long composition, *20*

Note a sign that shows the pitch and the length of tone, *14*

Ostinato an accompaniment pattern repeated over a over, *122*

Percussion Family instruments played by shaking or striking, including the trap set, celesta, chimes, chestra bells, and timpani, *63*

Phrase a complete musical idea, *37*

Pianissimo (*pp*) very soft, *90*

Piano (*p*) soft, *34*

Pitch the highness or lowness of a musical sound, *1*

Presto very fast, *89*

Rhythm the pattern of long and short notes and res *202*

Ritardando a slowing of the tempo, *172*

Staccato a series of tones that are separated by short lences, *91*

String Family instruments played by plucking or bo ing strings, including the violin, viola, cello, and doul bass, *60*

Syncopation a type of rhythm that is created when t accents in a melody occur at a different time from t accented beat, *178*

Tempo the speed of the beat, *88*

Theme an important melody, *13*

Tie a musical addition sign used to join two or mo notes, *80*

Timbre the distinctive sound made by a particular i strument, *196*

Tonal Center the pitch to which all tones in a so seem to return; the home tone, *22*

Tone Row a series of pitches, *196*

Variation a musical idea that is repeated with som change, *13*

Woodwind Family wind instruments usually made of wood metal, including the piccolo, flute, oboe, clarinet, and ba soon, *61*

58. My Momma Told Me

Traditional Song Game

My mom - ma told me, mm,_____ if I was good - ie, mm,_____
told her, mm,_____ I kicked a boul - der, mm,_____

That she would buy me, oh,_____ a rub - ber
Now she won't buy me, oh,_____ a rub - ber

1. dol - ly, mm,_____ My aunt - ie
2. dol - ly, mm._____

11. Weave Me the Sunshine

Words and Music by Peter Yarrow

Moderately bright

Chorus

Mm. Weave, weave, weave me the sun - shine out of the fall - ing rain.

Weave me the hope of a new to - mor - row and fill my cup a - gain.

A - gain, now.

On - ly you__ can climb that moun - tain, shine on me a-

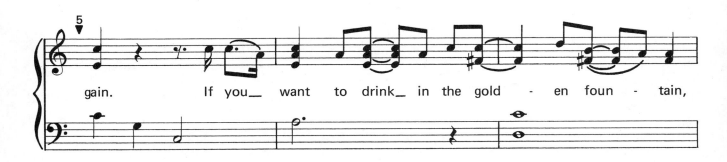

gain. If you__ want to drink__ in the gold - en foun - tain,

Repeat chorus twice and fade out second time

shine____ on me a - gain.____ Sing it with me.

12. Peace Like a River

Old Southern Hymn

1. I've got peace like a riv - er, I've got peace like a riv - er, I've got
2. I've got joy like a foun-tain, I've got joy like a foun-tain, I've got
3. I've got love like the o - cean, I've got love like the o - cean, I've got

peace like a riv - er in my soul.   I've got peace like a riv - er, I've got
joy like a foun-tain in my soul.   I've got joy like a foun-tain, I've got
love like the o - cean in my soul.   I've got love like the o - cean, I've got

peace like a riv - er, I've got peace like a riv - er in my soul.
joy like a foun-tain, I've got joy like a foun-tain in my soul.
love like the o - cean, I've got love like the o - cean in my soul.

23. Pop Goes the Weasel

Traditional

All a - round the cob - bler's bench, the mon - key chased the wea - sel. The mon - key thought 'twas all___ in fun; Pop! (clap) goes the wea - sel.

24. Bye Bye, Blackbird

Words by Mort Dixon

Music by Ray Henderson

Pack up all my cares and woe, Here I go, sing-ing low. Bye

bye, black - bird._____ Where some - bod - y waits for me,

sug - ar's sweet, so is she. Bye bye, black - bird._____

No one here can love and un-der-stand me. Oh, what hard-luck

sto-ries they all hand me. Make my bed and light the light.

I'll ar-rive late to-night. Black-bird,___ bye bye.___

19. The Silver Birch

Russian Folk Tune

Sil - ver birch a - lone in a mead - ow, stand - ing all a -
lone in a mead - ow. Soon a shep - herd boy comes
stroll - ing. With his sheep and goats, he's stroll - ing.

244

31. Do Your Ears Hang Low?

Traditional

1. Do your ears hang low? Do they wob-ble to and fro? Can you
2. Do your ears flip flop? Can you use them for a mop? Are they

tie them in a knot?__ Can you tie them in a bow? Can you
string-y at the bot-tom? Are they cur-ly on the top? Can you

flip them o'er your shoul-der like a Con-ti-nen-tal sol-dier? Do your ears hang low?
use them for a swat-ter? Can you use them for a blot-ter? Do your ears flip flop?

21. School Days

Music by Gus Edwards

Words by Will D. Cobb

School days, school days, Dear old gold-en rule days. Read-in' and writ-in' and 'rith-me-tic, Taught to the tune of a hick-'ry stick.

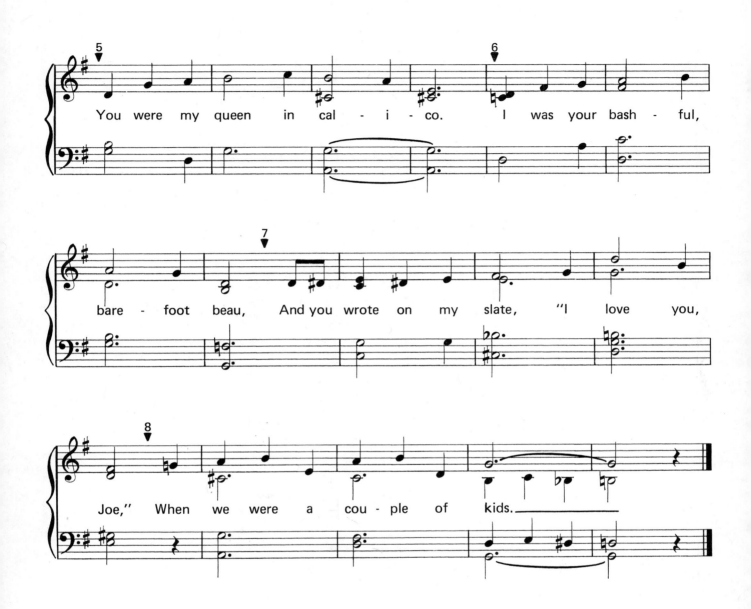

You were my queen in cal - i - co. I was your bash - ful, bare - foot beau, And you wrote on my slate, "I love you, Joe," When we were a cou - ple of kids.

22. Three Jolly Fishermen

Traditional

1. There were three jol - ly fish - er - men, _____ There
2. The first one's name was A - bra - ham, _____ The
3. The sec-ond one's name was I - saac, _____ The
4. The third one's name was Ja - cob, _____ The
5. They all sailed up to Jer - i - cho, _____ They

were three jol - ly fish - er - men,
first one's name was A - bra - ham,
sec-ond one's name was I - saac,
third one's name was Ja - cob,
all sailed up to Jer - i - cho,

Fish - er, fish - er, men - men - men,
A - bra, A - bra, ham - ham - ham,
I, ___ I, ___ zak - zak - zak,
Jay, ___ Jay, ___ cub - cub - cub,
Jer - ry, Jer - ry, co - co - co,

Fish - er, fish - er, men - men - men, There were three jol - ly fish - er - men.
A - bra, A - bra, ham - ham - ham, The first one's name was A - bra - ham.
I, ___ I, ___ zak - zak - zak, The sec-ond one's name was I - saac.
Jay, ___ Jay, ___ cub - cub - cub, The third one's name was Ja - cob.
Jer - ry, Jer - ry, co - co - co, They all sailed up to Jer - i - cho.

186. The Riddle Song

American Folk Song

1. I gave my love a cher-ry that has no stone; I
2. How can there be a cher-ry that has no stone? How
3. A cher-ry when it's bloom-ing, it has no stone; A

gave my love a chick-en that has no bone; I gave my love a ring that
can there be a chick-en that has no bone? How can there be a ring that
chick-en when it's pip-ping, it has no bone; A ring when it's roll-ing, it

has no end; I gave my love a ba-by, there's no cry-in'.
has no end? How can there be a ba-by, there's no cry-in'?
has no end; A ba-by when it's sleep-ing, there's no cry-in'.

249

26. Janišek the Highwayman

Transcribed by Benjamin Suchoff

Bela Bartók

Who's rid-ing down the street? No one I'd like to meet! Jan-i-sek the high-way-man will

catch you if catch he can! (clap)

28. The Wells Fargo Wagon

From "The Music Man"
by Meredith Willson

120. Down by the Riverside

Spiritual

1. Gon - na lay down ____ my sword and shield, ____ } (Clap,
2. Gon - na put on ____ my long white robe, ____ }

clap) Down ____ by the riv - er - side, ___ (Clap, clap) Down ___ by the riv - er - side, ___ (Clap,

clap) Down _____ by the riv - er - side, ____ Gon - na
Gon - na

254

lay down ____ my sword and shield, ___ } (Clap,
put on ____ my long, white robe, ___ }

clap) Down ____ by the riv - er - side, ___ Oh,

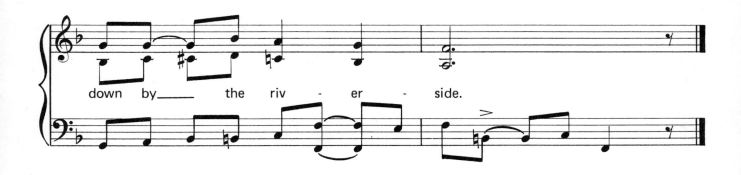

down by ____ the riv - er - side.

32. The Happy Wanderer

Words by Antonia Ridge

Music by Friedrich W. Moller

In marching tempo

1. I love to go a-wan-der-ing A-long the
2. I love to wan-der by the stream That danc-es
3. I wave my hat to all I meet And they wave
4. High o-ver-head, the sky-lark wing; They nev-er

moun-tain track._____ And as I go, I love to
in the sun._____ So joy-ous-ly it calls to
back to me._____ And black-birds call so loud and
rest at home._____ But just like me they love to

Refrain

sing, My knap-sack on my back._____
me, "Come! Join my hap-py song."_____
sweet From ev-ery green-wood tree._____
sing, As o'er the world we roam._____

Val - de -

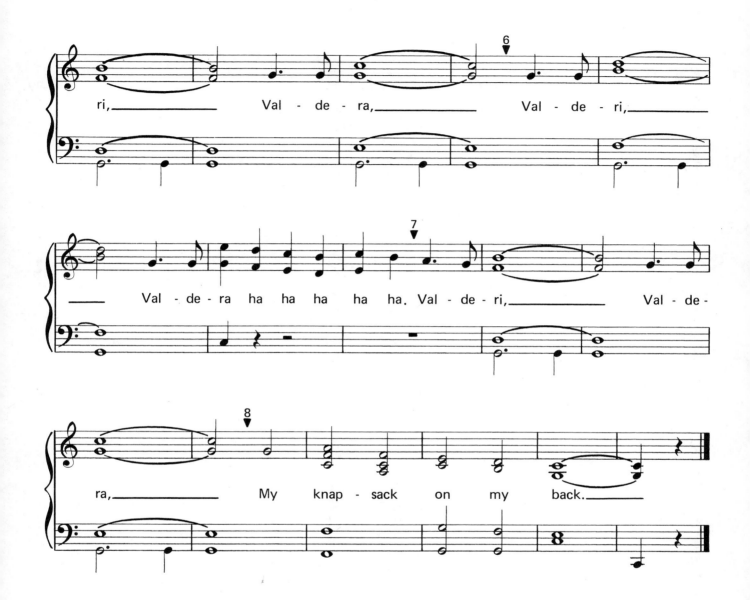

ri,_____ Val - de - ra,_____ Val - de - ri,_____

_____ Val - de - ra ha ha ha ha ha. Val - de - ri,_____ Val - de -

ra,_____ My knap - sack on my back._____

85. Who Did?

Traditional

(Second time go to second ending.)

1. Who did, who did, who did, who did, Who did swal - low Jo, Jo, Jo, Jo?
2. Whale did, whale did, whale did, whale did, Whale did swal - low Jo, Jo, Jo, Jo.
3. Ga - briel, Ga - briel, Ga - briel, Ga - briel, Ga - briel blow your trum, trum, trum, trum.
4. Dan - iel, Dan - iel, Dan - iel, Dan - iel, Dan - iel in the li, li, li, li.

1.

Who did, who did, who did, who did, Who did swal - low Jo, Jo, Jo, Jo? *(Back to Verse 1)*
Whale did, whale did, whale did, whale did, Whale did swal - low Jo, Jo, Jo, Jo.
Ga - briel, Ga - briel, Ga - briel, Ga - briel, Ga - briel blow your trum, trum, trum, trum.
Dan - iel, Dan - iel, Dan - iel, Dan - iel, Dan - iel in the li, li, li, li.

2.

Who did swal - low Jo - nah? Who did swal - low Jo - nah?
Whale did swal - low Jo - nah, Whale did swal - low Jo - nah,
Ga - briel blow your trum - pet, Ga - briel blow your trum - pet,
Dan - iel in the li - on's, Dan - iel in the li - on's,

Who did swal - low Jo - nah down?
Whale did swal - low Jo - nah down.
Ga - briel blow your trum - pet loud!
Dan - iel in the li - on's den!

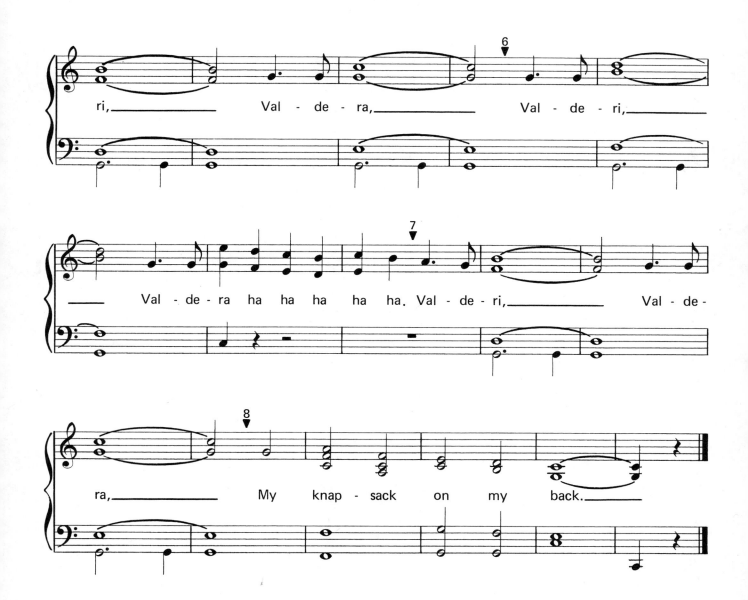

ri,_____ Val - de - ra,_____ Val - de - ri,_____

_____ Val - de - ra ha ha ha ha ha. Val - de - ri,_____ Val - de -

ra,_____ My knap - sack on my back._____

85. Who Did?

Traditional

(Second time go to second ending.)

1. Who did, who did, who did, who did, Who did swal-low Jo, Jo, Jo, Jo?
2. Whale did, whale did, whale did, whale did, Whale did swal-low Jo, Jo, Jo, Jo.
3. Ga-briel, Ga-briel, Ga-briel, Ga-briel, Ga-briel blow your trum, trum, trum, trum.
4. Dan-iel, Dan-iel, Dan-iel, Dan-iel, Dan-iel in the li, li, li, li.

1.

Who did, who did, who did, who did, Who did swal-low Jo, Jo, Jo, Jo? *(Back to Verse 1)*
Whale did, whale did, whale did, whale did, Whale did swal-low Jo, Jo, Jo, Jo.
Ga-briel, Ga-briel, Ga-briel, Ga-briel, Ga-briel blow your trum, trum, trum, trum.
Dan-iel, Dan-iel, Dan-iel, Dan-iel, Dan-iel in the li, li, li, li.

2.

Who did swal-low Jo - nah? Who did swal-low Jo - nah?
Whale did swal-low Jo - nah, Whale did swal-low Jo - nah,
Ga-briel blow your trum - pet, Ga-briel blow your trum - pet,
Dan-iel in the li - on's, Dan-iel in the li - on's,

Who did swal-low Jo - nah down?
Whale did swal-low Jo - nah down.
Ga-briel blow your trum - pet loud!
Dan-iel in the li - on's den!

46. The Colorado Trail

Cowboy Song
Arranged by Kurt Miller

Eyes like the morn-ing star. Cheek like a rose.

Lau - ra was a pret-ty girl, ev - ery - bod - y knows.

Weep, all ye lit - tle rains, Wail, winds,___ wail,

All a - long, a - long, a - long the Col - o - ra - do Trail.

42. Polly Wolly Doodle

Traditional

1. Oh, I went down South to see my Sal,
2. Oh, my Sal - ly is a maid - en fair,
3. Be - hind the barn, down on my knees,
4. He___ sneezed so hard with whoop-ing cough,

Sing Pol-ly wol-ly doo-dle all the day.

My___ Sal - ly is a spunk-y gal,
With___ curl - y eyes and laugh-ing hair,
I___ thought I heard a chick-en sneeze,
He___ sneezed his head and tail right off,

Sing Pol-ly wol-ly doo-dle all the day.

Refrain
Fare thee well, fare thee well, Fare thee well, my fair-y fay. For I'm going to Loui-si-an-a, for to see my Su-sy-an-na, Sing Pol-ly wol-ly doo-dle all the day.

78. Whether the Weather

Traditional

Wheth-er the weath-er be cold _____ Or wheth-er the weath-er be hot Or

wheth-er the weath-er be fair_____ Or wheth-er the weath-er be not, We'll

weath-er the weath-er what - ev - er the weath-er, Wheth-er we like it or not!

44. One Cold and Frosty Morning

Alabama Folk Song

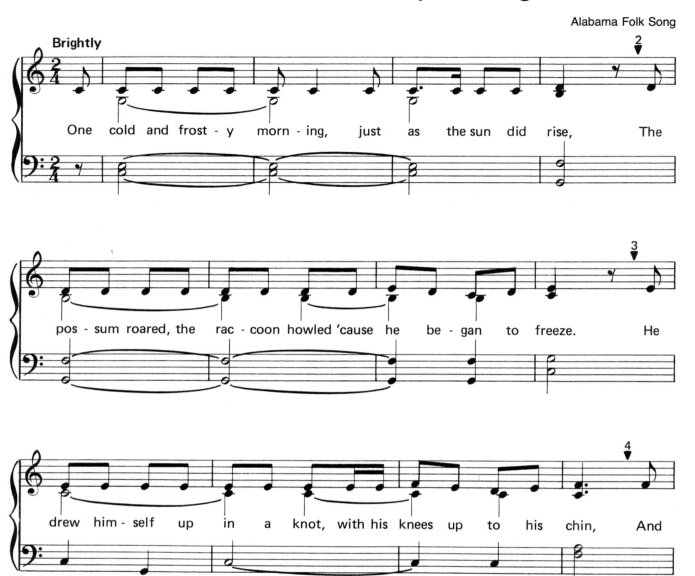

One cold and frost-y morn-ing, just as the sun did rise, The pos-sum roared, the rac-coon howled 'cause he be-gan to freeze. He drew him-self up in a knot, with his knees up to his chin, And

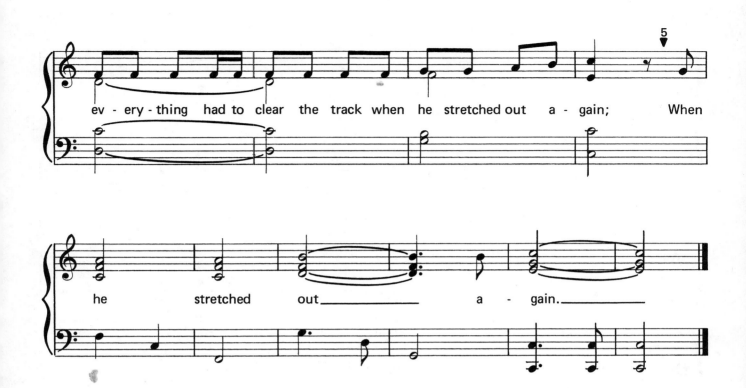

ev - ery - thing had to clear the track when he stretched out a - gain; When

he stretched out_____ a - gain._____

48. Woke Up This Morning

1960s Civil Rights Anthem

1. I woke up this morn - ing with my mind, _____ It was
2. Walk - in' and talk - in' with my mind, _____ It was

stayed ____ on free - dom. ____ I woke up this morn - ing with my
stayed ____ on free - dom. ____ Walk - in' and talk - in' with my

mind, ____ It was stayed ____ on free - dom. ____ I
mind, ____ It was stayed ____ on free - dom. ____ I

264

woke up this morn - ing with my mind,_____ It was
Walk - in' and talk - in' with my mind,_____ It was

stayed_____ on free - dom. Hal - le - lu,_____   Hal - le - lu,_____
stayed_____ on free - dom. Hal - le - lu,_____   Hal - le - lu,_____

_____ Hal - le - lu - jah!_____
_____ Hal - le - lu - jah!_____

54. Songmaker

Words and Music by Fred Willman

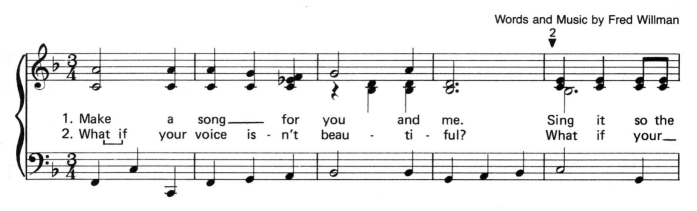

1. Make a song____ for you and me. Sing it so the
2. What if your voice is - n't beau - ti - ful? What if your____

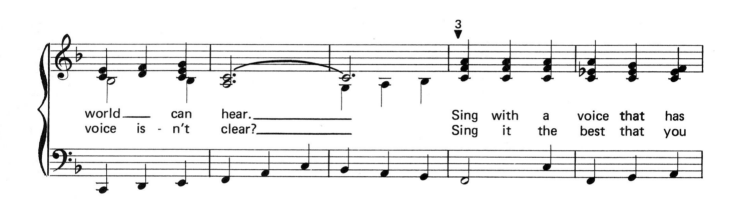

world____ can hear._____ Sing with a voice that has
voice is - n't clear?_____ Sing it the best that you

force - ful - ness, One that has____ no fear._____
can, my friend. If it's right, then the whole world will hear._____

Song - mak - er, song - mak - er, Tell what you have____ to

34. Gather 'Round

Words and Music by Margaret Dugard

Raise your voice with a joy - ous___ ring - ing, Gath - er 'round hear the

chil - dren sing - ing, Ding, dong, ding ring - a - ling, Ding, dong,

ding ring - a - ling, Give thanks and sing. Give thanks and sing.

Young folks gath-er 'round. Old folks gath-er 'round.

Gath-er 'round and join us sing-ing, Ding, dong, ding ring-a-ling Ding, dong,

ding ring-a-ling, Give thanks and sing. Give thanks___ and sing.

56. The Cat Came Back

Traditional

cat came back___ the ver - y next day!___ The cat came back!___

Thought he was a gon - er, but the cat came back!___ He

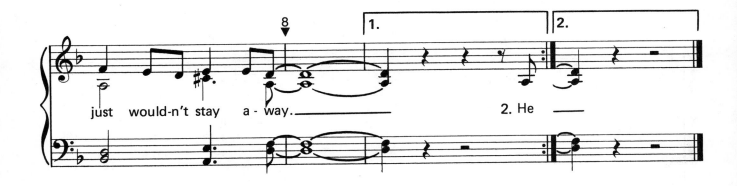

just would-n't stay a - way._____ 2. He ___

68. Sing Along

by Malvina Reynolds

1. I get but-ter-flies in my stom-ach when-ev-er I start to
2. Oh when I need a raise in pay and have to ask my
3. My con-gress-man's im-por-tant, he hob-nobs with big

sing. And when I'm at a mi-cro-phone, I shake like an-y-
boss, If I go to see him by my-self I'm just a to-tal
biz. He soon for-gets the guys and gals who put him where he

thing. But if you'll sing a-long with me, I'll
loss. But if we go to-geth-er, I'll
is. I'll just write him a let-ter, to

hol-ler right out loud. 'Cause I'm aw-ful-ly ner-vous,
do my right part right pret-ty. 'Cause I'm aw-ful-ly ner-vous,
tell him what I need. With a hun-dred thou-sand

lone - some. But I'm swell when I'm a crowd.
lone - some. But I make a fine com - mit - tee. Sing a-
sig - na - tures, why e - ven he can read.

long._____ Sing a - long._____ And

just sing "la la la la la" if you don't know the song. You'll

quick - ly learn the mu - sic, you'll find your - self a word. 'Cause

when we sing to - geth - er, we'll be heard!_____

71. On Top of Old Smoky

Kentucky Folk Song

1. On top of Old Smok - y _____ All cov - ered with
2. O court - ing's a pleas - ure, _____ But part - ing's a
3. A thief will but rob you _____ Of all that you
4. The grave will de - cay you _____ And turn you to

snow, _____ I lost my true lov -
grief, _____ And a false - heart - ed lov -
save, _____ But a false - heart - ed lov -
dust, _____ But a false - heart - ed lov -

er _____ By court - ing too slow.
er _____ Is worse than a thief. _____
er _____ Sends you to your grave. _____
er _____ You nev - er can trust. _____

80. My Name Is Yon Yonson

Traditional

76. Hurdy-gurdy Man

Translation by Merritt Wheeler

Music by Franz Schubert

In the vil - lage stands a hur - dy - gur - dy man, *(improvise on bells)*

Play - ing fro - zen - fin - gered, when and where he can. *(improvise on bells)*

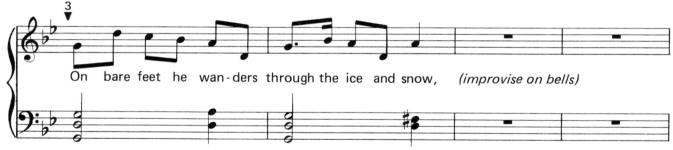

On bare feet he wan - ders through the ice and snow, *(improvise on bells)*

From GROWING WITH MUSIC SERIES, Book 6 TE, Wilson et al
(Englewood Cliffs, NJ: Prentice-Hall Inc. © 1970)

And his lit-tle cup swings emp-ty, to and fro. *(improvise on bells)*

And his lit-tle cup swings emp-ty, to and fro. *(improvise on bells)*

Play, old man, keep play-ing, and I'll go with_ you;

Play your hur-dy gur-dy till my songs are through._

110. Buffalo Gals

American Folk Song

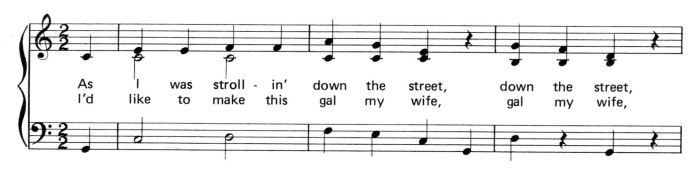

As I was stroll - in' down the street, down the street, down the street,
I'd like to make this gal my wife, gal my wife,

down the street, A pret - ty lit - tle gal I chanced to meet. Oh
all my life. I'd like to make her hap - py all her life. If

Refrain

she was sweet to see!
she would just have me!

Buf - fa - lo gals won't you

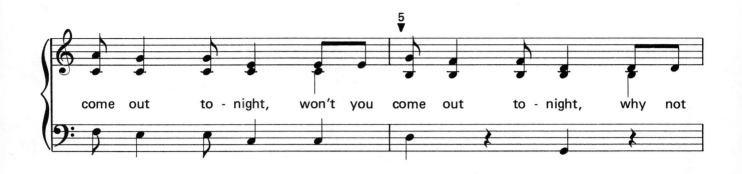

come out to-night, won't you come out to-night, why not

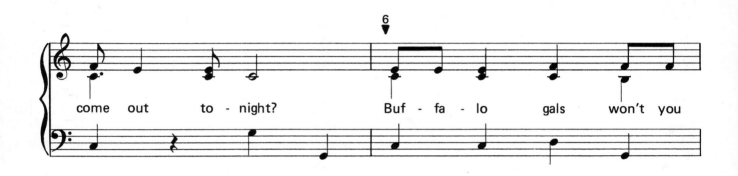

come out to-night? Buf - fa - lo gals won't you

come out to-night and dance in the light of the moon?

82. Follow Me

Traditional Carol

84. She'll Be Coming 'Round the Mountain

Traditional

(spoken)

1. She'll be com-ing round the moun-tain when she comes. (toot toot) She'll be
2. She'll be rid-ing six white hors-es when she comes. {(Whoa there!) She'll be
{(toot toot)

com-ing round the moun-tain when she comes. (toot toot) She'll be
rid-ing six white hors-es when she comes. {(Whoa there!) She'll be
{(toot toot)

com-ing round the moun-tain, She'll be com-ing round the moun-tain, She'll be
rid-ing six white hors-es, She'll be rid-ing six white hors-es, She'll be

com-ing round the moun-tain when she comes. (toot toot)
rid-ing six white hors-es when she comes. {(Whoa there!)
{(toot toot)

141. A Sailor Went to Sea

Traditional

A sail - or went to sea To see what he could see And all that he could see Was the deep blue sea.

75. Some People

Traditional

Some peo - ple talk a lot and don't say a thing, So it's bet - ter yet to let them sing!

100. You Can't Make a Turtle Come Out

Words and Music by Malvina Reynolds

You can't make a tur-tle come out._____ You can't make a tur-tle come

out._____ You can call him or coax him or shake him or shout. But you

can't make a tur-tle come out, come out. You can't make a tur-tle come out._____

86. Bye Bye Blues

Words and Music by Fred Hamm,
Dave Bennett, Bert Lown, and Chauncey Gray

88. Chickery Chick

Words by Sylvia Dee

Music by Sidney Lippman

Chick-er-y chick cha la cha la. Check-a-la rome-y in a ba-nan-i-ka.

Bol-li-ka, wol-li-ka, can't you see chick-er-y chick is me.

Ev-ery time you're sick and tired of just the same old thing,

93. Schnitzelbank

German American Song

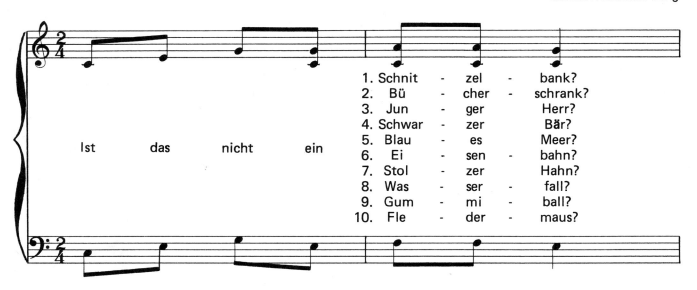

Ist das nicht ein

1. Schnit - zel - bank?
2. Bü - cher - schrank?
3. Jun - ger Herr?
4. Schwar - zer Bär?
5. Blau - es Meer?
6. Ei - sen - bahn?
7. Stol - zer Hahn?
8. Was - ser - fall?
9. Gum - mi - ball?
10. Fle - der - maus?

(to Refrain, 1st time only)

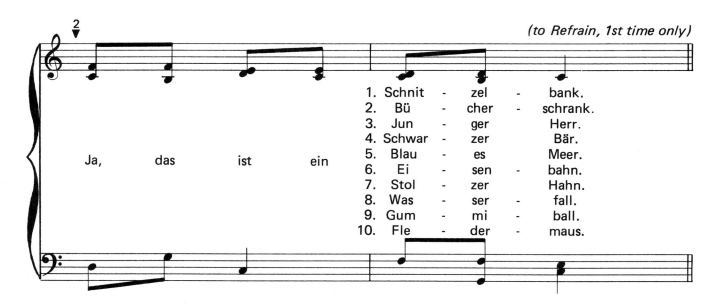

Ja, das ist ein

1. Schnit - zel - bank.
2. Bü - cher - schrank.
3. Jun - ger Herr.
4. Schwar - zer Bär.
5. Blau - es Meer.
6. Ei - sen - bahn.
7. Stol - zer Hahn.
8. Was - ser - fall.
9. Gum - mi - ball.
10. Fle - der - maus.

(to Refrain, 2nd time and thereafter)

3. 2. Bü - cher - schrank, 1. Schnit - zel - bank.

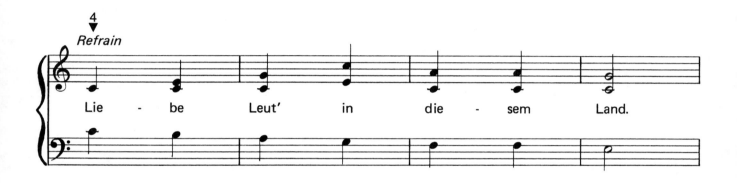

4. *Refrain*

Lie - be Leut' in die - sem Land.

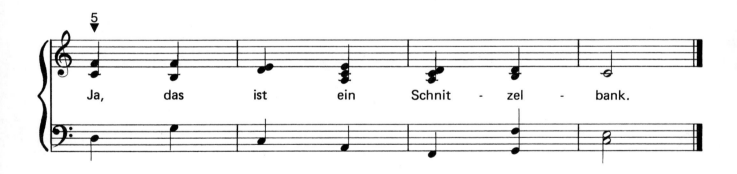

5. Ja, das ist ein Schnit - zel - bank.

103. Give a Little Whistle

Words and Music by Ned Washington
and Leigh Harline

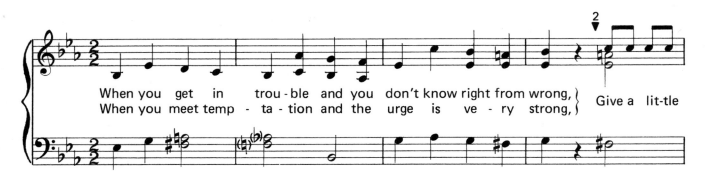

When you get in trou - ble and you don't know right from wrong, }
When you meet temp - ta - tion and the urge is ve - ry strong, }
Give a lit-tle

whis - tle!   (whistle)__   Give a lit-tle whis - tle!   (whistle)__

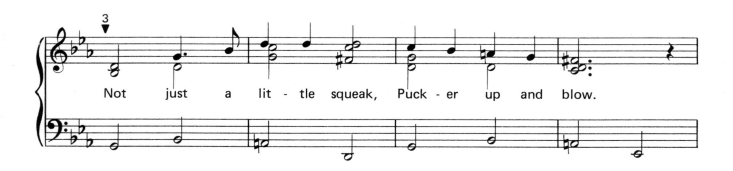

Not   just   a   lit - tle squeak,   Puck - er   up   and   blow.

And if your whis-tle's weak, yell "Ji-mi-ny Crick-et"!

Take the straight and nar-row path, and if you start to slide, Give a lit-tle

whis-tle! (whistle)___ Give a lit-tle whis-tle! (whistle)___ And

al-ways let your con-science be your guide.___

106. Sally Don't You Grieve

Spiritual

Oh, I want to go to hea-ven, Oh, I want to go to hea-ven, And I want to go
right, And I want to go right, I want to go to
hea-ven, I want to go to hea-ven, All dressed in
white. All dressed in white. {1. Oh, I want to go to
2. Oh,___ Sal - ly don't you

heaven, And I want to go right, I want to go to
grieve,___ don't you grieve ___ no more. Oh, Sal - ly don't you

hea - ven, All dressed in white.} Oh, Sal - ly don't you
grieve,___ don't you grieve no more.}

grieve, Don't you grieve no more.___

112. Brethren in Peace Together

Jewish Folk Song

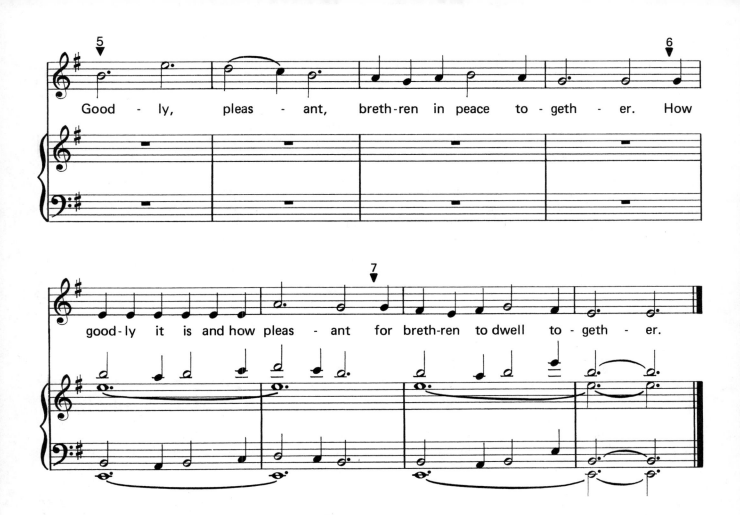

Good - ly, pleas - ant, breth-ren in peace to - geth - er. How

good - ly it is and how pleas - ant for breth-ren to dwell to - geth - er.

114. Lady From Baltimore

Southern Folk Song

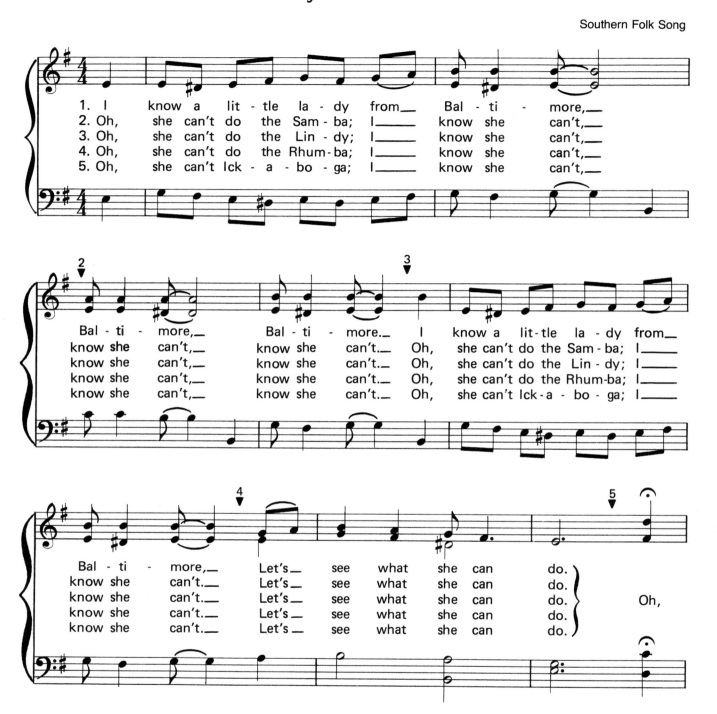

116. March of the Kings

French Folk Melody

Three great
Ce ma-

kings____ I met at ear - ly morn,____ With all their ret - i - nue were slow - ly
tin,____ J'ai ren - con-tré le train____ De trois grands Rois qui al - laient en voy-

march - ing. Three great kings____ I met at ear - ly morn,____ Were on their
a - ge, Ce ma - tin,____ J'ai ren - con-tré le train____ De trois grands

way to meet the new - ly born. With gifts of gold brought from far a-
Rois des-sus le grand che - min. Tout char - gés d'or les sui-vaient d'a-

way__ And val - iant war - riors to guard the king-ly treas - ure, With gifts of
bord__ De grands guer-riers et les gar-des du tré - sor,__ Tout char - gés

gold brought from far a - way__ And shields all shin-ing in their bright ar - ray.
d'or les sui-vaient d'a - bord__ De grands guer-riers a-vec leurs bou-cli - ers.

122. The Caravan

Syrian Folk Song

127. My Home's in Montana

Cowboy Song

1. My home's in Mon - tan - a; I wear a ban - dan - na. My spurs are of
2. When far from the ranch - es, I chop the pine branch - es To heap on my

sil - ver; my po - ny is gray. When rid - ing the rang - es, my
camp - fire, as day - light grows pale. When I have par - tak - en of

luck nev - er chang - es. With feet in the stir - rup, I'll gal - lop all day.
beans and of ba - con, I whis - tle a cheer - y old song of the trail.

126. I Ride an Old Paint

American Folk Song

128. So Long, Farewell

Words by Oscar Hammerstein, II

From *The Sound of Music*
Music by Richard Rodgers

bye._____ 3. We're glad to go. I can-not tell a
sun has gone to bed, and so must

lie.___ We flit, we float, we fleet-ly flee, we fly.___ 4. The
I.___ So long, fare-well, Auf Wie-der-sehn, a-

dieu. Good-bye,_____ good-bye,_____ good-bye._____

130. There Was an Old Woman

American Folk Song

(D. S. first time only)

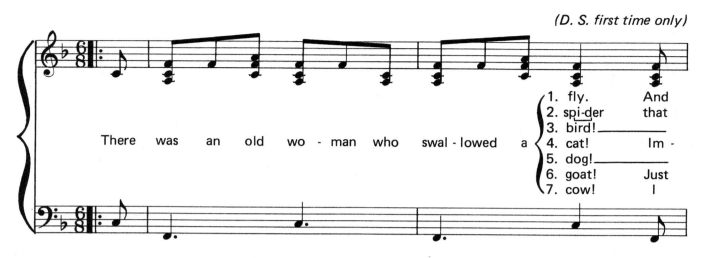

There was an old wo - man who swal - lowed a

1. fly.   And
2. spi-der   that
3. bird!_____
4. cat!   Im -
5. dog!_____
6. goat!   Just
7. cow!   I

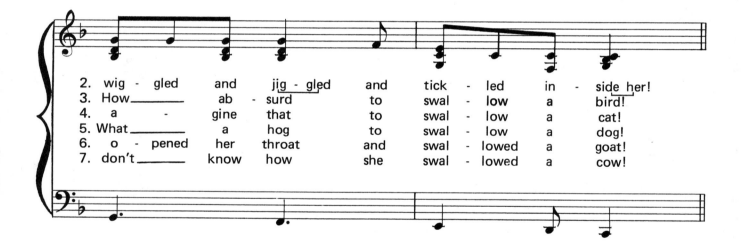

2. wig - gled   and   jig - gled   and   tick - led   in - side her!
3. How_____   ab - surd   to   swal - low   a   bird!
4. a - gine   that   to   swal - low   a   cat!
5. What_____   a   hog   to   swal - low   a   dog!
6. o - pened   her   throat   and   swal - lowed   a   goat!
7. don't_____   know   how   she   swal - lowed   a   cow!

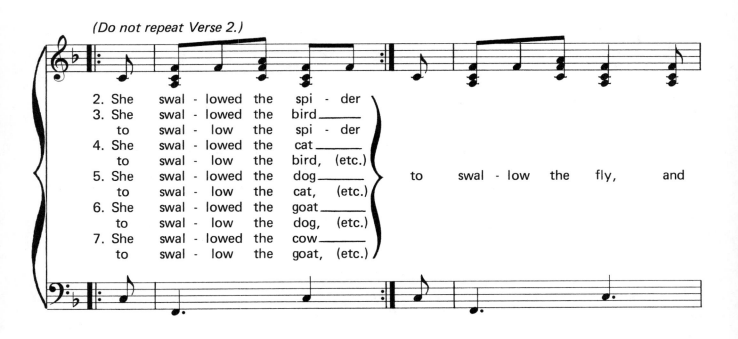

(Do not repeat Verse 2.)

2. She swal - lowed the spi - der
3. She swal - lowed the bird____
   to swal - low the spi - der
4. She swal - lowed the cat____
   to swal - low the bird, (etc.)
5. She swal - lowed the dog____
   to swal - low the cat, (etc.)
6. She swal - lowed the goat____
   to swal - low the dog, (etc.)
7. She swal - lowed the cow____
   to swal - low the goat, (etc.)

to swal - low the fly, and

(To Coda after Verse 7.)

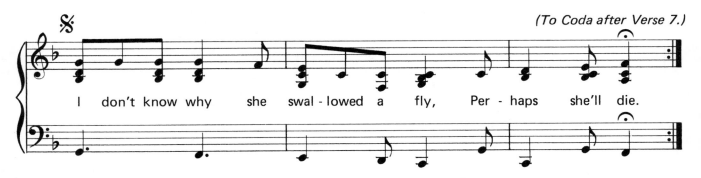

I don't know why she swal - lowed a fly, Per - haps she'll die.

Coda

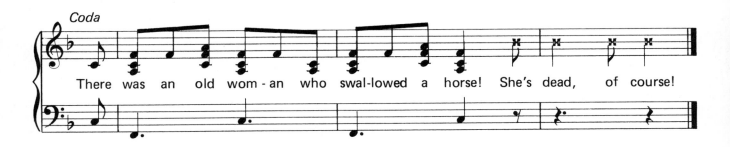

There was an old wom - an who swal-lowed a horse! She's dead, of course!

132. Lament for a Donkey

Spanish Folk Song

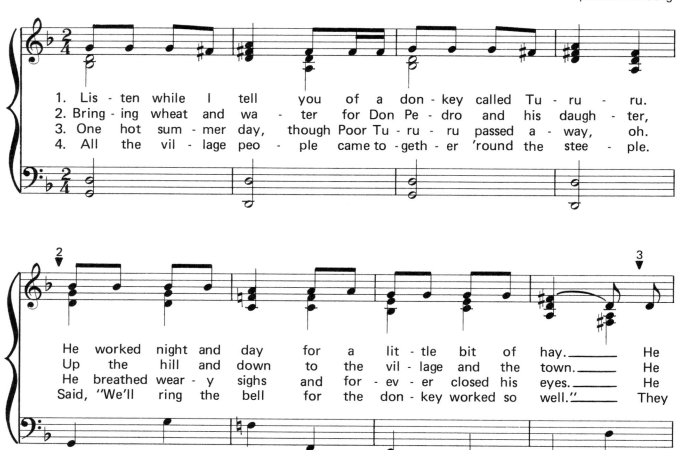

1. Lis - ten while I tell you of a don - key called Tu - ru - ru.
2. Bring - ing wheat and wa - ter for Don Pe - dro and his daugh - ter,
3. One hot sum - mer day, though Poor Tu - ru - ru passed a - way, oh.
4. All the vil - lage peo - ple came to -geth - er 'round the stee - ple.

He worked night and day for a lit - tle bit of hay._____ He
Up the hill and down to the vil - lage and the town._____ He
He breathed wear - y sighs and for - ev - er closed his eyes._____ He
Said, "We'll ring the bell for the don - key worked so well."_____ They

worked all night and day, just for a lit - tle hay. He
went up hill and down to the vil - lage and the town. He
breathed such wear - y sighs and for - ev - er closed his eyes. He
said, "We'll ring the bell for the don - key worked so well." They

worked all night and day, just for a lit - tle hay.
went up hill and down to the vil - lage and the town.
breathed such wear - y sighs and for - ev - er closed his eyes.
said, "We'll ring the bell for the don - key worked so well."

133. Gypsy Rover

English Ballad

1. The gyp - sy ro - ver came o - ver the hill, Bound through the val - ley so
2. She left her fath - er's cas - tle gate; She left her own true
3. Her fath - er sad - dled his fast - est steed; He roamed the val - ley all
4. He came at last to a man - sion fine Down by the riv - er
5. He's no gyp - sy, my fath - er, said she, My lord of free lands all

sha - dy. He whist-led and he sang till the green woods rang. And
lov - er. She left her ser - vants and her es - tate To
o - ver. He sought his daugh - ter at great speed And the
Clay - de. There was mu - sic and bright sun - shine For the
o - ver. And I will stay till my dy - ing day With my

he won the heart of a la - dy.
fol - low the gyp - sy ro - ver.
whist - ling gyp - sy ro - ver.
gyp - sy and his la - dy.
whist - ling gyp - sy ro - ver.

Ah - di - do ah - di - do - da - day. Ah - di - do ah - di -
Ah - di - do ah - di - do - da - day. Ah - di - do ah - di -
Ah - di - do ah - di - do - da - day. Ah - di - do ah - di -
Ah - di - do ah - di - do - da - day. Ah - di - do ah - di -
Ah - di - do ah - di - do - da - day. Ah - di - do ah - di -

day - dee; He whist-led and he sang till the green woods rang and
day - dee; She left_ her_ ser - vants and her es - tate to
day - dee; He sought_ his_ daugh-ter_ at great speed and the
day - dee;_ There was_ mu - sic and bright sun-shine for the
day - dee; And I_ will_ stay till my dy - ing day with my

he won the heart of a la - dy.
fol - low the gyp - sy_ ro - ver.
whist - ling_ gyp - sy_ ro - ver.
gyp - sy_ and his_ la - dy.
whist - ling_ gyp - sy_ ro - ver.

139. Groundhog

Traditional

1. Let's git a-go-in'. Whis-tle up your dog.
2. Ev-ery-bod-y read-y and ev-ery-bod-y set.
3. Too man-y rocks and too man-y logs.

Let's git a-go-in'. Whis-tle up your dog. We're off to the woods to
Ev-ery bod-y read-y and ev-ery-bod-y set. We'll catch a ground-hog,
Too man-y rocks and too man-y logs. Too much trou-ble to

catch ground-hog. Ground-hog!
you can bet. Ground-hog!
catch ground-hogs. Ground-hog!

140. Found a Peanut

Nonsense Song

1. Found a pea - nut, found a pea - nut, Found a pea - nut last__ night.
2. It was rot - ten, it was rot - ten, It was rot - ten last__ night.
3. Ate it a-ny - way, ate it a-ny - way, Ate it a-ny - way last__ night.
4. Got__ sick,__ got__ sick,__ Got__ sick__ last__ night.
5. Called the doc - tor, called the doc - tor, Called the doc - tor last__ night.
6. Had an op-er - a-tion, had an op-er - a-tion, Had an op-er - a-tion last__ night.
7. I died a-ny - way, I died a-ny - way, I died a-ny - way last__ night.
8. Went to heav - en, went to heav - en, Went to heav - en last__ night.
9. Woke__ up,__ woke__ up,__ Woke__ up__ last__ night.

night. Last__ night I found a pea-nut, Found a pea - nut last__ night.
night. Last__ night__ it was rot - ten, It was rot - ten last__ night.
night. Last__ night I ate it a-ny-way, Ate it a-ny - way last__ night.
night. Last__ night I got__ sick,__ Got__ sick__ last__ night.
night. Last__ night I called the doc - tor, Called the doc - tor last__ night.
night. Last__ night I had an op-er-a - tion, Had an op-er-a - tion last__ night.
night. Last__ night I died__ a-ny-way, I died a-ny - way last__ night.
night. Last__ night I went to heav - en, Went to heav - en last__ night.
night. Last__ night I woke__ up,__ I woke up__ last__ night.

144. Down by the Bay

Traditional

Down by the bay, (Down by the bay) Where the wa - ter - mel - ons

grow, (Where the wa - ter - mel - ons grow) Back to my

home, (Back to my home) I dare not go. (I dare not

142. So Long, It's Been Good to Know You

Words and Music by Woody Guthrie

So long, it's been good to know you, So long, it's been good to know you, So long, it's been good to know you, What a long time since I've been home, and I've got to be drifting along.

176. My Hat

German Folk Song

My hat it had three cor - ners,_____ Three cor - ners
Mein Hut er hat drei Eck - en,_____ Drei Eck - en

had my hat;_____ And had it not three
hat mein Hut;_____ Und hat er nicht drei

cor - ners,_____ It would not be my hat._____
Eck - en,_____ Dann ist er nicht mein Hut._____

145. Old Texas

Cowboy Song

146. I'm on My Way

Traditional

I'm on my way,_____ and I won't turn back.

I'm on my way,_____ and I won't turn back.

I'm on my way,_____ and I won't turn back.

I'm on my way, oh yes, I'm on my way!_____

148. Grizzly Bear

Southern Work Song

1. I'm gon-na tell you a sto-ry 'bout griz-zl-y bear, Jack o'
2. He had great long teeth like a griz-zl-y bear, He made a
3. Tell me who was the griz-zl-y bear,

Dia-monds was-n't noth-ing but a griz-zl-y bear. Oh, the
track in the bot-tom like a griz-zl-y bear. Oh, the
Tell me who was the griz-zl-y bear.

griz-zl-y griz-zl-y griz-zl-y bear, Oh, the

griz-zl-y, griz-zl-y, griz-zl-y bear.

149. Happiness Runs

Words and Music by Donovan Leitch

Hap-pi-ness runs in a cir-cu-lar mo-tion, Thought is like a lit-tle boat up-on the sea.

You can have ev-ery-thing if you let your-self be,

You can have ev-ery-thing if you let your-self be.

147. Apusski Dusky

Traditional Nonsense Song

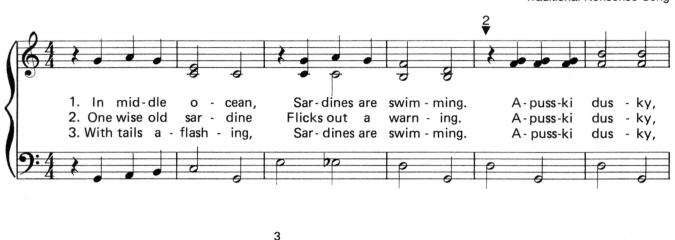

1. In mid-dle o-cean, Sar-dines are swim-ming. A-puss-ki dus-ky,
2. One wise old sar-dine Flicks out a warn-ing. A-puss-ki dus-ky,
3. With tails a-flash-ing, Sar-dines are swim-ming. A-puss-ki dus-ky,

a-puss-ki-du.   A boat sails o-ver,   Down comes a
a-puss-ki-du.   Swift through the wa-ter,   They dart a-
a-puss-ki-du.   So full of joy that   They're swim-ming

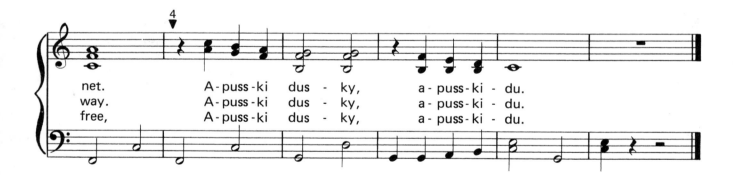

net.   A-puss-ki dus-ky,   a-puss-ki-du.
way.   A-puss-ki dus-ky,   a-puss-ki-du.
free,   A-puss-ki dus-ky,   a-puss-ki-du.

150. Portland Town

Words Adapted by B.A.

Music by Derroll Adams

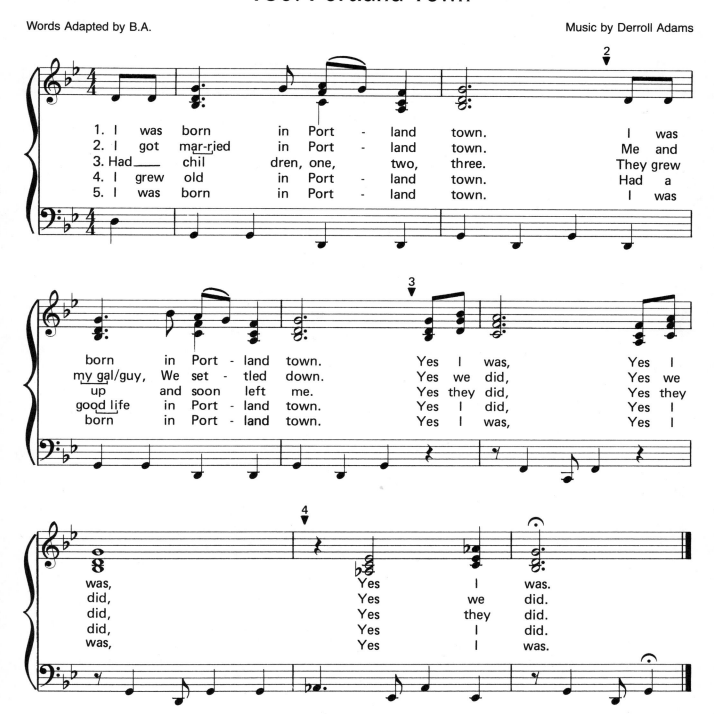

1. I was born in Port - land town. I was born in Port - land town. Yes I was, Yes I was, Yes I was.
2. I got mar-ried in Port - land town. Me and my gal/guy, We set - tled down. Yes we did, Yes we did, Yes we did. Yes we did.
3. Had chil - dren, one, two, three. They grew up and soon left me. Yes they did, Yes they did, Yes they did. Yes they did.
4. I grew old in Port - land town. Had a good life in Port - land town. Yes I did, Yes I did, Yes I did. Yes I did.
5. I was born in Port - land town. I was born in Port - land town. Yes I was, Yes I was, Yes I was.

154. We're Off to See the Wizard

Words by E.Y. Harburg

Music by Harold Arlen

We're off to see the Wiz-ard,___ the won-der-ful Wiz-ard of Oz.___ We

hear he is a whiz of a wiz, if ev-er a wiz there was.___ If

ev-er, oh ev-er a **wiz** there was, the Wiz-ard of Oz is one be-cause, Be-

cause, be-cause, be-cause, be-cause, be-cause,___ Be-

cause of the won-der-ful things he does. *(whistle)* _____ We're

off to see the Wiz - ard, ____ the won-der-ful Wiz - ard of Oz!

155. The Merry Old Land of Oz

Words by E.Y. Harburg

Music by Harold Arlen

Ha - ha - ha! Ho - ho - ho! and a coup-le of tra - la - las, That's

how we laugh the day a - way, In the mer-ry old land of Oz.

156. Ding-Dong, the Witch Is Dead

Words by E.Y. Harburg

Music by Harold Arlen

Ding - Dong, the witch is dead! Which old witch? the wick - ed witch.

Ding - Dong, the wick - ed witch is dead.

Wake up, you sleep - y head, rub your eyes, get out of bed.

Wake up, the wick - ed witch is dead!_____ She's

gone where the gob - lins go be - low,   be - low, be - low, yo -

ho   let's o - pen up and sing,   and ring the bells out.

Ding - Dong! the mer - ry - o,   sing it high,   sing it low,

Let them know the wick - ed witch is dead._____

157. Somewhere Over the Rainbow

Words by E.Y. Harburg

Music by Harold Arlen

1. Some - where o - ver the rain - bow way up high,
2. Some - where o - ver the rain - bow skies are blue,
3. Some - where o - ver the rain - bow blue - birds fly,

There's a land that I heard of once in a lull - a -
And the dreams that you dare to dream real - ly do come
Birds fly o - ver the rain - bow, why then, oh why can't

by.
true.
Some - day I'll wish up - on a star and

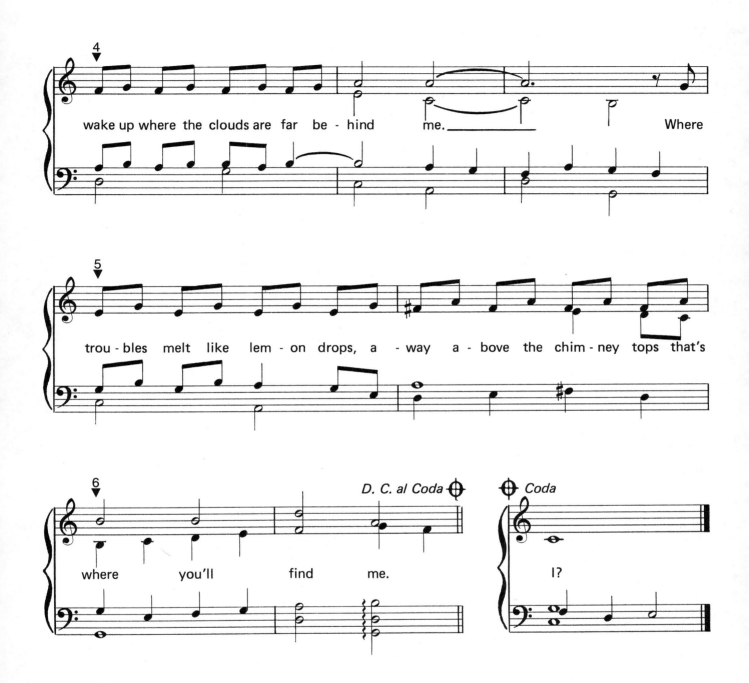

wake up where the clouds are far be - hind me. _____ Where

trou - bles melt like lem - on drops, a - way a - bove the chim - ney tops that's

D. C. al Coda

where you'll find me.

Coda

I?

152. Sing a Little

Traditional Round

la, la, la. Sing a lit-tle, sing a lit-tle, la, la, la.

Sing a lit-tle, sing a lit-tle, la, la, la. La, la, la, la, la, la, la, la, la, la.

162. Clouds

Words by Christina Rossetti

Music by Ruth Bampton

Wistfully

White sheep, white sheep, on a blue hill,

When the wind stops, you all stand still. When the wind blows, you

walk a - way slow. White sheep, white sheep, where do you go?

From GROWING WITH MUSIC SERIES, Book 2, Wilson, et al (Englewood Cliffs, NJ: Prentice-Hall Inc. © 1970)

162. Clouds

Words by Christina Rossetti

Music by Don Malin

Dreamily

White sheep, white sheep, on a blue hill,

When the wind stops, you all___ stand still. When the wind blows, you

walk a - way slow. White sheep, white sheep, where did you go?

163. Clouds

Words by Christina Rossetti

Music by Arthur Frackenpohl

White sheep, white sheep, on a ___ blue ___ hill, White sheep,

white sheep, on a ___ blue ___ hill, When the wind stops, you all ___ stand

still. When the wind blows, ___ you walk a - way slow.

White sheep, white sheep, Where do ___ you go? ___

165. Me and My Shadow

Words and Music by Billy Rose, Al Jolson and Dave Dreyer

Me and my sha - dow, Stroll-ing down the av - e - nue. Me and my sha - dow, Not a soul to tell our trou-bles to. And when it's

twelve o'-clock,____ We climb the stair.____ We nev-er knock,____ For

no-bod-y's there.____ Just me and my sha -

dow, All a - lone and feel - ing blue.____

172. The Unicorn

Words and Music by Shel Silverstein

1. *Andante:* A long time a - go when the earth was green,___ There was
2. *Allegro:* But the Lord seen some sin-nin' and it caused him pain,___ He says,
3. *Andante:* Now No - ah was there and he an - swered the call-in' And he
4. *Adagio:* Well, No - ah looked out through the driv - in' rain,___ But the
5. *Adagio:* Then the ducks start - ed duck-in' and the snakes start-ed sneak-in', And the
6. *Andante:* And then the ark start - ed mov-in' and it drift - ed with the tide,___ And the

more kinds of an - i - mals than you've ev - er seen. And they'd
"Stand back,___ I'm___ gon - na make it___ rain. So___
fin-ished up the ark___ as the rain start - ed fall-in'. Then he
U - ni - corns was hid - in'— play - in' sil - ly games. They were
el-e-phants start - ed el-e-phant-in' and the boat start - ed shak-in'. The___
U - ni - corns looked up___ from the rock___ and cried, And the

run a - round free while the world was be - ing born. And the
hey,___ Broth-er No-ah, I'll___ tell you what to do.
marched___ in the an - i - mals___ two___ by___ two, And___
kick - in' and a - splash-in' while the rain___ was___ pour-in'.
mice___ start - ed squeak-in' and the li - ons start - ed roar-in', And___
wa - ter came up and sort of float - ed them a - way. That's___

love - li - est of all was the U - ni - corn. There were
Go___ and___ build me a float - ing zoo. And you take
he___ sung___ out as___ they went through. "Hey Lord, I got you
Oh,___ them___ fool - ish___ U - ni - corns. And you take
ev - ery - one's a - board but them U - ni - corns. I mean the
why you've nev - er seen a U - ni - corn to this day. You'll see a

Refrain

Allegro: green al - li - ga - tors and long - necked geese,___
Rit: two al - li - ga - tors and a cou-ple of geese,___
Largo: two al - li - ga - tors and a cou-ple of geese,___
Accel: two al - li - ga - tors and a cou-ple of geese,___
Presto: two al - li - ga - tors and a cou-ple of geese,___
Accel: lot of al - li - ga - tors and a whole mess of geese,___

Hump - back ca - mels and chim - pan - zees,___
Two hump-back ca - mels and two chim - pan - zees,___ Two
Two hump-back ca - mels and two chim - pan - zees,___ Two
Two hump-back ca - mels and two chim - pan - zees,___ Two
The hump-back ca - mels and the chim - pan - zees,___
You'll see hump-back ca - mels and chim - pan - zees,___ You'll see

Cats and rats and e - le - phants but sure as you're born,___ the
cats, two rats, two e - le - phants but sure as you're born, Noah,___
cats, two rats, two e - le - phants but sure as you're born,___ I
cats, two rats, two e - le - phants but sure as you're born, Noah,___
No - ah cried,___ "Close the door___ 'cause the rain is pour-in',___ And
cats and rats and e - le - phants but sure as you're born,___ You're

1. — 5. | **6.**

love - li - est of all was the U - ni corn.
don't___ you for - get my___ U - ni - corns.
sure___ don't___ see your___ U - ni - corns.
don't___ you for - get my___ U - ni - corns.
we just can't___ wait for them U - ni - corns."
nev - er gon - na see no___ U - ni - corn.
(ritard, last time)

337

175. Once

Israeli Folk Song

Once a lad went for a walk to the vil - lage square.
On the road guess whom he met? A young

maid - en fair. Hey! Yum-pa - pa, yum - tsa - tsa, yum - tsa - tsa,

yum - pa - pa. Won't you join me, pret - ty maid, Come let us dance.

220. Sleigh Bells

Russian Folk Song

1. Mer - ry bells go ting - a - lin - gle, Toes and fin - gers freeze and tin - gle,
2. As we ride our song goes ring - ing, Through the air its ech - oes wing-ing,

With our friends we gai - ly min - gle, While the snow - flakes fall.
Till the world seems full of sing - ing: So we speed a - long.

Boys and girls, come out to - geth - er, Clad in coats of fur and leath - er
Through the town and by the riv - er, Where the birch - es sigh and shiv - er

Made to brave the cold - est weath - er, When the sleigh bells ring.
And the birds are si - lent nev - er, Join - ing in our song.

177. The Smoke Went Up the Chimney

American Camp Song

Oh, we pushed the damp - er in and we pulled the damp - er out, And the smoke went up the chim - ney just the same. Just the same, just the same, And the smoke went up the chim - ney just the same.

185. The Purple Bamboo

Chinese Folk Song

1. See I bring to you pur-ple bam-boo shoot, Now 'twill make a
2. You must try and grow like the bam-boo tall, Then those part-ing

love-ly flute; But those lips so small Can-not play at all
lips so small Soon will play the flute Made from bam-boo shoot;

On a love-ly gold-en__ flute. Ee - tee - tee,
Sil-very tunes will gent-ly__ fall.

Soon will come the hap-py day. day. My son the flute will play.

178. I'm Looking Over a Four-Leaf Clover

Words by Mort Dixon

Music by Harry Woods

I'm look-ing o-ver a four-leaf clo-ver that I o-ver-looked be-fore;_____ One leaf is sun-shine, the sec-ond is rain,___ Third is the ros-es that grow in the lane,___

No need ex - plain - ing, the one re - main - ing is some - bod - y I a - dore._____ I'm look - ing o - ver a four - leaf clo - ver that I o - ver - looked be - fore.

184. La Jesusita

Mexican Folk Song

seen. Tra la la la! Oh, dance with me, Je - su - si - ta, Oh, please, won't you dance with
lón. Ya-ya-ya - ya! Y quié - re -me, Je -su - si - ta, y quié - re - me por fa -

me? If you'll be my danc-ing part-ner, Then your faith-ful slave I'll be.
vor. Y mi - ra que soy tu a -man - te, y se - gu - ro ser - vi - dor.

188. Sir Eglamore

Old English Ballad

1. Sir Eg - la - more,__ that val - iant knight, Fa la
2. There starts a huge drag - on out of his den, Fa la
3. This drag - on had__ a plagu-ey hard hide, Fa la
4. The drag - on had__ him down and roared, Fa la

lank - y down dil - ly, He took up his sword and he went for to fight;
lank - y down dil - ly, Which had__ killed I know not how man - y men;
lank - y down dil - ly, Which could__ the strong - est steel__ a - bide;
lank - y down dil - ly, The knight__ was sor - ry for__ his sword;

Fa la lank - y down dil - ly. And as he rode o'er
Fa la lank - y down dil - ly. But when he saw Sir
Fa la lank - y down dil - ly. But as the drag - on
Fa la lank - y down dil - ly. The sword it was a

hill and dale, All arm - èd with a coat of mail,
Eg - la - more, If you'd but heard how the drag-on did roar!
yawn-ing did fall, He thrust his sword down hilt and all.
right good blade, As ev - er Turk or Span - iard made.

6 Refrain

Fa lank - y down, la lank - y down, Fa la lank - y down dil - ly.

210. This Is My Country

Words by Don Raye

Music by Al Jacobs

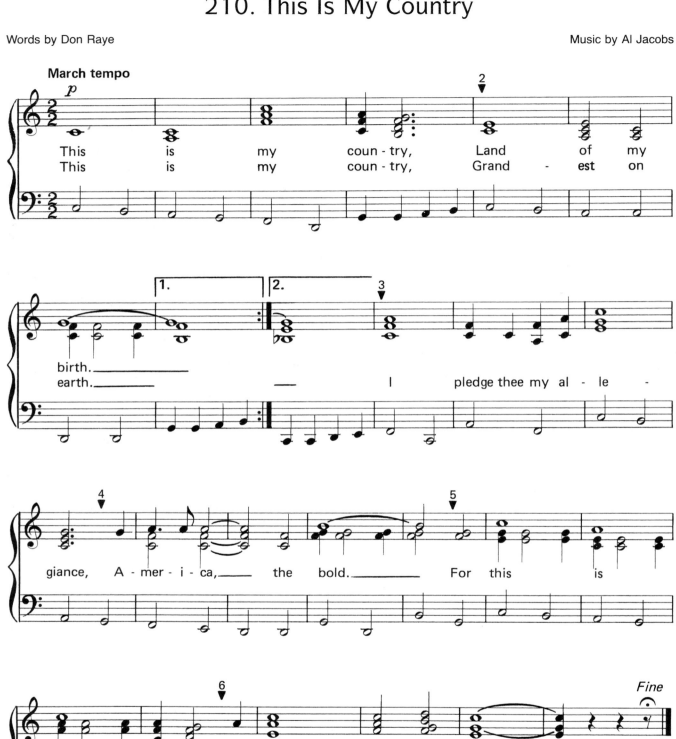

This is my coun-try, Land of my birth.
This is my coun-try, Grand-est on earth.

I pledge thee my al-le-giance, A-mer-i-ca, the bold. For this is my coun-try, To have and to hold.

212. Birthday Hallelujah

Words and Music by Malvina Reynolds

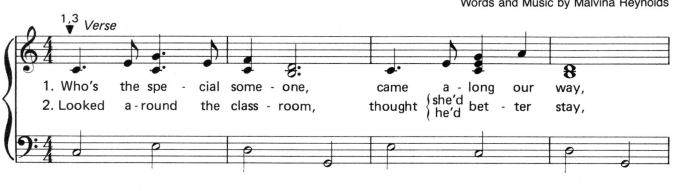

1. Who's the spe - cial some - one, came a - long our way,
2. Looked a - round the class - room, thought {she'd / he'd} bet - ter stay,

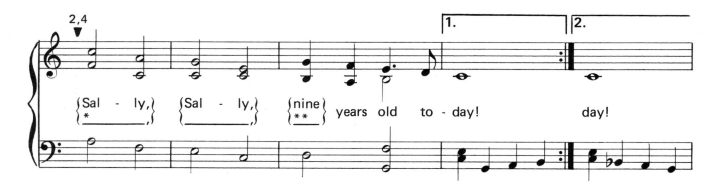

{Sal - ly,} {Sal - ly,} {nine} years old to - day! day!
*_____, *_____, **

Sing Hal - le - lu - jah, and {throw your fish - ing line. / chase the big, fat hen.}

Hold your hat, hold your specs, man the pumps, clear the decks,

* *Insert the name of the person who is celebrating a birthday.*
** *Insert the age of the person who is celebrating a birthday.*

350

Who knows what will hap-pen next, {Sal - ly} is {nine.}

229. Dayenu

Jewish Folk Song

I - lu ho-tsi, ho-tsi - a - nu, ho-tsi - a - nu mi-Mits-ra-yim, Ho-tsi - a -nu mi-Mits-ra-yim,

Da - ye - nu. Da - da - ye-nu,____ da - da - ye-nu,____

Da - da - ye-nu, da - ye-nu, da-ye-nu, da-ye-nu. ye-nu, da-ye-nu.

214. Sing a Rainbow

Words and Music by Arthur Hamilton

Red and yel-low and pink and green, pur-ple and o-range and blue,

I can sing a rain-bow, sing a rain-bow, sing a rain-bow, too.____

Lis-ten with your eyes; lis-ten with your eyes and sing ev-ery-thing you see.

You can sing a rain-bow, sing a rain-bow, sing a-long with me.

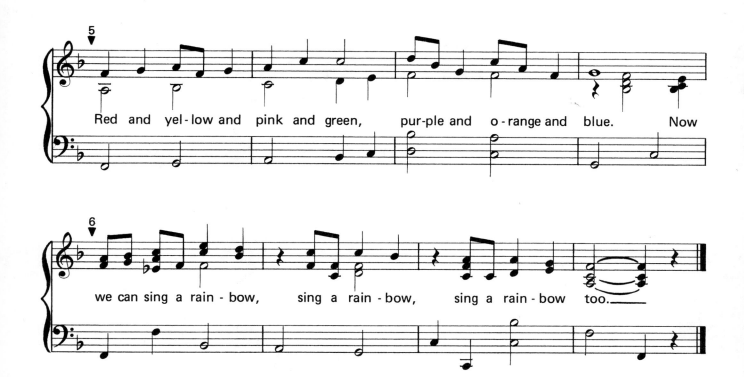

Red and yel-low and pink and green, pur-ple and o-range and blue. Now

we can sing a rain-bow, sing a rain-bow, sing a rain-bow too.

219. O Hanukah

Translated by Judith Eisenstein

Yiddish Folk Song

O Ha - nu-kah, O Ha - nu-kah, come light the me-no - rah, Let's have a par - ty, we'll

all dance the ho - ra. Gath-er 'round the ta - ble, we'll give you a treat,

Shin - ing tops to play with and pan - cakes to eat; And while we are

play - ing, the can - dles are burn - ing___ low.

One for each night, they___ shed a sweet light To re - mind us of days long a -

go.

mind us of days long a - go.

171. The Music Is You

Words and Music by John Denver

Mu - sic makes_ pic - tures and of - ten tells_ sto - ries,

All of it_ mag - ic and all of it_ true._ And

all of the pic - tures and all_ of the sto - ries And

all of_ the mag - ic, the mu - sic is_ you._

232. America, the Beautiful

Words by Katherine Lee Bates

Music by Samuel A. Ward

1. O beau-ti-ful for spa-cious skies, For am-ber waves of grain, For
2. O beau-ti-ful for pil-grim feet Whose stern, im-pas-sioned stress A
3. O beau-ti-ful for he-roes proved In lib-er-at-ing strife, Who

pur-ple moun-tain maj-es-ties A-bove the fruit-ed plain!
thor-ough-fare for free-dom beat A-cross the wil-der-ness!
more than self their coun-try loved, And mer-cy more than life!

A-mer-i-ca, A-mer-i-ca, God shed his grace on thee, And
A-mer-i-ca, A-mer-i-ca, God mend thine ev-ery flaw, Con-
A-mer-i-ca, A-mer-i-ca, May God thy gold re-fine, Till

crown thy good with broth-er-hood From sea to shin-ing sea.
firm thy soul in self-con-trol, Thy lib-er-ty in law.
all suc-cess be no-ble-ness, And ev-ery gain di-vine.

221. We Wish You a Merry Christmas

English Folk Song

We wish you a mer-ry Christ-mas, We wish you a mer-ry Christ-mas, We

Fine

wish you a mer-ry Christ-mas and a hap-py New Year.

Good tid-ings we bring for you and your kin; Good

tid - ings of Christ - mas and a hap - py New Year.

5
1. Now bring us some fig - gy pud - ding, Now bring us some fig - gy pud - ding, Now
2. We won't go un - til we get some, We won't go un - til we get some, We

(after Verse 2, D. C. al Fine)

7
bring us some fig - gy pud - ding, and bring some right here.
won't go un - til we get some, so bring some right here.

223. O He Did Whistle and She Did Sing

Words and Music by Richard Felciano

224. A' Soalin'

Words and Music by Paul Stookey,
Tracy Batteast, and Elena Mezzetti

Soal, a soal, a soal cake, Please, good mis-sus, a soal cake, An ap-ple, a pear, a plum, a cher-ry, An-y good thing to make us all mer-ry, One for Pe-ter, two for Paul, Three for Him who made us all.

(After Verse 3, D. C. al Fine)

226. A Valentine Wish

Words and Music by Natalie Sleeth

It was sent by in-tent, from a spe-cial friend!_____

3.

game!_____

Part I

Hope some-one sends me a Val-en-tine, { red and white, bold and bright. / bought with care, just to share. / trimmed with lace, just a trace. }

Part II

I will send you a Val-en-tine, { red and white, bold and bright. / bought with care, just to share. / trimmed with lace, just a trace. }

Hope some-one sends me a Val-en-tine, { to set my heart a-flame!_____ / and fails to sign her/his / and helps me play the }

I will send you a Val-en-tine, { to set your heart a-flame!_____ / and fail to sign my / and helps you play the }

1.

216. Hallowe'en

Words by Harry Behn

Music by John Wood

Mysteriously

1. To - night is the night when dead leaves fly Like witch - es on
2. To - night is the night when leaves do sound Like gnomes in their
3. To - night is the night when pump - kins stare Through brown sheaves and

switch - es a - cross the sky, When elf and sprite flit
homes far be - neath the ground, When spooks and trolls creep
leaves al - most ev - ery - where, When ghoul and ghost and

through the night, On a moon - y sheen, on a moon - y sheen.
out of holes Dark and moss - y green, dark and moss - y green.
gob - lin host Dance a - round their queen, for it's Hal - low - e'en!

230. Feed My Lambs

Words and Music by Natalie Sleeth

Feed my lambs, Tend my sheep, o - ver all a vig - il keep;

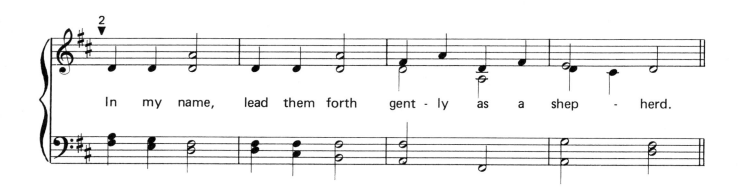

In my name, lead them forth gent - ly as a shep - herd.

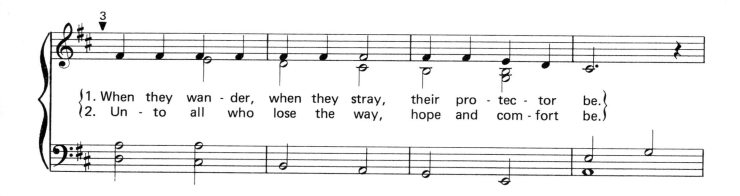

1. When they wan - der, when they stray, their pro - tec - tor be.
2. Un - to all who lose the way, hope and com - fort be.

As ye do un-to my flock, thus ye do to Me.

Feed my lambs, Tend my sheep, o-ver all a vig-il keep;

In my name, Lead them forth gent-ly, gent-ly,

as a lov-ing shep-herd of the lambs._____

234. The Star-Spangled Banner

Words by Francis Scott Key

Composer Unknown

1. Oh,— say, can you see by the dawn's ear-ly light, What so proud-ly we
2. On the shore, dim-ly seen thro' the mists of the deep, Where the foe's haugh-ty
3. Oh,— thus be it ev-er when— free men shall stand Be-tween their loved

hailed at the twi-light's last gleam-ing? Whose broad stripes and bright stars, through the
host in dread si-lence re-pos-es, What is that which the breeze, o'er the
homes and the war's des-o-la-tion! Blest with vic-t'ry and peace, may the

per-il-ous fight, O'er the ram-parts we watched were so gal-lant-ly
tow-er-ing steep, As it fit-ful-ly blows, half con-ceals, half dis-
heav'n-res-cued land Praise the Pow'r that hath made and pre-served us a

stream - ing? And the rock - ets' red glare, the bombs burst - ing in air, Gave
clos - es? Now it catch - es the gleam of the morn - ing's first beam, In full
na - tion. Then_ con - quer we must, for our cause it is just, And

proof through the night that our flag was still there. Oh, say, does that_ star-span - gled
glo - ry re - flec-ted now_ shines on the stream; 'Tis the star-span - gled_ ban - ner, Oh,
this be our mot-to: "In_ God is our trust." And the star-span - gled_ ban - ner in

ban - ner_ yet_ wave_ O'er the land_ of the free and the home of the brave?
long may_ it_ wave_ O'er the land_ of the free and the home of the brave!
tri - umph_ shall_ wave_ O'er the land_ of the free and the home of the brave!

222. Arruru

English Words by Elena Paz

Spanish Folk Melody

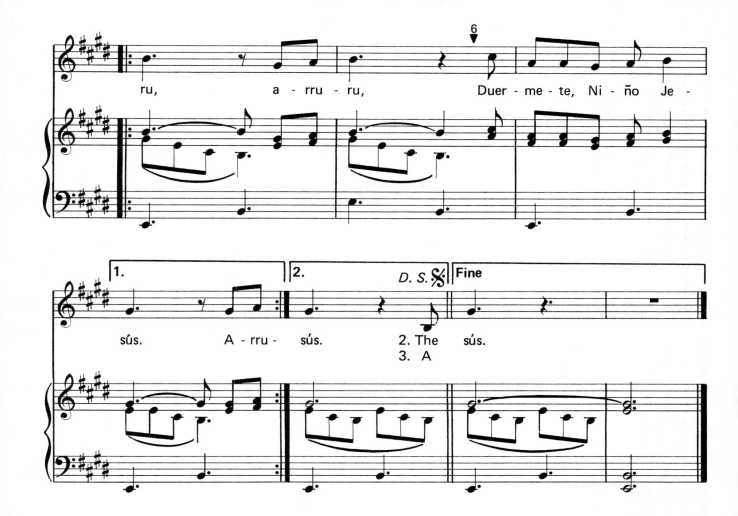

ru,   a - rru - ru,   Duer - me - te, Ni - ño Je -

1. sús.   A - rru - 2. sús.   D. S. %: Fine
                   2. The   sús.
                   3. A

124. Get Along, Little Dogies

Cowboy Song

As I was a-walk-ing one morn-ing for pleas-ure, I
His hat was thrown back, and his spurs were a-jing-ling. And

spied a cow-punch-er a-stroll-ing a-long.
as he ap-proached, he was sing-ing this song:

Whoop-ee

ti-yi-yo, get a-long, lit-tle do-gies. It's

your_____ mis - for - tune and none of my own. Whoop - ee

ti - yi - yo, get a - long, lit - tle do - gies. You

know that Wy - o - ming will be your new home.

187. Sweet and Low

Words by Alfred Lord Tennyson

Music by Joseph Barnaby

Sweet and low, sweet and low, Wind of the west - ern sea,____ Low, low,

breathe and blow, Wind of the west - ern sea,____ O - ver the roll - ing

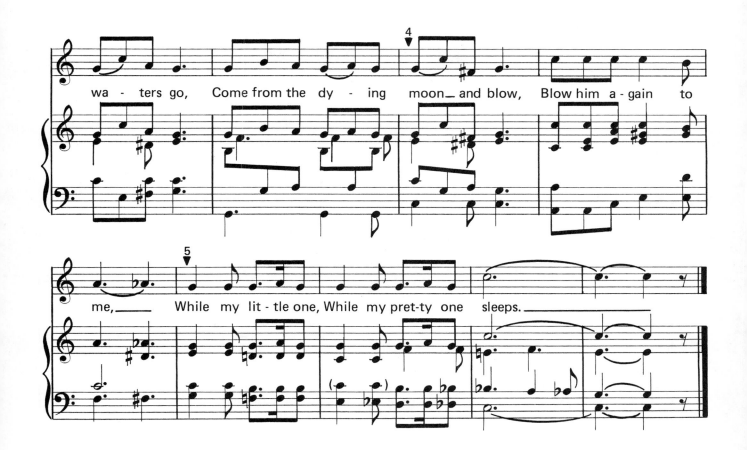

wa - ters go, Come from the dy - ing moon_ and blow, Blow him a - gain to

me,_____ While my lit - tle one, While my pret-ty one sleeps._____

Accidental A notational sign indicating that single tones within a measure should be raised or lowered a half step.

Accompaniment The musical background provided for a principal part.

Aerophone An instrument whose sound is made by blowing into an opening to vibrate a column of air.

Arpeggio The sound produced when the notes of a chord are sounded one after another rather than simultaneously.

Articulation The manner in which a tone is produced, smoothly (*legato*) or detached (*staccato*).

Beat The basic unit of time in music, usually organized within a certain meter into groups of two or three. The underlying pulse of the music.

Brass family Instruments made of brass or other metal on which sound is produced by blowing into a mouthpiece. Pitch changes result from altering the length of tubing through which the air moves. This family includes the trumpet, French horn, and tuba.

Call-response A musical form in which a musical idea is stated (usually by one voice) and echoed (usually by a group).

Canon A composition in whch one line of music is imitated strictly in another line of music at any pitch or time interval.

Chamber music Music for small instrumental ensembles in which one instrument plays each part.

Chord The simultaneous sounding of three or more tones.

Chordophone An instrument whose sound is produced by the vibration of stretched strings.

Chromatic scale In Western music the octave is divided into twelve half steps. When these half steps are played one after the other, they form a chromatic scale.

Coda A section added to the end of a composition as a conclusion.

Concerto A piece of music for one or more soloists and orchestra, usually in symphonic form with three contrasting movements.

Consonance A combination of tones within a given musical system that creates an agreeable effect or a feeling of repose.

Countermelody A melody added to another to provide rhythmic or harmonic contrast, or harmonic tone color.

Crescendo A gradual increase in volume.

Da Capo (D.C.) From the beginning. Indicates that the composition should be repeated from the beginning to the end or until the word *Fine* appears.

Dal Segno (D.S.) From the sign. Indicates that the composition should be repeated from the sign until the word *Fine* appears.

Decrescendo A gradual decrease in volume.

Descant A countermelody usually played or sung above the main melody of a song.

Dissonance A combination of tones within a given musical system that creates a disagreeable effect or a feeling of tension.

Dynamics The expressive markings used to indicate the degree of intensity of sound or volume. The most common are pianissimo (*pp*): very soft; piano (*p*): soft; mezzo piano (*mp*): moderately soft; mezzo forte (*mf*): moderately loud; forte (*f*): loud; fortissimo (*ff*): very loud; crescendo: increase in loudness; decrescendo or diminuendo: decrease in loudness.

Fermata Hold or pause.

Fine End or close.

Fugue A composition in which one or two themes are repeated or imitated by successively entering voices.

Glissando A rapid slide over the scale on a keyboard instrument or harp; also a ''smeared'' slur of no definite pitch intervals, possible on stringed instruments and the trombone.

Harmony The sound that occurs when two or more tones are produced simultaneously.

Home tone The tonal center, or first tone of a scale.

Idiophone An instrument whose sound is produced by the vibration of a solid material; the sound is initiated by striking, scraping, or rattling.

Imitation The repetition by one voice or instrument of a theme or melody previously sung or played by another voice or instrument, as in a round, canon, or fugue.

Improvisation Performing or creating music spontaneously without the use of printed music, notes, or memory.

Interlude A section of music inserted between the parts of a long composition. In this text, it often refers to brief instrumental sections between verses of songs on the recordings.

Interval The distance in pitch between two tones.

Introduction An opening section of a composition.

Key The key of a composition indicates the scale on which the work is based.

Key signature A number of sharps or flats present on a staff at the beginning of a piece or section that indicates its key or tonality.

Legato An indication that tones should be performed in a smooth, connected manner.

Major scale A scale consisting of seven different pitches and an eighth pitch that is a higher repetition of the first. All of the pitches, except the third and fourth and the seventh and eighth, are separated from each other by one whole step. The remaining pitches are separated from each other by a half step.

Marcato The performance of a tone in a marked or stressed manner.

Measure A group of beats, the first of which is usually accented. The number of beats in the group is determined by the meter signature. Measures are separated from each other by bar lines.

Melodic contour The shape of a succession of musical tones.

Melody A succession of tones having both motion and rhythm.

Membranophone An instrument whose sound is produced by vibrating a stretched skin or membrane.

Meter The organization of a specific number of beats into a group. The groupings are determined by the frequency of the underlying accents.

Meter signature A numerical indication found at the beginning of a piece of music or section that tells the number of beats and type of beat found in each measure.

Minor scale A scale consisting of seven different pitches and an eighth pitch that is a higher repetition of the first. All of the pitches except for the second and third and the fifth and sixth are separated from each other by one whole step. The remaining pitches are separated by a half step.

Mode A scalewise arrangement of tones that may form the basic tonal material of a composition; specifically refers to the medieval church modes.

Modulation The process of changing from one key to another during the course of a composition.

Motive The shortest recognizable unit of notes of a musical theme or subject.

Movement An independent section of a larger instrumental composition such as a symphony or concerto.

Octave The interval between two tones having the same name and located eight notes apart.

Ostinato A short pattern, repeated over and over.

Patschen A physical movement in which one slaps his or her thighs rhythmically.

Pentatonic scale A five-tone scale with no half steps between any two tones. The five tones include one group of two tones and one of three, separated by an interval of one and one-half steps. The scale can be produced on the piano by playing only the black keys.

Percussion family A group of instruments played by shaking or striking. This family includes the celesta, orchestra bells, timpani, maracas, woodblock, castanets, cymbals, drums, xylophone, glockenspiel, tambourine, and claves.

Phrase A natural division of the melodic line, comparable to a sentence in speech.

Pitch The highness or lowness of a musical sound, determined by the frequency of the sound waves producing it.

Pizzicato In string music, the sound produced by plucking the strings rather than bowing them.

Prime mark A marking that indicates the upper octave of notes; e.g. 1′ is higher than 1. Also used to describe sections of music that are similar; e.g. A′ is similar to A.

Pulse See *Beat*.

Rallentando A slowing down of tempo.

Rest A sign indicating silence in music.

Ritard A gradual slowing of tempo.

Rondo A musical form resulting from the alternation of a main theme with contrasting themes (**A B C A** etc.)

Root The note on which a chord is built. A chord is said to be in root position if the root is the lowest sounding note.

Round A melody sung or played by two or more musicians. Each musician or group starts at a different time and repeats the melody several times.

Scale A series of tones arranged in ascending or descending order according to a plan.

Score Printed music.

Sequence Immediate repetition of a tonal pattern at a higher or lower pitch level.

Slur A curved line placed above or below two or more notes of different pitch to indicate that they are to be sung or played without separation.

Sonata A composition for piano or some other instrument (violin, flute, cello, etc.), usually with piano accompaniment, which consists of three or four separate sections called movements.

Staccato An indication that tones should be performed in a short, detached manner.

Staff A group of five horizontal lines on and around which notes are positioned.

String family A group of instruments on which sound is produced by rubbing a bow against strings. Includes the violin, viola, cello, and double bass (bass viol).

Suite A musical form consisting of a set of pieces or movements.

Symphony A sonata for orchestra.

Syncopation The temporary displacement of a regular rhythmic pulse.

Tempo Rate of speed.

Texture The density of sound in a piece of music. This thickness or thinness of sound is created by the number of instruments or voices heard simultaneously.

Theme A complete musical idea that serves as the focus or subject of a musical composition.

Tie A curved line between two or more successive tones of the same pitch. The tones so connected are sounded as one tone that is equal in length to the combined duration of the individual tones.

Timbre The quality or "color" of a tone unique to the instrument or voice that produces it.

Tonal center The first degree of the scale on which a melody is constructed. Also called the *tonic*.

Tonality Feeling for a key or tonal center.

Unison All voices or instruments singing or playing the same pitch. The playing of the same notes by various instruments, voices, or a whole orchestra, either at the same pitch or in different octaves.

Variation The modification of a musical theme to create a new musical idea. This modification may be the result of melodic, rhythmic, or harmonic alteration.

Whole-tone scale A six-tone scale with one whole step between any two tones.

Woodwind family A group of instruments on which sound is produced by vibrating one or two reeds. Includes the clarinet, flute, oboe, and saxophone.

ACKNOWLEDGMENTS

Grateful acknowledgment is made to the following copyright owners and agents for their permission to reprint the following copyrighted material. Every effort has been made to locate all copyright owners; any errors or omissions in copyright notice are inadvertent and will be corrected as they are discovered.

"Apusski Dusky," traditional melody, words from *Apusskidu*, edited by B. Harrop. Reprinted and recorded by permission of A & C Black (Publishers) Limited, London. All rights reserved.

"Arruru," Spanish folk song translated into English by Elena Paz. Copyright © 1963 by Elena Paz Travesi. Reprinted and recorded by permission. All rights reserved.

"A Soalin'," words and music by Paul Stookey, Tracy Batteast and Elena Mezzetti, copyright © 1963 by Pepamar Music Corporation. Reprinted by permission of Warner Bros. Music. All Rights Reserved. Recording licensed through the Harry Fox Agency. All rights reserved.

"Birthday Hallelujah," words and music by Malvina Reynolds from *Songs for a New Generation*. Copyright © 1974 Oak Publications. Reprinted and recorded by permission of Schroder Music Co. (ASCAP). All rights reserved.

"Brethren In Peace Together," Jewish folk song paraphrased from Psalm 133:1, text adapted by Vincent Silliman, from *We Sing of Life*, copyright © 1955 by The American Ethical Union. Permission to reprint and record this song was granted by the American Ethical Union. Copyright 1955: The American Ethical Union Library Catalog number 54:11625. All rights reserved.

"Bye-Bye, Blackbird," words by Mort Dixon, music by Ray Henderson. Copyright 1926 (Renewed) WARNER BROS. INC. All Rights Reserved. Reprinted by Permission. Recording licensed through the Harry Fox Agency.

"Bye Bye Blues," words and music by Fred Hamm, Dave Bennett, Bert Lown and Chauncey Gray. Copyright 1930 by Bourne Co., Music Publishers. Reprinted by permission. All rights reserved. Recording licensed through the Harry Fox Agency.

"Chickery Chick," written by Sidney Lippman and Sylvia Dee, copyright © 1945 Sainty-Joy, assigned to Harry Von Tilzer Music Publishing Company (c/o The Welk Music Group, Santa Monica, California, 90401). International Copyright Secured. All Rights Reserved. Used by Permission. Recording licensed through the Harry Fox Agency.

"Clouds," music by Don Malin. From *Birchard Music Series, Book Three*. Copyright © 1962 Birch Tree Group Ltd. All rights reserved. Reprinted by permission. Recording licensed through the Harry Fox Agency.

"Clouds," music by Ruth Bampton, from *Growing with Music, Book 2* by Harry R. Wilson, Walter Ehret, Alice M. Snyder, Edward J. Hermann and Albert A. Renna. Copyright © 1970 by Prentice-Hall, Inc., Englewood Cliffs, NJ. Reprinted and recorded by permission. All rights reserved.

"Ding-Dong! The Witch is Dead," lyric by E. Y. Harburg, music by Harold Arlen. Copyright © 1938 (Renewed 1966) Metro-Goldwyn-Mayer Inc. Copyright © 1939 (Renewed 1967) Leo Feist, Inc. Rights throughout the world controlled by Leo Feist, Inc. Reprinted by permission of Columbia Pictures Publications. Recording licensed through the Harry Fox Agency.

"Down By the Bay," from *Sally Go Round the Sun*, by Edith Fowke. Excerpted and reprinted by permission of The Canadian Publishers, McClelland and Stewart Limited, Toronto. Recording licensed through Edith Fowke.

"Down By the Riverside," arranged by Buryl Red. Copyright © 1971 Generic Music. Reprinted and recorded by permission of the publisher.

Copyright © 1972 by Carl Fischer, Inc., New York. This arrangement copyright © 1988 by Carl Fischer, Inc., New York. All Rights Reserved. International Copyright Secured. Reprinted and recorded by permission.

"Gather 'Round," by Margaret Dugard. Copyright © 1984 by Margaret Dugard. Reprinted and recorded by permission. All rights reserved.

"Get Along Little Dogies," originally "Git Along Little Dogies," Copyright © 1975 by Chappell & Co., Inc. International Copyright Secured ALL RIGHTS RESERVED Used by Permission. Recording licensed through the Harry Fox Agency.

"Give a Little Whistle," by Ned Washington and Leigh Harline, copyright 1939 (Renewed by Bourne Co., Music Publishers. Reprinted by permission. All rights reserved. Recording licensed through the Harry Fox Agency.

"Hallowe'en," words by Harry Behn, music by John Wood, adapted from *The Little Hill*, copyright 1949 by Harry Behn, © renewed 1977 by Alice L. Behn. Adapted, reprinted and recorded by permission of Marian Reiner. All rights reserved.

"Happiness Runs" aka "Pebbles and the Man," words and music by Donovan Leitch, copyright © 1968 by Donovan Music Ltd. Reprinted by permission of Columbia Pictures Publications. All rights reserved. Recording licensed through the Harry Fox Agency.

"The Happy Wanderer," words by Antonia Ridge, music by Friedrich W. Moller. Reprinted in the United States and Canada and recorded by permission of Sam Fox Publishing Company. Reprinted outside the United States and Canada by permission of Bosworth & Co. Ltd., London. All rights reserved.

"Howdido," words and music by Woody Guthrie. TRO - © Copyright 1961 and 1964 Ludlow Music, Inc., New York, NY Reprinted by permission. Recording licensed through the Harry Fox Agency.

"How I Get Cool," reprinted by permission of the publisher from Smith, *Using Poetry to Teach Reading and the Language Arts: A Handbook for Elementary School Teachers* (NY: Teachers College Press © 1985 by Teachers College Columbia University. All rights reserved.) pp. 56 and 78.

"Hurdy Gurdy Man," translated by Merritt Wheeler, music by Franz Schubert, from *Growing with Music, Book 6, Teacher's Edition*, by Harry R. Wilson, Walter Ehret, Alice M. Snyder, Edward J. Hermann and Albert A. Renna. Copyright © 1970 by Prentice-Hall, Inc., Englewood Cliffs, NJ. Reprinted and recorded by permission. All rights reserved.

"If I Only Had a Brain (If I Only Had a Heart) (If I Only Had The Nerve)," lyric by E. Y. Harburg, music by Harold Arlen. Copyright © 1938 (Renewed 1966) Metro-Goldwyn-Mayer Inc. Copyright © 1939 (Renewed 1967) Leo Feist, Inc. Rights throughout the world controlled by Leo Feist, Inc. Reprinted by permission of Columbia Pictures Publications. Recording licensed through the Harry Fox Agency.

"I'm Looking Over A Four Leaf Clover," words by Mort Dixon, music by Harry Woods. Copyright © 1927 (Renewed) WARNER BROS, INC. All Rights Reserved. Used by Permission. Recording licensed through the Harry Fox Agency.

"I Ride An Old Paint," Copyright © 1975 by Chappell & Co., Inc. International Copyright Secured ALL RIGHTS RESERVED Used by Permission. Recording licensed through the Harry Fox Agency.

"Kookaburra," Australian round arranged by Sharon Beth Falk. Reprinted and recorded by permission. All rights reserved.

"Lament for a Donkey," Spanish folk tune, words adapted by Martha Harris, from *Growing with Music, Book 4* by Harry R. Wilson, Walter Ehret, Alice M. Snyder, Edward J. Hermann and Albert A. Renna. Copyright © 1966 by Prentice-Hall, Inc., Englewood Cliffs, NJ. Reprinted and recorded by permission. All rights reserved.

"This Is My Country," words by Don Raye, music by Al Jacobs. © Copyright 1940, Shawnee Press, Inc.; Delaware Water Gap, PA 18327. U.S. Copyright Renewed 1968. Copyright Assigned to Shawnee Press, Inc. All Rights Reserved. Reprinted by permission. Recording licensed through the Harry Fox Agency.

"The Three Fishermen," originally "Three Jolly Fishermen," from *The Fireside Book of Fun and Game Songs*, collected and edited by Marie Winn, musical arrangements by Allan Miller. Copyright © 1974 by Marie Winn and Allan Miller. Reprinted and recorded by permission of SIMON & SCHUSTER, Inc. All rights reserved.

"The Unicorn," words and music by Shel Silverstein. TRO - © copyright 1962 and 1968 Hollis Music, Inc., New York, NY Used by Permission. Recording licensed through the Harry Fox Agency.

"A Valentine Wish," words and music by Natalie Sleeth, from *Weekday Songbook*, copyright © 1977 by Hinshaw Music, Inc. Reprinted and recorded by permission. All rights reserved.

"Weave Me the Sunshine," words and music by Peter Yarrow, copyright © 1972 by Mary Beth Music. Excerpted, reprinted and recorded by permission.

"We're Off To See The Wizard," lyric by E. Y. Harburg, music by Harold Arlen. Copyright © 1939 (Renewed 1967) Metro-Goldwyn-Mayer Inc. All rights controlled and administered by Leo Feist, Inc. Reprinted by permission of Columbia Pictures Publications. Recording licensed through the Harry Fox Agency.

"The Wells Fargo Wagon" from *The Music Man* by Meredith Willson. © 1957, 1959, FRANK MUSIC CORP. and THE ESTATE OF MEREDITH WILLSON, © Renewed 1985, 1987 FRANK MUSIC CORP. and THE ESTATE OF MEREDITH WILLSON. International Copyright Secured. All Rights Reserved. Reprinted by permission of FRANK MUSIC CORP. Recording licensed through the Harry Fox Agency.

"Woke Up This Morning," copyright © 1975 by Chappell & Co., Inc. International Copyright Secured. ALL RIGHTS RESERVED. Used by Permission. Recording licensed through the Harry Fox Agency.

"You Can't Make A Turtle Come Out," words and music by Malvina Reynolds, from *Little Boxes and Other Handmade Songs* by Malvina Reynolds. © 1963 Schroder Music Co. (ASCAP). Reprinted and recorded by permission. All rights reserved.

PHOTO CREDITS

Pupil Book (page numbers refer to pupil pages)
HRW photos by Bruce Buck pp. 104, 134–135, 143, 211; Elizabeth Hathon pp. 18, 92, 160, 179, 186, 197 (all), 202 (all), 208, 209, 228; Richard Haynes pp. 6, 14, 19, 20, 23 (left), 34, 36, 38 (all), 40, 41, 52, 67 (all), 73, 77, 82, 89, 108, 136, 137, 138, 158, 159 (all), 198, 199, 213, 229; Rodney Jones, Inc. p. 70; Ken Karp pp. 60, 61, 62, 63, 76, 137, 195, 196, 198, 220; John Kelly p. 51; Ken Lax pp. 198, 199; John Lei pp. 192, 226, 227; Greg Schaler p. 27; Cliff Watts pp. 68, 69. pp. 4, 5, Nicholas Devore III/Bruce Coleman; p. 8, Culver Pictures; p. 12, Carmelo Guadagno & David Heald; p. 18 (center), Peter Vadnai/The Stock Market; (bottom), Bettmann Archive; p. 23 (center), Peter Krupenye; (right), Eric Levenson/The New York Baroque Dance Co.; p. 28, Lynton Gardiner, The Museums at Stony Brook, 1985, Gift of Railway Express Agency, 1951; pp. 32–33, Keith Gunnar/Bruce Coleman; p. 48, Francis Miller © Time-Life Inc.; p. 102, Martha Swope; p. 108, Three Lions; p. 109, Art Fotopolke/The Image Bank; p. 112, Paul Meredith/Click Chicago; p. 116, Scala/Art Resource; p. 118, Donald Smetzer/Click Chicago; pp. 122, 123, Tom Hollyman/Photo Researchers; pp. 124, 125, Martin Weaver/Woodfin Camp; p. 126, © 1982 Michael Furman/The Stock Market; p. 127, Timothy Eagen/Woodfin Camp; p. 129, Memory Shop; p. 145, Balthazar Korab/The

Image Bank; p. 146, Mickey Pfleger; p. 170, Bill Warren; p. 171, David Brownell/The Image Bank; p. 177, Dick Smith; p. 179, Art Fotopolke/The Image Bank, David Falconer, David Overcash/Bruce Coleman Agency; p. 181 (top), David Hiser/The Image Bank; (bottom), Giraudon/Art Resource; p. 182, Marc and Evelyne Bernheim/Woodfin Camp; p. 183 (top), Margot Granitsas/Photo Researchers; (bottom), Geoffrey Clements; p. 189, *Hours of the Duchess of Burgundy* (© 1450), Musee Conde, Chantilly, Giraudon/Art Resource; p. 190, *Going to the Wedding*, K. Rodko, Yugoslavia; Three Lions; p. 199 (bottom), © Kate Bader; p. 214, © 1985 Don King/The Image Bank; p. 223, John Lawlor/The Stock Market; pp. 230–231, Susan Leavines/Photo Researchers; pp. 232–233, Nicholas Devore III/Bruce Coleman; p. 235, Ted Thai/Time; Production editor: Beth Caspar

Teacher's Edition:
HRW Photos by Elizabeth Hathon appear on pp. ii–iii (top), xvi–xxi.

HRW Photos by Richard Haynes appear on pp. ii–iii (bottom).

ART CREDITS

Pupil Book (page numbers refer to pupil book)
pp. 6, 42, 58, 59, 106, 107, 124 Lisa Cypher; pp. 7, 86, 87 Michael Conway; pp. 16, 44, 147 Debbie Dieneman; pp. 24, 25 Nina Winters; pp. 30, 138, 188, 189 Marilyn Janovitz; pp. 40, 100, 101, 149, 193, 217 Sally Springer; pp. 126, 127 Steve Cieslawski; pp. 168, 169 Carolyn Virgil; p. 187 Thomas Thorspecken; pp. 9, 130, 144 Represented by Publisher's Graphics, Inc. Paul Harvey; pp. 21, 50 Helen Davies; pp. 71, 120, 216 James Watling; pp. 111, 221 Jane Kendall; pp. 136, 140, 141, 142, 143 Eulala Conner; p. 161 Jean Helmer; pp. 179, 201 Patti Boyd; p. 166 Steven Schindler; pp. 15, 67, 81 Represented by Philip M. Veloric Lane Yerkes; p. 22 Represented by Mulvey Associates, Inc. John Killgrew; p. 82 Sally Schaedler; pp. 85, 114.

p. 115 Les Gray; p. 224 Thomas Noonan; pp. 26, 27, 55, 69, 78 Represented by Asciutto Art Representatives Jan Pyk; pp. 56, 57, 89, 96, 97, 98, 99, 104, 139 Sal Murdocca; pp. 154, 156, 157, 158, 159 Anthony Accardo; pp. 204, 205, 206, 207 Loretta Lustig; p. 35 Represented by Lou Gullatt Guy Kingsbery; pp. 37, 53, 94, 152 Represented by Bookmakers, Inc. Michele Noiset; p. 113 Carolyn Croll; p. 75 Represented by Carol Bancroft and Friends Andrea Eberbach; pp. 164, 165 Jackie Rogers; pp. 172, 174 Susan Dodge; p. 218 Yoshi Miyaki.

All table of contents art for grades 2 through 8 rendered by Susan Dodge/represented by Carol Bancroft and Friends, Inc. All technical art prepared by Karen Hoodes, Jimmie Hudson, and Bud Musso. All black and white instrument art prepared by Jimmie Hudson, Brian Molloy, and Bud Musso.

Project Editor: Darrel Irving   Editorial Assistants: Kurt Briggs, Catherine Graetzer, Tim Kulp, June Lee, Susan Ratté, Liz Thomas

Teacher's Edition:
All technical art prepared by Vantage Art.

All illustrative art prepared by Jody Wheeler/Represented by Publisher's Graphics, Inc.

*Topic of special interest to teachers who use the Kodaly and Orff methods are indicated with a **K** and an **O**.*

ANIMALS, BIRDS, INSECTS
Apusski Dusky, 147
Bye Bye, Blackbird, 24
Caravan, The, 122
Cat Came Back, The, 56
Grizzly Bear, 148
Groundhog, 139
I Ride an Old Paint, 126
Kookaburra, 16
Lacadel Was a Ponderous Bear, 94
Lament for a Donkey, 132
One Cold and Frosty Morning, 44
Pop Goes the Weasel, 23
Sweetly Sings the Donkey, 15
Unicorn, The, 172
Why Shouldn't My Goose?, 15
You Can't Make a Turtle Come Out, 100

ART REPRODUCTIONS
Kwele tribal mask (Africa), 182
Peach Tree, Peonies and Cranes (*Shen Chu'uan*), 180
Pictorial quilt (*G. Hanchett*), 183
Region of Brooklyn Bridge Fantasy (*J. Marin*), 183
Renaissance country scene, 181
Rug/Tapestry (Mexico), 181
Several Circles (*W. Kandinsky*), 12

COMPOSED SONGS
A' Soalin' (*P. Stookey*), 224
Allelujah, 40
America, the Beautiful (*S. Ward*), 232
Birthday Hallelujah (*M. Reynolds*), 212
Bye Bye, Blackbird (*R. Henderson*), 24
Bye Bye Blues (*F. Hamm*), 86
Chickery Chick (*S. Lippman*), 88
Clouds (*R. Bampton*), 162
Clouds (*D. Malin*), 162
Clouds (*A. Frackenpohl*), 163
Ding-Dong, the Witch Is Dead (*H. Arlen*), 156
Feed My Lambs (*N. Sleeth*), 230
Gather 'Round (*M. Dugard*), 34
Give a Little Whistle (*N. Washington and L. Harline*), 103
Hallowe'en (*J. Wood*), 216
Happiness Runs (*D. Leitch*), 149
Happy Wanderer, The (*F.W. Moller*), 32
How Di Do (*W. Guthrie*), 8
Hurdy-gurdy Man (*F. Schubert*), 76
I'm Looking Over a Four-Leaf Clover (*H. Woods*), 178
Instruments, The (*W. Geisler*), 64
Janišek the Highwayman (*B. Bartók*), 26

Me and My Shadow (*B. Rose*), 165
Merry Old Land of Oz, The, (*H. Arlen*), 155
Music Is You, The (*J. Denver*), 171
O He Did Whistle and She Did Sing (*R. Felciano*), 223
Portland Town (*D. Adams*), 150
School Days (*G. Edwards*), 21
Sing a Rainbow (*A. Hamilton*), 214
So Long, Farewell (*R. Rodgers*), 128
So Long It's Been Good to Know You (*W. Guthrie*), 142
Somewhere Over the Rainbow (*H. Arlen*), 157
Songmaker (*F. Willman*), 54
Star-Spangled Banner, The, (*words by F. Scott Key*), 234
Sweet and Low (*J. Barnaby*), 187
This Is My Country (*A. Jacobs*), 210
Unicorn, The (*S. Silverstein*), 172
Valentine Wish, A (*N. Sleeth*), 226
Weave Me the Sunshine (*P. Yarrow*), 11
Wells Fargo Wagon, The, (*M. Willson*), 28
We're Off to See the Wizard (*H. Arlen*), 154
You Can't Make a Turtle Come Out (*M. Reynolds*), 100

CONTEMPORARY
Acadian Songs and Dances (excerpt) (*V. Thomson*), 42
Allegro from Percussion Music (*M. Colgrass*), 63
Bear Dance from Hungarian Sketches (*B. Bartók*), 26
Chorale from The Louisiana Story (excerpt) (*V. Thomson*), 104
Concerto for Orchestra, Second Movement (*B. Bartók*), 66
Meringue Boom (*Caribbean Folk Tune*), 36
Nuages from Nocturnes (*C. Debussy*), 160
On the Mall (*E.F. Goldman*), 48
Papa's Tune from Acadian Songs and Dances (*V. Thomson*), 104
Six Pieces for Orchestra, Third and First Pieces (*A. Webern*), 168
Symphony No. 1 in D Major (excerpt) (*G. Mahler*), 39
Unsquare Dance (*D. Brubeck*), 74
Variations on Pop Goes the Weasel (*L. Caillet*), 22

COWBOY SONGS
Colorado Trail, The, 46
Get Along, Little Dogies, 124
I Ride an Old Paint, 126

My Home's in Montana, 127
Old Texas, 145

CUMULATIVE SONGS
Schnitzelbank, 93
There Was an Old Woman, 130

DESCANTS
Colorado Trail, The, 47
Sleigh Bells, 220

FOLK SONGS—K, O
American
Buffalo Gals, 110
Down by the Riverside, 120
Face-Dance Song, 50
Grizzly Bear, 148
I Ride an Old Paint, 126
Jump Down, Turn Around, 105
Lady from Baltimore, 114
One Cold and Frosty Morning, 44
Peace Like a River, 12
Riddle Song, The, 186
Sally Don't You Grieve, 106
Smoke Went Up the Chimney, The, 177
There Was an Old Woman, 130

Australian
Kookaburra, 16

Chinese
Purple Bamboo, The, 185

English
Gypsy Rover, 133
Hey, Ho! Anybody Home?, 138
Merry Are the Bells, 7
Sir Eglamore, 188
Sweetly Sings the Donkey, 15
We Wish You a Merry Christmas, 221

French
March of the Kings, 116

German
My Hat, 176

Israeli
Once, 175
Zum Gali Gali, 118

Jewish
Brethren in Peace Together, 112
Dayenu, 229

Mexican
La Jesusita, 184

Russian
Silver Birch, The, 19
Sleigh Bells, 220

Spanish
Arruru, 222
Lament for a Donkey, 132

Classified Index of Activities and Skills

*Topics of special interest to teachers who use the Kodaly and Orff methods are indicated with a **K** and an **O**.*

ACTIVITY PAGES IN THE PUPIL BOOK

Create Your Own Gamelan Music, 200

Create Your Own Radio Program, 208–09
Creating Form, 105
Describe What You Hear, 164

Describe What You Hear by Talking, 170
Instruments of the Orchestra, 60–63